Unstable bodies

In a wide-ranging and provocative book, Jill Matus uses bio-medical, social scientific and literary texts to interrogate Victorian concepts of sexual difference. Departing from the usual critical focus on Victorian conceptions of the sexes as incommensurably different, she emphasises the powerful effects in Victorian culture of notions of sexual instability and approximation.

While ideas about mutable or ambiguous sexuality provoked fear and fascination, they also served Victorian middle-class ideology by offering 'scientific' ways of constructing racial, class and national identity in terms of the body.

Throughout this period fierce public debates raged around prostitution, infanticide, working-class sexuality, female reproduction and domesticity. Drawing on works by Elizabeth Gaskell, George Eliot and the Brontës, Matus explores the dialogue between literary and other discourses of sexuality.

Unstable bodies deepens our understanding of the way Victorians articulated problems concerning gender and sexual difference, many of which continue to engage us in the late twentieth century, and it will be an essential reference work for students and scholars working in Victorian literary and cultural studies, feminist studies, and the history of sexuality.

Jill L. Matus is an Associate Professor of English at the University of Toronto, Scarborough College

D0875019

UNSTABLE BODIES

Victorian representations of sexuality and maternity

Jill L. Matus

Manchester University Press

Manchester and New York

distributed exclusively in the USA and Canada by St. Martin's Press

Published by Manchester University Press
Oxford Road, Manchester M13 9NR, UK
and Room 400, 175 Fifth Avenue, New York, NY 10010, USA

Distributed exclusively in the USA and Canada
by St. Martin's Press, Inc., 175 Fifth Avenue, New York, NY 10010, USA

British Library Cataloguing-in-Publication Data
A catalogue record is available from the British Library

Library of Congress Cataloging-in-Publication Data
Matus, Jill L., 1952–
        Unstable bodies : Victorian representations of sexuality and
    maternity / Jill L. Matus
            p.   cm.
        Includes bibliographical references (p.   -   ) and index.
        ISBN 0-7190-4347-6 — ISBN 0-7190-4348-4 (pbk.)
            1. Women—Great Britain—Sexual behaviour—History—19th century
    2. Sexual ethics—Great Britain—History—19th century 3. Women
    and literature—Great Britain—History—19th century 4. Sex in
    literature. 5. Motherhood—Great Britain—History—19th century
    I. Title
    HQ29.M44   1995
    306.7'082—dc20   94-22957

ISBN 0 7190 4347 6 hardback
     0 7190 4348 4 paperback

Typeset in Monotype Dante
by Koinonia, Manchester

Printed in Great Britain
by Bell & Bain Ltd, Glasgow

Contents

In loving memory of my parents
Hazel and Edward Lazar

Acknowledgements

The thoughtful criticism and support of many friends and colleagues has contributed to the writing of this book. I am especially grateful to Henry Auster for his careful reading of the manuscript and for his support and challenging criticism at every stage of this project. Among those who gave generously of their time to read and comment on parts of the manuscript, or who offered information, shared ideas, or gave encouragement, I thank Jenny Altschuler, Donna Bennett, Alan Bewell, Russell Brown, Melba Cuddy-Keane, Betsy Ermarth, Heather Glen, Hans de Groot, Mary Hamer, Linda Hutcheon, Mary Jacobus, Heather Jackson, Maureen Lazar, and Denise Zarn. I thank also my editor, Anita Roy, at Manchester University Press whose enthusiasm sustained me, while her editorial judgement appropriately constrained me. A research grant from the Social Science and Humanities Research Council (SSHRC) funded some of the research for this project. Invaluable time for research and writing was provided by the Division of Humanities, Scarborough College, University of Toronto. I also thank New Hall, Cambridge for the congenial home it offered me in 1992-3.

My greatest debt is to my family. With almost unflagging good spirits, Geoffrey Matus bore countless levies on his generosity; not least was his willingness to incur chronic jet-lag during my year of research leave in Cambridge. My daughters Lauren and Hayley already know that they have borne much for the sake of this book; I hope they will also understand how they have inspired it.

Several parts of this book have been previously published. A version of part of Chapter Three appeared as 'Looking at Cleopatra: the exhibition and expression of desire in *Villette*' in *Victorian Literature and Culture*, 21; part of Chapter Four appeared as 'Disclosure as cover-up: the discourse of madness in *Lady Audley's Secret*' in *University of Toronto Quarterly*, 62:3 (1993), pp. 334-55. Chapter Five is a version of two articles, 'Saint Teresa, hysteria and *Middlemarch*', *Journal of the History of Sexuality* 1:2 (1990), pp. 215-40, and 'The iconography of motherhood: word and image in *Middlemarch*', *English Studies in Canada*, 17:3 (Sept 1991), pp. 283-300, which *ESC* awarded the F.E.L Priestley prize for its best essay of 1991. I thank the editors of these journals and their publishers for permission to use the material here.

Introduction: unstable bodies

Soon after its publication in 1859, *Adam Bede* was favourably reviewed in the *Saturday Review* for its portrait of village character and village humour. However, the reviewer took exception to the intrusion into the portrait of the 'rustic reality' of seduction, pregnancy and child-murder. He objected especially to details of Hetty's pregnancy, which were said to 'read like the rough notes of a man-midwife's conversation with a bride':[1]

> There is also another feature in this part of the story on which we cannot refrain from making a passing remark. The author of *Adam Bede* has given in his adhesion to a very curious practice that is now becoming common among novelists, and it is a practice that we consider most objectionable. It is that of dating and discussing the several stages that precede the birth of a child. We seem to be threatened with a literature of pregnancy.... Hetty's feelings and changes are indicated with a punctual sequence that makes the account of her misfortunes read like the rough notes of a man-midwife's conversations with a bride. This is intolerable. Let us copy the old masters of the art, who, if they gave us a baby, gave it us all at once. A decent author and a decent public may take the premonitory symptoms for granted.[2]

When John Blackwood read these comments he worried that they would trouble his sensitive author, so he sent the book to James Y. Simpson, Professor of Midwifery at Edinburgh University. Simpson reported that he found no tactless indelicacies in the account of Hetty's pregnancy, and, falling for the pseudonym, praised George Eliot as a 'great and glorious fellow', a 'Teniers and Titian of a novel writer'.[3] The fact that Blackwood immediately sought medical counsel on the question of the novel's indelicacy is worth scrutiny. Surely the leading gynaecologist of the day might be able to pronounce on the *accuracy* of representation (which he does when he offers that it was unrealistic for Hetty's baby to have cried so loudly and persistently since it was premature and probably weak at six or seven months). But what he was called upon to confirm was its *propriety*. Clearly, the field of an expert on matters of sexuality and reproduction embraced not merely issues of scientific accuracy but the appropriateness of their extra-medical provenance. And indeed, even a brief look at the titles of medical treatises of the period shows that morality, ethics and hygiene were legitimate areas of professional concern. Such texts form what Foucault calls the 'medicine of sex', a discourse largely directed to 'ensure the physical vigor and moral cleanliness of the social body', and they testify to what has been described as the 'monopolism exercised by the medical profession over scientific, biological, moral, ethical and empirical concerns'.[4] As Elizabeth Blackwell noted in *The Human Element in Sex* (1884): 'Medicine and morality being related to function and use, are therefore inseparable in a Christian state.'[5] Since both Victorian literature and medical science saw moral questions as their province, and since morality was organised to some extent around conceptions of appropriate sexual behaviour, it is perhaps not surprising that the territory of *Adam Bede* and the Professor of Midwifery at Edinburgh University should overlap. The institutions of literature and medicine were (and still are) both powerful cultural agencies. A central concern of this book is the relationship between their various and often contradictory representations of womanhood.

The review and Blackwood's appeal to Simpson indicate a cultural context which registers differing responses to the representations of sexuality and maternity that increasingly appear to be the territory of the literary text. In addition, the incident draws attention to the difference between what seemed in 1859 an area of dispute and concern – the bold representation of Hetty's pregnant state – and what today would not raise a readerly eyebrow. We are hardly likely to think of *Adam Bede* as a novel that breaks new ground in its treatment of pregnancy. Reviews such as this mark as contentious what we would surely bypass as insignificant, or perhaps even experience as evasive. The narrative offers but a few details and symptoms of Hetty's pregnancy, and those are euphemistically expressed. At one point, the narrator hints that there is 'a more luxuriant womanliness about Hetty of late'; a bit later we learn that 'after the first on-coming of her great dread, some weeks after her betrothal to Adam, she had waited and waited, in the blind vague hope that something would happen to set her free from her terror'; finally, on her flight from Hayslope a stranger's eyes wander to her figure and detect 'what the familiar unsuspecting eye leaves unnoticed'.[6]

That George Eliot's representation of Hetty's pregnancy could be considered offensive confirms the old stereotype of Victorian prudishness about the representation of sexuality and sexual relations. But the fact that the conservative *Saturday Review* objected to a growing 'literature of pregnancy' reveals that representational practices were not simply content with the way the old masters did it – the production of a baby 'all at once' and certainly without any hint about the act of conception, the circumstances of pregnancy, or more importantly, the subjective state of the woman approaching and experiencing motherhood. The old masters' method of delivery, miraculous and spontaneous, erased the experience of pregnancy or anticipated maternity. What the reviewer of *Adam Bede* refers to as a punctual charting of the pregnancy's progress is not merely 'obstetric accuracy of detail', gratuitous realism, but a part of the novel's representation of Hetty's desperation and subsequent abandonment of her child.[7] It allows George Eliot to show that the biological and physiological state of pregnancy does not carry with it a 'battery of predetermined maternal attitudes and patterns of behaviour'.[8]

The fact that 'new mistresses' rather than 'old masters' were commanding attention in the field of literature also bears on the nature of representations of female sexuality and maternity. A number of reviewers detected a woman's hand in *Adam Bede*, and while one might take issue with the observation that 'the position of the writer towards every point in discussion is a woman's position', it is clear that the nature of George Eliot's interest in cultural constructions of female sexuality aligns her with a growing number of Victorian women writers venturing to make such matters the subject of their fiction.[9] As Gillian Beer has pointed out, *Adam Bede* sets out to revise 'a powerful female text, that of Gaskell's *Ruth*', particularly in its idealisation of the fallen woman and her subsequent motherhood.[10] But before we consider their differences – George Eliot's 'determined and uncompromising' view of Hetty in contrast to Gaskell's idealisation of Ruth – we must notice first that both Gaskell and George Eliot are interested in the effect of anticipated maternity and the responses of the fallen woman to her position as unmarried mother.[11] What are the consequences of knowing that 'within the body ... there is an other'?[12] Ruth's response to the doctor's announcement of her pregnancy is unequivocal joy, even though her rescuers debate whether the prospective child should be seen as a cause for rejoicing or regret. Gaskell's plea for tolerance in the words of the minister to his sister suggests that while mother love may be natural, it can certainly be curdled by the world's harshness. 'The world's way of treatment is too apt to harden the mother's natural love into something like hatred. Shame, and the terror of friends' displeasure, turn her mad – defile her holiest instincts.'[13] He recognises that 'such a responsibility must be serious and solemn enough, without making it into a heavy and oppressive burden, so that human nature recoils from bearing it'.[14] While endorsing the naturalness of mother love, Gaskell also summons another response which she designates as equally natural – the recoil of 'human nature' from oppressive burdens. The fallen woman as mother is then torn between two natural propensities, one (maternal) toward her child, another (human) away from it when society makes bearing it a burden. In this way, Gaskell qualifies and makes problematic the categoric pronouncements about maternal instinct frequently rehearsed in medical and social texts. In *Adam Bede*, when Hetty finally confesses her abandonment of her baby to Dinah, she describes it in terms of a heavy weight hanging round her neck – a burden that she recoils from bearing. The qualification of maternal instinct in relation to other responses also applies to her situation, though it is made more complex through George Eliot's focus on Hetty's limited capacity for relationship in the first place. As Gaskell and George Eliot engage with the circumstances of sexual transgression and illegitimacy, and respond to the topical problems of seduction, prostitution and infanticide, the representation of pregnancy assumes textual importance. It is part of the way these novels explore conceptions of female nature and ideologies of motherhood circulating in Victorian culture.

In a series of essays, linked by shared concerns and similar topics, this book explores how literary, social and medical texts from the 1840s to the 1870s construct multiple and contesting versions of womanhood and female sexuality. As Martha Vicinus notes, the way society has been permeated by the discussion of the nature, definition, use and abuse of sexuality – what Foucault calls the discourse on sexuality – is a relatively recent historical construct.[15] One of my aims is to historicise the work of Victorian novelists in relation to biomedical and social scientific discussions of sexuality and maternity, and to consider particularly how women's writing participated in and shaped the way Victorian culture represented sexuality. There is now a substantial body of work that explores and even anthologises Victorian medical and scientific constructions of sexual difference.[16] How can it inform the way we read Victorian novels? In what ways do imaginative works engage with topical debates about the impact of female functioning on the mind and body? What do they say about the manner in which sexual difference shapes subjectivity? Both biomedical and literary texts are inflected by cultural assumptions and ideologies, and this is not a study of the influence of scientific texts on literary production, but rather an exploration of the shared cultural context that George Levine and Ludmilla Jordanova, among others, invoke in suggesting that literature and science belong to 'one culture', and are 'united in their shared location within cultural history'.[17] Rather than assuming that literature echoes or reflects views expressed elsewhere, I am looking here at how fictive works transform or help to shape topical conceptions of sexuality. Recent historicist criticism has argued that by locating literary texts in a differential field, we can observe how they underwrite or confront other constructions of reality, and how they function in relation to other discursive practices.[18] Such criticism has also proposed that literature participates in constructing a culture's sense of reality, that it is not simply reflective but helps actively to constitute the larger symbolic order by which a culture imagines its relation to the conditions of its existence. I share this view, but I want at the same time to suggest that the agency of literary texts is far from straightforward. The discourse of sexuality in the novel is itself an unstable body of representations.[19] Avoiding large claims or generalisations about the agency of literary texts, the essays in this book explore specific instances in which fictional texts rework and transform topical constructions of the natural propensities of women, in part confirming but also sometimes undermining and challenging the assertions about sexuality produced by other discourses.

Studies of Victorian 'sexual science' have emphasised how comparative anatomists, biologists, gynaecologists and physiologists confirmed the rigid categorisation of men and women as fundamentally different and provided authority for the culture's narrow ideals and ideological formulations.[20] However, biomedical responses to the question of sexual difference were never unanimous or univocal. One of my concerns, addressed in the first chapter, is to show that biomedical discourse offers varied and contradictory versions of sexual difference and female sexuality. And although critics have seen biomedical representations as the basis for misogynist, cramping ideals of femininity, such discourse may, especially on the question of sexual instability and bisexuality, appear more open, exploratory and less ideologically obedient than fictive imaginings. The interesting question then is what has become of these 'other stories' about difference and similarity that biomedical discourse has to tell? How are they are socially and culturally deployed and can they be traced in other forms of writing? It is clear that the strand of biomedical discourse emphasising sexuality as a dynamic and malleable process is detectable in early social scientific texts, for example, which assume the mutability of natural propensities in order to demonstrate that the working classes are in the process of becoming a different race or species by virtue of their morality and physical conditions. Behaviour and environment can alter physiology, and these conditions, it is claimed, are actually in the process of producing a new kind of reproductive female body. Gaskell's *Mary Barton* certainly demonstrates an awareness of such representations, registering a fascination with the potential abandon and wildness of that body, as well as a fear of its capacity for degeneration. Ideas about sexual instability and its power to change and redefine a community inform Gaskell's narrative and illuminate its need to tame and deliver the working-class heroine to conformity and stability.

The textual base of these essays comprises fiction, medical treatises, doctors' advice books, essays and letters in medical, social and cultural periodicals, travel writing, and early social science tracts. Techniques of poststructuralist analysis can be brought to bear on all discursive and signifying practices, but the difficulty of differentiating among the kinds of such practices and texts is a continuing concern in critical theory. If all texts are porous, self-divided, opaque and open to mutual intertextual influences, what then are the distinctions to be made between literary and other texts, and their treatments of the ideological?[21] Some forms of theoretical thinking over the last few years have suggested that distinctions among cultural texts are misleading, even untenable: either they obscure the way in which literary texts serve ideological interests or they ignore the fact that other texts, which claim to be factual and hence distinguishable from imaginative works, are themselves dependent on the rhetorical and imaginative constructions associated with the literary. How can history, for example, fulfil the role of a metalanguage able to explain

social and textual phenomena, if it always emerges as itself the product of a series of narrative and rhetorical devices?[22] It is one thing,
however, to argue that no texts are impervious to ideology or outside
of it, another to obliterate distinctions among kinds of writing.[23] Can
claims be made for the difference of specifically 'aesthetic' works
from other modes of representation? Is literature to be distinguished
from other kinds of writing by virtue of its aesthetic component and
its perceived power to exploit ambivalences more richly than other
texts? The question of whether literature's specificity inheres in
formal and aesthetic qualities is of course a complex and vexed one.
Claims for the aesthetic as a special formal and transhistorical essence
have provoked challenge, but at the same time, dissolving the
category Literature because it cannot be said to have an object seems
both unsatisfactory and unnecessary.[24] It is possible, though, to think
of the difference between imaginative and other texts as itself
historically specific and socially produced. If, as Mary Poovey has
argued, the work performed by different discourses is dependent on
the kinds of social authority they wield, then the social effects that
literature can produce will be different from those produced by law
or medicine, for example. Imaginative texts are able to 'mobilize
fantasies without legislating action', and can constitute a space in
which shared anxieties and tensions are articulated and symbolically
addressed.[25]

Victorian cultural arguments and social theory may have invoked
the authority of science to underwrite attempts to define and
prescribe social relations and to assert the natural and biological
character of sexual difference, but, as recent work has shown, science
itself depended on cultural assumptions about gender. Biological
accounts of reproduction and sexuality are not the origin from which
ideas about men and women and sexual difference then radiate and
circulate; rather the relationship between scientific knowledge and
cultural imperatives is one of interplay and exchange.[26] Once we
recognise that Victorian medical texts and narratives of reproductive
biology are to some extent dependent on the very assumptions about
gender that they are enlisted to prove, we undermine the argument
that biological sex – conceived of as irreducible and natural sexual
difference – is the basis on which the complex and shifting structure
of gender is built. One of the undertakings of feminist work has been
to distinguish between sex (as anatomical difference) and gender (as
the culturally variable, social organisation of difference). This

distinction was an important basis for disputing the legitimating power of the 'natural' and then for arguing that identities and behaviours were socially constructed and hence mutable.

Debates about how much is natural and how much constructed continue to hover, often unfruitfully, around the essentialist/constructionist opposition. But if the claims of biological narratives of reproduction to tell the truth about biological sex are already infused with assumptions about gender, what use is the distinction between sex and gender? Among others, Judith Butler has recently argued that sex – as that which is supposedly radically unconstructed – is itself a cultural construct. 'Gender is not to culture as sex is to nature; gender is also the discursive/cultural means by which "sexed nature" or a "natural sex" is produced and established as "pre-discursive".'[27] The distinction between sex and gender, Butler argues, turns out to be no distinction at all; she makes problematic any definition of these terms that relies on a pre-discursive (and hence transhistorical) notion of sexual difference.[28] I would argue that it is more useful to unsettle the distinction between 'sex' and 'gender' than to collapse or conflate the two categories. The distinction may be vexed, but it helps us to see that the 'difference between nature and culture is always a function of culture'. But if, as Nancy Armstrong argues, the construction of nature is one of culture's 'habitual tropes of self-authorization', we have also to recognise that the category 'nature' was for the Victorians, as it is now, the subject of considerable cultural dispute.[29] Not only did they continually cite sexual differences as testimony to social relations, but they also invested heavily in representing those differences as natural. Indeed, the struggle to manipulate distinctions between nature and culture (mutually dependent and politically powerful concepts) is an important part of the Victorian discourse of sexuality. Disputed constructions of 'nature' signal the cultural stakes involved in representations of sexual difference.

Deconstructing the sex/gender distinction reveals the mutual dependency and enmeshment of the terms, but what of the distinction between *sexuality* and gender? In *Epistemology of the Closet*, Eve Kosofsky Sedgwick argues that sexuality may be closely related to gender, but is nevertheless not reducible to it. She acknowledges the feminist difficulty with the sex/gender distinction, but observes that

the whole realm of what modern culture refers to as 'sexuality' and *also* calls 'sex'– the array of acts, expectations, narratives, pleasures, identity-formations, and knowledges, in both women and men, that tends to cluster most densely around certain genital sensations but is not adequately defined by them... is virtually impossible to situate on a map delimited by the feminist-defined sex/gender distinction.[30]

Although sexuality may be associated with procreation or the potential for it, Sedgwick notes that the 'distinctly sexual nature of human sexuality has to do precisely with its excess over or potential difference from the bare choreographies of procreation'.[31] Thus sexuality could occupy, even more than gender, a 'polar position' on the side of the symbolic, the constructed and the representational. What Sedgwick draws attention to is the way '*something* legitimately called sex or sexuality is all over the experiential and conceptual map'. It seems to represent a range of positions between the most 'intimate and the most social, the most predetermined and the most aleatory, the most physically rooted and the most symbolically infused, the most innate and the most learned, the most autonomous and the most relational traits of being'.[32]

Sedgwick's description of the space designated by sex/sexuality helps to clarify the Victorian understanding of this space, for although the term 'sexuality' rarely occurs in Victorian discourse, the strange territory of the bodily-but-the-psychic, the biological-but-the-socially-infused is certainly its concern.[33] Not unexpectedly, Victorian biomedical discourse tends to emphasise the first terms of Sedgwick's pairings – 'intimate', 'predetermined', 'physically rooted', 'innate' and 'autonomous' – but medical texts also convey a recognition that sexuality is subject to sociocultural moulding and that the psychic and the social are able to shape and influence the body's supposedly autonomous functioning.

Since cultural influences were acknowledged to shape, mould and especially distort 'natural' sexuality and sexual desire, it is clear that the Victorians did not therefore assume that grounding an identity in a biology of 'essential nature' was a stable way of insulating it from societal interference.[34] Rather, the threat of societal interference fuelled the urgency of social texts that attacked the evils of civilisation (or its lack) and stoked the power of the medical profession's claims to regulate the unstable and endangered body. Some of the ill effects of modern fashionable life were thought to be responsible for hysterical women and mothers who refused to nurse; the degraded conditions of working-class life produced a blighted and degenerating reproductive body. Similarly, the clamouring of women for financial independence and higher education augured the demise and atrophy of reproductive capacities, while the heinous marriage practices of foreign peoples could explain the sorry state in which some bodies and social groups found themselves. Arguments based on biology almost always served views about the right and proper relation of the sexes. Imprecations or dark rumblings about the state of culture and society, or comparisons of national identities and relative states of civilisation, are grounded in notions of what preserves natural propensities best and assert the dire results that must flow from ignoring that knowledge.

Most recent studies of Victorian conceptions of sexuality have emphasised the absolute and incommensurable distinction between male and female bodies in Victorian biomedical discourse and the ideological uses that this rigid binary served. But although being sexed was understood as a natural, pre-given biological condition, it was at the same time conceived of as unstable, even precarious, acquired at puberty rather than manifest at birth. The conception of sexual transitivity – a continuum of sexed being rather than a great divide between incommensurable opposites – also served important cultural purposes. It underwrote arguments about class and racial difference while still preserving the notion of sexuality as a natural, biological mandate. If enculturation could transform biological sexuality, either refining it or debasing it, then the careful monitoring and assessment of cultural tendencies and differences was a matter of great importance. Nature had made provisions for human sexuality, but culture was free to fall, as it were, and to distort or befoul nature's endowments. Debates and arguments about sexual differentiation from sameness take different forms or assume new connotations under the influence of evolutionary thinking later in the century, especially after Darwin's *The Descent of Man*. They reveal a range of representations about sex, nature and culture that could serve different and indeed competing interests.

In suggesting that representations of sexual difference in biomedical writing are neither homogeneous nor consistent, but multiple and contradictory, I draw on Foucault's view of sexuality as a cultural construct with a history, and his emphasis in *The History of Sexuality* on the

> complex and unstable process whereby discourse can be both an instrument and an effect of power, but also a hindrance, a stumbling-block, a point of resistance and a starting point for an opposing

strategy. Discourse transmits and produces power; it reinforces it, but also undermines and exposes it, renders it fragile and makes it possible to thwart it.[35]

Foucault's formulation of the possibility of 'reverse discourse' works against the idea of seamlessness, especially in so far as he draws attention to a multiplicity of discursive elements rather than dominant representations.[36] A well-known Victorian example of the appropriation of existing vocabularies or representations is the way feminist arguments against the contagious diseases legislation turned circulating notions of female passionlessness to their own ends. Nancy Cott has shown how views about passionlessness were in fact in the vanguard of feminist thought and were serviceable to women in gaining social and familial power.[37] Similarly, social science of the 1830s represented working-class women as morally and physically degraded, thereby serving the purpose of defining and distinguishing the healthy, middle-class body. But the same representations were also available to lobbyists for factory reform and working-class politicians, who used them to very different political ends. Competing and contradictory representations of the female body, sexuality and maternity offer possibilities of mobilising and developing oppositional formulations, enabling women writers to articulate positions that might become instrumental in political change. The volatility and instability of cultural representations and their deployment allows for a range of responses wider than either rebellious or collusive.

But as critics of Foucault have pointed out, his work presents the problem of differentiating among the forms that power takes. Even though he asserts that power is heterogeneous and productive, and that a counter vocabulary is always possible, his historical analyses tend to depict power as a monolithic and unidirectional force.[38] As Martha Vicinus has pointed out, it is unclear how change comes about for Foucault. Lack of agency is a problem in his work, for without the naming of 'persons, events, institutions and ideologies, resistance tends to float free from any historical specificity'.[39] If what is lacking in Foucault is an account of the relationship between discourse and social formation, it may be useful to think in terms of the concept of hegemony, provided that the process of social formation is understood as active and transformational, contradictory and conflictual.[40] A powerful example in this regard is Mary Poovey's *Uneven Developments: The Ideological Work of Gender in*

Mid-Victorian England, which emphasises both the emergence of oppositional formulations and the differentiation of power in social formation. Although she follows Foucault in pointing to the text as 'an ensemble of specific discursive practices', her analysis of ideology and gender explores the conditions and circumstances in which middle-class claims to social power were staked and established. Her work examines the unevenness of ideological formulation – uneven in the sense that it was experienced differently by each person by virtue of his or her position in the social formation, and uneven in that it was articulated differently by the various 'institutions, discourses, and practices that it both constituted and was constituted by'.[41]

While Foucault's emphasis on sexuality as a cultural construct with a history has proved enabling for studies such as Nancy Armstrong's *Desire and Domestic Fiction* or Anita Levy's *Other Women*, both these works claim a cultural agency for various discourses that does not take into account their instability. Following Foucault, Armstrong explores sexual relations as the site for changing power relations between classes and cultures, genders and generations. She argues that the history of women's writing is the history of the production of the gendered middle-class subject. Armstrong's study is useful in drawing attention to the power wielded by women's writing and to the contradiction in assuming that authors represent (or misrepresent) a prior and essential form of sexuality, rather than also participating in its production. Not only, however, are the ideologies of womanhood produced by the novel more various and contradictory than Armstrong suggests, but we need to ask how they compare to versions of 'woman' produced by other discourses.[42] Levy's interdisciplinary analysis of the construction of gender in sociology, anthropology, fiction and psychology broadens Armstrong's project to explore the discourse of sexuality in the human sciences as well as in fiction and their instrumentality in establishing and maintaining middle-class hegemony.[43] Her use of Gramsci allows her to focus on the intellectuals and professionals of the dominant class, authorised 'to pronounce the "truth" about individuals, cultures, and historical moments with impunity'.[44] But her trenchant study of the formation of class and gender does not demonstrate the unevenness and conflict of hegemonic struggle or illuminate the multiple and contradictory representations produced in social scientific and literary texts. The title of my study draws attention, therefore, not just to the bodies that biomedical and cultural discourses elaborated as unstable, but to the representations themselves as an 'unstable body' of discourse.

In 'Sex in mind and in education' (1874) Henry Maudsley apologises for having to speak plainly about medical and physiological matters in a literary forum such as the *Fortnightly Review*, and Elizabeth Garrett Anderson, responding to his article, doubts that 'such a subject can be fully and with propriety discussed except in a professional journal'.[45] The sense conveyed is that medical literature may discuss matters of sex and sexuality explicitly; doctors are licensed to speak plainly among themselves, but the public should not be exposed to such delicate subjects. Unlike texts of popular advice, aimed at a lay audience, specialised medical texts were written largely for professional brethren, even if not solely medical.[46] Thus the preface to William Acton's *Functions and Disorders* claims that the book will be valuable to physiologists, comparative anatomists, surgeons and advocates. While some works, like Acton's, did sell in large numbers and successive editions, for the most part biomedical texts had a limited circulation and readership. But the discourse of sexuality certainly proliferated in fervent public discussions about the birth rate, especially the hyperbreeding of the poor, public health, the death rate, prostitution, infanticide, and the female propensity to derangement and insanity.[47] My discussions of literary texts are organised in most cases around specific moments of intense social and cultural debate in which conflicting representations of sexuality erupt: the debate concerning working-class sexuality in the 1840s, the politics of female passionlessness and the debates about prostitution in the 1850s; the attempts to recuperate a notion of maternal instinct in response to rising rates of infanticide and the horrors of baby farming in the 1860s; the controversy in medico-legal discourse around the maternal insanity plea in the 1850s and 1860s.

Public discussion and debate was one way in which women readers and writers became familiar with the discourse of sexuality, and literature was one of the few means by which women writers could take part in it. As recent critics have argued, participation in literary discourse offered Victorian women an opportunity for conceptualising their own sexuality; their representations could alter and influence the way such matters were understood, a fact that clearly provoked some anxiety in Victorian culture.[48] In writing about the false morality of lady novelists (an essay in which he discusses how Gaskell erred in *Ruth*), W. R. Greg explained that women cannot be expected to have first-hand experience or knowledge of the deep truths of 'the science of sexual affections', which was (and ought to remain) a male domain of knowledge. By naming such knowledge 'science', Greg already suggests that it is beyond the reach of a woman:

> She may possibly have enjoyed (or suffered) opportunities of observing the workings of the sentiment in some one of her friends; but its wilder issues and its fiercer crises are necessarily and righteously hidden from her sight. She may, by dint of that marvellous faculty of sympathy and intuition which is given to those who have felt profoundly and suffered long, be able to divine much which she cannot discover, and to conceive much which she has never seen or heard; and the pure and God-given instincts which some women possess in so rare a measure may enable her to distinguish between the genuine and the false, the noble and the low; – but many of the saddest and deepest truths in the strange science of sexual affection are to her mysteriously and mercifully veiled; and the knowledge of them can only be purchased at such a fearful cost, that we cannot wish it otherwise. The inevitable consequence, however, is,that in treating of that science she labours under all the disadvantages of partial study and superficial insight.[49]

Greg conveys a sense of the 'fearful cost' attendant on 'the strange science of sexual affection'. Women writers can only treat this science with 'partial knowledge and superficial insight', because knowledge and experience are necessarily denied them. In their fiction, however, we see that women did indeed take its 'wilder issues and fiercer crises' as their subject matter. That 'strange science' and its political implications are, as the following chapters explore, very much the terrain of women's writing in representations of feminine desire, working-class sexuality, prostitution, racially-inflected sexuality, and maternal instinct and its aberrations. By focusing on the texts of women writers, I pursue both Greg's perception that a particularly female cultural agency in representing sexual affections and relations is dangerous and misleading, and the question of what opportunities for self-representation women took when they wrote about sexuality and maternity.

The first chapter deals with the construction of 'natural propensities'. The term 'propensity' itself signals activity, the possibility of movement or change. It is a leaning or weighting towards one course rather than another, but not a rigid, entirely predictable script. Propensities may be natural, but they are nevertheless unstable and mutable. Such perceptions have two important consequences. One is the demand for and rationalisation of surveillance and protection; the other is the explanation of differences among races, classes and nations. Also evident in biomedical discourse is a reliance on analogies between human sexuality and plant and animal reproduction. Since discourses of human sexuality relied on what was known of plant and animal reproduction, tracing the varied construction of 'nature' in Victorian biomedical discourse means looking at the strategies for distinguishing human from plant and animal reproduction and thinking about the deployment of analogies from the natural world, particularly the comparison of human and animal behaviour.[50] Victorian anatomists and physiologists find themselves pondering such questions as whether menstruation is the equivalent of heat in animals or an instance of the obvious difference between humans and the lesser creation. If the nervous system of the pre-copulatory female frog is such that 'the slightest touch will then produce those states of the nervous system which, at other times can only be produced by narcotic poisons, or by energetic galvanic action', does it follow that when women are subject to increased ovarian action, they are also more irritable and sensitive?[51] If the cerebellum is the seat of sexual instinct, why are monkeys, whose cerebellum is small, so salacious that they are often excited to violent demonstrations 'by the sight even of a human female'?[52]

Applied biology and its more or less obvious political implications rely on similar persuasion by analogy. But how differently do William Acton and Anne Brontë use the example of the glow-worm when discussing the question of human physical attraction! And what does George Eliot tell us about views of human sexuality and maternal instinct through Bartle Massey's remarks about his promiscuous dog, whom he addresses as if she were a woman? When the *Saturday Review* publishes discussions of women's work entitled 'Queen Bees and Working Bees', what view of bee behaviour and sexual differentiation is invoked as a contrast to human organisation? What assumptions reassure Sir James Chettam that 'as the smallest birch-tree is of a higher kind than the most soaring palm' a man's mind will always be superior to a woman's?

Chapters Two, Three, Four, and Five extend this exploration of ideas about sexual instability through readings of a selection of literary texts. Chapter Two examines the representation of working-class mothers and wives in social scientific writing of the 1840s and focuses on the way prevailing conceptions of unstable working-class sexuality shape Gaskell's *Mary Barton*. Chapter Three considers the representation, production and politics of desire. The first two sections of this chapter explore anxieties provoked by the possibly disruptive sexuality of governesses and fallen women. Anne Brontë's concern with confession in *Agnes Grey* and Gaskell's interest in the function of the sexual closet in *Ruth* signal the participation of these novels in the vexed discussions of desire and passionlessness at the mid-century. The third section of this chapter considers Charlotte Brontë's *Villette* and its engagement with reciprocal constructions of sexuality and race in the figure of Cleopatra as a latter-day harem slave. Written at the same time as *Ruth*, *Villette* engages not with doctrines of essential passionlessness, but with apparently contradictory constructions of the sexualised Oriental 'other'. Chapter Four examines ideologies of motherhood and particularly the problems of recuperating notions of maternal instinct in the face of maternal aberrations. It explores the medical and social debates about wet-nursing, baby-farming and infanticide in the late 1850s and 1860s, which expose ideological contradictions in prevailing representations of motherhood. Turning to the way two very different novels engage issues raised in debates about maternal deviance, the chapter discusses George Eliot's *Adam Bede* and Lady Emma Caroline Wood's *Sorrow on the Sea*. The last section of Chapter Four explores constructions of maternal insanity in Mary Elizabeth Braddon's *Lady Audley's Secret*. Chapter Five, 'From hysteria to maternity', focuses not like other chapters on a specific moment of social debate, but on pervasive and restrictive social and scientific assumptions about the essentially reproductive nature of women and the stabilising effect of marriage and motherhood. It explores George Eliot's engagement with these issues in *Middlemarch* and the way she probes the gendered distinction between productive and reproductive work in the case of Dorothea Brooke, who until she settles into her social place as a relatively stable body is regarded as the 'dangerous part in the family machinery'.

Unstable Bodies focuses on canonical and noncanonical fictional texts because both 'closet' concerns about the instability of sexuality. An unabashed sensation novel such as *Lady Audley's Secret* or *Sorrow on the Sea* may bring to light what the high culture and ethical morality of a novel by George Eliot obscures, so that reading such texts in conjunction illuminates both. Positing women as an object of investigation, the discursive contradictions *Unstable Bodies* explores allow women writers to mobilise an army of fictional possibilities in representing sexuality and maternity. In order to address the question of how female subjectivity is constituted by such discursive contradictions, I turn first to explore the alertness in biomedical texts to the malleability of sexed being and to suggest the social and political implications of sexual difference conceived as responsive to physical environment and moral conditions.

Notes

1. *Saturday Review* (26 February 1859), pp. 250–1, quoted in D. Carroll (ed.), *George Eliot: The Critical Heritage* (London, Routledge, 1971), pp. 73–6; see also the account of this incident in G. S. Haight, *George Eliot: A Biography* (New York, Oxford University Press, 1968), p. 276.
2. Carroll, *George Eliot*, p. 73.
3. Simpson's letter to Blackwood (4 March 1859) is cited in Haight, *Biography*, p. 277.
4. M. Foucault, *The History of Sexuality* vol. 1, trans. R. Hurley (Harmondsworth, Penguin, 1981), p. 54; R. Morgan, *Women and Sexuality in the Novels of Thomas Hardy* (London, Routledge, 1988), p. 1.
5. E. Blackwell, *The Human Element in Sex: Being a Medical Enquiry into the Relation of Sexual Physiology to Christian Morality*, 2nd edn, (London, Churchill, 1884), p. 12.
6. G. Eliot, *Adam Bede*, ed. S. Gill (Harmondsworth, Penguin, [1859] 1980), pp. 405, 411, 422.
7. The reference to 'obstetric accuracy of detail' is from a later review in the *Examiner* (5 March 1859), p. 149.
8. E. Badinter, *The Myth of Motherhood: An Historical View of the Maternal Instinct*, trans. R. DeGaris (London, Souvenir Press, 1981), p. xx.
9. A. Mozley, *Bentley's Quarterly Review* (July 1859); cited in Carroll, *George Eliot*, p. 90.
10. G. Beer, *George Eliot* (Sussex, Harvester, 1986), p. 59.
11. Dickens referred to George Eliot's conception of Hetty's character as determined and uncompromising in his letter, 10 July, 1859; see Carroll, *George Eliot*, pp. 84–5.
12. J. Kristeva, *Desire in Language: A Semiotic Approach to Literature and Art*, ed. L. S. Roudiez (New York, Columbia University Press, 1980), p. 237.
13. E. Gaskell, *Ruth*, ed. A. Shelston (Oxford, Oxford University Press, [1853] 1985), p. 120.
14. E. Gaskell, *Ruth*, p. 120.
15. M. Vicinus, 'Sexuality and power: a review of current work in the history of sexuality', *Feminist Studies*, 8 (1982), p. 135.
16. See, for example, P. Jalland and J. Hooper (eds.), *Women from Birth To Death:*

The Female Life Cycle in Britain 1830–1914 (New Jersey, Humanities Press, 1986).

17. G. Levine (ed.), *One Culture: Essays in Science and Literature* (Madison, University of Wisconsin Press, 1987), p. 26; L. Jordanova (ed.), *Languages of Nature: Critical Essays on Science and Literature* (London, Free Association Books, 1986), p. 15.

18. For further discussion on this point, see J. Howard, 'The new historicism in Renaissance studies', in A. Kinney and D. Collins (eds.), *Renaissance Historicism: Selections from English Literary Renaissance* (Amherst, University of Massachusetts Press, 1987), p. 17.

19. On the agency of domestic fiction, for instance, see N. Armstrong, *Desire and Domestic Fiction: A Political History of the Novel* (Oxford, Oxford University Press, 1987); and on the novel in relation to the human sciences, see A. Levy, *Other Women: The Writing of Class, Race, and Gender, 1832–98* (New Jersey, Princeton University Press, 1991).

20. See, for example, C. E. Russett, *Sexual Science: The Victorian Construction of Womanhood* (Cambridge, Mass., Harvard University Press, 1989).

21. This description of texts is derived from Howard, 'New Historicism', p.. 15.

22. T. Bennett, *Outside Literature* (London, Routledge, 1990), p. 52.

23. See the discussion of this point in H. Glen, *Charlotte Brontë: The Imagination in History* (forthcoming); on the distinction between science and literature, S. Shuttleworth and J. Christie (eds.), *Nature Transfigured: Science and Literature, 1700–1900* (Manchester, Manchester University Press, 1989), p. 3, point out that 'to reduce science to literature by insisting that science is a kind of writing, or to reduce literature to science by insisting that its codes also give a higher or privileged access to the real, are simplifications offering only the most banal of realisations'; see also Stephen Greenblatt's discussion of the 'powerful if conceptually imperfect differentiation between the literary and the nonliterary', in 'Shakespeare and the exorcists', in P. Parker and G. Hartmann (eds.), *Shakespeare and the Question of Theory* (London, Methuen, 1985), p. 164.

24. Responding to this debate, and particularly Terry Eagleton's views in *Literary Theory: An Introduction* (Oxford, Basil Blackwell, 1983), Tony Bennett has recently argued that although the boundaries of the literary cannot be secured, that does not mean that there is no place for a theory of literature that will theorise its object 'as a set of social rather than formal realities and processes', *Outside Literature*, p. 139.

25. M. Poovey, *Uneven Developments: The Ideological Work of Gender in Mid-Victorian England* (Chicago, University of Chicago Press, 1988), p. 124.

26. See T. Laqueur, *Making Sex: Body and Gender from the Greeks to Freud* (Cambridge, Mass., Harvard University Press, 1990), pp. 10–11.

27. J. Butler, *Gender Trouble: Feminism and the Subversion of Identity* (London, Routledge, 1990), p. 7.

28. What, for example, do we understand by 'the anatomical differences of sex' in the following definition of the sex-gender system as the 'social-historical, symbolic constitution, and interpretation of the anatomical differences of sex'? See S. Benhabib, 'The generalized and the concrete other', in S. Benhabib and D. Cornell (eds.), *Feminism as Critique* (Cambridge, Polity Press, 1987), p. 80.

29. N. Armstrong, *Desire and Domestic Fiction*, p. 262, n.6.

30. E. K. Sedgwick, *Epistemology of the Closet* (Berkeley, University of California Press, 1990), p. 29.

31. Sedgwick, *Epistemology*, p. 29.

32. Sedgwick, *Epistemology*, p. 29. I prefer her formulation to the usual assumption that gender is wider than sexuality, and to the reduction of sexuality to 'sexual feelings'; on this point, see L. Jordanova, *Sexual Visions: Images of Gender in Science and Medicine between the Eighteenth and Twentieth Centuries* (Brighton, Harvester, 1989), p. 13, who argues that 'whereas "sexuality" implies the experience of sexual feelings, "gender" can be applied to anything.'

33. Two nineteenth-century usages in the O.E.D suggest that 'sexuality' maps a vast terrain. In one case it is defined as 'the characteristic of the male and female reproductive elements' (genoblasts); in another, where a gynaecologist denies that the 'sexuality' of the woman is destroyed by the removal of ovaries, the term suggests not so much reproductive capacity or even sexual feelings but feminine attributes and social role.

34. These terms are Sedgwick's; see *Epistemology*, p. 43.

35. Foucault, *The History of Sexuality*, p. 101.

36. Foucault, *The History of Sexuality*, p. 100; see P. Dews, 'Power and subjectivity in Foucault', *New Left Review*, 144 (1984), pp. 72–95; see contrastingly J. Sawicki, 'Feminism and the power of Foucauldian discourse', in J. Arac (ed.), *After Foucault: Humanistic Knowledge, Postmodern Challenges* (New Brunswick, Rutgers University Press, 1988), pp. 161–78, and L. McNay, *Foucault and Feminism: Power, Gender and the Self* (Cambridge, Polity Press, 1992), pp. 5, 38–44.

37. N. Cott, 'Passionlessness: an interpretation of Victorian sexual ideology, 1790–1850', *Signs*, 4:2 (1978), p. 235.

38. See the discussion of this point in L. McNay, *Feminism and Foucault*, pp. 38–41, where McNay notes that when Foucault comes to talk of the hystericisation of the female body, his implication is that female experience was thoroughly circumscribed by notions of a pathological and hysterical sexuality, leaving little room to then consider the ways in which women did not passively absorb socially prescribed feminine roles.

39. Vicinus, 'Sexuality and power', p. 139.

40. See J. Weeks, 'Foucault for historians', *History Workshop*, 14 (1982), pp. 114–16; see also Rod Edmond's discussion of Raymond Williams and hegemony in *Affairs of the Hearth: Victorian Poetry and Domestic Narrative* (London, Routledge, 1988), p 39, n. 28.

41. Poovey, *Uneven Developments*, pp. 17, 3.

42. See S. Shuttleworth, 'Empowering fictions: the history of sexuality and the novel', *The Eighteenth Century*, 30:3 (1989), pp. 51–61.

43. Levy's purpose is 'to show how the history of discovering and universalizing women that is the project of the human sciences is part of the larger formation that we call middle-class culture' (*Other Women*, p 8).

44. Levy, *Other Women*, p 13.

45. H. Maudsley, 'Sex in mind and in education', *Fortnightly Review*, 15 (1874), p 466; E. G. Anderson, 'Sex in mind and education: a reply', *Fortnightly Review*, 15 (1874), p 582.

46. Acton's *Functions and Disorders* is unusual in having reached fourteen editions. Dr George Drysdale's *The Elements of Social Science* (1854) went through thirty-five English editions – some 88,000 copies by 1905. For a fuller discussion of Drysdale, see E. K. Helsinger, R. L. Sheets and Wm. Veeder (eds.), *The Woman Question: Social Issues, 1837–1883*, vol. 2 (Manchester, Manchester University Press, 1983), pp. 65–71.
47. See J. Weeks, *Sex, Politics and Society: The Regulation of Sexuality Since 1800*, 2nd edn. (London, Longmans, 1989), p. 19.
48. See M. Poovey, 'Speaking of the body: mid-Victorian constructions of female desire', in M. Jacobus, E. Fox Keller, and S. Shuttleworth (eds.), *Body\Politics: Women and the Discourses of Science* (London, Routledge, 1990), pp. 30, 38.
49 W. R. Greg, 'False morality of lady novelists', *The National Review* (January 1859), pp. 148–9.
50. Charles Webster notes that the origins of ethology illustrate the dialectic between the human and biological sciences: a transference of ideas about human society to the animal order, and then their return to provide a biological rationale for behaviour within the family. See C. Webster (ed.), *Biology, Medicine and Society 1840–1940* (Cambridge, Cambridge University Press, 1981), p. 3.
51. E. J. Tilt, *On Diseases of Women and Ovarian Inflammation* (London, Churchill, 1853), p. 85.
52. Wm. Carpenter, *Principles of Human Physiology; with Their Chief Applications to Pathology, Hygiene and Forensic Medicine* (London, Churchill, 1842), p. 207.

Chapter one

Sexual slippage and approximation in Victorian biomedical discourse

While Victorian theories of sexual differentiation certainly emphasised the great difference between the sexes and the natural complementarity of male and female, they were also very much concerned with the instability of that difference. My aim in this chapter is to explore the social and political implications of Victorian representations of sex as a dynamic process, responsive to environment and habit, dependent on a permeable and mutable body. I want to show that even though theories of sexual instability may have been dangerous and anxiety-provoking they could also serve ideological purposes. Victorian cultural politics may have needed the scientific legitimation of ineradicable sexual difference, but theories of sexual fluidity were especially useful in formulating ideas about differences among women of different classes and cultures.

A critical and contentious debate within twentieth-century feminism has revolved round the contingency of the category 'Woman': what are the grounds for feminism if a special, timeless and universal realm of female experience is denied? If being a woman is a 'state which fluctuates for the individual, depending on what she and/or others consider to characterise it', the notion of an 'underlying continuity of real women, above whose constant bodies changing aerial descriptions dance' becomes deeply problematic.[1] Further, feminist theorists have recently been drawing attention to the way one's sense of oneself as a sexed and gendered being 'intersects with class, racial, ethnic, sexual and regional modalities of an identity that is discursively constituted'.[2] How does one conceptualise the category 'Woman' in relation to variables of class, race, nationality, religion, and so on? In *Regulating Womanhood*, Carol Smart points to a problem with what she describes as the additive approach. We cannot simply prefix variables to the 'dominant theoretical categorisation', and proceed to talk of black women, or working-class women, operating on the assumption that their 'Womanness' is 'held fast in some way'.[3] In contrast to the additive approach, theorists have suggested concrete, historically specific analyses of how class, gender and race interact, and a rejection of 'models' in favour of an examination of shifting meanings.[4]

I want to argue that a focus on sexual instability in Victorian biomedical discourse addresses these issues in interesting ways. Far from being held fast, 'Womanness' in Victorian biomedical narratives is indeed a category that accommodates change and produces politically consequential conceptions of difference. Racial and national modalities of identity inflect the notion of 'Womanness', as they inflect even the supposedly natural and biological sexuality usually assumed to be common to all women. One reason therefore for exploring the emphasis on sexual approximation and similarity in biomedical texts is that it may help us to understand the ways in which such writing produced accounts of differences among women even as it insisted on what was essential to all women.

According to the Foucauldian view that sexuality is constituted through representation, biomedical literature is an important participant in constructing what we have come to understand by Victorian sexuality. To pursue Foucault's terms we would say that sexuality is never logically prior to its written representation; however much it is represented as natural – a matter of biological fact – sexuality belongs to culture, and its history is thus the history of its discourses.[5] Recent explorations of the narratives of reproductive biology have shown how scientific representations of sex are deployed ideologically and how the grounding of sexual difference in ostensibly natural facts both reflects and serves ideologies of gender. Such studies have also shown that the rigid distinction between male and female, which prescribed the nature and destiny of individuals in each category, was a Victorian cultural imperative.

Yet sex and sexuality were ambiguous and vexed categories in the biomedical writing of the period, and the nature and extent of distinction between male and female much debated and contested. The very notion of sexual difference was complicated, hedged and indeed given form by questions of sexual sameness and continuity. To scrutinise the writings of Victorian physiologists, reproductive biologists, and medical doctors, is to find some uncertainty about what distinguishes the sexes, and the extent to which sexuality belongs to culture rather than nature. The question of sexual approximation and mutability has persisted in different forms. Seen in a larger framework, we can identify it in the environmentalism of the eighteenth century, the Darwinian notion that humankind's ancestors were hermaphroditic, the late nineteenth-century interest in the 'man-woman' and androgyny, and the Freudian concern with bisexuality and a genderless libido.[6] Disputes surrounding questions of stable sexual difference and the incommensurable differentiation between sexes enable us to historicise Victorian narratives of sexual difference and to question the idea that scientific and medical authority simply confirmed and underwrote rigid ideals of femininity. Rather than consensus about the nature of sexuality and the essential differences between male and female, conflicting and sometimes contradictory formulations make up the discursive history of reproductive biology.

In his illuminating study, *Making Sex*, Thomas Laqueur has argued that the age-old model of a 'one-sex' body with two genders gave way gradually, post-Enlightenment, to the notion of two incommensurably different sexes underwriting two genders. In the first model, women are considered lesser or imperfect men; in the second, they are radically different from men and specialised for a particular social destiny because of their reproductive physiology.[7] The shift in models shows us that theories about sex are enlisted to either a greater or lesser extent in the ideological work of gender. The two-sex paradigm accommodates a binary model of difference articulated upon sex, and does important ideological work in representing difference as natural, bodily, anatomical. Although a biology of difference served Victorian middle-class hegemony in oppressive ways, underpinning and justifying specific forms of social organisation dependent on the representation of 'Woman' as essentially sexually differentiated, such a biology, Laqueur argues, was politically ambivalent, capable of being used to promulgate different and competing social interests.[8] The ideological use of the sexed body was indeed complex and diverse, rather than monolithic or conspiratorially misogynistic, but the development of ideas about difference was similarly complex and diverse, interwoven with disputes and debates about the basic similarity of the sexes. Victorian theories about sexual similarity, approximation and instability are, however, a relatively unremarked aspect of their production of gender. While Laqueur certainly acknowledges the continuity of ideas about the kinship between the sexes, he does not dwell on the importance of these in nineteenth-century constructions of sexuality; his concern is with the way in which sexual differentiation became a cultural imperative.

Ornella Moscucci's history of gynaecology, *The Science of Woman*, pays greater attention to the question of sexual kinship in Victorian medical literature, pointing to the Victorian interest in hermaphroditism, male menstruation, and the conception of sexuality as a dynamic process, rather than a static essence. While Moscucci is most insightful about Victorian beliefs in the basic bisexuality of humankind and the vexed distinctions between sexual characteristics bestowed by nature or acquired by culture, she explains these concerns by suggesting that they 'stemmed from the comparative approach itself' and that the Victorians needed to temper emphasis on the difference between man and woman lest they 'obscure racial categories and undermine the unity of the human species in relation to the lower animals'.[9] Further questions need to be asked both about the ideological service of theories that detracted from the belief in incommensurable difference and whether they underwrote resistances to dominant formulations.

Victorian debates revealing the ambiguity of the categories male and female not only augment our sense that the 'natural' facts of sex are discursively produced, but draw attention to the operations of cultural transmission. If models of undifferentiation had served greater political and economic ends, no doubt sexual difference could have been minimised in social theory and discourse. The overwhelming sense conveyed in Victorian social discourse that male and female bodies are rigidly differentiated may mean that ambiguities about sexual categorization were merely omitted as irrelevant in cultural appropriations of medical knowledge. But such a conclusion assumes that the relationship between medical discourse and the larger culture is simply one of cause and effect; medical science discovers, interprets, and disputes, culture appropriates only what is ideologically useful. The interplay between scientific findings and cultural imperatives cannot, however, be adequately represented as a one-way street.[10] The persistence of ideas about sexual approximation in biomedical discourse suggests that they reflect and serve ideological needs. Potentially unsettling, questions about ambiguous sexuality open the door to a scrutiny of the relationship between nature and culture, and structure debates about biological determinism and environmentalism. For example, if the body is open to change and influence, or if environment, nutrition and social life have the potential to destabilise and alter the work that 'sexing' ought to do, then culture and, as far as possible, environment have to be regulated and controlled. The Victorians avowed that Dame Nature may have done a wonderful job providing for sexual differentiation, but she certainly left some doors open. That meant that the possibility of sexual slippage needed to be monitored, but of course, it could also be exploited. At the same time that ideas about universal and essential sexual differentiation served to underpin the Victorian doctrine of separate spheres, so concepts of sexuality as a dynamic and unstable process, responsive to environment and culture, allowed ideologically important distinctions to be made between classes and races. The anatomical differences of working-class women, prostitutes, Oriental and African women, for example, could be explained by the fact that the body's sexed nature was dynamic and open to change. Nature could be shaped, improved upon or indeed perverted by culture.

Sex as a continuum

A good place in which to track medical assumptions of sexual approximation is the debate about education for girls and women which was gathering steam in the 1870s. The famous Maudsley/ Garrett Anderson exchange marks a moment when medical discussion of sexual difference 'comes out' in a literary periodical in order to enter public debate over pressing gender issues. Henry Maudsley's apologies for having to discuss matters of sex 'out of a medical journal' and for using 'plainer language than would otherwise be fitting in a literary journal' have already been mentioned; they draw attention to his authority as a doctor and his license to speak about matters of sex, as well as to the specialised nature of scientific discussion, usually conducted among professionals in medical journals and appropriately inaccessible text books.[11]

I want to focus on Maudsley's figuring of sexual difference, not to make again the argument that medical expertise underwrote oppressive gender distinctions, but to point out how even his terms of stringent difference are dependent on, and admit, instability and similarity. Maudsley begins by invoking Plato's account of sexual origins. Like Freud, he reads the Platonic fable selectively, in his case to illustrate and support his theory of sexual differentiation and complementarity. The story in Plato's *Symposium*, recounted by Aristophanes, tells of the way people were divided initially into three sexes: male, female, and male–female. When Zeus severed these double persons (for they each had two heads, two of each limb, and so on) the hermaphrodite or androgyne divided into male and female, whereas the other two sexes became two females and two males. Since each half longed to be reunited with his or her other half, the story constitutes an account of the origins not so much of sexual difference, but of sexual desire.[12] However, complementarity, rather than questions of heterosexual or any other desire, was Maudsley's concern when he invoked the Platonic story in order to mount arguments against similar education for men and women:

> It was an Eastern idea, which Plato has expressed allegorically, that a complete being had in primeval times been divided into two halves, which have ever since been seeking to unite together and to reconstitute the divided unity. It will hardly be denied that there is a great measure of truth in the fable. Man and woman do complement one another's being. This is no less true of mind than it is of body; is true of mind indeed as a consequence of its being true of body.[13]

Since the fable is purely for him an allegory of sexual difference and complementarity, Maudsley does not dwell on the figure of the androgyne or hermaphrodite, the divided unity, and, according to James Young Simpson, the truly representative human specimen. Yet even in Maudsley's insistence on difference, there is the assumption that sexual (therefore mental) difference begins at puberty and represents the parting of ways previously very close. Rather than defining human beings from the moment of birth, sexuality comes into the picture only much later. Boys and girls are alike physically and mentally, he explains, although a girl's passion for her doll shows a 'forefeeling of her future functions'.[14] After the years of reproductive activity, ways converge and the sexes come to resemble each other once more. Aberrations show how related the normal positions of men and women are: men 'whose reproductive organs are in some way mutilated approach the state of women in their bodily form, voice and mental qualities, while women whose reproductive organs remain from some cause in a state of arrested development, approach the mental and bodily habits of men'.

Rather than woman being 'undevelopt man', in Tennyson's famous phrase, 'undevelopt' woman approaches man.[15] The continuum on which sexuality is seen to exist suggests difference, but not of an incommensurable and unbridgeable kind. The differences are temporary; yet, Maudsley implies, so crucial are they for the time in which they operate, that they must be allowed to dictate all social practices. As Maudsley's opponents could have pointed out, there is no logical reason why such difference could not be minimised as opposed to maximised. One could say that boys and girls, old men and women are alike and the differences occasioned by specialisation for reproduction are no reason for suddenly treating them as opposites, categories altogether and thoroughly different. And indeed, Elizabeth Garrett Anderson's response to Maudsley argues on this basis: why should any organ or set of organs require exceptional attention? If women can continue to eat beef and bread with as much benefit as men even though they are marked by special physiological function, why can they not continue to be educated in the same way? [16] Arguing that menstruation is the body's way of getting rid of what it has in excess, that surplus nutritive material is disposed of rather than a deficit being incurred, she asks why a woman's system should be considered depleted or overtaxed by menstruation. She admits, however, that rapid growth in young womanhood could be taxing the nutritive powers, but suggests that those in charge of the education of young women can make allowances for these special conditions. After all, she humbly submits, 'No one is proposing that girls of seventeen or eighteen should be allowed to try for a place in the Cambridge Honours' List.'[17] Girls under eighteen are not admitted at Girton, and final examinations take place three years or more later.

As the Maudsley / Garrett Anderson debate shows, the question of difference shapes itself against that of similarity, and indeed, the sometimes urgent and anxious assertion of an incommensurable divide between the sexes is a response to the more fluid implications of continuity or similarity, which blur boundaries and suggest that what men and women have in common may be greater than, or at least as important as, what differentiates them. However, the question of difference is never a neutral one: it is always a question of better or worse, superior or inferior. To say that the sexes are basically similar, but that women are inferior men, is different from saying that the sexes are basically similar and equal. The oppositional pairs of similar\different and inferior\equal line up in such as way that similar–inferior is usually set against different–equal. In 1875 Antoinette Brown Blackwell could still say that 'current physiology seems to be grounded on the assumption that woman is undersized man, with modified organs and special but temporary functions' – the similar–inferior combination. In the light of such hierarchical ordering, she obviously finds the promise of different–equal – 'equal halves' making a 'perfect whole' – more amenable.[18] Despite her belief that science can underwrite a complementarity of equals, she ends up with a rather traditional division of qualities based on the doctrine of separate spheres. Although she criticises the way science has been used by Spencer and Darwin to support notions of female inferiority, her vision of gendered difference does not appear markedly different from theirs.[19]

If sexual difference can be understood as a position on a graduated scale, the intriguing question is what factors, internal and external, determine that position. Writing in the early 1840s, the neuro-physiologist Thomas Laycock rehearses the well-known view that 'woman is but an imperfectly developed male'. In explaining why woman must be so regarded, Laycock quickly asserts that imperfect does not mean inferior, it is just that 'the primary formative nisus' in women is not 'sufficiently powerful to carry the individual through all the phases of masculine developement'. A more energetic nisus would have 'so influenced the general system, that the bones and muscles would have attained the masculine size, and the ovaria would have been testes, with all the special points of sexual difference dependent on the latter'.[20] If greater or lesser energy in the system determines whether ovaries become testes, then sexual difference can be understood as the result of differing positionality on a continuum. But what factors affect and control development and location on that continuum? Simply allowing or arresting development determined sex in the case of certain animals. Naturalists were fascinated by the way in which, when necessary, worker bees could 'make' queens out of grubs that would have become workers by merely enlarging the cell size and continuing to feed the grub royal jelly. Can it be, asks William Kirby, author of one of the Bridgewater Treatises, that trivial circumstances can change

> the very passions, tempers and manners? That the very same foetus, if fed with more pungent food, in a higher temperature and in a vertical position, shall become a female destined to enjoy love, to burn with jealousy and anger, to be incited to vengeance, and to pass her time without labour – that this very same foetus, if fed with more simple food, in a lower temperature, in a more confined and

horizontal habitation, shall come forth a worker zealous for the good of the community, a defender of the public rights, enjoying an immunity from the stimulus of sexual appetite and the pains of parturition – laborious, industrious, patient, ingenious, skilful – incessantly engaged in the nurture of the young; in collecting honey and pollen, in elaborating wax; in constructing cells, and the like![21]

Kirby's highly anthropomorphising description links the insect and human world, preparing the reader for the next step in his argument: stranger sexual changes than this take place among human beings. Surely the well-known fact that sometimes men have breasts and women beards is a more violent instance of change than the case of a 'worker bee, which may be regarded as a sterile female', assuming the secondary characteristics of a fertile female? Arguing for the importance of food and environment as factors influencing sexual development, Kirby also cites the example of tightly swathed or malnourished infants who grow up imperfect and sterile. We should not be surprised therefore that the control of development through nutrition and environment determines fertility, sterility, size and function in bees.[22] Kirby's turn here to evidence from the world of human beings in order to bolster an observation about animal life parallels the practice in biomedical texts of frequent recourse to examples from the animal and even vegetable kingdom to explain and interpret human physiological processes. It also shows that Kirby is able to draw on an established sense of human sexuality as a dynamic, even malleable condition.[23]

Kirby's resort to analogy raises the interesting question of the inescapable rhetoricity of biomedical writing. Moments of analogical assertion and disputation are important in revealing both the imaginative and ideological impetus – the cultural imperatives of interpretation – behind the choice of one parallel situation or association over another. Since many claims about human sexuality relied heavily on the use of analogy, one way of handling opposing views was to disallow the analogical reasoning on which they depended, or to substitute a more telling or appropriate analogy in its place. This is well illustrated in James Young Simpson's discussion of recent developments in embryology. Simpson begins by accepting the still persuasive homology of male and female organs. As he pointed out in his essay on hermaphroditism, originally published in Todd's *Cyclopaedia* (1839), the view of the respective organisations of the two sexes in which the female is regarded as an inverted male, with testicles and penis turned in, is by no means obsolete: 'This doctrine of analogy between male and female organs has, with various modifications, been very generally admitted by modern physiologists, and in some of its bearings it has been made, more particularly of late years, the subject of considerable discussion.'[24] Simpson then proceeds to reveal how embryology as a branch of enquiry supports notions of a basic human bisexuality, dealing with views that oppose his by objecting to what he sees as an inappropriate implicit analogy. Simpson regards the embryonic state as neutral, that is, either male or female organs can develop from it; 'unity of type' exists between the genital organs of the two sexes. He takes issue therefore with the view that the embryo itself is hermaphroditic, disputing this doctrine of the 'original but temporary double-sexed character of all embryos'. Although the existence of a double-sexed character is the 'normal and permanent sexual type in most plants and many of the lower orders of animals', he cannot, he says, allow this implicit analogy. 'This argument by analogy certainly cannot by any means be considered as a sufficient basis for the establishment of so broad and important a generalization in philosophical anatomy.'[25] We see, however, that argument by analogy and persuasive evidence drawn from observations about the mechanisms of plant and animal generation is fundamentally important in biomedical representations of human sexuality. For example, the analogy of human and vegetable reproduction supports the claim that foetal life commences before the ovum has entered the uterus; menstruation is described as 'flowers' because 'as these precede fructification in vegetables, so does menstruation indicate in woman the capability of being fecundated'.[26] An argument for the heightened nervous susceptibility of women proceeds from observations about pre-copulatory frogs:

> In the beginning of spring, just before the period of copulation, the nervous system of frogs is endowed with a most remarkable degree of irritability. The slightest touch will then produce those states of the nervous system which, at other times can only be produced by narcotic poisons, or by energetic galvanic action. It is a matter of daily observation, that when women are subject to increased ovarian action, they are also more irritable, more impressible to cold, to noise, and other physical agents.[27]

Concerned to distinguish human sexuality from that of other living creatures, yet drawn to the similarity of principles of sexual functioning and organisation, biological explanation is necessarily comparative. But which analogies are appropriate? In the case of human ovulation, was ovulation coitally induced as in some mammals such as rabbits, or did the human female ovulate spontaneously and cyclically during 'heat' like other mammals? Part of the problem was the lack of observable evidence. As one doctor explained, it was a question of working with the evidence at hand. He notes that although several points on the question of ovulation require elucidation, yet, 'from the analogy which is known to exist in the structure of the ovum and foetus of the human species and that of quadrupeds and birds, we are enabled to bring together the detached observations which chance has thrown in our way, and thus give a connected account of the generative process in man, imperfectly as that process has as yet been observed'.[28]

The difference between allowable evidence and unwarranted, but rhetorically powerful yoking of dissimilar situations is a problematic (though not frequently discussed) question in biomedical texts. Foucault has drawn attention to the incongruity between nine-teenth-century discourses of human sexuality and what was known at the time about the physiology of animal and plant reproduction.[29] In its recourse to analogy, biomedical discourse displays its dependency and reliance on knowledge about the world of animal and plant reproduction; it also highlights the ideological dimension involved in interpreting plant and animal reproductive behaviour in relation to that of human beings.

The emphasis on sex as a spectrum of possibilities, and the difference between male and female sexuality as a matter of degree rather than kind, persists in biomedical texts of the nineteenth-century despite growing cultural insistence on and deployment of sexual difference as an ontological category. Victorian physicians opine that the sex of an individual at birth cannot be determined on the basis of its genitalia alone and regard pre-pubescent boys and girls as sexually neutral.[30] As Maudsley's discussion bears out, only at puberty can one distinguish between the male and the female of the species, for at this time the organs controlling sexual difference begin to exert their influence on the body. The sense of sexuality as a dynamic process is also clear from Maudsley's references to the reproductive period as the time when anatomical and psychological differences become important.[31] Further, his recognition of the way the sexes approximate each other when men are mutilated or women malformed signals the possibility of one sex merging into the other, the collapse of unstable or precarious difference in convergence. If sexuality is not a static essence, and if one is not sexed once and for all, then presumably culture has to regulate the individual carefully so that anatomy conforms with prescribed social destiny.

At the same time as they searched for *the* particular spring in the human body that controlled and determined sexuality at puberty, physicians and physiologists also considered what caused the approximation of male to female and female to male. These fields of enquiry were opposite sides of the same coin. By the 1840s and 1850s Victorian medical texts are emphasising the ovaries as 'the workshop of generation' and attributing all the peculiarities of the human female – the development of the pelvis, the uterine system, the mammae, the function of menstruation – to these 'essential organs of reproduction'. Edward Tilt voiced a representative opinion when he announced that 'it is on account of the ovaries that woman is what she is'.[32] If the ovaries were what made woman, then what was the effect of their removal, absence or a change in their condition? Women who have no ovaries become masculine – their skin is brown, their mammary glands undeveloped. In one such case history, the woman's pelvis was also masculine, and the 'subpubic angle' measured only sixty-three-and-a-half degrees instead of the usual ninety-five. Tilt also had the idea that nefarious Eastern practices of removing the ovaries robbed women of their typically female form. He explained that the fate of certain unfortunate Eastern women testifies to the fact that a woman without ovaries approaches the condition of a man: 'The destruction of the ovaries by artificial means, to serve the morbid jealousy of Eastern despots, is followed by the arrest of that characteristic luxuriance of form in women, and by their assuming the drier texture, the harder outline, and the angular harshness of men.'[33] And yet, as Ornella Moscucci points out, although there was enormous controversy over the practice of ovariotomy in the next decades – the 'unsexing' of women – no actual evidence was offered that ovariotomised women had lost their 'feminine characters', though women did apparently report decreased sexual desire. Thomas Laycock asserted that when ovaries or testicles are removed, 'All sexual desire is annihilated, certain sexual characteristics disappear, and, so far as a mere negation of these will allow, the individual approaches in form to the opposite sex.'[34] He thought it impossible, however, for women to develop male characteristics that were actually dependent on the *presence* of the testicles.[35] It would be 'contrary to our every day's experience in lower animals. We never see the spayed sow have the boar's tusks or neck bristles; nor the spayed heifer with the massy neck and short thick horns of the bull.'[36]

Laycock suggests that a *change* in the ovaries, rather than their *removal*, 'partly approximates them in structure and influence on the system to the testes, and partly destroys their influence on the general system'.[37] Observations about male plumage in female pheasants, the subject of a paper to the Royal Society (1827), could be explained by this principle. Laycock cites a Mr Yarrell, who focused on several female birds that assumed the appearance and plumage of the male, finding that the intensity of 'virilescence' was in direct proportion to the extent of lesion or malformation in the female organs of generation.[38] Laycock confirms, therefore, that there is a sound physiological reason for the belief popularly held that 'those women who have hair on the upper lip seldom bear children. In aged females, especially those who have always been unmarried, there is most usually a slight beard; the voice becomes strong', and the individual has a lean, meagre appearance.[39] Few mid-Victorian fictional texts deploy marked physical details in representations of sexual indeterminacy or androgyny, but Wilkie Collins' description of Marian Halcombe in *The Woman in White* is a striking exception. Collins represents her masculine qualities through the 'dark down on her upper lip', which was 'almost a moustache'. However, her figure is decidedly female – 'comely and well-developed, yet not fat ... her waist perfection in the eyes of a man'. The combination of masculine and feminine traits provokes a sensation described as 'oddly akin to the helpless discomfort familiar to us all in sleep, when we recognise yet cannot reconcile the anomalies and contradictions of a dream'.[40] As an androgynous heroine, she transgresses the rigidly gendered division of qualities associated with the strictly differentiated, clearly-sexed body, but, significantly, only the dark, morally ambiguous Count Fosco appreciates and desires her. The novel closes with her conventionally desirable sister's marriage and motherhood: she herself remains an onlooker.

On the question of perplexing approximations or amalgamations of male and female – the anomalies and contradictions of which Collins speaks – James Young Simpson's influential essay 'Hermaphroditism' is a point of reference in many Victorian medical texts.

As evidence of the fundamental similarity of the sexes, the hermaphrodite is important in understanding Victorian efforts to reconcile the concept of sexual difference with the idea of a human nature common to both sexes. [41] Simpson argues that the representative human body is really neither male nor female, but hermaphrodite. The 'natural history characters of any species of animal are certainly not to be sought for solely either in the system of the male or that of the female'. They are to be found in 'those properties that are common to both sexes … combined together by nature upon the bodies of an unnatural hermaphrodite, or evolved from the interference of art upon the castrated male or spayed female'.[42] When it came to individual development, the male surpassed the female, who was left 'more in possession of those characters that are common to the young of both sexes' and which the male would not have lost had his testicles been removed. But as regards the species, he concluded, the development of the female was more perfect. Characteristically self-sacrificing, female development is geared to the good of the species; ambitious and self-interested, the male perfects himself. Having given the female representative status, Simpson immediately follows with a qualification: since the female is specialised for reproduction, she constitutes the standard of the species to a lesser extent than she would if she were not so specialised.[43] Related to the debate about the relative perfection of the sexes is the question of women's greater longevity, which exercised medical powers of explanation. Although the organs of *animal* life in the male' gave him greater size, the development of the organs of *'vegetative'* life gave woman greater 'vital tenacity than man' and prolonged her life to a greater length.[44] According to Ann Richelieu Lamb in *Can Women Regenerate Society?* such vital tenacity was simply biological justice: women live longer than men to make up to them for the time that they, by their organisation, have been appointed to spend on others.[45] If women also seemed to be ahead of men in that girls begin to mature earlier than boys, one could explain away that advantage by saying, as J. McGrigor Allan does, that the most complex organism takes longest to reach full development:

> In the animal and vegetable kingdoms we find this invariable law–rapidity of growth inversely proportionate to the degree of perfection at maturity. The higher the animal or plant in the scale of being, the more slowly does it reach its utmost capacity of development. Girls

are physically and mentally more precocious than boys. The human female arrives sooner than the male at maturity.... The quicker appreciation of girls is the instinct, or intuitive faculty in operation; while the slower boy is an example of the latent reasoning power not yet developed. [46]

In considering what characteristics are particular and sexual as opposed to general to the species, Simpson offers the tentative but nevertheless startling opinion that the 'full development of the mammary glands is a character proper to the species in general, rather than one peculiar to the female system alone. Perfect males sometimes have developed mammae and give milk.'[47] William Carpenter's *Principles of Human Physiology* also draws attention to instances of male breasts and lactation: 'The strong desire to furnish milk, together with the irritation of the gland through the nipple, have often been effectual in producing the secretion in girls, old women, and even in men.'[48] The 'essential character of the gland is the same in the male as in the female', and, he notes, there are several cases on record in which infants have been suckled by men.[49] He cites one in Maryland, where in 1837 a professor exhibited to his obstetrical class a 'coloured man, fifty five years of age, who had large, soft, well-formed mammae'. The man had officiated as a wet-nurse for many years in his employer's family. To allay doubts about this nurse's masculinity, Carpenter adds that 'his genital organs were fully developed'.[50]

If breasts were not exclusively a female characteristic, menstruation was also, according to some experts, not a solely female activity. All beings functioned under a primal law of periodicity, and vicarious haemorrhages, periodic and seasonal changes affected men too. Although Todd's *Cyclopaedia of Anatomy and Physiology* dismissed the notion of male periodicity, Dr Allen Thomson, the author of the essay 'Generation', nevertheless saw the opposing view as worthy of comment: 'It has attempted to be shewn that the male is subject to a periodical plethora in some respects similar to that which gives rise to menstruation in the female, but without any just reason, unless we choose to consider as such the gradual accumulation of seminal fluid, which frequently takes place in healthy men of sanguine temperament, and which gives rise to its periodical emission.'[51] But Laycock's publications on the fundamental periodicity of all life supported ideas of analogous 'periodical plethora' in both male and female. Questions of vicarious male bleeding, biological cycles and periodicity were discussed throughout the century, indicating, in effect, a concern with the larger question: should the difference between male and female be seen as a matter of degree rather than of kind?[52]

Nature and culture

Clear distinctions between social and biological factors, nature and culture, are problematic, which is well illustrated in the cases of hermaphroditism discussed by Simpson. There are instances, he explains, when the indeterminacy of sex is such that only by dissection after death can the 'true or predominant' sex be discovered. In determining sex the sexual desires of the malformed individual ought to be of very little weight.[53] His observation implies that desire is a matter of social construction, so that a man (anatomically speaking) can behave and desire as a woman, if he has been brought up and identified as such. Simpson illustrates this principle in the case of an elderly woman who, after death, was discovered to have male internal organs. She had lived all her life as a woman, and 'though there was never any menstruation, yet, from being constantly employed in domestic occupation, the mental character was feminine, and the married state had been willingly entered into'.[54] Self-identification and social conditioning make sexual desire and preference unreliable indicators of the 'true' sex. Simpson discusses another case, reported in 1846, of a fifty-eight-year-old subject who had lived her life as a woman until she was in her late thirties, even though at seventeen the testes were found to be descending and she developed a 'copious beard'. She was examined by three doctors and pronounced to be a hypospadiac or malformed male. They provided the subject with a certificate; he 'assumed the masculine attire'.[55] As this case history demonstrates, anatomical confusion appears to be important mainly in how it affects the subject's social position. The certificate authorises the subject's assumption of masculine dress, suggesting that unauthorised assumptions would wreak social havoc. As Thomas Laqueur points out in his discussion of similar earlier confusions, 'to be a man or a woman was to hold a social rank, to assume a cultural role, and not to *be* organically one or the other of two sexes. Sex was still a sociological, not an ontological, category.'[56] By no means resolved, the tension between the sociological and ontological is persistently inscribed in Victorian medical texts.

The recognition that social and environmental factors could shape and influence sexual functioning and development informs the range of interpretations of functions such as menstruation. Far from being a universal function among women, menstruation was represented in some medical texts as an effect of civilisation. One doctor describes it as the body's protest against inadequate sexual fulfilment, the unfortunate result of 'social habits, which do not permit women to enjoy sexual intercourse when they feel the want of it'.[57] Widespread recognition was given to the influence on menstruation of social and environmental factors; climate, race or stock, national customs all affected the time of first menstruation, the deferral of which for as long as possible was generally felt to be a good thing: 'Warm rooms, a sedentary life, particular kinds of reading, and some bad habits are all hurtful in this respect', warned Todd's *Cyclopaedia*. Since early menstruation was taken as a sign of primitive and hence inferior races, the claim that women of the working classes were approaching the condition of such 'others' was a potent and disturbing one. But John Roberton, a Manchester surgeon who spent nearly twenty years researching the claims about the onset of puberty in different cultures concluded that the effect of climate and culture made little appreciable difference, and that assertions of the inferiority of races whose 'menstrual commencement is eight, nine or ten years' cannot hold. He was referring to arguments which explained differences between primitive tribes and civilised nations by emphasising the importance of culture acting on nature. Such arguments claimed that it was not nature that had specially fitted the South Sea Islanders to 'the functions of propagation at the period of life [six to seven years] now mentioned' but their 'barbarous and debased state of civilisation', which was responsible for early unions.[58]

While some doctors saw menstruation as the response in women to the way civilisation had interfered with nature, others regarded it as evidence of progress. Arguments influenced perhaps by Darwinian thinking represented menstruation as evidence of an advanced evolutionary stage in the human female. If it could be argued that menstruation was unknown among primitive women, who were thought to be continuously pregnant, and represented an adaptation to relieve the uterus of surplus blood, it could also be claimed that menstruation was analogous to a more frequent oestrus, which meant that civilisation had 'improved women's biological capacity to bear children'.[59] Civilisation was not, however, always responsible for improvements: often it was blamed for sad deviations from an earlier, more natural state of things. According to medical experts, the suffering of women in childbirth was due to their 'artificial habits of life' and not to the 'form and make' that nature had bestowed on them.[60] Arguing for the importance of good medical attention, Michael Ryan noted that where women live according to nature's laws, childbirth is safe, but 'among the higher and middle classes, indeed all classes of civilised society' where nature's laws were often forgotten or violated, or 'where the constitution is impaired by the luxury or dissipation of modern times', the process of childbearing is attended by danger.[61]

Darwin observes in *The Descent of Man* that the progenitor of vertebrates was surely hermaphroditic, and that at some early time, both sexes of Man were bearded, but he does not pay much attention to present dangers of approximation since his concern there is with the evolutionary differentiation of the sexes through sexual selection.[62] Although Darwinian theories of sexual selection linked greater sexual differentiation to the evolutionary process, the very instability of evolutionary change confirmed earlier views that environmental changes could affect sexuality and gave rise to the spectre of the process of differentiation reversing itself. When Spencer addressed the restiveness of women who demanded to participate in worldly activities and thus seemed to want to disrupt the progression of complementarity, he represented their 'anti-differentiation' as a step back in time toward savagery:

> When we remember that up from the lowest savagery, civilization has, among other results, caused an increasing exemption of women from bread-winning labour, and that in the highest societies they have become most restricted to domestic duties and the rearing of children we may be struck by the anomaly that in our days restriction to indoor occupation has come to be regarded as a grievance, and a claim is made to free competition with men in all outdoor occupations.[63]

Darwin saw no reason to deny that like any other instinct, social instinct is greatly strengthened by habit. 'It is not improbable that after long practice virtuous tendencies may be inherited'; only the 'transmission of moral tendencies' could explain the differences that people believe to distinguish races. The moral nature of man has reached its present standard because of the effects of 'habit, example, instruction, and reflection'.[64] In *The Descent of Man* Darwin also recognises and addresses the problem of distinguishing between constitutional and external influences. The preface to the second edition calls attention to the importance of environmental influences on corporeal and mental changes. Here Darwin defends himself against the imputation that he has attributed all changes of corporeal structure and mental power exclusively to the 'Natural selection of such variations as are often called spontaneous'. Emphatically he states that 'Great weight must be attributed to the inherited effects of use and disuse, with respect both to the body and mind.'[65] The emphasis on use and disuse reassures a readership (anxious about uncontrolled and spontaneous change) that monitoring and regulation are effective and change is under human power and control. In his conclusion, however, weighing up the relative power of internal constitution and external influence, he concludes that variations in an organism depend much more on the constitution of that organism, than on 'the nature of the surrounding conditions; though new and changed conditions certainly play an important part in exciting organic changes of many kinds'.[66] However delicately Darwin tries to balance the relative weight of constitution and environment here, my point is that he underscores ideas of the constitution's receptivity and capacity for change. And what aspect of the constitution more sensitive to change than the reproductive system? In *The Variations of Animals and Plants Under Domestication* (1868) he had indeed warned that the reproductive system was very susceptible to alterations in the environment, and that 'changed conditions of life have an especial power of acting injuriously on the reproductive system'.[67]

Since social and environmental factors could change and mould human sexuality, Victorian medical texts anxiously extrapolated from current trends and predicted dire bodily responses to cultural developments, stressing the body's tendency to degeneration and responding to feminist attempts to widen women's educational and vocational spheres with predictions of atrophy and masculinisation. Maudsley's strictures on education, for instance, can be seen in this context. He warns that female breasts will atrophy and become 'by disuse as rudimentary' as they are in the male sex.[68] Maybe, he remarks sarcastically, it is the plan of evolution to bring forth a 'race of sexless beings' who will 'carry on the intellectual work of the world, not otherwise than as the sexless ants do the work and the fighting of the community'.[69] Infertile worker bees and sexless ants –

the principle of division of labour taken yet further than two sexes – could indeed provide analogies for the neutral condition that was thought to exist before puberty; the threat of such 'sexlessness' could then be enlisted against women who sought to change the social status quo. If the difference between men and women is inextricably linked to social changes and altering environments, then women might become more like men if they assumed male habits and occupations. Victorian cultural monitors continually predict the loss of femininity or the approach of androgyny in threatened changes: 'We do not want our women to be androgynous', wrote the author of 'Queen Bees or Working Bees?', *Saturday Review* (1859): 'We had rather do what we can for the Governesses' Institution ... than realize Miss Parkes' utopia of every middle-class girl taught some useful art.'[70] The essay closes with the well-known lines from Tennyson's *The Princess*:

> For woman is not undevelopt man
> But diverse: could we make her as the man,
> Sweet love were slain; his dearest bond in this,
> Not like to like, but like in difference.

The lines following these, which sound an ideal differentiation that yet allows greater approximation, were less quotable:

> Yet in the long years liker must they grow;
> The man be more of woman, she of man.[71]

The sexual instincts

Conceptions of the relative weight of cultural and natural factors are shaped by views about instinct, propensity, and Lamarckian notions of the ability to acquire characteristics through education and influence. Alexander Walker, for example, distinguished three kinds of instinct: the first is propensity, which he described as involuntary and unconscious. The second is a subspecies of the first, 'subsequent to individual experience' and dependent on individual instruction. It becomes habit, alters the organisation, and acquires the generic character of excluding all process of reasoning. The third is a product of the second, which no longer affects individuals but the race. Acquired habits become hereditary and assume the character of instinct. Further, in acquiring some propensities, we lose others.[72] Thus women who turn away from their proper sphere and seek to behave like men, will eventually lose their womanly instincts. Walker, applying physiology to the moral relations between the sexes, pronounced: 'A learned and philosophical lady is indeed not less out of character, nor less ridiculous, than those beings originally of opposite sex who lose the characteristics of men to grace an Italian stage. Those are alike monstrous who possess more or less, either physically or morally, than nature prescribes.' Concerned to refute 'Mrs Wolstonecraft [sic]' and reaffirm Rousseau, Walker further observed: 'When a woman, indeed, is notorious for her mind, she is in general frightfully ugly, and it is certain that great fecundity of the brain in women usually accompanies sterility or disorder of the matrix.'[73]

Discussions of sexual propensities work to distinguish human sexual instinct from that of animals and to qualify reference to corporeal desires with an emphasis on a psychical, mental or moral element. The control of 'the intellectual and moral powers of the mind' is the crucial distinction not only between humankind and the beasts but among different classes and races of men. Cultural differences in sexual behaviour could be used to explain different states of civilisation: 'Hence the immense variety we observe in the effects of the exercise of the sexual passions on different people, and hence the various modifications which they undergo from the state of civilization among different nations.'[74] Not only could the moral component of sexual desire be used to distinguish human beings from beasts, and primitive tribes from civilised peoples, but it could also distinguish nations and classes from one another.

William Carpenter compared the largely instinctive actions and behaviour of animals to those of humankind, guided largely by reason or the will.[75] As far as sexual instincts are concerned, 'Man' is prompted by a 'powerful instinctive desire, which he shares with the lower animals' to the use of the sexual organs for the continuance of his race, but what distinguishes Man from the animals is the 'engraftment (so to speak) of the psychical attachment, upon the mere corporeal instinct'.[76] In man, the sexual instinct is of a 'very compound' nature. It is usually under the control of the will, and although it may prompt one, much as feelings of hunger and thirst, to find means of gratification, nevertheless that process is subject to reason and moral sentiment.[77] Writing in the 1860s, Henry Maudsley represented 'naked lust' as an animal instinct found only in human beings whose brains are 'ill-constituted or imperfectly developed'.

When the brain is properly constituted and naturally developed 'the sexual desire undergoes a complex development in consciousness; from its basis are evolved all those delicate, exalted and beautiful feelings of love that constitute the store of the poet, and play so great a part in human happiness and in human sorrow'.[78] Medical texts that emphasise the combined operations of the reason, the imagination and the moral feelings that make up desire do not therefore underwrite the frequent portrayal (in social debates about prostitution and seduction) of male sexuality as naturally and unregenerately animal. Nevertheless, the view that male sexual instincts need to be satisfied and that women must be sacrificed in the process was not uncommon. It led the *Medical and Times Gazette* to criticise the work of rescue societies on the grounds of an 'unanswerable' objection. To 'snatch a brand from the fire' simply meant 'the precipitation of another brand into it' – the supply of prostitutes would always equal the demand.[79] This view of sexual instinct reveals how the belief in natural (therefore 'unanswerable') male propensities can serve a strategy for making women responsible for sexual control. An answering strategy, as Elizabeth Blackwell's work reveals, was to code male lack of control as inferiority, and hence to encourage a high valuation of self-control: 'It is an insult to the male nature to infer that it is inferior to the female nature, because it does not possess the power of individual self-balance.'[80]

How are sexual feelings and the reproductive function related to the brain and its parts? 'Mental feeling and local affection relating to sex are very intimately associated together; on the one hand, the local irritation of the genital organs exciting mental desire, and on the other, the erection and other signs of affection of the sexual organs being immediately caused by all those ideas and passions of the mind which bear a relation to sex.'[81] Whether the cerebellum was the seat of sexual desire, as many phrenologists claimed, was a contested point among physiologists. William Carpenter considers the claims of phrenology, but concludes that monkeys (known to be particularly salacious, often being excited to violent demonstrations 'by the sight even of a human female'), have a very small cerebellum compared to man, whose sexual impulse is much less violent. [82] When Mary Elizabeth Braddon indignantly defended herself against charges that her sensation fiction encouraged 'the lurking poison of sensuality', she summoned phrenological evidence, though she was clearly aware that such evidence was not universally credited: 'And to you, Lord Lytton, as a phrenologist, I may venture to say – without fear of provoking ridicule – that all those who have examined my head phrenologically know that this sin is one utterly foreign to my organization, that indeed, the great weakness of my brain is the want of that animal power.'[83] According to phrenologists, men had a greater capacity for amativeness than women, since the male cerebellum was larger than that of the female. Women, however, had a greater propensity to love their young. Such 'philoprogenitiveness', claimed George Combe, distinguished the female from the male brain.[84] Further, as the heads of infanticides supposedly showed, this capacity to love the young was developed only feebly in some women. But as Cynthia Eagle Russett observes, phrenologists did not pursue the idea that a kinship surely existed between the brains of both men and infanticidal women, since both showed a lesser capacity to love the young than that found in normal women.[85] Combe also noted that the function of philoprogenitiveness was to help the mother through her toils of raising the young, while Maudsley observed more caustically that if it wasn't for maternal instinct, mothers might be provoked to disgust, first with the process of parturition itself – essentially a mode of excretion – and then with the 'base services which the child exacts' from the mother.[86]

Clearly, the representation of female desire and sexual instinct has significant implications in Victorian biomedical texts. One reason is that it focuses the opposition between agency and instrumentality in explanations of conception and ovulation. Did the discovery of spontaneous ovulation in 1843 and the recognition that female 'heat' or passion was unnecessary for conception endorse and facilitate the relegation of women to a passive social role? Certainly, the discovery that ovulation occurs secretly, quietly and involuntarily suggested that women were the instruments through which reproductive forces worked rather than themselves the agents of willed activity, whose bodily functioning was under conscious control. But although cases proving that orgasmic heat was unnecessary for conception laid the framework for a doctrine of female passionlessness and passivity, that doctrine was by no means orthodox or representative during the Victorian period. Many biomedical texts continued to assert that ovulation and fecundation were the effect of sexual excitement; others accepted that conscious excitement was not necessary in either men or women, but that in both 'internal excitement' effected the physiological reactions necessary for conception. The account in

Todd's *Cyclopaedia*, for instance, asserts that the immediate consequence of sexual union upon the female internal generative organs
is their great excitement, a state which helps in releasing the ovum
from the ovary and sending it (already 'fecundated') to the uterus.
The emphasis on 'internal' excitement allows the author to absorb
the knowledge that women do not have actively to enjoy or even be
conscious of intercourse in order to conceive. Yet the author does
not focus on women alone, but suggests even-handedly that no one
need feel pleasure: 'It is most erroneous to suppose, as some have
done, that these [sexual] feelings are in either sex necessary to insure
the fecundating power of the one, or the liability to conception of the
other.'[87]

I want to explore two formulations from the 1850s, one endorsing
a version of female desire as analogous to male; the other linking
female human behaviour to animal behaviour and expounding a
theory of passionlessness. In each case, the representation is shaped
by its service in a larger argument, which suggests that mid-Victorian
ideology had need of contradictory constructions of female desire. In
attempting to think of female desire as analogous to male, Edward
Tilt advises that we remember how powerfully the causes of desire
operate on man, and 'as they promote in him the secretion of the
seminal fluids, we may therefore infer that they produce on woman
an analogous effect'. He proceeds to think how much of a woman's
lifetime is occupied by the various phases of the generative process,
and how 'terrible is then the conflict within her, between the
headlong impulse of passion and the dictates of duty'. Tilt discusses
various conditions in women that are the result of unsatisfied desire
and sexual stimulus. 'The absolute privation of sexual stimulus is no
doubt a cause of sub-acute ovaritis in women whose passions are
strong, especially when they are excited to their satisfaction by many
of the fashionable amusements of civilised society. Then women
suffer from one of the many forms of hysteria, sometimes caused by
ovarian inflammation.'[88] The absence of sexual stimulus in those
who are accustomed to it, may also give rise to ovarian irritation.
Thus young widows, or prostitutes, who are placed in confinement
or in institutions where they may be reclaimed, are subject to
'hysterical symptoms and abdominal pains hitherto unexperienced
by them'.[89]

Tilt also emphasised that psychical causes tend to exaggerate
desires which, 'though natural in themselves, may be pampered by

bodily and mental inactivity, and unduly excited by thoughts, books, pictures, conversation, music, and the fascinations of social intercourse'. If birds lay their eggs under the influence of impressions 'calculated to promote sexual feelings, such as the crowing of their mate', and if animals have spurious pregnancies, we must admit 'the influence of sexual incitements of a psychical nature on the formative power of the ovario-uterine organs, and we may fairly infer that similar incitements of the minds of females have a stimulating effect on the organ of ovulation'. When the organs that prompt such desires cannot be relieved by 'natural orgasm' they are placed in a state of vital turgescence, from which a morbid condition may result.[90] Tilt's emphasis on 'sexual incitements of a psychical nature' in female animals underpins his representation of the ovario-uterine organs as 'the seat of mischief, a fit soil ... for disease to spring from or to take root in'.[91] Since his intention is to prove the susceptibility of the body to ovarian disturbance, he needs the notion of ungratified desire as a source of such disturbance in the ovarian economy. Female desire is therefore figured as a powerful destabiliser of the female sexual economy and fundamentally analogous to male.

While Tilt represents desire in male and female as analogous and considers that psychical causes are capable of generating strong female desire, William Acton insists on the difference between male and female and aligns the human female closely with the animal world.[92] Rousseau had argued that there is no violent competition among human males for females in the state of nature because women, unlike other female animals, do not have alternating periods of heat and abstinence and are thus always sexually available. Acton believed, in contrast, that women do have the equivalent of periods of heat. In a state of nature, wild female animals will not allow the approach of the male except when in a state of rut, and this occurs at long intervals and only at certain seasons of the year. 'The human female would not differ much in this respect from the wild animal, had she not been civilised, for as I shall have occasion again and again to remark, she would not for her own gratification allow sexual congress except at certain periods.'[93] Throughout *The Functions and Disorders* Acton displays an interest in comparative anatomy and draws on examples of sexual behaviour among animals to underpin his discussion of human sexuality. His introduction affirms that the 'comparative anatomist will judge how much light his investigations on the animal kingdom have thrown upon sexual relations in Man'.

In successive revisions of *The Functions and Disorders* he adds further supportive examples from the animal kingdom. Analogies and associations with the animal world help Acton make the claim that the mysteries and opacities of female reproductive behaviour are made manifest by associating them with the more transparent behaviour of animals.[94] In order to suggest the female distaste throughout nature for the sexual act, he cites the wincing pain experienced by female cats, and the following anthropomorphised instance of mating behaviour among frogs:

> In some [animals] the act must, we would think, be an unmitigated distress and annoyance to the female. The female frog, for instance, is not only encumbered with an abdomen distended with ova, but is obliged to carry about her husband on her back as long as he may see fit, as he is provided by nature at this period with an enlarged thumb, which enables him to keep his hold, past the power of the female to shake him off. [95]

Sex, from the female's point of view, is represented as yet another instance of being uncomfortably under the male thumb. Acton's sympathy for the imagined female distaste for sex is in fact an expression of his displaced anxiety about the dangers of sex for the male system. Throughout nature the sexual act exhausts animal systems: male fish die, the buck rabbit falls on his side and 'the whites of his eyes turn up and hind legs are spasmodically agitated'. Nervous shock affects the spinal cord, and even a healthy man will become drowsy and languid, and experience temporary depression. Acton warns that 'an act which *may* destroy the weak should not be tampered with, even by the strong'.[96]

Human females then, according to Acton, are like other female animals in that their moments of receptivity are periodic and in the interests of conception, but they are different (civilised) because a sense of duty and unselfishness renders them available to their husbands. Nevertheless, their 'natural repugnance' for connection means that male desire itself will cool and that intelligent, civilised men will not indulge in intercourse more than once in seven to ten days. Paradoxically, the physiology of female passion, which is analogous to animal receptivity, becomes the agent of civilisation's progress. Female passionlessness in Acton's seminal economy and social world is thus of crucial importance, and his formulation of desire quite outdoes Rousseau, who argued in *Emile* that the Supreme Being has joined modesty to the unlimited desires of women in order to constrain them.⁹⁷ In Acton's view, nature and culture have combined to make the female stance of repugnance / willingness just the right one for ensuring the continuity of the species yet saving men from depleting themselves by dangerous indulgences.

The politics of instability

The recognition of the body's unstable and dynamic sexuality was responsible for great social concern about population, reproduction, the labour force and social relations; it also provided a rationale for regulation and control. While specialised medical texts discuss questions of sexual approximation and biological instability, popular advice texts, not unexpectedly, omit such theorising and explanation. Nevertheless, the transmission of medical thinking on these topics informs advice texts in a number of ways. The unarticulated assumption that control of the body and its environment is important because the body is open, permeable and subject to change, underlies advice about the onset of puberty, menstruation and its irregularity or suppression, pregnancy and early motherhood, breast-feeding and child-rearing. Middle-class sexuality has to be guarded and monitored. The female body, especially, because it was seen primarily as a reproductive body, demanded special attention and regulation if it was to keep a proper hold on its 'natural' sexuality.⁹⁸

Medical regulation and intervention depend on representations of the body as fragile and remarkably subject to deviation from good health. Indeed, so precarious is the body's hold on nature's sexing that physiology and pathology sometimes become indistinguishable. Cultures that do not take good care of their women, by implication, lose what nature has prescribed, or fail to develop what nature has provided. Not only do 'the state and morals of the women' function metonymically as a culture's claims to civilisation and progress, but by logical extension the progress of medical care for women becomes similarly an index of a culture's civilisation: 'The state of the obstetric art in any country may be taken as a measure of the respect and value of its people for the female sex; and this, in turn, may be taken as a tolerably true indication of the standard of its civilization.'⁹⁹ In this quotation, the nature of obstetric art joins a long list in ethnographic and medical discourse of standards for civilisation that relate to sexuality and its management: the turn from polygamy to monogamy, the special character of the English home, the late age of menstruation among Western women.

I have been suggesting that ideas about sexual slippage and ambiguity were most ideologically useful in Victorian enterprises of 'othering' – the construction, particularly, of other classes, races and nationalities. In these discursive productions, the body's responsiveness to change is an important ground on which the environment and social behaviour of other classes and cultures can be proven inferior. While it may have been convenient to argue for the essential reproductive function and maternal instinct of all women, it was also necessary to be able to point to differences among different classes and nations of women and to argue for the perverting modifications of particular moral and physical conditions. So, for example, the effects of factory life on the morals and bodily functioning of working-class women allowed social theorists to represent the labouring classes as a race apart and working-class culture as degenerative and contaminating. Views about the prostitute's body are particularly revealing of the way concepts of class and gender construct each other reciprocally. Especially before the 1850s, theories about the anatomical and physiological differences of prostitutes from other women function either as warnings of the dangers of a life of sin or to suggest that such a life is embarked on only by those whose bodies already deviate from the norm. Despite the fact that they appear to be the most sexual of women, prostitutes are really 'unsexed' and partly masculinised. Citing Parent Duchatelet's work on prostitution, Thomas Laycock says that the characteristic 'embonpoint of these women' has been explained by the 'use of mercury and the warm bath, inactivity of life, rich food, &c'. It is his view, however, that this fullness and plumpness, as well as the 'harsh voice of prostitutes, has a sexual origin'. Excessive fatness in young women, he notes, is 'most usually associated with a morbid state of the ovaria'.[100] It is well known that 'the removal, wasting or developement of the testes or ovaries' affects sexual appendages and voice. The same characteristic hoarse voice is found in prostitutes as in aged unmarried women. 'It ought to be observed that this approximation to the voice of man is caused, probably, by some change in the ovaries, analogous to that of hybrid birds, prostitutes being, notoriously, sterile.'[101] Paradoxically, the most sexualised woman is, in fact, not fully a woman at all, her masculinisation detectable in her voice and the (alleged) fact that she is unable to bear children. 'The ovaries of prostitutes' concurred Tilt, 'are seldom without some morbid lesions.'[102] But did an originary anatomical difference lead some women to a life of prostitution, or did that life produce the ill-effects that then defined the prostitute? As the speculations of the many investigators of prostitution – the great Social Evil – reveal, this was a vexed and variously answered question. The doctrine of passionlessness can be seen as an attempt to solve that question by bypassing it. Rather than pathologising the desire of the prostitute, Greg, Acton and others offered a version of essential female nature as passionless.

This chapter has sought to unsettle the notion that Victorian medical texts and the narratives of reproductive biology present a unified or coherent representation of female sexuality or sexual difference. In so doing, it has drawn attention to their contradictory formulations of female desire, prostitution, sexual instinct and to the role of analogy with animal life in defining the nature of human reproductive behaviour. I have sought also to argue that only when we recognise the Victorian concern with sexual instability and the various ways in which 'nature' is constructed in discussions of sexuality can we appreciate what studies of Victorian sexuality have tended to emphasise – an anxious concern with disciplining, regulating and monitoring the sexual body. The chapters that follow explore not so much the echoes or reflections of these ideas about sexuality as a dynamic process, but their implications and transformations in specific social debates and literary representations.

Notes

1. D. Riley, *'Am I That Name?': Feminism and the Category of 'Women' in History* (Minneapolis, University of Minnesota Press, 1988), pp. 6–7.
2. These are Judith Butler's terms in her discussion of Riley in *Gender Trouble: Feminism and the Subversion of Identity* (London, Routledge, 1990), p. 3.
3. C. Smart, 'Disruptive bodies and unruly sex: the regulation of reproduction and sexuality in the nineteenth century', in C. Smart (ed.), *Regulating Womanhood: Historical Essays on Marriage, Motherhood and Sexuality* (London, Routledge, 1992), p. 9.
4. See Smart, 'Disruptive bodies', p. 11.
5. Foucault's formulation has been the subject of some debate; see N. Armstrong, *Desire and Domestic Fiction: A Political History of the Novel* (Oxford, Oxford University Press, 1987), pp. 10–11; and S. Gilman, *Sexuality: An Illustrated History Representing the Sexual in Medicine and Culture from the Middle Ages to the Age of AIDS* (New York, John Wiley, 1989), pp. 2–

4, who takes issue with Foucault by insisting on the existence of the libido, 'of an intrinsic, if shapeless and unfocused force, within all human beings that provides the extraordinary power always associated with all our constructs of sexuality' (p. 2); for an appraisal of the debate see M. Vicinus, 'Sexuality and power: a review of current work in the history of sexuality', *Feminist Studies*, 8 (1982), pp. 133–56.

6. See L. Jordanova, *Sexual Visions: Images of Gender in Science and Medicine between the Eighteenth and the Twentieth Centuries* (Brighton, Harvester, 1989), pp. 246; and L. Birkin, *Consuming Desire: Sexual Science and the Emergence of a Culture of Abundance, 1871–1914* (Ithaca, Cornell University Press, 1988), who overstates Darwin's emphasis on sexual differentiation out of sameness as the origin of later sexologies.

7. T. Laqueur, *Making Sex: Body and Gender from the Greeks to Freud* (Cambridge, Mass., Harvard University Press, 1990).

8. See C. Gallagher and T. Laqueur (eds), *The Making of the Modern Body: Sexuality and Society in the Nineteenth Century* (Berkeley, University of California Press, 1987), p. ix; T. Laqueur, *Making Sex*, p. 197; for a discussion of the reasons for increased scientific attention to women, see L. Schiebinger, 'Skeletons in the closet: the first illustrations of the female skeleton in eighteenth-century anatomy', in *The Making of the Modern Body*, pp. 42–82; she argues that post-Enlightenment science responded to social needs in finding ways to deal with the 'woman problem'.

9. O. Moscucci, *The Science of Woman: Gynaecology and Gender in England 1800–1929* (Cambridge, Cambridge University Press, 1990), p. 16; see also a reworking of her first chapter in 'Hermaphroditism and sex difference: the construction of gender in Victorian England', in *Science and Sensibility: Gender and Scientific Enquiry 1780–1945*, ed. M. Benjamin (Oxford, Basil Blackwell, 1991), pp. 174–99.

10. Laqueur, *Making Sex*, pp. 10–11.

11. H. Maudsley, 'Sex in mind and in education', *Fortnightly Review*, 15 (1874), p. 466.

12. My account here follows Rachel Bowlby's in her discussion of Freud's misremembering of the fable; see 'Walking, women and writing: Virginia Woolf as *flaneuse*', in I. Armstrong (ed.), *New Feminist Discourses* (London, Routledge, 1992), pp. 26–7.

13. Maudsley, 'Sex in mind and in education', p. 472.

14. Maudsley, 'Sex in mind and in education', p. 470. The similarity of boys and girls is often assumed, but also contested. See T. Laycock, *Treatise on the Nervous Diseases of Women* (London, Longman, 1840), who says, 'It is commonly stated that there is little difference in the general appearance of the sexes before puberty. This may be true with regard to the period of infancy; but a single glance at an assembly of boys and girls of various ages, from two to ten years, will convince the observer that there is more harshness of outline, greater proportionate magnitude, and a less delicate expression of countenance in the boys' (pp. 77–8). See however R. B. Todd's *Cyclopaedia of Anatomy and Physiology* (London, Sherwood, 1839–54) where Dr. Allen Thomson in the entry on 'Generation' notes that in youth the sexes do not differ materially (p. 439).

15. Maudsley, 'Sex in mind and in education', p. 470; his references to mutilated men and women suffering from arrested development expose a contradiction that puzzled medical writers. If woman was supposed to be imperfect or undeveloped man, then her 'arrested development' should have made her even less like a man.

16. E. G. Anderson, 'Sex in mind and education: a reply', *Fortnightly Review*, 15 (1874), p. 586.

17. Anderson, 'Sex in mind and education: a reply', p. 589.

18. A. B. Blackwell, *The Sexes Throughout Nature* (New York, 1875), p. 232.

19. See the discussion of Blackwell in E. K. Helsinger, R. L. Sheets and Wm. Veeder (eds.), *The Woman Question: Society and Literature in Britain and America, 1837–1883*, 3 vols (Manchester, Manchester University Press, 1983), pp. 106–8.

20. Laycock, *A Treatise on the Nervous Diseases of Women*, pp. 78–9.

21. Wm. Kirby and Wm. Spence, *An Introduction to Entomology: or Elements of the Natural History of Insects*, vol. 2 (London, Longman, 1817), p. 132. See also Laycock's discussion of 'periodic changes of insects', *Treatise*, pp. 56–9.

22. Kirby, *An Introduction to Entomology*, pp. 128–36; he also cites the following example: a cow has two calves, of which one is male and the other female, the female will always be sterile, and 'partakes of the characteristics of the other sex'. More recently, discoveries about the sex of male and female turtle and crocodile eggs suggest that temperature is the key factor in sex determination.

23. When Darwin argues in *The Descent of Man, and Selection in Relation to Sex*, 2nd edn. (London, John Murray, 1874) that social instinct is, like any other instinct, strengthened by habit, he too draws on the social instincts of bees. 'If for instance, to take an extreme case, men were reared under precisely the same conditions as hive bees, there can hardly be a doubt that our unmarried females would, like the worker-bees, think it a sacred duty to kill their brothers, and mothers would strive to kill their fertile daughters; and no one would think of interfering' (p. 99).

24. Sir J. Y. Simpson, 'Hermaphroditism', in *The Works of Sir James Y. Simpson, Bart* ,vol. 2, ed. Sir W. G. Simpson (Edinburgh, Adam Black, 1871), p. 501.

25. Simpson, 'Hermaphroditism', p. 517. He refers to the views of Knox, recently published in the *Edinburgh Journal of Science*, vol. ii, p. 322.

26. Laycock, *Treatise on the Nervous Diseases of Women*, pp. 40–1.

27. E. J. Tilt, *On Diseases of Women and Ovarian Inflammation* (London, Churchill, 1853), p. 85.

28. Todd, *Cyclopaedia*, p. 451.

29. See Foucault, *The History of Sexuality*, pp. 54–5.

30. See Moscucci, *The Science of Woman*, p. 16.

31. On the contrast between sexuality as dynamic process or static essence, see Moscucci, *The Science of Woman*, p. 16.

32. Tilt, *On Diseases of Women*, p. 24.

33. Tilt, *On Diseases of Women*, p. 27.

34. Laycock, *Treatise on the Nervous Diseases of Women*, p. 11.

35. Though he notes that others have claimed that the voice becomes harsh like a man's and there is frequently a formidable beard, and hair on different

parts of the body, Laycock doubts such changes. He says that although he
has searched diligently, he has never found an instance of this sort.

36. Laycock, *Treatise on the Nervous Diseases of Women*, p. 12.
37. Laycock, *Treatise on the Nervous Diseases of Women*, p. 22.
38. For a discussion of Yarrell's paper, read before the Royal Society in 1827, see
    Tilt, *On Diseases of Women*, p. 26; Laycock, *Treatise on the Nervous Diseases of
    Women*, p. 21.
39. Laycock, *Treatise on the Nervous Diseases of Women*, p. 22.
40. W. Collins, *The Woman in White* (Harmondsworth, Penguin, [1859–60]
    1974), pp. 589.
41. This point is made by Moscucci, *The Science of Woman*, p. 17; she takes issue
    with Laqueur's emphasis on difference, which she sees as fundamental to
    the articulation of masculinity and femininity, but insists that kinship was
    also important. In *Making Sex*, Laqueur does say of the nineteenth century
    that despite the most impassioned defense of two sexes, of ineradicable
    'organic difference ... proved by all sound biology' the one-sex model lived
    on. The openness of nineteenth-century science to either a two- or a one-sex
    model can be seen, he argues, in the way that denunciations of prostitution
    and masturbation reproduced an earlier discourse of the unstable individual
    body, open and responsive to social evil (p. 21).
42. Simpson, 'Hermaphroditism', p. 490.
43. Simpson, 'Hermaphroditism', pp. 490–1.
44. Tilt, *On Diseases of Women*, p. 56.
45. [Anne Richelieu Lamb] *Can Woman Regenerate Society?* (London, Parker,
    1844), p. 178.
46. J. M. Allan, 'On the differences in the minds of men and women', *Journal of
    the Anthropological Society*, 7 (1869), p. cxcvii; he notes that 'for male and
    female there is no serious difference of opinion or object until the age of
    puberty. Then, how great the difference! The boy, springing into manhood,
    is at once and for ever developed, and, so far as sex is concerned, completed.
    Whereas the woman, for a period varying from twenty to thirty years, is an
    admirably constructed apparatus for the most mysterious and sublime of
    nature's mysteries – the reproductive process.'
47. Simpson, 'Hermaphroditism', p. 492.
48. Wm. Carpenter, *Principles of Human Physiology; with Their Chief Applications
    to Pathology, Hygiene and Forensic Medicine* (London, Churchill, 1842), p. 343.
49. Carpenter, *Human Physiology*, p. 569; see also Todd, *Cyclopaedia*, vol. 3, p.
    250, where the author notes that the glandular structure of the male and
    female breast, discovered by Sir Astley Cooper, explains most satisfactorily
    those recorded cases in which the infant was suckled by the male parent
    after the death of the female. The most authentic instance of this is cited in
    Humboldt's travels.
50. Carpenter, *Human Physiology*, p. 569; see Laycock, *Treatise on the Nervous
    Diseases of Women*, p. 25, who cites various case histories, and observes that
    'in effeminate men the mammae are frequently somewhat developed'.
51. Todd, *Cyclopaedia*, p. 441.
52. See the discussion of periodicity and male menstruation in Moscucci, *The
    Science of Woman*, pp. 18–20.

53. Simpson, 'Hermaphroditism', p. 430.
54. Simpson, 'Hermaphroditism', p. 453.
55. Simpson, 'Hermaphroditism', p. 479.
56. Laqueur, *Making Sex*, p. 142.
57. See Tilt, *On Diseases of Women*, p. 32, who is citing a variety of opinions about menstruation.
58. Todd, *Cyclopaedia*, p. 442; having taken a plank out of such racist arguments, Roberton is proud that his work is endorsed by the ethnologist and monogenist, James Prichard, in his influential *Natural History of Man*; see *Essays and Notes on the Physiology and Diseases of Women, and on Practical Midwifery* (London, John Churchill, 1851), p. 22.
59. See Moscucci, *The Science of Woman*, p. 25.
60. J. T. Conquest, *Letters to a Mother* (London, 1848).
61. M. Ryan, *A Manual of Midwifery*, 4th edn. (London, 1841).
62. Darwin, *Descent of Man*, p. 602.
63. H. Spencer, *Principles of Sociology*, vol. 1, 3rd edn. (London, Williams and Norgate, 1897–1906; reprint, Westport, Conn., Greenwood, 1975), p. 756.
64. Darwin, *The Descent of Man*, p. 612, p. 124.
65. Darwin, *The Descent of Man*, p. v.
66. Darwin, *The Descent of Man*, p. 608.
67. C. Darwin, *The Variations of Animals and Plants Under Domestication*, vol. 20 *The Works of Charles Darwin* ed. P. H. Barrett and R. B. Freeman (London, William Pickering, 1988), p. 124.
68. Maudsley, 'Sex in mind and in education', p. 477. William Acton too deals with the question of atrophy in service of his argument against sexual excess. Responding to George Drysdale's advocation of regular sexual exercise for both men and women, and insisting on the need for continence he argues: 'I may state that I have never seen a single instance of atrophy of the generative organs from this cause' (*Functions and Disorders of the Reproductive Organs* [London, 1857], p. 57).
69. Already, he remarks, invoking a spectre of atrophy, 'those in whom the organs are wasted' have to resort to the 'dressmaker's aid in order to gain the appearance of them; they are not satisfied unless they wear the show of perfect womanhood' (Maudsley, 'Sex in mind and in education', p. 477).
70. 'Queen bees or working bees?', *Saturday Review* (12 November 1859), p. 576.
71. A. Tennyson, 'The Princess: A Medley', in *From Tennyson: A Selected Edition* vol. 7, ed. C. Ricks (Essex, Longman, 1969), pp. 259–64.
72. A. Walker, *Woman Physiologically Considered as to Mind, Morals, Marriage, Matrimonial Slavery, Infidelity and Divorce* (London, Baily, 1840), pp. 14–21. Walker's discussion serves to introduce a diatribe against Wollstonecraft and her views on female education.
73. Walker, *Woman Physiologically Considered*, pp. 42–3. The *Saturday Review* found similarly that 'a strong-minded woman is like a pretty man; the merit is unnatural to both' ('Feminine wranglers', *Saturday Review*, 18 [1864], p. 112). Describing the 'man-rivalling' woman, Coventry Patmore in the *North British Review* noted that she was 'seldom handsome', and thought that she 'retaliates Nature's injuries by injuries to Nature, not knowing that it is in the power of every well-conditioned woman to fulfil the duty of being

lovely,' ('The social position of women', *North British Review*, 14 [1851], p. 528). Literary reviews often have recourse to judgement in terms of the 'unsexing' of women – the unwomanly woman, the mannish woman (also known as the strong-minded woman) and the womanish man. The aggressive heroines of women's fiction are found to be 'unsexed'. The strongest term of disapprobation paid to a male writer is to find him feminine, unmanly or effeminate.

74. Todd, *Cyclopaedia*, p. 443.
75. Carpenter, *Human Physiology*, p. 197.
76. Carpenter, *Human Physiology*, p. 619.
77. Carpenter, *Human Physiology*, p. 73.
78. H. Maudsley, *The Physiology and Pathology of the Mind* (London, Macmillan, 1867), p. 133.
79. *Medical Times and Gazette* (18 February, 1860), p. 170; see the discussion of this article in S. Mitchell, *The Fallen Angel: Chastity, Class and Women's Reading, 1835–1880* (Ohio, Bowling Green University Popular Press, 1981), p. 102.
80. E. Blackwell, *The Human Element in Sex: Being a Medical Enquiry into the Relation of Sexual Physiology to Christian Morality*, 2nd edn. (London, J. and A. Churchill, 1884), p. 28.
81. Todd, *Cyclopaedia*, p. 444.
82. Carpenter, *Human Physiology*, p. 207; on the question of the cerebellum as the seat of desire see also Todd, *Cyclopaedia*, p. 444; G. Combe, *Elements of Phrenology* (Edinburgh, Maclachlan and Stewart, 1855), p. 64ff; see his defence against Carpenter's objections to the functions of the cerebellum (p. 224).
83. Quoted in R. Wolff, 'Devoted disciple: the letters of Mary Elizabeth Braddon to Sir Edward Bulwer-Lytton, 1862–1873', *Harvard Literary Bulletin*, 22 (1974), pp. 5–35, 129–61.
84. Combe, *Elements of Phrenology*, p. 66.
85. On this point see Russett, *Sexual Science*, p. 19.
86. Maudsley, *Physiology and Pathology of the Mind*, p. 389.
87. Todd, *Cyclopaedia*, p. 447.
88. Tilt, *On Diseases of Women*, p. 148.
89. Tilt, *On Diseases of Women*, p. 147; he quotes Parent Duchatelet who says that only 8 out of every 105 prostitutes suffers from hysteria, but when they enter the Magdalene institutions they are troubled with hysterical symptoms. This may have been less on account of unsatisfied desire than the result of the activities prescribed by reforming institutions; see E. J. Bristow, *Vice and Vigilance: Purity Movements in Britain since 1700* (Dublin, Gill and Macmillan, 1977), p. 65: 'A number of staple occupations had been suggested for the inmates, from weaving of Turkish carpets, which after all kept harems happily occupied...'.
90. Tilt, *On Diseases of Women*, p. 147.
91. Tilt, *On Diseases of Women*, p. 8.
92. In 1857, Acton reprinted from the 3rd edition of his *Practical Treatise on Diseases of the Urinary and Generative Organs* the section on functional disorders, which he had there treated for the first time. This section he then

expanded and printed separately as *The Functions and Disorders of the Reproductive Organs* (reprt. from the 3rd edn., London, Churchill, 1857). Since Havelock Ellis held Acton up as the epitome of sexually repressive attitudes that came to seem typically Victorian, a great deal has been written about his views, and he has been characterised variously as representative, orthodox, extreme, innovatory. See S. Marcus, *The Other Victorians: A Study of Sexuality and Pornography in Mid-Nineteenth-Century England* (New York, Basic Books, 1966); Helsinger *et al.* (eds.), *The Woman Question*, pp. 58–72 on the Drysdale / Acton debate; J. Maynard, 'The worlds of Victorian sexuality: work in progress', in *Sexuality and Victorian Literature* ed. D. R. Cox, *Tennessee Studies in Literature*, vol. 27 (Knoxville, University of Tennessee Press, 1984), pp. 251–65; F. Mort, *Dangerous Sexualities: Medico-Moral Politics in England since 1830* (London, Routledge, 1987), p. 79; J. Weeks, *Sex, Politics and Society: The Regulation of Sexuality since 1800* (Essex, Longman, 1981), p. 39.

93. Acton, *Functions and Disorders* (6th edn., 1885), p. 184.
94. Laqueur makes this point in relation to the hidden process of ovulation; see Gallagher, *The Making of the Modern Body*, p. 30.
95. See Acton, *Functions and Disorders* (3rd edn., 1862), n. 1, p. 84.
96. Acton, *Functions and Disorders*, (3rd edn., 1862), p. 87.
97. On Rousseau's views see Laqueur, *Making Sex*, p. 199. Carpenter also noted that the highest degree of bodily vigour is inconsistent with a frequent indulgence in sexual intercourse: 'Nothing is more certain to reduce the powers, both of body and mind, than excess in this respect' (*Human Physiology*, p. 620).
98. On the ideological implications of representations of menstruation see S. Shuttleworth, 'Female circulation: medical discourse and popular advertising in the mid-Victorian era', in M. Jacobus, E. Fox Keller and S. Shuttleworth (eds.), *Body\Politics: Women and the Discourses of Science* (London, Routledge, 1990), pp. 47–68.
99. W. T. Smith, 'Introductory lecture to a course of lectures on obstetrics, delivered at the Hunterian School of Medicine, 1847–48', *The Lancet*, 2 (1847), p. 371.
100. Laycock, *Treatise on the Nervous Diseases of Women*, p. 24.
101. Laycock, *Treatise on the Nervous Diseases of Women*, p. 32.
102. Tilt, *On Diseases of Women*, p. 146.

Chapter two

The making of the moral mother: representations of working-class sexuality in *Mary Barton*

When Elizabeth Gaskell took up her pen in *Mary Barton* to engage with ongoing debates about the nature and condition of the working classes, she turned her attention not only to class relations in the marketplace but to topical representations of domestic life and the moral and sexual behaviour of working-class women.[1] We have been taught to think of *Mary Barton* as a 'condition-of-England' novel because of its concern with class conflict in the new northern manufacturing towns and its factory and strike scenes. But economic, political and class issues are not only manifest in the relations of the marketplace or in strike and factory scenes. If we recognise the importance of gender as an analytic category in scrutinising social and cultural formations, we need to attend also to Gaskell's representations of domestic life, mothering and attitudes to women's work, which are as politically charged as her treatment of strikes and unemployment.[2] To read *Mary Barton* in relation to a range of contemporary texts that address the 'problem' of working-class sexuality and morality is to see how the novel engages with articulations of class difference in prevailing contemporary representations of sexuality.

Ideas about the openness of sexuality to cultural and environmental influence are nowhere more evident than in middle-class constructions of class difference. Grounded in beliefs about sexual instability, the work of early social scientists represents the working, labouring and 'lower' classes as belonging to a separate race or species by virtue of their sexual and moral behaviour. In showing that the environment, morality, and physicality of one group distinguished it from other groups, middle-class social scientists drew on notions of an unstably sexed body whose altered reproductive functioning reflected moral decline and foretold widespread degeneration. Whether depravity had bred destitution or vice versa was the subject of considerable discussion among philanthropists, reformers and social scientists during the 1830s and 1840s, but whatever the cause, the result was a class of people as physically and morally 'other' as a separate species or race.[3]

As the previous chapter has shown, Victorian biomedical discourse represents sexuality as a dynamic process, susceptible to moral and cultural influence. It was not, we recall, that nature had specially fitted the South Sea Islanders to 'the functions of propagation' at the age of six or seven years, but their 'barbarous and debased state of civilization' that was eventually responsible for their early maturation.[4] The example of nature altered by depraved culture also suggests that moral, sexual and marital behaviour can be taken as an index of a culture's degree of civilisation, which is judged according to middle-class norms. Since a psychical component – the moral sense – is supposed to temper and refine brute sexual urge in human beings, talk about a culture's moral condition is usually talk about its sexual arrangements and attitudes, that part of culture which influences sexuality and shapes even the physicality of a people. Working-class sexual habits and morality – most evident in domestic conditions – are represented as cultural determinants, and defined as a 'social problem' of critical importance. Indeed, working-class domesticity, it can be argued, was *the* social problem that gave birth to Victorian social science, and as countless reports and theories on the moral and physical condition of the working classes show, Victorians believed that the 'condition of England' was to be seen, accounted for, and modified in the home.[5]

Throughout the 1840s the public discourse of poverty and immorality focused on women's responsibility for the regulation of the home, the observation of sanitary laws and the inculcation of habits of thrift, providence, and temperance, which would ameliorate the condition of the working classes. As social researchers recorded statistics about the nature of employment, income, education and production, they also inquired into household organisation, domestic economy, and sleeping arrangements.[6] Since the process of moralising the category 'Woman' was well under way at this time, mothers and housewives ultimately shouldered the blame for immoral households – dirty and disorderly living quarters, sexual laxity, the loosening of family ties, poor attitudes to education, a lack of nutritious food and even bad table manners. Time and again, observers remark that all depends on the wife and mother: if a man was careful in choosing his wife, he would secure prosperity. W. R. Greg, who had a great deal to say about the moral condition of the labouring classes, pronounced in a review of *Mary Barton* that among the working population the lack is not material but moral, and prosperity depends on whether a man marries a 'sluggard and a slattern, or a prudent and industrious woman'.[7] The best wives are those who have had a 'good industrial training in the well-regulated household of persons of a higher condition'.[8]

Because they anticipated the effects of morality on physicality, social scientists turned their attention to female sexuality and bodily function, considering the age of puberty and menstruation, conditions of birth, nursing, and child-rearing practices. Responsive to moral and environmental conditions and reproducing changes in successive generations, the working-class female body is found to differ from other female bodies in its early maturation and menstruation, reduced fertility, perversions of maternal instinct, and the assumption of masculine form through muscular development and physical labour.[9] An array of scientific and medical authority is cited to show that the moral condition of the working classes, dependent on (and reflected in) the state and morals of the women, is perilously degenerate. [10] One might argue that the Victorian preoccupation with domesticity and the nature of female function and sexuality among the labouring classes was a way of not dealing with problematic economic relations, that it was an attempt to manage class and economic issues by writing them as sexual issues. By centring their focus on the domestic habits of the industrial poor, middle-class social analysts were certainly able to deflect attention from labour and wage matters, to offer reasons for endemic poverty and disease, and to regulate the socialisation of an indispensable labour force. But more than deflection was at stake here: to claim that class differences were written into the body's sexuality was to naturalise them; to insist that the nature of the home was an index and reflection of that sexuality was to make the domestic sphere crucial to the production of a gendered social hierarchy.

But the moral and sexual nature of working-class women was not the focus of middle-class observers alone. Working-class radicals and Chartist leaders depended on similar 'scientific' evidence about the effects of the factory system on maternity and sexuality in their struggle for factory reforms and the franchise. In this context too, the same representations could be tailored and used to serve different ideological interests and political ends. If one wrote deploring the factory system and militating for its reform, then the reports of W. R. Greg and James Kay Shuttleworth could help to show how detrimental it was to put women to work. In *The History of the Factory Movement*, Samuel Kydd (writing pseudonymously as 'Alfred') records that the publications of Greg and Kay 'accelerated the growth of public opinion in favour of factory legislation' and that it was the custom of 'Mr. Oastler and others to read extracts therefrom, corroborating the parliamentary evidence on the question, and either leaving out or replying to the educational and economical theories of the authors'.[11] He notes later that although 'Mr. Greg and Dr. Kay would probably have felt shocked at being associated with Mr. Oastler and Mr. Bull, yet the labours of the former contributed practically toward the same end as the latter – the physical, moral and mental elevation of those employed in factory labour'.[12] They were enlisted to show that if the factory system had never existed, manufacture would not have 'lowered its victims beneath the level of brutes in their habits', and 'perverted the superior reason' of men and women from 'an appreciation of the homely virtues of domestic life to an admiration of that which was sensual and vicious'.[13] To emphasise further how texts were appropriated and contested, we may notice that when W. R. Greg's brother, Robert Hyde Greg, published a vigorous defense of the factory system in 1834, he dealt with his brother's previous damning account by saying that it was *little more than a college thesis* written without any real acquaintance with factories or factory populations. He explained that his brother had 'imprudently adopted as facts, the *misrepresentations of a heated partizan of the "Ten Hours Bill"*'.[14]

While middle-class reporting implied that a debased morality bred poverty and destitution, men and women of the working classes insisted that the inhumane factory system and the exploitation of female labour was responsible for the destruction of their domestic life and social organisation. Both agreed that the reproductive health of the social group was at risk. In an influential pamphlet, 'The Rights of Women' (1840), one of the Chartist leaders, R. J. Richardson, urges the working women of England to demand equal right to the suffrage. He reminds his audience that Queen Victoria is a woman, legitimating women's entitlement to political power and the vote. 'If a woman is qualified to be a queen over a great nation... a woman in a minor degree ought to have a voice in the election of the legislative authorities.'[15] If women contribute to the wealth of the kingdom by their labour in the fields, dairy farms, factories, they should be allowed to vote. It is interesting to note, however, that Richardson is speaking only of widows and spinsters. He rather conventionally regarded married women as 'one' with their husbands and thought that they did not need to vote independently. His argument is that single women should use their vote to help elect a government that would allow working-class life to assume its proper shape and allow them to take their proper place in it. They will presumably then no longer need a public voice.

Richardson's apparently radical views on women's suffrage are enlisted to serve a position on domesticity and the sexual division of labour little different from that of bourgeois ideology and its vision of separate spheres; both are a response to the complex threat that working women posed to labour and sexual relations. He deals with that threat by mustering evidence on the natural function of women, the corruption of childbearing and child-rearing, the dangers to women's bodies and the future of their offspring. Both factory and agricultural work distort women's natural capacities. Working like men in the fields yet naturally unfit for such toil, women become masculine, and, as he explains, the

> force of all those tender passions implanted by God in the breast of woman to temper the ruggedness of man, become weakened, her real virtues forgotten, and her proper usefulness destroyed.... To the women I say, endeavour to throw off the degradation of predial slavery, return to your domestic circles and cultivate your finer feelings for the benefit of your offspring. How can you expect to be free, when you are willing slaves, and nourish in your lap a new race of hereditary bondsmen?[16]

Factories are figured as hideous dens where the 'pith of womanhood' is 'dried up and withered', and girls become 'women and mothers years before their natural period'. Factory mothers have to return to work a few days after giving birth and must leave the 'innocent babe to the *care* of a nurse, who, with bottle teat and Godfrey's cordial, keeps the little victim quiet until the mother returns from the mill to her meals'.[17] The woman who does not have a husband should find one to toil for her; the woman who does have one should go home and minister to his comforts. 'The Rights of Women' reveals how the subject of female sexuality and motherhood functions as an important arena in which to press class interests, assert grievances and challenge dominant constructions of class difference.[18]

Mary Barton's relationship to this politically charged discourse of working-class morality, domesticity and sexuality is complex: the novel is simultaneously an indictment of dominant constructions of the industrial poor and an endorsement of middle-class liberal values. It is engaged in detailing the heterogeneity of working-class culture (though not, as some critics have noticed, the corporate culture of the working classes), offering explanations for excessive and embittered behaviour among poverty-stricken workers, enlisting the reader's understanding and sympathy for the plight of the industrial poor, as well as sometimes reinforcing and underwriting the association of the working classes with a lack of discipline, a need for regulation, and a disorder both wild and dangerous.[19] After detailing the privations that the poor have suffered, for example, the narrator concedes to public opinion about vice, then encouragingly pledges her own faith in virtue: 'The vices of the poor sometimes astound us *here*; but when the secrets of all hearts shall be made known, their virtues will astound us in far greater degree. Of this I am certain.'[20]

The novel's difficulty in representing and explaining the condition of the working classes from a liberal, middle-class perspective is manifest in its textual unevenness. The narrator often hastens to anticipate the arguments and prejudices of her middle-class readers, either modifying or conceding them, but then at once mounting an impassioned defence of her working-class subjects that nevertheless subtly endorses middle-class prejudices, corroborating their views of the working classes as needy, child-like, uneducated, precipitous, dangerous. A well-remarked example is the representation of John Barton and the working class as a whole as Frankenstein (metonymically meaning the monster). In her creation scenario, delinquent middle-class parenting has spawned a monster, outraged and uneducated, soulless yet visionary. On another occasion, the narrator explains the power of trade unions, or combinations, as possessing the 'mighty agency of steam; capable of unlimited good or evil. But to obtain a blessing on its labours, it must work under the direction of a high and intelligent will; incapable of being misled by passion or excitement. The will of the operatives had not been guided to the calmness of wisdom.' After this meditation on the necessity of wisdom to guide power and the absence of wisdom among working men, she plunges hastily back into the narrative: 'So much for generalities. Let us now return to individuals' (p. 203).

Gaskell was not alone in her discomfort with public discourses of working-class poverty and immorality and her simultaneous reliance on them. Within the complex social fabric of liberal middle-class Manchester life in the 1840s, ambivalence and discomfort were especially strong among Unitarian social managers – educationalists, clergymen, temperance advocates, doctors, philanthropists.[21] Signs of strain are particularly evident in the history of the Unitarian Domestic Mission, with which Elizabeth Gaskell and her husband were closely involved and from whose reports she literally lifted some of her descriptions of poverty-stricken dwellings in *Mary Barton*.[22] The history of the Domestic Mission reveals significant tensions and contradictions between its stated aims when established, and its subsequent experiences of home visiting through the late 1830s and 1840s. As initially conceived, the missionary was supposed to

> establish an intercourse with a limited number of families of the neglected poor – to put himself in close sympathy with their wants – to become to them a Christian advisor and friend – to promote the order and comfort of their homes, and the elevation of their social tastes – to bring them into a permanent connection with religious influences – and, above all, to promote an effective education of their children, and to shelter them from corrupting agencies.[23]

If the Domestic Mission began as part of a 'liberal offensive to make inroads into working-class life', to ensure the effective sociali-sation of the labour force, it did not, according to John Seed, proceed unproblematically. The aim of penetrating and reshaping the domestic lives of the poor seemed hardly applicable as the economic situation of the late 1830s and 1840s deteriorated. Unitarian ministers in the Domestic Mission, first George Buckland and then John Layhe, were forced to confront contradictions between the dominant middle-class ideology of poverty and what they were seeing in the daily lives of impoverished families among the working classes.[24] In the face of grinding poverty, injunctions about thrift, prudence and good housekeeping struck the minister as horribly irrelevant: 'The only place for learning what poverty is, and its influence on the temper, dispositions and habits of its unfortunate subjects, is the destitute abode itself, surrounded by half-clad and famishing children.'[25] The 'germ' of *Mary Barton* may well have been Gaskell's experience of similar abodes: report has it that she was 'trying hard to speak comfort, and to allay those bitter feelings against the rich which were so common with the poor, when the head of the family took hold of her arm, and grasping it tightly said, with tears in his eyes, "Ay, ma'am, but have ye ever seen a child clemmed to death" '.[26]

Like the mission reports, Gaskell's text registers the contradictions and confusions of a growing rift between the public discourses of poverty and moral management on the one hand, and the experience and practice of those who were witnessing working-class distress through regular contact and visitation on the other. In the context of the Ministry to the Poor, Gaskell's text is itself a domestic mission of another kind, designed to penetrate the homes of the middle-class reading public and inform them of a widespread social alienation that could only be addressed through personal involvement and direct interaction.[27] Home visiting is a fundamental structuring device in *Mary Barton*; the narrator frequently takes the middle-class reader into the homes of a variety of working-class subjects: the Wilsons visit the comfortable Bartons in the opening chapters, Mary visits Alice Wilson in her tidy cellar, George and John Barton visit the impoverished Davenports in their shockingly squalid conditions, Will Wilson visits Job Legh to chat about mermaids and flying-fish, and so on. The home is in *Mary Barton,* as much as in the investigations of early social science and the Domestic Mission reports, the place where the condition of England can best be read. But what was to be read was open to challenge. In the earlier Mission reports of home visitation, domestic disorder is consistently linked to vice: 'Whenever I visit a more than ordinarily wretched habitation, I feel a suspicion that vice must be there; a suspicion which subsequent enquiry too often justifies.'[28] Like the later reports, which abandon such equations, Gaskell's text is defensive of working-class domestic pride and reluctant to see wretched conditions as symptomatic of immorality and vice. To think of this novel as attempting to build its fictional form from the basic stuff of the Domestic Mission reports, goes some way to explain its problematic generic affiliations and the difficulty critics have articulated in identifying its form.[29]

In terms of its concern with domestic order, *Mary Barton* is not, as it were, itself a tidy and well-regulated house; Elizabeth Barrett Browning thought the novel powerful but 'slovenly' in style.[30] Although it can suggest simply 'carelessness' or 'lacking in thoroughness', 'slovenly' is a term used frequently in the 1840s to describe both working-class women and the state of their homes, connoting a slackness of appearance that suggests inner disorder and failure of discipline.[31] The unsettled and disruptive texture of *Mary Barton* can be taken to express an identification and association with its disorderly and unregulated subjects. The struggle between the expression and control of powerful passionate feelings informs the text at many levels: Gaskell's preface warns of 'hands clenched and ready to strike' (p. xxxvi), 'wild romances' trouble the lives of people you might pass in the street, the prostitute Esther has a nature 'violent and unregulated', John Barton's association with trade unions and Chartism links him to that which is 'wild and visionary', and Mary, figured as a 'wild' rose, has energy and passion of considerable transgressive potential. Indeed, the unsolved dilemma of the text is how to endorse education, regulation and self-restraint (associated with sexual and moral stability) while not relinquishing the best of working-class culture (associated with energy, spirit and passion).

I have been suggesting that the style and form of *Mary Barton* signal Gaskell's uneasy involvement with public discourses of poverty and moral laxity. I want now to focus specifically on three aspects of contemporary discussion that figure importantly in the novel: the question of female labour and its effect on the moral and physical condition of women, the rhetoric of degeneration and community health, and the representation of indigent mothers. These issues will serve to highlight the politics of gender with which the novel's emphasis on domesticity is concerned.

During Mary Barton's visit to the recently widowed Mrs. Wilson, the older woman and her sister-in-law air views about working women that resonate with contemporary debates on the sexual division of labour in working-class life. Mrs. Wilson wonders how Prince Albert would like

> his missis to be from home when he comes in, tired and worn, and wanting someone to cheer him; and maybe, her to come in by and by, just as tired and down in th' mouth; and how he'd like for her never to be at home to see to th' cleaning of his house, or to keep a bright fire in his grate. Let alone his meals being all hugger-mugger, and comfortless. I'd be bound, prince as he is, if his missis served him so, he'd be off to a gin-palace, or summut o' that kind (p. 140).

Mrs Wilson declares that because she had worked in a factory before she was married, she knew nothing about housekeeping and began married life by burning her husband's dinner to a nasty brown mess.

Work before marriage is bad enough, but matters are even worse when women go to work afterwards: 'I could reckon up... nine men I know, as has been driven to th' public-house by having wives as worked in factories; good folk too, as thought there was no harm in putting their little ones out at nurse, and letting their house go all dirty, and their fires all out...' (p. 139). She is of the opinion that Queen Victoria should stop women working because work inter- feres with their function as homemakers. Eventually in this conversation the women find themselves trying to understand the thorny problem of Victoria's authority as queen and her duty as wife, bound to submit to her husband: they conclude that Albert is the one to approach, because even though Victoria is the monarch, she must surely do what her husband says. Somewhat more knowledgeable about matters of legislation than the older women, Mary Barton doubts that Victoria and Albert make the laws at all, and thereby excuses herself from expressing an opinion on the contradiction that the queen embodies as sovereign power and obedient wife. Mary's silence on this issue is significant, since the narrative has just been at pains to show her own preference for power and self-direction over obedience. More than a humorous instance of 'local colour' in the novel, Mrs Wilson's views about factory work and domesticity invoke a range of topical concerns that swirl around the nature of working-class sexuality.

Victorian analyses of the effects of factory work associated 'factory girls' with everything from crude language, licentiousness and prostitution to infertility and defective reproductive capacities.[32] W. R. Greg regretted that a 'large number of ... female hands are notoriously immoral characters', and advised that they should have to produce 'certificates of their being persons of at least *tolerably* correct behaviour'.[33] Citing a variety of medical opinions, Leon Faucher's *Manchester in 1844* showed that factory women fail the most important test of womanhood: they are less fertile and less able to reproduce than normal (middle-class) women who lead well- regulated lives. One doctor declared that the fecundity of women diminished in proportion as they practised early intercourse, especially when that intercourse was promiscuous. Another added that 'the ill-regulated excitement which takes its source in a premature development of the sexual propensities, tends to destroy the power of re-production'.[34] Clergymen underwrote this view: 'The number of women who abandon themselves to prostitution in the manufacturing districts is so great, that they have lost the power of conceiving.'[35] Commentators even blamed the high temperature in the factories because it acted like the tropical sun, encouraging puberty before 'age and education have matured the moral sentiment'.[36] As Dr Michael Ryan noted, 'heat has a considerable influence in bringing animals, as well as plants, to a premature maturity. In the cotton mills of Manchester and Glasgow, and in many manufactories, which are kept at high temperatures, girls arrive early at a state of puberty.'[37] Thus the discourse of class and gender overflowed into the discourse of race and geography. As the factory becomes the equivalent of a different climate and geographical location, an intemperate zone, female workers are seen as if they were members of a different race or tribe. Like dark women in tropical climates, whose sexuality is represented as reflecting a depraved and uncivilised condition, factory women too are marked by a quasi-racial as well as sexual otherness. Victorian discourses on prostitution also link loose women with highly sexualised, racially-inflected others; an assumed synonymity of factory workers and prostitutes is thus not surprising.

When Gaskell tells us that Mary Barton is not allowed to work in a factory because her father objects to it 'on more accounts than one', she gestures to the range of evils detailed in the texts we have just examined (p. 26). More specifically, Barton seems to attribute his sister-in-law's downfall to the independence and wilfulness she developed in her work in the factory. But if Mary is saved from the factory and its attendant dangers, we notice that she does still have to work. Her choice and the conditions of work reflect ideological contradictions in attitudes to female employment. As Sally Alexander has pointed out, it was not that Victorians did not expect women of the lower classes to work, but rather that they tried to encourage only those sorts of work coinciding with what was regarded as women's natural sphere; the kind of work where women might compete with men was discouraged.[38] Similarly, the dependence of so many middle-class governesses on work did not for a long time create much pressure for wider opportunities for female employment. In the late 1850s, when middle-class feminists began to urge that 'every middle-class girl be taught some useful art', anxious reactions in the press envisioned the collapse of class boundaries that such training of women could provoke. Middle-class women who worked would descend to the level of the worst wives – those to be found among women of the labouring classes: 'Stunted children, a dirty home, social duties neglected, daughters uncared for, the marriage vow slighted, home comforts unknown – these are in practice the results of female labour.'[39]

Although the threat of dysfunction attended all female labour, sweated needlework was not so frowned upon for women as was factory work. Thus Mary and her friend Margaret sit up nights ruining their eyes as they concentrate on their stitching. Needlework or the taking in of washing, which is what the herbalist Alice Wilson does for a living, disrupted family life least, and were therefore acceptable female employments.[40] Since her father has ruled out work in a factory, Mary must choose between domestic service, which she refuses to consider because of the limitations it will place on her independence, and millinery or dressmaking, traditionally women's jobs. Like factory work, however, these occupations were also associated with overwork, poor conditions, prostitution, sexual irregularity, and even hysteria. Thomas Laycock noted that hysteria was 'often seen amongst sempstresses and lace workers and others of the female populations of large towns, confined for many hours daily at sedentary employments, or in heated manufactories'. By associating in numbers, he argued, they excited each other's passions.[41] At the very least, gregarious employment was felt to give a 'slang character' to a girl's appearance and habits. And indeed, the narrator sees Mary's apprenticeship at Miss Simmonds as a bad influence, encouraging her vanity and love of finery (themselves emphatic signs of the prostitute). From the other apprentices she also acquires a taste for popular romances that fill her head with foolish ideas (p. 91). The question of whether some kinds of work were more feminine and hence more appropriate than others is complicated by the fact that as a milliner's apprentice Mary appears to be no less vulnerable to the attentions of the mill-owner's son Harry Carson than if she were working, like Esther, in the factory.[42] As we have seen, anxieties about morality, work and its effect on the female body focused on reproductive capacities, the distortion of natural propensities and dangers to the health of ensuing generations. The spectre of racial degeneration occupied both bourgeois and working-class representations of the working-class mother. On the one hand, middle-class observers feared that the 'flawed reproductions' of women of the 'lower' classes were likely to lower the fibre of the nation as a whole; on the other, the degenerate, working-class mother also offered a way of explaining shockingly high rates of infant mortality.[43] Moral depravity, occasioned by anything from working outside the home to demanding the vote, was causing mothers to lose their child-rearing instincts, and resulting in negligence and the perpetuation of vicious habits.

Middle-class observers who inspected the dwellings of the poor and compiled sanitary reports debated whether charity and social aid would help or exacerbate social problems. Influenced by Malthusian doctrine, many saw improved sanitation and social welfare as helping to preserve the unfit and encouraging degeneration, but others felt that social improvements were essential to prevent racial decline. A favourite argument of early-twentieth-century eugenists was that the slowly declining nation would not be able to fight a war, and that Boer war recruits and conscripts for the First World War were inferior human specimens.[44] Such anxieties about the degeneration of the British folk are anticipated in Victorian representations of the condition of the labouring classes. Faucher reports that

> the operatives are pale and meagre in their appearance, and their physiognomy has not that animation which indicates health and vigour. Female beauty is not to be found amongst them, and the declining vigour of the men is replaced by a febrile energy. The officers of the regiments, raised in Lancashire, affirm that the men cannot bear much fatigue. It is evident that the race is degenerating.[45]

Gaskell invokes and considers the question of physical degeneration in Manchester's working classes through her descriptions of John Barton, the Wilson twins, factory girls, and Mary herself. John Barton is a 'thorough specimen of a Manchester man', born of factory workers, 'bred up in youth, and living in manhood, among the mills'. Gaskell describes him as 'below the middle size and slightly made; there was almost a stunted look about him; and his wan, colourless face, gave you the idea that in his childhood, he had suffered from the scanty living consequent upon bad times and improvident habits' (p. 4). Jem Wilson's baby twin brothers who fall ill and die are also evidence that there is simply not enough to go round: the pair were never strong and 'seemed to have but one life divided between them. One life, one strength, and in this instance... one brain; for they were helpless, gentle, silly children, but not the less dear to their parents... They were late on their feet, late in talking, late every way; had to be nursed and cared for when other lads of their age were tumbling about in the street' (p. 84). Mrs

Wilson herself is 'a delicate fragile-looking woman, limping in her gait', her 'little, feeble twins inheriting the frail appearance of their mother' (p. 4). Such descriptions signify perhaps the degeneration brought about by poverty and 'improvident habits'. But while Gaskell points frequently to the observable differences in the factory population when compared with other groups, those differences are not necessarily degenerative.[46] The novel opens with a description of a group of merry factory girls, 'not remarkable for their beauty': they have 'sallow complexions and irregular features' (p. 3). Gaskell hastens to add, however, that they are notable for their 'acuteness and intelligence of countenance'. They contrast with Mary's country-bred mother, whose beauty is fresh, but whose countenance is 'somewhat deficient in sense'. We are later told that the urban daughter's sense and spirit surpass her rural mother's, and that Mary is deluded in imagining that her mother would have been able to solve her problems and protect her. Indeed, Mary seems to have the best of both town and country: she is beautiful like her mother and aunt, but she also has 'something of keen practical shrewdness about her' (p. 91).

The power of transmission of female reproductive capacity could inspire powerful and threatening images of the dissolution of class boundaries. Corruption in a man was bad enough, but as texts of the period often lament a corrupted woman poisoned the very fountain of life; violations of her constitution could produce dreadful aberrations in offspring.[47] Aggressive women, for example, could give birth to sons who were colour-blind or haemophiliac. Changing the constitutional bent of women by allowing them to vote or work could therefore 'radically change the biological and *moral* health of a nation'.[48] An interesting locus of anxiety, which peaked in the 1860s, was the question of breastfeeding. Since wealthier classes relied on working-class mothers to supply their infants with milk, there was considerable debate about how the nurse's state of mind and her milk could affect the child. As wet-nurses, working-class mothers represented convenience, but were also associated with danger since they might through their milk impart to their little charges 'the germs of libertinism, criminality and alcoholism'.[49] Heredity was considered 'a dynamic process beginning with conception and ending in weaning', and the period of nursing was therefore a very important one, in need of regulation by professional advice.[50] While medical men applauded the mother's natural desire to nurse her own child, and indeed averred that it was dangerous (for different reasons from working-class and middle-class points of view) that anyone else take care of it, doctors also warned that it was not healthy to nurse the child excessively or beyond a certain age. Nine months was the recommended time for weaning, or earlier if the mother was weak. After twelve months, it was believed, suckling would do the child more harm than good and would 'moreover injure the mother's health'.[51] Middle-class women, in turn, took it upon themselves to pass on such knowledge to their 'lower' sisters; one of the aims of the Women's Sanitary Movement was to instruct women of the labouring classes in infant care by distributing tracts such as 'How to manage a baby' and 'The mother: her duty first towards her unborn and then to her newly born infant'. Another aim of the movement, more obviously self-interested, was to use the institutions developed to diffuse sanitary knowledge in order to build up a much needed 'class of intelligently-trained nursery maids'.[52]

Gaskell's representation of Mrs Davenport, an indigent nursing mother, invokes some of these concerns about inadequate mothering among the labouring classes. But again, the relationship between Gaskell's text and the social and medical texts I have been citing is complex. The scene in the novel where George Wilson and John Barton visit the Davenports exemplifies that the novelist is both defensive and critical of Mrs Davenport. As the narrative focuses our attention on the ill and nearly starved woman, she is vainly endeavouring to nurse her child:

> When he [Wilson] turned round again, he saw the woman suckling the child from her dry, withered breast.
> 'Surely the lad is weaned!' exclaimed he, in surprise. 'Why how old is he?'
> 'Going on two year,' she faintly answered. 'But oh! it keeps him quiet when I've nought else to gi' him, and he'll get a bit of sleep lying there, if he's getten nought beside. We han done our best to gi' the childer food, howe'er we pinched ourselves' (pp. 71–2).

Gaskell's representation defends this poverty-stricken mother's valiant, if fruitless, efforts to nurse her child, even as it suggests her own unwise depletion in the image of the 'dry, withered breast'. Subsequently, the town board and her neighbours help the widow to pay her arrears and rent; she earns money to feed her family by taking in 'some little children to nurse, who brought their daily food with them, which she cooked for them, without wronging their helplessness of a crumb' (p. 83). Despite her abject poverty, Mrs Davenport is not, Gaskell emphasises, the unscrupulous nurse or child-minder of many tracts against factory work, where litanies of 'wronged helplessness' abound. Gaskell notes, however, that Mrs Davenport is quite prepared to lie to the factory inspector 'and persuade him that her strong, big, hungry Ben, was above thirteen' so that he would be allowed to work and earn (p. 84). And when John Barton is going to London, she begs him to tell the Parliament folk what a 'sore trial it is, this law o' theirs, keeping childer fra' factory work, whether they be weakly or strong' (p. 100). Through her treatment of the desperately needy Mrs Davenport, Gaskell shows that pronouncements about good mothering are limited in value by social and economic circumstances, unsettling the notion that mothers who would want their children to work a long day even before they are thirteen must be monstrous.

By historicising the concern in *Mary Barton* with morality and motherhood among women of the labouring classes, we see that sexuality, conceived of as unstable, is a powerful means of constructing class difference. Gaskell's novel responds to such constructions in plotting Mary's progress and fate. Just as social texts focus repeatedly on the immorality and licentiousness of working-class women as a metonymy for the overall state of the class, Gaskell's novel is centrally concerned to save the heroine from following the example of unstable sexual and maternal behaviour characteristic of her family.

The complex responses in *Mary Barton* to representations of the moral inadequacy and sexual promiscuity of working-class women are most clearly apprehended in the threatening similarities between Mary and her aunt Esther, a prostitute. The factory girl who becomes a prostitute allows Gaskell to acknowledge this great 'Social Evil', testify to the effects of a degraded life, and offer on the question of prostitution a variety of conflicting responses ranging from sympathy to condemnation.

Some early reviewers praised the representation of the prostitute Esther as realistic, but others (Maria Edgeworth, for example) did not see what she had to do with the rest of the novel. Esther is of obvious importance in the novel because the similarities between aunt and niece are heavy-handedly drawn: hers is the fate Mary is in danger of repeating. But she is also important in that the novel's ambivalent attitudes to working-class motherhood and sexuality are inscribed in her representation. On one level, the text urges us to see Esther's descent into prostitution as the unhappy result of seduction and betrayal: her only fault has been to love 'above her station'. Class morality as well as the double standard in judging male and female sexual behaviour are similarly Gaskell's concern in Harry Carson's plan to use and 'ruin' Mary. On another level, the text suggests that Esther's contributory negligence, as it were, is considerable. Seduction and abandonment may be the immediate cause of her street-walking life, but the text hints that they have resulted from Esther's own moral susceptibility, signalled most clearly through her sartorial vanity. As the author of *Women's Work* admonished, 'incalculable mischief has been wrought by the passion for vanity, and fondness for dress . . . . And by this foolish vanity, [young women] expose themselves to numberless evils and temptations; and many a young woman who would have gone through life innocently and happily, has, by dress and display thrown herself into the seducer's power, and ended her days guiltily and wretchedly.'[53] Victorian treatises emphasise 'love of finery' as one of the major causes of prostitution – a connection with a strong class dimension, for many observers believed that loose women began their downward path through the desire to imitate their social superiors.[54] As John Barton in the novel exclaims: 'I see what you'll end at with your artificials, and your fly-away veils, and stopping out when honest women are in their beds; you'll be a street-walker' (p. 6).

If the text seems divided on Esther's culpability for her own fate, it also expresses ambivalence about the competence and reliability of women's efforts as mothers and sisters on behalf of each other. Thus the question of Esther's responsibility goes beyond her own situation: she is seen as being partly to blame for her sister's death in childbirth because of her 'hysterical' grief in response to Esther's disappearance. At least it is Esther whom John holds responsible for his woe: 'Dost thou know it was thee who killed her, as sure as Cain killed Abel?' (p. 144). Gaskell emphasises that John Barton's troubles begin domestically with his wife's death. Though he feels outrage at the disparity between rich and poor and is maddened by losing his job and by seeing his fellow workers' distress, it is the death of his wife that triggers his moral and social alienation, taking away 'one of the ties which bound him down to the gentle humanities of earth' (p. 22). The social role of woman as the softening, humanising yet firm anchor of male energy and desire, that would otherwise be anarchic and destructive, is invoked again later in Jem's distress after he has been refused by Mary. He warns her that she will be responsible for his future moral corruption:

'Mary, you'll hear, may be, of me as a drunkard, and may be as a thief, and may be as a murderer. Remember! when all are speaking ill of me, you will have no right to blame me, for it's your cruelty that will have made me what I feel I shall become' (p. 151).

In fact, however, he turns out to be a success at his work, patenting an engineering design for which he receives enough to establish an income for his mother and aunt. But since the narrative's end is to realise Mary's womanly potential to become a sound moral anchor, he must be shown to have need of her. She does not so much rescue him from himself, but rather rescues both of them eventually from the confusion that her own instability appears to have created.

As the stories of Mary, Esther, and the elder Mary confirm, once the maternal centre is loosed, things fall apart. Susceptible in the final stages of pregnancy and grieving (perhaps excessively, the narrator implies) over her sister's departure and moral transgression, Mrs Barton is an unstable centre, and her death is the explicit cause of her daughter's confused values and imperfect moral education as well as her husband's confusion and alienation. At Jem's trial, Mary begins by explaining her situation with the early loss of her mother: 'For you see, sir, mother died before I was thirteen, before I could know right from wrong about some things; and I was giddy and vain, and ready to listen to any praise of my good looks...a mother is a pitiful loss to a girl, sir; and so I used to fancy I could like to be a lady, and rich, and never know want any more' (p. 383). Without maternal ministry, both husband and daughter lose their moral direction. Perhaps Esther too might claim that the early loss of her own mother left her vulnerable to moral confusion. Since their mother's death Esther's sister, much her senior, had been 'more like a mother to her' but far from having kept Esther safe, the attention seems only to have spoiled her (p. 6). Indeed, maternal powers appear limited, even when exerted for the survival of children. Esther becomes a 'street-walker' in a desperate but vain attempt to provide for her illegitimate daughter. When she turns her attention to the orphaned Mary, who reminds her of her dead child, this interference, though well motivated, leads eventually to the false accusation and trial of Jem.

Although it looks to the world that Jem is on trial because of Mary's irresponsible flirtation, it is in fact Esther who has drawn him into involvement with Harry Carson.

Nevertheless Esther does prove to be the means by which Mary is empowered to rescue Jem. In an important scene she masquerades as a respectable woman to visit her niece and give her the evidence that she imagines incriminates Jem. Before she arrives, Mary has a vision that her mother is coming to help her and when Esther suddenly enters she addresses her as 'Mother'. Mary's longing for her mother expresses a wish to return to childhood and deny the vortex of passion, jealousy and sexuality in which she has become implicated. Instead of the desired mother-rescuer, her fantasy of rescue yields a flawed quasi-mother, whose unwitting gift to Mary is not magical rescue but the difficult knowledge of her father's guilt.[55] By handing over the bit of the inscribed Valentine that Mary knows exonerates rather than incriminates Jem, Esther enables Mary's rescue of him and allows her to proceed with clarity and determination, if alone. Yet this empowerment of Mary by her disreputable aunt is indirect, mistaken and never explicitly acknowledged as helpful in the text; her attempts to help are coded rather as bungling, and the end of the chapter sends her weeping into the streets in a paroxysm of self-condemnation. The text allows Esther's estimation of herself to stand: 'How could she, the abandoned and polluted outcast, ever have dared to hope for a blessing, even on her efforts to do good? The black curse of Heaven rested on all her doings, were they for good or for evil' (p. 277). This moralistic self-condemnation is the last we hear of Esther till her death at the end of the novel.

Unlike Esther's sexual transgressions, John Barton's murder of Carson is presented as an instance, an individual aberration whose staining or contaminating effects are contained. When Mary sees him after her illness, she embraces him as her own dear father. 'His crime was a thing apart, never more to be considered by her.' Esther may change her clothes, but it is her degradation that makes her identity and is never a thing apart. Though in both cases the wages of sin are death, Barton at the end knows he is supported and forgiven, while Esther, having crept home to die, hardly registers that she is taken in and tended.

In tracing the book's representation of social transgressions, we can see Esther as John Barton's structural counterpart, even though Gaskell invests greater narrative time and energy in his alienation and degradation than hers. Esther, a prostitute, is 'violent and unregulated'; unemployed, John Barton grows increasingly morose, takes opium, occasionally beats his daughter and dies a murderer. In each case, Gaskell creates situations that vitiate gendered visions of happiness: Esther's sexual transgression expresses her moral collapse, John Barton's political confusion and act of vengeance express his. The degradation of each, the text suggests, springs from strong feeling unguided by education and wisdom. Gaskell links the two – the abandoned girl and prospective criminal – in the following vision, which does not specifically refer to John and Esther but foreshadows their respective fates:

> You cannot read the lot of those who daily pass you by in the street. How do you know the wild romances of their lives; the trials, the temptations they are even now enduring, resisting, sinking under? You may be elbowed one instant by the girl desperate in her abandonment, laughing in mad merriment with her outward gesture, while her soul is longing for the rest of the dead, and bringing itself to think of the cold-flowing river as the only mercy of God remaining to her here. You may pass the criminal, meditating crimes at which you will to-morrow shudder with horror as you read them (p. 70).

As if to cement their bond as similar examples of degradation, John and Esther are buried in the same grave. Their 'wild romances' suggest the turbulence and distress, which, the narrator implies, are common enough beneath the masks of public anonymity.

If we look at the way redemption is sought in the next generation, we see that the novel could as well have focused on how Jem avoids becoming a John Barton, as it focuses on how Mary avoids becoming an Esther. Jem's career, the antithesis of John Barton's, is a self-help story much approved of by the middle class. Unaided by charity, he betters himself through his own exertions and the opportunities provided by industry's need for technological improvements. Yet the text is far more interested in the 'moral making' of Mary than the 'self-helping' of Jem, because the question of the moral mother at the heart of working-class domestic life is a central concern. As critics have noted, the question of whether Mary will follow her aunt's course is abruptly resolved fairly early in the novel.[56] For a time, Mary's future is presented as a forked path: vice or virtue, but she soon abandons her flirtation with the mill-owner's son, her dreams of upward mobility, and loses all interest in finery. The text dispenses briskly with any apparent impediments to virtue and Mary's route to moral solidity is very soon a sure thing. The point of Mary's attempts to exonerate Jem and her endurance of his trial is to distinguish her from the susceptibility, volatility and excess associated with her mother and aunt. And despite its certainty, Mary's instalment as the virtuous mother and wife in the final pages inscribes also a sense of loss for the passion, spirit and energy that respectability and stability seem to exclude.

We can trace the record of that ambiguous loss by looking at the different attitudes to Mary's energetic independence encoded in the narrative. In this respect, it is useful to focus on Gaskell's use of flower images, which function generally in the novel to suggest both sexuality and class and which, in Mary's case, register a tension between the wild and the domestic. The traditions linking female sexuality and flowers are many, from Linnaean botanical classification to biomedical analogies explaining human in terms of plant reproduction.[57] Not only were the Victorians fascinated by the language of flowers, as a substantial body of flower literature suggests, but nature stories involving plants and flowers were frequently used to exemplify morals.

Botanical taxonomy had, since the eighteenth century, recapitulated aspects of sexual hierarchy.[58] In so doing it offered a way of talking about gender roles, social organisation and even, in the 1790s, revolutionary culture. As Alan Bewell has shown, James Gillray's *New Morality* could satirise the productions of Wollstonecraft, Godwin, and Coleridge as outgrowths of Jacobinism – 'Jacobin Plants'. Botanical discourse at this time, responding to Linnaean sexual classification, also gave wide analogical scope to the discussion of different modes of femininity in terms of floriculture. 'Wild' flowers, luxuriants, ornamentals, monstrous and beautiful but infertile double-flowers could find analogues in attributes favoured or deplored in women.[59] For example, Wollstonecraft introduces *A Vindication of the Rights of Women* with a scathing attack on domestic flowers and ornamental women in which she castigates current ideals of domestic womanhood and education practices:

> The conduct and manners of women, in fact, evidently prove that their minds are not in a healthy state; for, like the flowers which are planted in too rich a soil, strength and usefulness are sacrificed to beauty; and the flaunting leaves, after having pleased a fastidious eye,

fade, disregarded on the stalk, long before the season when they ought to have arrived at maturity. One cause of the barren blooming I attribute to a false system of education, gathered from the books written on this subject by men who, considering females rather as women than human creatures, have been more anxious to make them alluring mistresses than rational wives .[60]

The possibilities of discussing female sexuality, education, and status through the association of women and flowers, and her use of flower analogies suggests a context, albeit one modified by changing ideas about women, botany and sexual classification, for early Victorian flower analogies. Thus Gaskell's figuration of Mary as a blooming 'wild' flower is a means of setting up a contrast with class-inflected ideals of womanhood, since she specifically compares the 'wild-rose' to the cultivated flowers of the garden from which Harry Carson could have had his pick. Kathleen Tillotson refers to the characters in *Mary Barton* as Gaskell's 'common flowers of human nature', a figure which underscores the text's focus on working-class or humble life.[61] Those flowers in the text that are *not* 'common' perform a significant comparative function because they signify the cultivation of ornamental femininity as opposed to the wholesome and natural womanliness of 'wild' flowers. Harry Carson's youngest sister, for example, is metonymically associated with a new breed of hothouse rose that she cajoles her father to buy for her, even though a small specimen costs half a guinea (p. 77). She declares she cannot live without her flowers and scents and is horrified when asked to content herself with 'peonies and dandelions' – such lowly plants do not deserve to be called flowers. Another scene describes their aspirations to gentility and cultivation as the Carson sisters sit languidly in the elegant drawing room, one sleepily reading 'Emerson's Essays', another copying manuscript music. The air, which is 'heavy with the fragrance of strongly-scented flowers' from the conservatory, seems cloying, stagnant and unvital (p. 238). The Carson's flowers sweeten the air inside as if there were no poverty and destitution lying beyond their doors, just as when John Barton goes to London, he sees that the hangers-on of carriages use nosegays against the 'bad smells' of the streets through which the carriage passes. In contrast to the expensive conservatory, we may recall the two unpruned geraniums that stand on the windowsill of the Barton's to defend them from 'out-door pryers', confirming that the Bartons are just as protective of their privacy as Gaskell's middle-class readers, despite prevailing generalisations about working-class slovenliness and lack of modesty or restraint.

Gaskell uses the language of flowers not only to mark class boundaries and signify status, but also to indicate Mary's vitality, wildness and energy. The floral terms in which Mary is figured allow Gaskell to explore the questions of class, morality and sexuality that connect and confuse representations of working-class women, fallen women and prostitutes. At first sight it would seem that Gaskell's flower images reproduce exactly what Mary Wollstonecraft objected to – the association of women with sweetness, blushing ignorance and pleasing ornamentality. Mary is repeatedly imaged as 'reddening like a rose', or flushing like a 'carnation'. But on one occasion she is seen 'blushing rosy red, more with anger than with shame', which suggests that the floral images are multivalent and signify more than maidenly modesty or shame (p. 10). Mary's association with the 'luxuriant bunch of early spring roses' given to her by Harry Carson is ambiguous. 'Early spring' and 'luxuriant' suggest a natural health, vitality, and abundance, but 'luxuriants' in botanical discourse were cultivated flowers, associated with degeneration and the botanist's interference in nature, and opposed to 'wild' or natural flowers. Jem expresses resentment about Carson's attentions to Mary by remarking bitterly that the mill-owner's son has 'all the glories of the garden at his hand', and should not have culled Jem's own 'fragrant wild-rose' (p. 194). 'Wild' as Jem uses it suggests Mary's wholesome, natural, and uncultivated state and is synonymous with 'common'. But it also carries connotations of danger, rebellion, and resistance to training – qualities that Jem has to contend with in Mary. Numerous details in the way Mary relates to Jem and her father reveal that she is quite contrary – quick to anger, resentful of any form of domination and appropriation, obstinate and perverse.

The valency of the adjective 'wild' (itself a wild-card in the novel) is inflected by the description of the 'scrambling and wild luxuriance' of the flowers in the opening paragraph of the novel. Having described the Green Heys fields as a place beloved of the labouring people because it connects them to the natural world, Gaskell focuses on an old farm and its garden:

> The porch of this farm-house is covered by a rose tree; and the garden surrounding it is crowded with a medley of old-fashioned herbs and flowers, planted long ago, when the garden was the only druggist's shop within reach, and allowed to grow in scrambling and wild

luxuriance – roses, lavender, sage, balm (for tea), rosemary, pinks and wallflowers, onions and jessamine, in most republican and indiscriminate order (p. 2).

The narrator lovingly details the garden's varied contents, revelling in its abundance and generous disorder, and yet stressing that though the plants are 'allowed to grow in scrambling and wild luxuriance', the garden seems to thrive. We may pause, however, over 'crowded' and 'indiscriminate', which are frequent terms of disapprobation in the discourse of the moral and physical conditions of the poor, associated with the disorder and promiscuousness of their homes, while 'republican' conjures up threatening associations with working-class political disturbances and the aims of Chartism. Indeed, in the last paragraph of the preface the author has just warned the reader of the state of feeling among the factory-people in England and recent events on the Continent that make clear the explosive potential of working-class discontent. Luxuriance and disorder are all very well in a garden, the vital spirit of which the narrator happily associates with the Manchester working people who throng to the fields, but *their* potential republicanism and disorder are not tolerable.

For Victorian nature writers such as Margaret Gatty, the vision of horticultural unrestraint in Gaskell's garden might well have called forth a moral lesson on the virtues of regulation and order. Indeed, Gatty's story 'Training and Restraining' offers itself as an apt gloss on Mary Barton's possible fate as a 'wild' flower. It features a wicked (male) wind who chides the flowers for accepting their loss of freedom at the gardener's hand and seduces them with stories of the freedom of their wild cousins in the fields. When the wind returns in his 'wildest mood' the flowers think of their time approaching 'with a sort of fearful pleasure'.[62] Eventually they lie bruised and spattered on the ground. The child, who weeps for her garden and her ruined flowers, learns the necessity of discipline and restraint:

> I know I should once have argued that if it were their *natural* mode of growing it must therefore be the best. But I cannot say so, now that I see the result. They are doing whatever they like, unrestrained....[63]

The parable's emphasis on the seductive, forceful wind and the flowers' fall and soiling makes it suggestive of moral and sexual license and encourages the association of disorder with immorality. Mary is spirited, responsive, headstrong and dangerously exposed to the perils of unrestraint in her flirtation with Harry Carson. Her association in the book's imagery with the wild rose, and the rose with luxuriance, abundance and passion have the potential both to unsettle and reinforce contemporary representations of working-class women. Mary's energy, and blooming vitality are attractive, undercutting perceptions of an enfeebled and degenerating female population, yet in the aura of unrestrained and self-indulgent desire that those attractive qualities evoke they also reinforce other aspects of the representation of working-class women as sexual, immoral and unregulated.

When do spirit, energy and resistance become excessive and dangerous? The mill fire that Mary has a hankering to see is a paradigm of unruly desires, readable on one level as a Gatty-like warning on the dangers of undisciplined feelings. The wind-driven flames, as she observes with fascination, seem to be 'licking the black walls with amorous fierceness'. The flames are triumphant and destructive, suggesting perhaps that Mary's encouragement of Harry Carson is tantamount to playing with fire. When the fire is out of control, Mary wishes she were away and 'clings to Margaret's arm, longs to faint, to be insensible and escape from the oppressing misery of her sensations' (p. 58). Perhaps the context of the fire more obviously suggests a conflagration between workers and masters personalised in John Barton's intense response to the plight of the working people, which becomes dangerous as he is associated with Chartism and trade unions – all that is 'wild and visionary'.[64] But this double layered meaning of the fire, of energy unleashed and out of control, manifests itself in gendered ways – in the obvious political power of working-class men, united by their common purpose, and the implicit sexual politics in the invidious perception of working-class women. But whereas Gaskell is unequivocal about the danger of Barton's proletarian rage and the error of his ways of expressing it, she seems to be ambivalent about relinquishing the abundance, vitality, and luxuriousness associated with Mary, even though these qualities signal disorder and danger. The novel enacts a rescue of its heroine by installing her as a stable moral, maternal centre. But despite its conventional ending, *Mary Barton* does not merely perpetuate middle-class ideals of stability and the separation of spheres. Especially in the use of flower imagery and its associations with a botanical discourse of sexuality, the novel inscribes reservations about regulation, control and a maternal ideal that constrain energy and passion.

The crisis of defending Jem and protecting her father allows Gaskell to test Mary's balance and self-regulation. Mary rehearses the dangerous excesses of emotion associated with Esther, whose account of her self-blame and transgressive past is expressed with a 'wild vehemence' bordering on insanity and anticipates the terms used to describe Mary's response to the news of Jem's arrest (p. 89). She blames herself bitterly for the madness and jealousy she has provoked, imagines that she will go mad, and feels her pulses careering through her head with 'wild vehemence' (p. 272). Mary imitates Esther too in appearing for a time as a shamed and promiscuous woman. With Carson's death, she attracts, like Esther, the opprobrium of the public woman. Mrs Wilson calls her a 'vile flirting quean' and 'a dirty hussy' (pp. 264, 267). Margaret temporarily withdraws her friendship and wonders if Mary is not a girl devoid of the 'modest proprieties of her sex' (p. 294). In Liverpool, the wife of the gruff boatman who helps her imagines that she is a prostitute, but resolves not to turn her from the house even if she is 'the worst woman in Liverpool' (p. 369). She becomes the titillating focus of public speculation through newspaper coverage of the murder, and at the trial the prosecutor practically salivates over the cross-class love-triangle apparently at the heart of the case.

During Jem's trial Mary again experiences a rite of passage through the emotional excesses associated with her mother and aunt. Considerable narrative attention focuses on her sensations and experiences – her reeling head, the strange wonder in her brain, the preternatural sensitivity of all her faculties. Against the dictates of modesty, she must confess publicly what 'a woman' should only whisper in the greatest privacy; against the injunctions of the law, she must keep private her knowledge of her father's guilt. This is a balancing act of some magnitude and is represented as a threat to her sanity during her weeks of delirium, causing Jem to fear not just for her life, but also that she may remain 'a poor gibbering maniac all her life long (and mad people do live to be old sometimes, even under all the pressure of their burden)' (p. 398). Like the excessive 'hysterical grief' that rendered a 'shock to the system' and caused her mother's death, Mary's raving threatens her consciousness and even her life. This crisis of sanity and identity serves as a purgation of the instability and wildness associated with Mary's maternal history. When she recovers she is docile and gentle. Nevertheless, we do see Mary exerting herself once more after her illness, urging Jem vehemently to help find her Aunt Esther, even if it is too late to save the dying woman.[65] The search for Esther and the scene of her death again emphasise the wildness she represents: looking for her is a 'wild chase', she is like a wounded deer, a 'wild animal', and when brought home to die she wonders 'wildly' if her life has been a dream (p. 460).

By the end of the novel, the dangerous instabilities of Manchester life – sexual, reproductive, moral and economic – are left behind and a vision confirming stability offered in their place. Gaskell's epilogue shows us a low, wooden house, shaded by one primeval tree, an orchard stretching beyond the garden. The peace and spaciousness of the garden, bathed in the sunlight of an Indian summer, make it seem very different from the garden of the opening paragraph, where plants grow in 'scrambling and wild luxuriance' (p. 2). The ending expresses Gaskell's wish that industrialisation might yet retain the values she, like others, associates with the land, community, and natural sources of affection.[66] If the closing of *Mary Barton* expresses yearning, it is not for a return to an idealised, pre-industrial age. Jem is to work as an instrument maker at an Agricultural college, a 'comfortable appointment, – house, – land, – and a good percentage on the instruments made' (p. 443). He will be using his engineering and technological skills, but the family is to live a rural rather than urban life. The vision is entirely consistent with demands for social organisation that affirm household and kinship and a connection to the land. It is a dream that also, like Chartist ideals of social reorganisation, distances woman from human law and knowledge – culture – and installs her 'closer to nature and the animal world'.[67] Attempting to modify 'wild' to that which is natural, wholesome, and unspoiled, rather than untamed and disordered, the closing scene envisions a domesticated wildness, in which we see a rather muted Mary. We focus on her watching for her husband's return from the town, speaking softly and seriously and being slightly eclipsed by her mother-in-law: her little son prefers to cling to his grandmother than come to his mother, and when Jem makes his wife and mother guess the news from England, he pronounces that 'the old woman has twice the spirit of the young one' (p. 464). Mary is apparently no longer quite so contrary and her Canadian garden, we can assume, does not grow in 'republican and indiscriminate disorder'. Gaskell's vignette of family life in Canada suggests the orderliness of a sexual division of labour in which a strong maternal centre guarantees a stable domestic and family life, but it also provokes a sense of regret that Gaskell's vision of order and stability exact a price of spirit, independence and desire.

Notes

1. Critics have often pointed to the way the difficult issues of class alienation are raised but then marginalised in the novel as narrative attention shifts from John Barton to his daughter. See R. B. Yeazell, 'Why political novels have heroines: *Sybil, Mary Barton* and *Felix Holt*', *Novel*, 18 (1985), pp. 126–44.

2. For discussion of the ways in which the articulation of a concept of class relied on the work of gender, see J. Scott, *Gender and the Politics of History* (New York, Columbia University Press, 1988), p. 45. Among recent critics who point to the political implications of the domestic in *Mary Barton* see H. Schor, *Scheherazade in the Marketplace: Elizabeth Gaskell and the Victorian Novel* (New York, Oxford University Press, 1992), pp. 13–44.

3. Edwin Chadwick's *Report on the Sanitary Condition of the Labouring Population of Great Britain* (1842) quotes a source who finds members of the labouring population that have 'voluntarily reduced themselves to the condition of savages'; they are transformed into something little better than wild beasts, for moral perceptions and social nature seem to the middle-class observers to have been destroyed among them. Certain areas will 'soon be occupied by a race lower than any yet known' and one observer expresses horror at the thought of 'so many savages living in the midst of civilization'. See Chadwick's *Report*, ed. M. W. Flinn (Edinburgh, Edinburgh University Press, [1842] 1965), pp. 201, 202; this vast document, compiled by Chadwick from the Poor Law Commissioners reports, cites data gathered from all over the country. Though Chadwick himself is said to have been convinced that inadequate housing and bad living conditions bred disease and intemperance and immorality, the reporters he cites often ascribe the miserable circumstances of the poor to defects in character, even race. The document as a whole contains conflicting answers to the question: Do people make their environment or does the environment make the people? See also J. P. Kay [later Shuttleworth], *The Moral and Physical Condition of the Working Classes Employed in the Cotton Manufacture in Manchester* (Manchester, James Ridgway, 1832), p. 21. His report invokes the notion then current in medical and anthropological literature that the habitual behaviour of human groups in different environments might become part of their hereditary physical make-up, implying that cultural phenomena were readily translatable into 'racial tendencies'. On this point, see G. W. Stocking, Jr., *Victorian Anthropology* (New York, Free Press, 1987), p. 64.

4. Todd, *Cyclopaedia*, p. 442.

5. On the way in which the working-class family was constructed as a problem in need of expert treatment, see J. Seed, 'Unitarianism, political economy and the antinomies of liberal culture in Manchester 1830–50', *Social History*, 7:1 (1982), pp. 1–25.

6. See A. Levy, *Other Women: The Writing of Class, Race, and Gender, 1832–1898* (New Jersey, Princeton University Press, 1991), Chapter 2.

7. A. Easson (ed.), *Elizabeth Gaskell: The Critical Heritage* (London, Routledge, 1991), p. 177.

8. Chadwick, *Report*, p. 195.

9. W. Johnson, *The Morbid Emotions of Women: Their Origin, Tendencies, and Treatment* (London, Simpkin, 1850), pp. 10–11, tells how 'fish women' were known to have such a mass of muscle in their legs that a gentleman once maintained that 'these daughters of the wave ought to be classed as a third sex, which he proposed to call "Amphibio-female"'.

10. See B. Taylor, *Eve and the New Jerusalem: Socialism and Feminism in the Nineteenth Century* (London, Virago Press, 1983), p. 28.

11. S. Kydd, *The History of the Factory Movement*, 2 vols (London, Simpkin, 1857), p. 260.

12. Kydd, *Factory Movement*, p. 269.

13. Kydd, *Factory Movement*, p. 270.

14. R. Greg, *The Factory Question and The Ten Hours Bill* (London, James Ridgway, 1834), pp. 69–70; see Samuel Kydd, who says that 'partizan' identified himself as Mr Fletcher, a surgeon in Bury, Lancashire who then published a letter in the *Times* demanding an apology from R. H. Greg, and challenging him to 'refute any fact or argument' he had made (*Factory Movement*, p. 270). In *Mary Barton* Gaskell evokes this context of medical evidence and advocation for the Ten Hours Bill when John Barton tells of his experience at the Infirmary where he helped the surgeon sort his papers. He learns that the greater part of accidents *as comed in, happened in th' last two hours o' work*, when folk getten tired and careless. Th' surgeon said it were all true, and that he were going to bring that fact to light' (p. 95).

15. D. Thompson (ed.), *The Early Chartists* (London, Macmillan, 1971), p. 117.

16. Thompson, *The Early Chartists*, p. 119.

17. Thompson, *The Early Chartists*, pp. 121, 122.

18. The reactions of working-class women to injunctions against female employment were varied and complex. Some protested that industrious women were being driven out of their jobs, and berated their men for being 'a' bad as their Masters'. Others felt that if taking on waged work and still having to be responsible for domestic duties was the choice, then let men be the primary breadwinners. See Taylor, *Eve and the New Jerusalem*, pp. 110–12.

19. See A. Shelston, 'Elizabeth Gaskell's Manchester (1)', *Gaskell Society Journal*, 3 (1989), pp. 41–82; he points out that Gaskell fails to acknowledge the strength of corporate working-class culture because her 'emphasis falls on the domestic dimension' (p. 65).

20. E. Gaskell, *Mary Barton*, ed. E. Wright (Oxford, World's Classics, [1848] 1987), p. 64. Subsequent references are to this edition and will be incorporated in the text.

21. See J. Seed, 'Unitarianism', who notes that social managers, or 'agents of organized virtue', undertook various efforts to 'restructure family life in order to ensure its role as an efficient socializer'. Such intervention in the social lives of the poor may be compared to a similar process being implemented in the workplace, where management was developing 'increasingly efficient means of controlling and manipulating the labour process' (p. 13).

22. See the discussion of Gaskell's appropriations in M. C. Fryckstedt, *Elizabeth Gaskell's* Mary Barton *and* Ruth: *A Challenge to Christian England* (Stockholm, Almqvist & Wiksell, 1982), pp. 87–97.

23. J. Drummond and C. B. Upton, *The Life and Letters of James Martineau*, vol. 1 (London, 1902), p. 89; quoted in Seed, 'Unitarianism', p. 14.

24. See Seed, 'Unitarianism', p. 18.

25. *Seventh Report of the Ministry to the Poor* (1841), pp. 4, 5; quoted in Seed, 'Unitarianism', p. 19.

26. M. Hompes, 'Mrs. E.C. Gaskell', *Gentleman's Magazine*, 55 (1895), p. 124.

27. John Seed's point is that the tension between an 'inchoate structure of feeling' and established public discourse on poverty belongs not only to *Mary Barton* and the Domestic Mission reports, but has roots in 'structural tensions and boundaries within liberal culture' ('Unitarianism', p. 20). Liberal Manchester culture was a complex social group in which ministers, missionaries and other agents of social reproduction were never merely the 'ventriloquist's dummy' of industrial interest ('Unitarianism', p. 23).

28. See *Fifth Report* (1839), p. 25; quoted in Seed, 'Unitarianism', p. 17.

29. See C. Gallagher, *The Industrial Reformation of English Fiction: Social Discourse and Narrative Form 1832–1867* (Chicago, Chicago University Press, 1985) which discusses the way the novel 'tries on' a variety of modes: tragedy, melodrama, sentimental romance, farce and domestic fiction. While it is possible to see what forms Gaskell rejected, Catherine Gallagher observes, 'it is difficult to identify the narrative mode that she adopted' in the interests of best reflecting working-class reality (p. 70).

30. Easson (ed.), *Elizabeth Gaskell: The Critical Heritage*, p. 187.

31. For example, Chadwick's *Report* quotes an account of what happens when a 'good, well-washed servant marries a labourer'. She is seen later, 'her face dirty, hair tangled, cap ill-washed and slovenly put on', her house wet and impossible to keep in order (p. 196).

32. On the sexual promiscuity of factory women, see L. Faucher, *Manchester in 1844: Its Present Condition and Future Prospects*, trans. with copious notes appended by a member of the Manchester Athenaeum (Manchester, Heywood, 1844), p. 46. Faucher's translator was Joseph Culverwell, a member of William Gaskell's Cross Street Congregation; see E. Burney, *Cross Street Chapel Schools* (Manchester, Didsbury, 1977), p. 19.

33. W. R. Greg, *An Inquiry into the State of the Manufacturing Populations* (London, James Ridgway, 1831), p. 35.

34. Faucher, *Manchester in 1844*, p. 46.

35. Faucher, *Manchester in 1844*, p. 46. Such views perform double service as condemnation and reassurance. Their reduced abilities to conceive classify factory women as deviant; at the same time, anxieties about the indiscriminate breeding of the poor can be secretly allayed by a belief in their inability to conceive, which promises their extinction as a quasi-species.

36. Faucher, *Manchester in 1844*, p. 46.

37. M. Ryan, *A Manual of Midwifery, and Diseases of Women and Children* (London, Bloomsbury, 1841), p. 60. In exploring the question of climate, puberty and reproductivity, the Manchester Statistical Society (1842–3) heard papers entitled, 'Early marriage in Oriental countries as evidence of

early puberty' and 'On the alleged influence of climate on female puberty in Greece'. These papers were the work of John Roberton, who also published 'On the period of puberty in Esquimaux women', *Edinburgh Medical and Surgical Journal*, 63 (1845), pp. 57–65. For a discussion of Roberton's work proving that humankind is one species and one family, see Chapter One; for a list of papers given at the Statistical Society, see T. S. Ashton, *Economic and Social Investigations in Manchester 1833–1933: A Centenary History of the Manchester Statistical Society* (London, 1934).

38. See the discussion of acceptable women's work in S. Alexander, *Women's Work in Nineteenth-Century London: A Study of the Years 1820–1850* (London, Journeyman's Press, 1983), pp. 10–11.
39. 'Queen bees or working bees?', *Saturday Review* (21 February 1857), p. 173.
40. See Alexander, *Women's Work*, pp. 10–11.
41. See T. Laycock, *A Treatise on the Nervous Diseases of Women: Comprising an Inquiry into the Nature, Causes, and Treatments of Spinal and Hysterical Disorders* (London, Longman, 1840), p. 210. Contradictorily, hysteria was also supposed to affect isolated and bored young women who lacked occupation and responsibility.
42. On the muffled connection between economic and sexual exploitation in the novel see R. Bodenheimer, 'Private grief and public acts in *Mary Barton*', *Dickens Studies Annual*, 9 (1981), pp. 195–216.
43. As testimony to the ideological work of differing images of motherhood, we may note that the contrary vision of buxom working-class women with their broods of lusty babies was used to chide middle-class women to do their duties as mothers and reproducers. See S. Shuttleworth, 'Demonic mothers: ideologies of bourgeois motherhood in the mid-Victorian era', in L. Shires (ed.), *Rewriting the Victorians: Theory, History, and the Politics of Gender* (London, Routledge, 1992), p. 32.
44. See C. Webster (ed.), *Biology, Medicine and Society 1840–1940* (Cambridge, Cambridge University Press, 1981), pp. 3–4.
45. Fauster, *Manchester in 1844*, p. 72; since the editor and translator of *Manchester in 1844* does not always agree with the author, his notes are interesting evidence of contesting interpretations about the condition of the Manchester labouring classes. He admits that the *Manchester Guardian* in August 1843 represented people as believing that the 'stature of the race, in the manufacturing districts, is declining, and that the recruiting officers find great difficulty in obtaining men of the proper height'. But he sees this as a sign of social progress that the working classes are reluctant to enlist: 'The men of the manufacturing districts are too well off, and have too much sense to join a profession which is daily growing disreputable. They begin to see that bad governments could not exist... if the working classes refused to enlist and take up arms against their fellow creatures. A red coat and a daily ration is, after all, a poor exchange for the loss of liberty.' See Faucher, *Manchester in 1844*, editor's note 32, p. 72.
46. Similarly, although the contrast between the feeble twins and their quick and hearty older brother Jem supports prevalent notions about the decline of working-class vigour, the implicit comparison could simply reflect beliefs about the formation of twins.

47. See Alexander, *Women's Work*, p. 10; C. Smart (ed.), *Regulating Womanhood: Historical Essays on Marriage, Motherhood and Sexuality* (London, Routledge, 1992), p. 3, notes that by mid-century issues of sexuality, motherhood and reproduction had certainly become matters of public policy and concern.

48. S. C. Gilman, 'Political theory: left to right, up to down', in J. E. Chamberlin and S. L. Gilman (eds.), *Degeneration: The Dark Side of Progress* (New York, Columbia University Press, 1985), p. 172.

49. J. E. Winters, 'The relative influences of maternal and wet-nursing on mother and child', *Medical Record*, (1896); quoted in Gilman, 'Political theory', p. 172.

50. Gilman, 'Political theory', p. 171.

51. Doctors warned that if children are suckled after they are twelve months old, they are generally pale and unhealthy, and the mother is usually emaciated and nervous; see H. P. Chavasse, *Advice to Wives on the Management of Themselves During the Periods of Pregnancy, Labour and Suckling* (London, Longman, 1843), p. 88.

52. See P. Williams, 'Women, medicine and sanitary reform: 1850–90', in M. Benjamin (ed.), *Science and Sensibility: Gender and Scientific Inquiry, 1780–1945* (Oxford, Basil Blackwell, 1991), pp. 60–88; also M. A. Baines, 'Address to the National Association for the Promotion of Social Science', *National Association for the Promotion of Social Science Transactions*, (1859), pp. 531–2.

53. See *Women's Work: or Hints to Raise the Female Character* (London, Clarke, 1844), p. 176. Other hints of Esther's unregulated and undisciplined nature are supplied in details of her resistance to education. She remembers Jem's beautiful and orderly handwriting as a contrast to her own 'misspelt scrawl' (p. 276).

54. See M. Valverde, 'Love of finery: fashion and the fallen woman in nineteenth-century social discourse', *Victorian Studies*, 32:2 (1989), pp. 169–88.

55. See M. Homans, *Bearing the Word: Language and Female Experience in Nineteenth-Century Women's Writing* (Chicago, Chicago University Press, 1986), p. 233, who considers this scene in the context of a 'drama among men about men's passions'. My reading emphasises how the relations of Mary to her mother and aunt are not a marginalised aspect of a male drama, but constitute a drama of morality and sexuality that is a crucial part of the political field in which John Barton and Harry Carson interact.

56. See the discussion of this point in Yeazell, 'Why political novels have heroines', pp. 126–44.

57. Thomas Laycock, we remember, refers to menstruation as 'flowers' because it precedes fecundation; the ovaries are frequently described as fruit blossoms, and the woman is said to bud as surely and as incessantly as the plant; see Laycock, *Treatise*, p. 40 and Laqueur, *Making Sex*, p. 224.

58. L. Schiebinger, 'The private life of plants: sexual politics in Carl Linnaeus and Erasmus Darwin', in Benjamin (ed.), *Science and Sensibility*, p. 143.

59. See A. Bewell, '"Jacobin Plants": botany as social theory in the 1790s', *Wordsworth Circle*, 20:3 (1989), pp. 132–9.

60. M. Wollstonecraft, *A Vindication of the Rights of Woman: With Strictures on Political and Moral Subjects* (London, J. Johnson, 1792), pp. 3–4.

61. K. Tillotson, *Novels of the Eighteen-Forties* (London, Oxford, 1954), p. 222.
62. M. Gatty, *Parables from Nature* (London, Bell and Daldy, 1855), p. 91.
63. Gatty, *Parables from Nature*, p. 96; for further discussion of her parables, see N. Scourse, *Victorians and Their Flowers* (London, Croom Helm, 1983).
64. Gaskell keeps Mary well away from Chartist or Owenite influences, both of which during the 1830s and 1840s had strong female following and participation, and might have fired Mary's spirit of independence and channelled her energies. For assessments of women's involvement in political organizations see D. Jones, 'Women and Chartism', *History*, 68:222 (1983), pp. 1–21; and D. Thompson, *The Chartists* (London, Temple Smith, 1984).
65. Patsy Stoneman has recently argued that Mary is effaced at the end of the novel: having exerted herself for her menfolk, she no longer has an active role to play. See *Elizabeth Gaskell* (Brighton, Harvester, 1987), p. 85.
66. For a discussion of Chartist ideals, see S. Alexander, 'Women, class and sexual differences in the 1830s and 1840s: some reflections on the writing of a feminist history', *History Workshop Journal*, 17 (1984), pp. 125–49.
67. Alexander, 'Women, class and sexual differences', p. 141.

Chapter three

Confession, secrecy and exhibition

Confession and secrecy are the shaping conditions for representing female desire and passion in *Agnes Grey* and *Ruth*. Yet criticism of these works has largely denied their engagement with such questions, regarding Anne Brontë's novel as a dispassionate and stoic account of governessing, and Gaskell's as evading the problem of desire through emphasis on its heroine's unknowing fall. Each text dwells on the subjectivity and experiences of a contentious and controversial figure in Victorian cultural discourse, for both the governess and the fallen woman focus anxieties about unregulated sexuality. The position of each is unstable in the Victorian symbolic economy, and hence provocative. The governess, whose task is to supervise the moral growth and education of her charges, must be one whose 'unimpeachable morality' demands that desires and longings of her own be bracketed, sacrificed, thwarted. Anne Brontë writes in 1847 with a knowledge of these constraints, imagining a narrator who reveals yet conceals her intense and passionate inner world. Hired to watch over others, the governess withdraws herself from their surveillance, yet is also urged to confess the desires and aggression that destabilise her position as one to whom mother's work can be entrusted. The confessional structure of *Agnes Grey* serves indeed to elaborate a notion of passionate subjectivity which is the more thoroughly policed for being discursively elaborated. Female subjectivity is therefore constituted by the discursive contradiction that repression itself generates the highly elaborated Victorian discourse of (repressed) passion.

In the early 1850s, when Gaskell writes *Ruth*, the doctrine of passionlessness is beginning to challenge earlier constructions of the fallen woman and prostitute as aberrantly sexualised. Gaskell draws on the idea of passionlessness to articulate Ruth's innocence, but questions that doctrine's essentialist implications in her representation of Jemima Bradshaw. By dealing with the effects of Ruth's sexual secret on another young woman, Gaskell explores the nature of what we now refer to as 'the closet', and how it works to structure and regulate social relations and to shape subjectivity.

Constructions of women of other cultures as wickedly and excessively sexualised persisted in Victorian culture, alongside and in apparent contradiction to arguments about the essential passionlessness of all women. Here again explanations centring on perceptions of sexual instability could resolve the contradiction. Views of both passionlessness and licentiousness hinged on the cultural management of sexuality: if protected from 'exciting causes', Greg and Acton could argue, all women would be sexually inert, but living in cultures that exploited and stimulated sexuality, they developed differently and bore the signs of their culture's corruption and mismanagement. On the basis of malleable sexuality – though she was not proposing a version of passionlessness – Elizabeth Blackwell argued that without proper physical education, women could not possibly develop either strong minds or strong bodies. 'Contrast the pictures of harem life, given by modern observers in the East', she advises. Women deprived of sound cultural management of their faculties become a 'by-word for meanness, and licentiousness, and falsehood'.[1] Published at the same time as *Ruth*, Charlotte Brontë's *Villette* invokes racially-inflected representations of Eastern women as licentiously sexualised and wonders about her own culture's problematic constructions of female sexuality and passion. Brontë's narrator focuses on a painting of a latter-day 'Cleopatra', which enables her to articulate the problems in constructing a version of female passion that is not associated with prostitution, cheap solicitation and exhibitionistic display. In much the same way that Harriet Martineau recorded her horror of the way Eastern women in the harem lived in the grip of 'that one interest', she regretted that Charlotte Brontë had given 'passion ... too prominent a place in her pictures of life', creating heroines whose cravings for love were vehement and morbid. Like Martineau and other travellers to the East, Charlotte Brontë offers a deflating version of harem sensuality, but unlike Martineau, she saw a world of difference between the sexual surfeit of the stereotypical harem slave and the passionate desire of Lucy Snowe to be seen and to be loved.

Agnes Grey and the 'animal side of life'

If *Mary Barton*'s engagement with the politics of working-class domesticity and sexuality makes for a disorderly fictional house,

Agnes Grey is by contrast a model of good housekeeping, often eliciting praise for its economical, well-regulated and tidy craft. But the estimate of the youngest Brontë's work as even and orderly, in contrast to the exciting, turbulent and disturbing novels of her sisters, is often dismissive – a way of damning it with faint praise. Its most enthusiastic proponent, George Moore, extolled *Agnes Grey* as 'the most perfect prose narrative in English letters', unjustly overlooked and underrated.[2] According to Moore, the tendency to underappreciate Anne's work follows Charlotte Brontë's own initiative in dismissing her youngest sister as a literary competitor. Charlotte emphasised Anne's quiet and sterling virtues; describing Anne as 'long-suffering, self-denying, reflective, and intelligent', she observed that her youngest sister lacked the power, the fire, and the originality of Emily. 'A constitutional reserve and taciturnity placed and kept her in the shade, and covered her mind, and especially her feelings, with a sort of nun-like veil, which was rarely lifted.'[3] Charlotte pronounced the choice of subject for *The Tenant of Wildfell Hall* an entire mistake; she preferred *Agnes Grey*: 'The simple and natural – quiet description and simple pathos are, I think, Acton Bell's forte.'[4]

Whether because of Charlotte's initiative or not, reviewers have also tended to find the novel's virtues reflecting Anne's in its simple and stoic forbearance or muted resignation:

> One feels that the sensibility of the author is too highly strung and too exhausted for her to engage in even the shadow of a struggle. A dull half-light illumines these pages which are filled with accounts of small unhappinesses suffered without murmur, small happinesses accepted with a gentle gratitude with scarcely the strength to smile. Resignation is the soul of this little book.[5]

In the same spirit, Inga-Stina Ewbank notes that 'in her anxiety to picture life that is drab, Anne Brontë sometimes produces art that is dull' and that her 'dispassionateness of style at times verges on boredom'.[6]

The evaluation of the novel as sombre, resigned and dispassionate does not, I want to argue, begin to take adequately into account its engaged and passionate narrator, a young woman who will crush fledglings with a large stone before a cruel pupil can mutilate them, and who finds herself violently shaking a provoking child, or forcefully dashing a poker into the cinders to ease her irritation. Nor does such an evaluation seem to describe the young woman who looks forward to exerting herself in the world; literally throbs with hope and excitement when the man to whom she feels attracted displays interest in her; wishes fervently for beauty and the power to attract him; experiences 'deep delight' in thinking of him; 'burns' with indignation when falsely maligned; and derives 'secret gratification' when she realises she is a contender for his attentions. While critics have observed that *Agnes Grey* is a narrative of growth and maturation, unusual in allowing its female protagonist independence and insisting on the importance of women being able to support themselves, they have not usually read it as a novel of intense passions, concerned with competition and triumph, and meditating on the mysterious and perplexing nature of sexual attraction.[7] Though accounts of Anne's life and comparisons with *Wuthering Heights* and *Jane Eyre* may have shaped impressions of *Agnes Grey* as muted and sombre, and though the narrator herself is partly responsible for encouraging these perceptions, it is curious how consistently the desiring and passionate subjectivity of the narrator has been overlooked. Even George Moore, who appreciated the 'heat' in Anne Brontë's *The Tenant of Wildfell Hall*, did not find it in the delicate and moderate *Agnes Grey*, the narrative he (not unlike Charlotte) characterised as 'simple and beautiful as a muslin dress'.[8]

Agnes Grey is at the same time overtly a record of the governess' limited powers and suffered indignities and a submerged documentary of self-assertion, conflict and competition. The narrator is continually embattled, first against the anarchic and destructive tendencies of children, later against the sexually competitive and manipulative behaviour of the young woman in her charge. In her first venture out of a family circle where she has been somewhat babied and coddled, she intends to exert her powers in a receptive world, and attempts to impress herself upon her charges. But in practice, and to her disillusionment, she finds she has very little effect on ungovernable and intractable children in a household whose moral standards leave much to be desired. In her next venture, she again leaves her secluded family circle, but this time, estimating her powers of change more accurately, she begins to worry that she may succumb to what she sees as the dangerous moral influences of her environment. She no longer imagines that she can mark or shape those around her, but is instead worried about how she is being marked and shaped – how she may degenerate in uncongenial moral surroundings. By figuring her young charges in terms of animals, she underlines the precarious distinction between the human and the bestial. By likening herself in her second situation to a lone civilised being among savages, she draws attention to the dangers of moral infection and conveys her fear that she is less likely to humanise others than they are to degrade her. We see that both the Murray daughters are 'unnatural' women: the elder is a selfish coquette who will later devalue motherhood and refuse to nurse her daughter; the younger, a big-boned, boyish young woman who does not want to cross the boundary from unsexed adolescence into young womanhood, is given to swearing like the grooms, enjoys a chase where the leveret 'cries like a child' and cares only for horses. In social texts of the period, it is usually the governess who is seen as a danger to the household's stability. From Brontë's point of view in *Agnes Grey*, however, the young governess is the one at risk, her own moral nature necessarily destabilised in such corrupting surroundings. While the thrust of the governess' narrative is to disqualify her employers' claims to moral superiority and attest to her own, she obliquely confesses to the very emotions and desires that subvert the bland and dispassionate face of feminine respectability to which she lays claim. That claim allows the narrator at the end of the novel to offer her marriage as a stabilising of sound middle-class values. Yet this apparently conservative position is complicated by Agnes Grey's insistence that women should be able to support themselves and that enormous satisfaction can be derived from self-supporting and rewarding work. Even as the novel appears to confirm formulations of the domestic and maternal ideal, it also challenges an important foundation of the separate spheres system – the financial dependence of wives and daughters.

Framed by the narrator's promise to lay her story candidly before the reader and to disclose what she could not tell an intimate friend, *Agnes Grey* begins like a confession, but of what?

> All true histories contain instruction; though, in some, the treasure may be hard to find, and when found, so trivial in quantity that the dry, shrivelled kernel scarcely compensates for the trouble of cracking the nut. Whether this be the case with my history or not, I am hardly competent to judge; I sometimes think it might prove useful to some, and entertaining to others, but the world may judge for itself: shielded by my own obscurity, and by the lapse of years, and a few fictitious names, I do not fear to venture, and will candidly lay before the public what I would not disclose to the most intimate friend (p. 1).

The promise of the opening paragraph may set us wondering what nature of divulgences can be offered to the public that could not be made to a confidante. Agnes Grey does indeed tell all about the families for whom she works and the trials of governessing, but beyond 'the darker side of respectability' in her employers, her narrative discloses her own internal world of desire and emotion. Although this inner world is revealed in the course of the narration, it is not entirely owned; the narrator cannot fully associate herself with her violent and passionate feelings and the desire for self-assertion that her narrative records.

If Victorian culture deemed violent feelings, passionate desire, jealousy, and triumph unwomanly, they were thought particularly transgressive in a governess. The figure of the governess, as Mary Poovey has shown, highlights some of the contradictions in mid-Victorian conceptions of female nature and the domestic ideal. Since the governess was a working woman, she was like men and women of the working classes, but since she was well-born and genteel, she was also like the middle-class mother, whose educative and child-rearing duties she was hired to perform.[9] Governessing focused anxieties about working women, class boundaries, the preservation of the domestic ideal of maternity. It presented the threat of potentially unruly female sexuality that was not naturally and happily channelled into reproductivity. As Poovey notes, the governess was 'expected to preside over the contradiction written into the domestic ideal – in the sense both that she was meant to police the emergence of undue assertiveness or sexuality in her maturing charges and that she was expected not to display willfulness or desires herself'.[10] The question of the governess' sexuality was anxiously focused in one way on her powers of self-control and denial – in so far as she was useful to middle-class households, could she be trusted to regulate and discipline herself appropriately? The question of sexuality was also focused in another way to demonstrate handily that it was neither natural nor desirable for women to work. Any woman denied the expression of sexuality in maternity would suffer and wither and lose her feminine characteristics; the large number of governesses in lunatic asylums testified to this.

Agnes begins her narrative by informing her readers that all true histories contain instruction, but wonders whether the 'nut' in this case is worth cracking, because the 'kernel' may be dry and shrivelled.[11] The image of a dried out kernel, un-plump and withered, suggests a life of hardship from which bitter truths are to be learned, and appears to deny the possibility of fulfilment, growth, ripeness. While apparently self-abnegating, the opening sentence is also a persuasive way of priming the reader for a joyless nut, a narrative whose kernel is neither rewarding, sweet nor ripe. Other hints in the novel – the old pressed primrose leaves that the narrator still keeps – suggest a present life that feeds on dried relics of the past and corroborate the associations raised by the image of the withered kernel. Brontë's terms of blight and fruit here correspond to those used in contemporary debates about the situation and plight of governesses, who were unfortunate enough to have to earn their own bread and denied (until or unless rescued by an offer of marriage) the expression of their natural propensities for mother-hood. The terms in which they are represented often imply sexual repression and the bodily costs of thwarted instincts: governesses were known to fade before their 'bloom' was gone, 'snap from the stalk', or prolong a 'withered, sickly life'.[12]

The promise of a candid exposure, which we have seen the opening paragraph also offers, works against the image of the nut that has to be cracked – possibly a tough one with a bitter kernel, at that. There is a tension then between the narrator's declared open-ness toward the reader, and the association of the narrative's truth with the nut's kernel. Agnes admits that she consistently dissembles to hide her feelings from her employers and pupils, but she claims to tell the privileged reader all. Yet in the course of this 'laying bare,' she will confess that there are limits to what she can divulge:

> I began this book with the intention of concealing nothing that those who liked might have the benefit of perusing a fellow creature's heart; but we have *some* thoughts that all the angels in heaven are welcome to behold – but not our brother-men – not even the best and kindest amongst them (p. 110).

Such censored material has always to do with the governess' passionate feelings. Moreover, in spite of her careful orchestration, we may discern an even more aggressive and triumphant self than the apparently dispassionate, but deeply passionate one she authorises. The textual effects of confession, reserve and reticence produce a narrator whose subjectivity is more complex than criticism of this novel has generally allowed or the narrator herself acknowledges.

Unlike the usual governess, who is alone and forced to seek employment, Agnes actually wants to try her powers in the world and assert her independence.[13] Even though her family is needy, they urge her not to go out to work. She contradicts therefore a common and enduring assumption, even among feminists in the 1860s, that no woman would want to work unless she were driven by absolute necessity. Agnes not only has a mother who is alive and well, a relatively uncommon situation in Victorian fiction, but Mrs Grey is decisive, active, and so capable that she has somewhat inhibited the exercise of managerial qualities in her daughters, the younger of whom now wants to affirm her own competence. She longs 'to go out', 'to enter', 'to act', 'to exercise', 'to show', 'to convince' (p. 9). As for her pupils, she intends to 'train the tender plants, and watch their buds unfolding day by day' (p. 10).

Initially, the names of her employers and their homes – Bloomfield and Wellwood – signify the possibilities for growth she has imagined in the adventure of 'cultivating' young children. Mrs Bloomfield may refer to the smallest boy as the 'flower of the flock', but the images of flowers and 'unfolding buds' are too gentle for the brutal world of juvenile urges, resistances and cruelties that she encounters. Instead of unfolding, buds are found to harbour vicious tendencies that must be nipped. Agnes begins to modify the metaphors that represent her pupils, gradually abandoning horticultural metaphors of plant training for zoological terms that better signify their undisciplined bestiality. Thus her pupils have no more notion of obedience than a 'wild, unbroken colt'(p. 24), and they quarrel over their 'victuals like a set of tiger cubs' (p. 38). When their father finds them grinding egg-shells in the nursery, he berates Agnes for letting them behave 'worse than a litter of pigs' (p. 38). Fanny Bloomfield 'bellows like a bull' (p. 30), and later at Horton Lodge, John Murray is as 'rough as a young bear, boisterous, unruly, unprincipled, untaught, unteachable' (p. 65). Rosalie is a dog in the manger – she behaves towards Agnes in relation to Mr Weston like a greedy animal which, 'when gorged to the throat, will yet gloat over what they cannot devour, and grudge the smallest morsel to a starving brother' (p. 142).

Agnes has come from a home where animals are highly valued and loved; taking leave of her pets, she kisses both her favourite silky white-fantail pigeons, and (to the scandal of the maid) the cat. But when her charges behave like animals, she finds them unruly and wild rather than lovable. The figuring of children as animals forcibly suggests the brutality of Wellwood, a world in which the 'persecution of the lower creation' is an index of moral degradation. What view of childhood does Agnes's representation of her charges imply? These children do not appear to come 'trailing clouds of glory', but filled to the brim with unruly, evil and 'vexatious propensities' that training and education must stamp out. Havelock Ellis was later to observe that 'the child is naturally, by his organization, nearer to the animal, to the savage, to the criminal, than the adult'. Henry Maudsley also expressed the view that children would be 'terrific criminals' if they 'had strong passions, muscular strength, and sufficient intelligence'.[14] A child of nine or ten, as 'frantic and ungovernable' as the children at Wellwood are at six or seven, would be a 'maniac', Agnes observes. At Horton Lodge, however, young John Murray is 'frank and good-natured in the main' and might have been a 'decent lad had he been properly educated' (p. 65). Agnes does not therefore necessarily support the view, not uncommon at the time, that children 'come into the world with evil passions, perverted faculties, and unholy dispositions'.[15] As advice literature on how mothers should manage themselves and their children was never tired of pointing out, it was the mother's duty to prevent the growth of 'headstrong passions and vicious thoughts'. Since the 'first days of humanity are under woman's guidance; impressions are then formed never to be obliterated – the young mind is then as pliable as wax, and will receive any form or stamp'.[16]

Victorian science was much occupied with the close relationship between women and children, developmentally and intellectually. Well before Darwin observed that the children of both sexes resemble the mature female more closely than the mature male, scientists had been arguing that woman stands midway between child and man. The female ends her growth before the male ends his, retains her childish roundness and generally more closely resembles the child in her bodily development than the male. Like the child, she is in danger of being overwhelmed by emotions and the inability to discipline them properly through the exercise of will and reason.[17] Only nineteen, and aware that 'many a girl of fifteen, or under, was gifted with a more womanly address', Agnes is leaving home to prove that 'little Agnes' is indeed a competent adult. 'Though a woman in my own estimation', she remarks of her family's opinion of her, 'I was still a child in theirs' (p. 6). Were Agnes to appear out of control, or given, like her charges, to vent her feelings violently, she would forfeit her own precarious claim to self-discipline and regulation. Her narrative cannot therefore acknowledge the extent to which she finds herself impassioned, out of control, and sometimes reduced to the level of those she has hoped to raise.

On her arrival at Wellwood, Tom Bloomfield initially makes the governess watch him 'manfully' apply whip and spurs to his rocking-horse. Shocked, Agnes hopes to wean him from such brutal delights, but later she longs herself to chastise him with a 'good birch rod', and wishes that his ill-treated dogs would turn round one day and bite him, if only they could do so with impunity (p. 25). When Mary Ann refuses to pronounce a particular word in her lesson Agnes sees it as her 'absolute duty' to force the child to obey and perform (p. 27). As urgings, threats and entreaties avail nothing in relation to the child's 'absurd perversity' she finds herself shaking Mary Ann 'violently by the shoulders' or pulling her hair. The child shrieks loudly, because, says Agnes, she knows how her governess hates the noise. When the cries bring Mrs Bloomfield to the scene, Agnes's version is that Mary Ann is naughty and has been 'screaming in a passion' (p. 28). Unable to discipline the children by gentle exhortation and example, Agnes longs increasingly to exercise force and physical chastisement. As if to corroborate the governess' experiences of the children at Wellwood as violent and impervious to her initial, missionary-like zeal, Betty the nursemaid attests that she can only manage the children by 'hitting 'em a slap sometimes' and giving the little ones 'a good whipping' (p. 41). The difference between Betty and Agnes is that the maid acts on her urge to punish the children physically, while the governess experiences the urge but largely restrains herself. What is significant, though, is the extent to which Agnes's own desire to vent her aggressive feelings in response to the children's 'vexatious' and 'incorrigible propensities' remains unexamined.[18]

The 'heart of darkness' to which governessing leads is covertly demonstrated through one of the most distressing incidents in the novel – the killing of the fledgling birds. In order to prevent their slow mutilation and torture at Tom's hands, Agnes crushes them by dropping a large stone upon them. The attitudes of Tom, his uncle and his mother are the subject of the narrator's comments, and although she imagines beforehand that the act will sicken her, she says nothing subsequently about her reactions to this desperate mercy-killing. In this regard, Mrs Gaskell's account of a conversation with Charlotte Brontë about *Agnes Grey* may illuminate the shifting and unstable subject positions of 'victim' and 'inflicter' that she experiences at Wellwood:

> I was speaking to her about *Agnes Grey* ... and alluding more particularly to the account of the stoning of the little nestlings in the presence of the parent birds. She said that none but those who had been in the position of a governess could ever realise the dark side of 'respectable' human nature; under no great temptation to crime, but daily giving way to selfishness and ill-temper, till its conduct towards those dependent on it sometimes amounts to a tyranny of which one would rather be the victim than the inflicter.[19]

According to Gaskell's account, Charlotte suggests that the governess is the one dependent on 'it' – the '"respectable" human nature' of her employers. But what of the dark side of respectable nature belonging to the governess herself, who finds herself, even in fantasy, in the position of 'inflicter' on 'those dependent' on her? A victim of her desires to lash out, the governess experiences a dissonance in her self-conception, or at least in her self-representation. Although Gaskell makes it clear that the dark side of respectability belongs to the employers, who she trusts 'err rather from a density of perception and an absence of sympathy, than from any natural cruelty of disposition', *Agnes Grey* reveals how positions of victim and inflicter are potentially blurred and unstable.

The first movement of *Agnes Grey* concerns, as I have already suggested, a failed attempt to impress oneself on an intractable world and to mould or shape it according to one's lights, while the next explores the need to defend against one's own impressibility and to resist absorbing undesirable influences. Unable to train young plants, or even to compel young rebels by force to what is right and good, Agnes leaves her first situation without reflecting on the effects of such interactions on herself. But after she has spent some time in the Murray household, and is less caught up in sheer physical battle with her charges, she begins to worry about the way her life as a governess degrades her and to fear the degenerative effects of her associations. At Horton Lodge she is not urged to subdue the undisciplined by force, but is subjected instead to the moral and intellectual short-comings of a social world more insidious in its influence than Bloomfield: 'Habitual associates are known to exercise great influence over each other's minds and manners. Those whose actions are for ever before our eyes, whose words are ever in our ears, will naturally lead us, albeit against our will – slowly – gradually – imperceptibly, perhaps, to act and speak as they do' (p. 97).

The Bloomfield children came to be seen largely in terms of unruly and incorrigible animals, but they were also described as 'turbulent rebels' who resisted all efforts to 'humanize' them. Though the Murrays are socially superior, living among them is more explicitly like life among savages:

> If one civilized man were doomed to pass a dozen years amid a race of intractable savages, unless he had power to improve them, I greatly question whether, at the close of that period, he would not have become, at least, a barbarian himself. And I, as I could not make my young companions better, feared exceedingly that they would make me worse – would gradually bring my feelings, habits, capacities to the level of their own (p. 97).

The language of this passage associates governessing with the dangers of living among savages and barbarians. Agnes seems to identify herself as the traveller or missionary susceptible to a new moral environment: might she not too descend to unspeakable horrors by imitation and assimilation? Drawing on a discourse of exploration, race and civilisation, the narrator attempts to explain the power of a group to reproduce its values (or lack of them) in inevitably impressionable others.

The images of New Zealand perform similar work. On arriving at Horton, the narrator asks the reader to imagine what it must feel like to suddenly wake some morning and find oneself at 'Port Nelson in New Zealand' (p. 58). While Anne Brontë may have been thinking simply of a faraway place to which people she knew, such as Mary Taylor, had emigrated, New Zealand was also associated with hostile and violent aborigines, capable of the most barbarous and inhuman practices.[20] In 1846, Governor Grey attempted to quell 'trouble with the Maori people of the area'.[21] Although Anne could not have seen it, a letter from Mary Taylor in 1849 corroborates such conflicts and military intervention: 'The Maoris are quiet and we begin to wish for another disturbance for fear the troops should leave the country.'[22]

Stationed at an outpost in 'uncongenial soil', 'governess' Grey finds herself fighting an invisible battle with the barbarians. At home, she has been accustomed to hold herself aloof from unsuitable influences, since the genteel if impoverished Grey family has kept itself in social seclusion from a neighbourhood that offered no

society. 'Our only intercourse with the world consisted in a stately
tea-party, now and then, with the principal farmers and tradespeople
of the vicinity, just to avoid being stigmatized as too proud to consort
with our neighbours' (p. 2). Brontë intensifies the representation of
Horton Lodge as a place of dangerous determinants through Agnes's
comments on the Horton servants. She complains that none of them
can appreciate or reciprocate her efforts to stand up for them. 'All
servants, I am convinced, would not have done so; but domestic
servants in general, being ignorant and little accustomed to reason
and reflection, are too easily corrupted by the carelessness and bad
example of those above them, and these, I think, were not of the best
order to begin with' (p. 69). They are a cogent reminder to Agnes of
the degenerative effects of habitual example and association, and
although she may be of a different order, she is not immune to
Horton's effects either.

She has not been there long before she begins to fear that her
'intellect [is] deteriorating', her 'heart petrifying', and her 'soul contrac-
ting' (p. 97). Anxious lest her 'very moral perceptions' might become
'deadened', her 'distinctions of right and wrong confounded', and all
her 'better faculties sunk', she is fortunate to be rescued by the
presence of Mr Weston (pp. 97–8). Significantly, her fantasies of
degeneration usher in a confession of her interest in the new curate,
an attraction she justifies in terms of a redemption. As the 'gross
vapours' of earth gather in on her 'thus it was that Mr. Weston rose
at length upon me, appearing like the morning star in my horizon, to
save me from the fear of utter darkness' (p. 98). Before she begins to
dwell on him, 'never a new idea or stirring thought came to me from
without, and such as rose within me were, for the most part, miserably
crushed at once, or deemed to sicken and fade away because they
could not see the light'; but after he becomes the focus of her thoughts
and desires, he is the light that nurtures new growth and stirring
thoughts (p. 97). She represents her ideas and thoughts as plants
having struggled feebly in the dark, etiolated, sickening and fading
for want of light, which Weston then provides. Those nurtured
thoughts remind one of the earlier image of herself as a 'thistle seed
borne on the wind to some strange nook of uncongenial soil, where
it must lie long enough before it can take root and germinate,
extracting nourishment from what appears alien to its nature, if
indeed it ever can' (p. 58). The combined effect of the images is to link
Weston powerfully with the conditions of her growth and fruition.

Whereas Jane Eyre fears that her love for Rochester eclipses her love for her maker, Agnes conveniently makes Weston his emissary, an agent of redemption and a justifiable object of worship. And yet, later, she does own that her conscience secretly reproaches her that she mocks God 'with the service of a heart more bent upon the creature than the creator' (p. 135). Quieting her conscience about her love for Weston, she insists: 'It is not the man, it is his goodness that I love' (p. 135). When hopes of a relationship with Mr Weston seem dashed, she berates herself for feeling so joyless and despondent, saying, 'I should have made God my friend, and to do His will the pleasure and the business of my life; but Faith was weak, and Passion was too strong' (p. 148). One reason for spiritualising her passionate feelings about Weston is her difficulty with the 'animal' in relation to the intelligent and moral being. The tendency to think in terms of these distinctions is clear in her judgement of Matilda, the second Murray daughter. As an animal, Agnes owns, Matilda is 'all right, full of life, vigour, and activity', but as an intelligent being, she is barbarously ignorant, and as a moral agent, 'reckless, headstrong, violent, and unamenable to reason' (p. 64).

If her first foray into the outside world exposed Agnes to her own startling capacity, when provoked, for violence, aggression and frustration, her second situation exposes her to other passions and the battle to assert yet conceal them in the face of opposition. Her second set of charges are merely older versions of the first; they have from infancy been suffered to tyrannise over nurses, governesses, and servants. Just as Agnes responded at times with superior force to the assaults of the delinquent Bloomfields, so she now engages Rosalie Murray's attempted tyranny, in the form of torment and competition, with her own quietly subversive stratagems. In assessing the Murrays, Agnes has realised that her task is to render the girls 'superficially attractive' and as showily accomplished as possible without present discomfort to themselves (p. 60). She was also advised in her correspondence with Mrs. Murray that her educational accomplishments were less important than 'unimpeachable morality' and obliging disposition (p. 53). The governess has been hired therefore to teach the '"accomplishments" that would attract a good husband without allowing the sexual component of these accomplishments to get the upper hand'.[23]

The young women whom she is supposed to supervise are both at the age when, according to medical discourses of reproduction, women become marked by sexual difference for their reproductive role. We have been told that 'at sixteen, Miss Murray was something of a romp, yet not more so than is natural and allowable for a girl of that age; but at seventeen, that propensity, like all other things, began to give way to the ruling passion, and soon was swallowed up in the all absorbing ambition, to attract and dazzle the other sex' (p. 63). The question of Miss Murray's changing propensities, however, invokes the recognition that Agnes herself is a marriageable woman. This fact is further brought to our attention when she declares her preference for the respectable clerical marriage her sister is about to contract in contrast to Rosalie's dreams of Ashby Park and marriage based on power and prestige. 'The "Coming Out"' is a chapter that ostensibly narrates Rosalie's launch into the world of husband-attracting. There is no official or social 'coming out' for Agnes; nonetheless she begins to think about what function beauty has in attracting men, and what her own appealing qualities are. Later she compares herself as the poor man with one sheep (one possible admirer) to Rosalie – the rich man with a thousand flock (many admirers). Another image – Rosalie as the greedy dog denying a scrap to his starving brother – similarly reveals her sense of being a player, albeit a disadvantaged one, in the business of courtship and marriage.

From the time Miss Murray begins to respond to 'the ruling passion', the narrative is structured to deal with awakened sexuality, in both the governess and her elder charge. Brontë follows 'The "Coming-Out"' with two short chapters whose function is to introduce the various men in the neighbourhood with whom Rosalie intends to flirt, and to bring to attention the new curate whom Miss Murray scorns as an 'insensate, ugly stupid blockhead' until she sees that her governess is interested in him (p. 77). Chapter XI finds Agnes virtuously and suddenly intent on visiting poor Nancy Brown in a rather obvious narrative ploy that allows her to hear about and then meet and talk with Mr Weston. Thereafter the narrative follows the progress of her relationship with him and the impediments to it.

The narrative highlights her walk to Church so that she can converse with Mr Weston, though its ostensible reason is to show how invidious her ambiguous social status is – she does not like to walk behind the group because it makes her seem like a domestic, but she also does not like to walk beside Rosalie and company because no one acknowledges her as a social equal or talks to her. The contemplation of nature provides a handy way of solving these social discomforts, so she often hangs back to 'botanize and entomologize among the green banks and budding hedges' (pp. 106–7). Marginalisation has its rewards, for Mr Weston joins her and helps her to gather some wild flowers she has admired. Though his short sermon on the toughness of the human heart seems to capture the sense of stoicism associated with Anne Brontë herself, and to articulate an antidote to the desiring self the narrator is about to expose to the reader, we are again misled. The narrative's emphasis turns out to be not on the toughness of the human heart, but rather on its capacity to swell, throb, and overflow.

As Agnes begins to fantasise about the curate's need for a partner, the Murray girls tease her with 'malicious glee' about her fondness for Mr Weston. Hot, irritable and defensive, Agnes denies any interest in Mr Weston, and when they soon turn their thoughts back to Captains and Lieutenants, she can turn hers to curates. The moment Agnes returns home, she confirms their perceptions by falling on her knees to pray, her heart 'overflowing with one earnest wish' (p. 111). Since we see that Rosalie is quite right about her governess' interest in Weston, the intensity of Agnes's denials merits some scrutiny. Certainly, Rosalie debases what seems pure and selfless into a superficial flirtation, so Agnes is stung to fierce protest. But the incident also focuses the narrative's representation of desire, as Brontë demonstrates the split between the outer and inner self that the governess' position appears to demand. Only to the reader can she expose something of 'what I would not disclose to the most intimate friend' (p. 1). If we return to the opening paragraph, we see therefore, that as much as it is a confession about the indignities a governess may suffer, the narrative is also a veiled confession of passion. What Agnes wants to disclose is the nature of her own desire, habitually and necessarily under cover. What we see also, however, is that desire may be hidden, but it is neither passive nor powerless, especially in the face of sexual competition.

The next time Mr Weston falls in beside her while she is walking once again behind Rosalie and her friends, she notices with satisfaction (and throbbing heart) that he is 'less bent on communicating his own thoughts and predilections than discovering mine' (p. 130). At exactly this point, Rosalie accosts him with a sweet smile and begins to walk beside him and talk to him with 'all imaginable cheerfulness and affability', engrossing him 'entirely to herself' (p. 131). Rosalie's interest in Mr Weston is awakened only when she sees him paying attention to the governess and gleans that Miss Grey has strong feelings for him. In response to this competitive appropriation of Mr Weston, Agnes feels wronged, listens with envy and observes with anxiety and apprehension as Rosalie appears vivacious and charming. Through the torments of insecurity, listening to her pupil gloat that she has 'fixed' the man and shot him through the heart, Agnes resolves to let not 'one glimpse of my feelings appear' (p. 132). Yet she is not without power either, and one subtle triumph follows another. Although she must watch Rosalie scheming to meet Mr Weston at the cottages in order to visit the sick, she wins a round when Mr Weston offers her his umbrella and smilingly persuades her to accept his offer after she has politely declined it, and then even hands her into the carriage. 'One glance he gave, one little smile at parting – it was but for a moment, but therein I read, or thought I read, a meaning that kindled in my heart a brighter flame of hope than had ever yet arisen' (p. 135). Witnessing that leave-taking, Rosalie has an 'unamiable cloud upon her pretty face'; the governess, triumphant, smiles 'placidly'. As the carriage moves forward, Rosalie is further angered because Mr Weston does not look back to receive the bow that she meant for him. 'I saw she was out of humour, and I derived a secret gratification from the fact; not that she was vexed, but that she thought she had reason to be so. It made me think my hopes were not entirely the offspring of my wishes and imagination' (p. 136). Gathering intelligence from the smallest of signs, reading the meaning of gestures, and observing changing expressions minutely, Agnes chalks up her own quiet victories.

'As I am in the way of confessions,' the narrator begins a chapter entitled 'Confessions', 'I may as well acknowledge that, about this time, I paid more attention to dress than ever before' (p. 138). She owns too that she often stares at herself in the glass, critically assessing her appearance and attractiveness. Her admission ushers in a consideration of cultural valuations of female beauty, and far from endorsing the conventional wisdom about the greater importance of the mind and heart, Agnes Grey declares that external beauty in a woman is a gift that ought to be appreciated.[24] Her meditation on the way beauty renders some animals more lovable and lack of it means that others are despised or at best tolerated, supports widely held views of the link between loveliness and the very condition of being a woman. 'A woman's face', declared Alexander Walker, 'whatever may be the vigor or extent of her intellect, whatever the importance of the objects that occupy her, is always, in the history of her life, an obstacle or a reason.'[25] In another work devoted solely to the subject of beauty, the same author expressed a corollary of the common view that specifically linked the bodily or corporeal beauty of woman to her sexual functions: the soft, rounded form and voluptuous contours were taken as proof that she was specially formed for reproduction. Indeed, it was during the period of reproductivity, from puberty to menopause, that the face and frame of woman was supposedly most pleasing and most beautiful. After menopause, as many doctors agreed, women became angular and sharp, their upper lips grew downy, and they lost their womanly temper and feelings. Beauty was a sign, therefore, of the specialised function of women, and indeed, a means of ensuring that they fulfilled it.[26]

Agnes insists that although external beauty is liable to be over-rated, it is a gift for attracting others; it must, therefore, be appreciated as God-given rather than scorned. Drawing like so many discursive writers on an analogy from the natural world, Agnes, who has an amateur's interest in entomologising, says:

> As well might the humble glow-worm despise that power of giving light, without which the roving fly might pass her and repass her a thousand times, and never light beside her; she might hear her winged darling buzzing over and around her; he vainly seeking her, she longing to be found, but with no power to make her presence known, no voice to call him, no wings to follow his flight; ... the fly must seek another mate, the worm must live and die alone (p. 139).

It is probable that Anne Brontë was familiar with the peculiar nature of the glow-worm from her reading of Goldsmith's *History of the Earth*, for her account of the worm glowing to attract her winged mate is not dissimilar from his.[27] Her particular use of this piece of natural history contrasts illuminatingly with William Acton's later invocation of the glow-worm in his widely read and often revised treatise on *The Functions and Disorders of the Reproductive Organs*. In the third edition, Acton included a short section on 'Sexual Attrac-tion', which comprised little more than an explanation of the glow-worm's luminosity.[28]

> The devices, so to speak, which nature employs to bring the sexes together are among the most interesting facts of zoology. No one can fail to notice the wonderful design evinced in bringing the sexes together by means of a phosphorescent light, as is the case with luminous insects.... 'The object of the light appears to be to attract

the male, since it is most brilliant in the female, and in some species, if not all, is present only in the season when the sexes are destined to meet, and strikingly more vivid at the very moment when the meeting takes place. The torch which the wingless female, doomed to crawl upon the grass, lights up at the approach of night, is a beacon which unerringly guides the vagrant male to her "lone illumined form", however obscure the place of her abode.'[29]

On the question of sexual attraction, Acton is prepared to let the example of the glow-worm suffice, implying that nature's marvellous devices also apply in the case of human beings. Offering the glow-worm as a sufficiently illuminating analogy, he refrains, however, from explaining exactly how nature has gone to work in the case of the most complex species. The function of the analogy is possibly twofold: first, it allows him to suggest that female sexuality belongs in the realm of the animal and instinctual, and second, since he is not really interested in the subject of human sexual attraction, the analogy allows him to dispose handily of its more complex operations. His subject in this text is the nature and right management of the male seminal economy, particularly problems presented by strong male sexual feelings and the temptations of self-abuse or profligacy. And although it is in this work that he makes his much quoted pronouncement about the absence of female desire, it occurs merely as an *obiter dictum*:

> There is so much ignorance on the subject, and false ideas as to women's sexual condition are productive of so much mischief, that I need offer no apology for giving here, before we proceed, the true state of the case.... I should say that the majority of women (happily for them) are not very much troubled with sexual feeling of any kind.[30]

The normal state of affairs is that 'the best mothers, wives and managers of households' feel only the passion of 'love of home, children, and domestic duties' and suffer intercourse as a means to a maternal end without desiring 'any sexual gratification' for themselves.[31] When ready to conceive they allow access, like animals in heat, but at no other time.[32] Acton also notes that 'the physiologist will not be surprised that the human female should in these respects differ but little from the female among animals'.[33] For the most part, women have a 'natural repugnance for cohabitation' and allow it out of a laudable wish to gratify their husbands. All this, Acton implies, is as it should be; indeed, the natural disinclination of women will serve to sober male desire, which will dwindle to a healthy level, for a rational hard-working man should not expend his energies in frequent intercourse.

In Brontë's rather different use of the same analogy, Agnes's confessions about her sense of herself as a physical being are bound up with her desire for Mr Weston and her preparedness to assert herself and compete for him. Whereas the glow-worm analogy allows Acton to link the human female to the 'lower creation', and to avoid exploring the question of human sexual attraction, it serves Brontë essentially to assert what he denies. First, it allows her to talk obliquely about, rather than avoid, the delicate matter of physical beauty and sexual attraction, and second, it enables her to shift the discussion away from beauty to the more mysterious and marvellous ways in which attraction works. Although she has argued that a woman's beauty is the human equivalent of the glow-worm's beckoning light, her own case demonstrates that attraction can be based on something more profound and less explicable than physical beauty. Even though Agnes judges herself plain, she does indeed attract the curate Mr Weston, 'lighting up' in his presence and revealing her opinions and thoughts to him. This 'glow', however, is something that she attempts to keep strictly hidden from those around her, just as the glow-worm was thought able to do. According to some naturalists, the glow-worm could extinguish or conceal her light at will – a necessary provision to guard her from the attacks of nocturnal birds.[34] If the narrator's capacity to attract is analogous to the glow-worm's, we see that she too protects herself from 'predators' by concealing and denying her power of attraction. It is, however, a power that her charge, Rosalie Murray, recognises and attempts to compete with as she engineers meetings for herself with Mr Weston and thwarts Miss Grey's opportunities to see him. Nevertheless, Agnes Grey's apprently self-abnegating narrative demonstrates her triumph – not only is she preferred by Mr. Weston, but there was really no contest, in spite of Rosalie's great beauty, her determined machinations to lure Mr Weston, and her attempts to tarnish Agnes in his eyes.

As soon as Rosalie is married to Lord Ashby and Miss Grey's 'incarceration' is over, she sets the record straight on any lies that Rosalie and Matilda have told Mr Weston. They have said she was a perfect book-worm, completely absorbed in study and 'lost to every other pleasure'; she dismisses that as a 'scandalous libel. These young ladies are too fond of making random assertions at the expense of their friends, and you ought to be careful how you listen to them' (p. 156). She also enlightens Mr Weston about Rosalie Murray's short-comings: 'I should not call her *dis*honest, but it must be confessed, she's a little artful' (p. 166). He says he knew Rosalie was 'giddy and vain', but 'artful' helps him to account for 'some things that puzzled me a trifle before' (p. 166). Far from helpless, Agnes records her victory with some satisfaction, revealing how she surpasses her recent charge's beauty, charms, wiles, power and confidence, none of which enabled Rosalie to 'fix' Mr Weston.

After Agnes has returned home to her widowed mother, Brontë delays the reunion of Agnes and Mr Weston for a number of reasons. One is to sustain narrative suspense, another to distinguish love from dependency: Agnes must be able to stand alone practically and financially. The third, as the novel moves towards conventional closure, is to affirm the superiority of Agnes as potential mother and wife over Rosalie, now Lady Ashby. Since the visit to Ashby Park is described as a 'great sacrifice' for Rosalie's sake, undertaken 'out of violence' to Agnes's feelings, we wonder why she makes it. Agnes hints that she hopes to learn something of Mr Weston, but since she learns nothing except that he has left Horton, there is more to it than that. The visit demonstrates Rosalie Murray's misery, the extent of which removes any need to gloat; the narrator, who is 'not disposed to censure her now', allows herself only the briefest of sanctimonious reflections on greed and the desire for title and power (p. 174). Within a year, Rosalie has become plump, lost her complexion, exuberance and vivacity, whether from dissipation or 'some other evil'. Rosalie already has a child, but she can take no pleasure in her baby daughter, whom she sees as potential competition – 'What pleasure can I have in seeing a girl grow up to eclipse me?' (p. 185). She refuses to be 'troubled with nursing it', confesses that she has no idea of how to bring her child up 'in the way it should go', and wants Miss Grey to come and be its governess and 'make a better woman of it than its mama' (p. 174). Rosalie's refusal to nurse her child and her confessions of maternal inadequacy help to define the domestic ideal of motherhood that Agnes herself will uphold.

The epilogue, depicting Agnes as an exemplary wife and mother, is an endorsement of middle-class claims to moral and therefore social superiority. The class discrepancies and financial instabilities that troubled the marriage of Agnes's parents have no part in hers; Agnes surpasses even her admirable mother in her prudent and responsible husband, managing on his modest income by 'practising economy' and attempting never 'to imitate ... richer neighbours' (p. 198). Every year something is laid by for the children and for charity.[35] We can be sure that there will be no governesses in the Weston household – mother's work will be done by mother. Yet if the novel endorses middle-class ideology by insisting that mothers ought not to delegate their responsibilities, it also challenges the ideology that prescribes female financial dependency and proscribes vocational opportunities for women.

As controversy about the situation of the governess and the question of female employment continued during the next decades, social observers sought to retrench the separation of spheres by advertising the dangers of allowing others to take over the mother's sacred mission. Although Agnes is critical of the mothers that hire her and acerbic about their abdication of motherly responsibility, she does not conclude from this that all would be right if each woman stuck to the business of finding a husband and mothering her children. She does argue, though, that governessing is an impossible profession. In each household that employs her, the mother is barely involved with her children yet is still intent on dispensing advice and curtailing the governess' authority. With superb irony, Mrs Murray bewails the fact that Miss Grey lacks a mother's innate sensitivity to her children's well-being: 'Oh! if you – if *any* governess had but half a mother's watchfulness – half a mother's anxious care' (p. 114). She is also quick to blame the governess for having failed to form her daughter's tastes: 'Who is to form a young lady's tastes, I wonder, if the governess doesn't do it!' (p. 152). Mrs Murray's hints on the vocation of governessing present a picture of ample supply and tough competition. Only those succeed who 'devote themselves body and soul to their calling'; they cannot afford to 'yield to indolence or self-indulgence' for they will be 'speedily distanced by wiser competitors' (p. 153). Her advice on what it takes to succeed emphasises the governess' self-abnegation in the cultivation of her pupils: 'If she wishes to prosper in her vocation she must devote all her energies to her business; all her ideas and all her ambition will tend to the accomplishment of that one object' (p. 152). As one who tends and trains the plants, the governess must not ask to bloom herself.

The tendency in social debates to cast the problem of governess-ing in terms of the delinquency of mothers meant that the issue could be represented as one of conflict among women. 'Whether it be right or wrong, as a general rule, for mothers to delegate their most sacred trust to hired strangers, we are not here to discuss', stated the author of 'Hints on the modern governess system' *Fraser's Magazine* (1844), but then proceeded to show how 'the miseries of the governess are the result of women having been untrue to themselves'. The modern governess system is 'a case between woman and woman. Before one sex demands its due from the other, let it be just to itself.'[36] Pre-sumably if women are true to themselves, there will be no governesses, for every mother will attend to imparting those principles to her children that her maternity specially framed her to impart. To read Brontë's novel in the context of debates about the ambiguous social and sexual position of the governess in mid-Victorian society is to see that it too sounds arguments (to be made more forcibly in coming decades) that mothers should not be employing others to do their work, whether as wet-nurses or governesses. But while *Agnes Grey* quietly endorses the idea that mother's work should not be hired out, it takes the question of female employment, self-sufficiency and independence very seriously. After the death of her father, Agnes and her mother determine to open their own school, and Brontë brings home the enormous difference between working 'as a hireling among strangers' and running a school of one's own (p. 169). According to the arguments against working women which mounted during the next decades, Mrs Grey should have regarded herself simply as a woman who had failed in the business of a woman's life. If the business of a woman was to be married, then any woman who did not marry or lost her husband, had failed: 'the mischance of the distressed governess and the improvident widow, is that of every insolvent tradesman'. [37] Mrs Grey, by contrast, refusing her elder daughter's help, sets about seeing how she and Agnes can 'gather honey' for themselves. Her metaphor suggests the sweetness of productive employment and self-sufficiency, as well as the indefati-gable activity of the honey-bee.

But what happens to the social and sexual division of labour when women gather their own honey? The association of working women with bees is raised by the titles of two articles on female inheritance, education and employment that appeared in the *Saturday Review* in

1857 and 1859. Neither discussion invokes the analogy except through its title, 'Queen bees or working bees?', and at first glance the alternatives serve merely to delineate two kinds of women – mothers and workers – and to ask, perhaps, 'Who would rather be a worker if she could be a queen?' The idea that the worker bees were female was entertained as far back as Aristotle's time, though Aristotle himself rejected it on the grounds that nature would 'never give offensive armour to females'.[38] Nineteenth-century naturalists describe working bees as imperfect females, for although they take on some mothering functions, they can never be mothers themselves. The *Saturday Review* articles strongly oppose the idea of female employment and deploy the bee metaphor perhaps to suggest that labouring women are bound to sacrifice or forfeit their femininity and reproductive capacity. But the analogy is further suggestive because in the social organisation of bees, the males, or drones are superfluous to the hive's busy productivity. Workers are not only responsible for honey-making, the nursery, and cell production, but also for the merciless ousting and killing of the drones when these have outlived their fertilising function. The threatening idea of working women who might compete with men, take over their work and reduce them to redundancy is also evident in anxious responses to the questions of female education, independence and vocation. In its strong line on these questions *Agnes Grey* is again a text more uneven and peculiar than its critics have allowed.

Through its confession of the governess' secret inner life, the novel raises the question of the self's stability in relation to the intractable and yet corruptive power of the world. Desire, represented as a form of moral resistance and a means of survival, comes to strengthen the permeable and susceptible self. It is figured as a redemption from moral numbness and a stay against degradation. Love also means, eventually, founding a 'colony' of one's own, in which approved moral values can be entrenched, strengthened, transmitted. As we have seen in the previous chapters, medical and social scientific discourse used images of animality and savagery to assert the inferiority of other cultures and classes; in *Agnes Grey* such images help to define a solid middle-class ideal that challenges the pre-eminence of both the newly wealthy Bloomfields and the older squirearchy. But if the union of Agnes and her curate installs Agnes as the paradigmatic middle-class mother and wife, the novel also transgresses middle-class formulations of female dependency by insisting on self-sufficiency and acknowledging the power and indeed pleasure of respected productivity. Although by the end of the novel Agnes appears to fulfil a middle-class maternal ideal, the revelations of her confession – aggression, active desire, pride in productivity and independence – also destabilise its apparent homogeneity.

Passionlessness and prostitution in *Ruth*

Since this novel's publication, critics have noticed that no sinner was ever more blameless and innocent than Gaskell's Ruth. Indeed, W. R. Greg felt that in order to justify her long repentance she ought to have been made more culpable. Some years after its publication, he discussed the novel in *The National Review* and criticised its 'false morality' in making Ruth so innocent yet so unforgiven. Assuming that Gaskell meant to show that one-time offenders should not be branded for life, and indeed are capable of regaining good standing after proper probation and repentance, Greg would like the novel to demonstrate that those who sin can be forgiven if they are duly penitent. If Mrs Gaskell, he writes, was 'anxious above all things to arouse a kinder feeling in the uncharitable and bitter world towards offenders of Ruth's sort', she should not have given in to the

> world's estimate in such matters, by assuming that the sin committed was of so deep a dye that only a life of atoning and enduring penitence could wipe it out. If she designed to awaken the world's compassion for the ordinary class of betrayed and deserted Magdalenes, the circumstances of Ruth's error should not have been made so inno-cent, nor should Ruth herself have been painted as so perfect. If she intended to describe a saint (as she has done), she should not have held conventional and mysterious language about her as a grievous sinner.[39]

We ought to recall, though, that 'offenders of Ruth's sort' conform exactly to Greg's own characterisation of fallen women in his 1850 review essay on prostitution, where he argued for the passionlessness of women in general and suggested that a fall from 'pure unknowingness' was indeed typical of fond and foolish female nature, framed to 'yield to desires' it did not share.[40] Even so, Greg's assumption that Gaskell's work is designed to canvas sympathy and awake compassion for the betrayed and deserted Magdalene warrants questioning. I want to suggest that the novel is interested rather in engaging the vexed question of female desire and how that question was currently being treated in medical and social scientific representations linking passionlessness and prostitution. The question is not whether Mrs Gaskell has 'given in' to the world's estimate, but how she holds it up to scrutiny.

My discussion of biomedical discourse in Chapter one drew attention to Victorian concerns about sexual ambiguity and slippage. The doctrine of essential female passionlessness is, in those terms, an attempt to fix and stabilise questions of female response, implying that sexual desire is not a natural propensity among women anywhere. Such a view denies the earlier theories of Laycock, Tilt and others who had argued for the power of desire to perturb ovarian function, and it repudiates earlier notions of the prostitute as physiologically aberrant.[41] What is at stake in representations of female passionlessness and what cultural politics do such representations support? Debates in the 1850s over the question of female desire and the difference between the prostitute and the respectable woman can be seen as preparatory for the battle about the Contagious Diseases legislation that developed in the following decades. If one could argue, as Greg did, that prostitutes are just like other women in that all women lack sexual desire, and argue further, as William Acton did, that prostitution is a transitory state through which multitudes of women pass, then how would one tell the morally and physically corrupt woman from others? At least if sexuality is dynamic and unstable, one can tell the effects of moral climate on the body – the prostitute's hoarse voice, for example, or the precocious puberty of licentious peoples. The point, for Acton, is that one cannot tell good women from bad, but one can register and inspect all those known to be prostitutes so as to check the spread of disease. In this way, a doctrine of essential passionlessness serves regulationism. Yet the idea of women as passionless was also to prove useful to the feminists of the 1870s who entered the political arena to challenge and question male power in the form of police, law-makers and medical men.[42] They adapted the representation of passionlessness for their political purposes, protesting the view of fallen women as pollutants of men, and depicting them instead as innocent 'victims of male pollution'.[43] Like those later feminist interventions against the Contagious Diseases Acts, Gaskell's novel lays the fault of sexual exploitation at the door of a polluting, male-ordained class morality. It represents female unknowingness as productive of enormous vulnerability and dependency and shows how the innocence so prized in women is in fact another name for dangerous ignorance. More tellingly, *Ruth* shows how secrets about illicit sexuality and sexual transgressions structure and sustain vulnerability and victimisation. But passionlessness is not a doctrine to which Elizabeth Gaskell fully subscribes. By making the effects of Ruth's secret on Jemima Bradshaw an important part of the novel, Gaskell challenges essentialist views about female passionlessness and considers how Jemima's sudden enlightenment about Ruth's sexual past becomes a means of social resistance.

As it turns on the closeting and subsequent revelation of a young mother's identity as a fallen woman, the narrative explores the way mid-Victorian social organisation depends on sexual secrets. The novel goes beyond merely sympathising with women who are punished for sexual ignorance; it expresses indignation at the shame and social stigma sexual transgressions attract and explores the secrecy they breed. By looking at the function that secrecy performs in the structure of the novel, we see also how the text explores the way illicit sexual identity functions to define and uphold middle-class claims to social superiority.

One of the ways to approach the categorisation of the fallen woman is to ask (as Eve Sedgwick asks of the homosexual closet) how it works, what enactments it performs and what relations it creates.[44] Without wishing to deny the specificity of the gay closet, I see some ways in which current analyses of closeting can apply to fictional representations of the fallen woman's attempts to avoid public exposure and humiliation. If we take the closet to be a metaphor for the construction of a framework that manages sexual taboos and controls the sexual activity of people in particular cultures, then its application to the mid-Victorian context is capable of generating some interesting questions. What is it that needs to be closeted? What culture- and class-specific norms make the closet necessary, and what could not be endured if the truth were told? How does the keeping and giving away of secrets affect social relationships? Is the fallen woman one whose desires run differently from the sanctioned norm, and in what ways does she threaten the continuity of a particular kind of sexual and reproductive social system? Questions such as these direct attention to why in *Ruth* so much narrative power is derived from the implications of secrecy, detection and disclosure.

As some nineteenth-century reviewers recognised, this is a novel like so many Victorian novels about secrets – how they are made, why they are kept, and how their keeping and giving away affects relationships in a far-reaching manner. In his review of *Ruth* in *The Leader*, George Henry Lewes seems to apprehend the novel's closeted truth, but then sidesteps the sexual questions which are at the heart of that truth. By insisting that this is a novel working out a moral problem rather than a 'social novel', he severs the two issues that are most cogently linked in the novel – the social meanings of sexuality and the veiling or closeting of truth. Lewes proposes that *Ruth* is really a novel about truth and truth seeming, about a lie that the widow poseur is one who is entitled to the respect and sympathy a pregnant widow would command. His insistence that the book is really concerned with the saving power of openness allows him to hold forth about 'Truth':

> *Very* rare are the cases wherein Truth … would not be the wisest and the directest course…. Had the Bensons confronted conventionalism, they would have awed and conquered it. Their own high characters would have been a coat of mail against which the sarcasms, the sneers, the comments, and the virtuous indignation of a small provincial town (and everyone knows what they are!) would have been powerless; while Ruth's real goodness and purity, so befriended, would soon have won for her universal sympathy and respect…. Tell the truth and act the truth, then all will be well. Truth is better than contrivance.[45]

The text is concerned not simply with how things go wrong when we don't tell the truth – it is not a moral fable – but why people resort to secrecy and how what we now call closets function in polarising and policing sexual identity. It is true that the dissenting minister must confront a moral dilemma in that he aids and abets the creation of the closet. But by suggesting that the minister's white lie and a general failure to tell the truth are the book's true concern, Lewes misses Gaskell's focus on the function of the closet in producing and regulating sexual and social identity.[46]

In *The Novel and the Police*, D. A. Miller astutely observes that secrecy can function as 'the subjective practice in which the oppositions of private/public, inside/outside, subject/object are established, and the sanctity of their first term kept inviolate. And the phenomenon of the "open secret" does not, as one might think, bring about the collapse of those binarisms and their ideological effects, but rather attests to their fantasmatic recovery.'[47] If telling the truth does not bring about the collapse of those oppositions which in the first place provoked secrecy, then assurances that all will be well if the truth is told are not likely to be convincing. G. H. Lewes seems naive in dismissing what Ruth fears as 'conventionalism', which ought to be conquered and awed.[48] But if transgressive behaviour is harshly judged and punished, then those without social power may find it necessary to live the lie rather than 'come out', only to occupy the second term in Miller's list of binaries. Secrecy and subterfuge are dispensable only when one occupies a position of relative power and independence in 'confronting conventionalism'.

What complicates Ruth's situation is not merely her own reputation, but the consequences to her child. Gaskell is careful to show that until the minister learns of Ruth's pregnancy, he does not think of creating a false identity for her. He is reminded by his sister of the dreadful case of Thomas Wilkins, who 'went to sea and was drowned' after the 'obnoxious word in the baptismal registry told him that he must go forth branded into the world'.[49] Keeping the obnoxious word from the registry is a matter of some importance in a social world that sets great store by legitimacy. The novel suggests that harsh sanctions breed a world of secrets and closeted identities. We glimpse this world when the respected surgeon, the recipient of many secrets, trades 'secret for secret' with Ruth and confesses his own illegitimate status (p. 441). Gaskell suggests that if the difference between the surgeon with a secret and the exposed Thomas Wilkins is the difference between life and death, then dissembling looks like a reasonable option, and it is clearly in that spirit that the minister's sister Faith tells Ruth that they will buy her a black gown and call her a widow.

Although the community in which she lives is prepared to accept the story of her tragic widowhood, she does not fool everyone. Sally, the Benson's old and outspoken servant, arrives in Ruth's room one evening, widow's cap and a pair of scissors in hand. As the daughter of a parish clerk, she is sensible of her own claims to respectability and means to protect that of her employers: 'Sit down and let me snip off your hair, and let me see you sham decently in a widow's cap tomorrow' (p. 145). The narrator draws attention to Ruth's hair, variously described as long, wavy, glossy, luxuriant, chestnut, and dishevelled. Sally is representative of traditional opinion in associating Ruth's luxuriant hair with a luxuriant sexuality, and she finds it offensive. Cropping her hair is a way to ensure that Ruth will never be able to 'let her hair down' again, a means of controlling the 'loose' woman. It reinforces the notion that to protect respectability – 'sham decently' – one needs to control sexuality. Informing her employers of the deed, Sally says that the 'bonny brown hair' was 'fitter for a bride in lawful matrimony than for such as her' (pp. 147–8).

The scene raises many folkloric and literary associations. Like the witch who cuts Rapunzel's hair in an archetypal story of sexual control, Sally shears the young woman's beautiful tresses as if to destroy her powers of attraction. But the tresses themselves are described as floating on the air, like the 'pendant branches of the weeping birch' (p. 144). References to 'floating', 'weeping', and 'pendant branches' associate the hair with Ophelia, who hung on 'pendant boughs' and fell into the 'weeping brook', floating a while, only to sink and drown. The cutting of the tresses, it is suggested, is like Ophelia's drowning – untimely, a casualty of innocence and beauty. Like Ophelia, Ruth seems also to be dissociated from and insensible to the meaning of the 'drowning'; she neither struggles nor mourns.

Anticipating that Ruth will not give up this symbol of her sexuality and her power to attract, Sally has entered Ruth's room with 'relentless purpose' and lays 'no light hand' on her shoulder; her pair of scissors is 'formidable' and she cuts 'in a merciless manner' (p. 145). 'I clipped her pretty roughly at first' she later says. Yet the text suggests that Ruth's locks are not 'raped': she willingly submits to Sally's will. It is as easy for Sally to cut Ruth's hair as it is for Bellingham to seduce her, because in neither case does she appear to be conscious of parting with anything of value. Sally is won over precisely because Ruth is unresisting and shows no vanity or knowledge of the value of what she is losing. 'Yon girl's secret is safe enough for me' she says (p. 148).[50] Yet perhaps because Ruth does not seem to care about her hair, Sally cannot explain to Ruth why she has wanted to cut it, so she merely declares that it is not 'wholesome' to have long hair. The 'chestnut tresses' are so lovely, however, that the old woman has not the heart to throw them away, but literally closets them in a 'safe corner of her drawer' (p. 146).

The violence and poignancy of the scene are disturbing, as Sally's desire to exercise rough discipline meets with such pliancy and powerlessness that it gives way to a sense of loss. The shorn locks become a token of Ruth's absent self-awareness; they are also now truly objects to be secretly admired, rather than a part of herself that Ruth can own, and their consignment to the safe drawer underlines the fact that the most deeply closeted secret in the novel is not Ruth's fall, but desire itself and any awareness of sexuality on her part.[51] Gaskell must present Ruth as innocent and unknowing, but if we trace the development of her relationship with Bellingham and her later refusal of his marriage proposal on the beach, we will see how the narrative attempts to have it both ways.

In the early chapters of *Ruth*, when Gaskell writes about Ruth's responses to Bellingham, her attraction to him is deliberately shown to be unconscious, but as the narrator is careful to point out, it is there. When they meet at a ball where Ruth is present with other apprentices to attend to the ladies' gowns, he gives her a camellia after she mends the hem of his dancing partner. The narrator admits that Ruth watches him with interest, 'yet she had no idea that any association made her camellia precious to her. She believed that it was solely on account of its exquisite beauty that she tended it so carefully. She told Jenny every particular of its presentation, with open, straight-looking eye, and without the deepening of a shade of colour' (pp. 17-18). That night she dreams joyfully that he presents flower after flower to her.

Whereas Ruth is initially dissociated from her desires and emotions, she is later more knowing, even though the narrative obscures the nature of that knowledge. During an important scene in which Bellingham/Donne confronts her on the beach and eventually offers marriage, he forces her to acknowledge that she was happy with him: 'Your heart will not allow you to prevaricate, and you know you were happy', he insists (p. 296). She blushes and admits it. Five times attention is drawn to the fact that she was happy with him. We may wonder why the narrative is so insistent about admitting past happiness, especially since, if we recall the descriptions of their time together in Wales, Ruth seemed anything but happy. Certainly after she hears a child repeat his parents' judgement of her as a bad woman, Ruth begins to sense the 'estimation in which she was henceforth to be held', grows pensive, wishes to conceal from Bellingham the nature of her sadness, and provokes his admonishment for her 'melancholy reveries' (p. 75). But even before this moment, she is always anxious not to vex Bellingham, who is irritated by her lack of power to amuse him. She finds solace only in the 'kind soothing balm which gentle mother Nature offers to us all in our seasons of depression' (p. 66).

Clearly, Gaskell has a difficult task satisfying various demands in the representation of Ruth's feelings for Bellingham: she must love him and admit that she was happy with him or the seduction and their subsequent time together would be more culpable yet. But she must also be dissociated from feelings of attraction and desire for him if she is to qualify for an innocent fall. While it would not do to show an initiated Ruth enjoying awakened sexuality in her sojourn in Wales, it will also not do, later in the novel, to deny that she was happy with him. Although she later accuses him of bad faith and refuses to marry him, she must struggle with memories of happiness and his lingering emotional power over her. After they part on the beach, therefore, she sinks to the ground, dizzy and overcome with feeling, then suddenly rouses herself with a 'quick desire to see him again', and cries sadly that she has spoken so angrily and bitterly to him (p. 304). Ruth's struggle with her feelings of attachment and her repudiation of Bellingham leave her in a 'taciturn languor'; for a few days she forgets about her son, who has, before Bellingham reappeared, been the repository of all her emotional investment. She is summoned back to 'vehement energy' by hearing that the boy is ill, clearly a speedy retribution for her responsiveness to the inadmissible passionate or sexual hold that Bellingham has over her, and her neglect of maternal feelings, fleeting though both have been.

Having put Ruth carefully into the closet as a pregnant widow, Gaskell's narrative strategy is then to take her out about half way through the novel and to have her live the secret in the 'open'. As Miller's analysis of the open secret suggests, the disclosure does not dismantle the categories that the secret was supposed to occlude; it merely declares them. The reactions, therefore, of those around Ruth to the divulgence of her identity as a woman unworthy of respect, a poseur, contaminant, and sexual deviant are the novel's central concern. Just as the gay closet 'is not a feature only of the lives of gay people', Ruth's uncloseted secret of sexual misbehaviour is shown to structure the lives of those around her.[52] The told secret becomes a catalyst of enormous importance: it allows Gaskell to explore how Leonard responds to his illegitimacy – an unconvincing and histrionic part of the novel; it forces others to confront the damaging effects of harsh categorisations and to weigh up the relative enormity of other crimes (the draconian Mr. Bradshaw has to own that his son's moral and fiscal delinquency is far greater than Ruth's sexual misdemeanours); it allows Gaskell to engage with contemporary discussions about moral pestilence and the contaminating effects on others of the fallen woman as potential prostitute; and most importantly, it provides an occasion for another young woman in the novel, Jemima Bradshaw, to contemplate the nature of her own unruly passions and desires.

When Gaskell expressed concern about the outrage with which some readers responded to the novel, she took heart from the fact that she had made people talk and think a little on 'a subject which is so painful that it requires all one's bravery not to *hide one's head like an ostrich* and try by doing so to forget that the evil exists' [my italics].[53] The metaphor of the ostrich and determined self-deception also serves Greg in the opening paragraph of his essay 'Prostitution':

> Statesmen see the mighty evil lying on the main pathway of the world, and, with a groan of pity and despair, 'pass by on the other side'. They act like the timid patient, who, fearing and feeling the existence of a terrible disease, dares not examine its symptoms or probe its depth, lest he should realise it too clearly, and possibly aggravate its intensity by the mere investigation. Or, *like a more foolish animal still, they hide their head* at the mention of the danger, as if they hoped, by ignoring, to annihilate it.[54] [my italics]

Like other concerned Victorians in the 1850s, Gaskell is determined not to be an ostrich about this social evil; she therefore addresses herself to many of the concerns swirling around the contested figure of the prostitute in the late 1840s and 1850s just as she responded to the discourse of working-class women in *Mary Barton*. But is the evil to which Gaskell refers the same thing as the social evil of prostitution? Nineteenth-century definitions of prostitution are so wide that the distinction between the fallen woman and the prostitute is in many formulations a nice one. Wardlaw's lectures, for example, define any voluntary surrendering of virtue as an act of prostitution, whether for money or not. But one act did not make the perpetrator a prostitute, Wardlaw argues, just as the first act of thievery does not make the person who commits it a thief. A 'character' cannot be formed by a solitary act, and 'prostitute' and 'thief' are 'designations of *character*'.[55] Wardlaw's distinction between one act and a vocation, as it were, a solitary deviation and habitual commission, leaves the status of the fallen woman ambiguous. Having committed an act of prostitution, she is not a prostitute, but she is also not what she was before she committed that act; she is neither quite on probation, nor redeemable. For Greg, to speak practically is to speak proleptically. Practically speaking, therefore, once fallen the woman is a prostitute, since her struggles to retrieve that 'first, false, fatal step' are usually vain. And indeed, for a powerful example of the inevitable downward career of the fallen or seduced woman, Greg turned to Gaskell's description of the apparently unredeemable Esther in *Mary Barton*.

The pathologising of the prostitute suggested a woman distinguished from the bourgeois norm by her unruly desires, and her barrenness, as one treatise on prostitution put it, 'a marking by nature of her own restrictions'.[56] If, as we have seen in *Mary Barton*, the associations of prostitution with working-class women served to reinforce class boundaries, what contributed to shift such representations, and why did a paradigm of passionlessness begin to serve political purposes through the 1850s and 1860s? Certainly, middle-class hygienics of the previous decades had some conception of acceptable pleasure for women.[57] So handbooks on marriage refer to the part played by sexual and emotional relations between husband and wife, and emphasise the healthiness of sexual desire in the service of marriage, conjugal love and family. Frigidity and reserve in either party will defeat procreation, Michael Ryan explains, and 'a want of love' is 'a certain cause of barrenness'.[58] It was thought therefore that rape hardly ever caused impregnation, and pregnancy was testimony to mutual enjoyment. The radical Richard Carlile observed that 'healthy human beings so far differ from the generality of other animals, that their desires and modes of living lead them to desire intercourse at all seasons; and where debility is not produced by excess, health is confirmed by the stimulating and pleasing excitement'.[59] By the 1840s, however, many biomedical texts were responding to Theodor von Bischoff's observation of spontaneous ovulation in mammals and extrapolating to human beings to find the processes of ovulation, menstruation and conception to be involuntary and periodic. Although medical authority was, as we saw in Chapter One, never unanimous about these questions, and popular opinion continued to hold to the enjoyment theory of conception, some biomedical literature both reflects and supports the erasure of female desire in social discourse.[60]

The most emphatic early statement of passionlessness in conjunction with prostitution is to be found in Greg's review essay, which departs from earlier pathologising constructions of the prostitute. In his scenario, the woman is blameless, powerless and passionless. She is in a worse position than an animal because even among cattle 'the sexes meet by common instinct and a common wish; – it is reserved for the human animal to treat the female as a mere victim for his lust'.[61] Greg's now well-known essay proposes that all women, prostitutes included, know no desire until they 'are exposed to exciting causes'.[62] In contrast to the early work of Michael Ryan, he argues that 'in men, in general, the sexual desire is inherent and spontaneous, and belongs to the condition of puberty. In the other sex, the desire is dormant, if not nonexistent, till excited; always till excited by undue familiarities; almost always till excited by actual intercourse.'[63] Commentators have erred, Greg insists, by confusing consequences and causes. Women fall because they desire only to please and because they are vulnerable when unprotected. 'Their affections are engaged, their confidence secured; thinking no evil themselves they permit caresses which in themselves, and to them, indicate no wrong, and are led on ignorantly and thoughtlessly from one familiarity to another, not conscious where those familiarities must inevitably end, till ultimate resistance becomes almost impossible.'[64] The vision of a world in which sexually driven women exercise their urges is, for Greg, a hellish apocalypse: 'If the passions of women were ready, strong, and spontaneous... even remotely approaching the form they assume in the coarser sex, there can be little doubt that sexual irregularities would reach a height, of which, at present, we have happily no conception.'[65] Greg's arguments, offering socially desirable behaviour as biological fact, turn on his notion of the essential nature of woman. Prescription masquerades as description in the hope that the former becomes the latter if one prescribes often and effectively. All women would be pure if placed in the right environment and protected from 'exciting causes', which indicates social control of the female environment as useful and fitting. The version of women as lacking desire is a reassuring one for Greg because it underwrites the protecting and monitoring of women in their separate and therefore safe, domestic sphere. The evil of prostitution exists not because some women are 'unnatural' – licentious, and depraved – but because they are victims of a system whose double standards are heinous. It remains therefore to clean up the public environment and to encourage men to abjure fornication and return to true gentlemanly and chivalric ideals. But since men are unlikely to achieve such self-control in the near future, the best option is to mitigate the evils of prostitution. Here Greg offers concrete measures as opposed to hortatory moral observations. He launches an argument for surveillance, registration, forcible inspection, and the establishment of asylums and hospitals to deal with syphilitic prostitutes, who are spreading the disease. The threat of syphilis and its control through control of the prostitute turns out to be his major concern already discernible in the opening paragraph in his analogy of the timid patient who fears 'disease' and fails to 'probe its depth'.[66]

Frank Mort has suggested that William Acton's work was innovative in the way it contrasted pure and impure women; previous representations of the pathology of prostitutes had not juxtaposed the 'unnatural' woman with an asexual norm, and by doing so Acton helped to 'generate an intellectual climate favourable to regulationism'.[67] Mort is right about Acton's support of regulationism, but Acton's argument does not, I think, depend on the difference of prostitutes from other women. It depends rather on their alarming similarity. Acton does not represent prostitutes as unnatural; indeed, he begins his treatise by dispelling the notion that prostitutes can be distinguished from other women by the nature of their aberrant desires: 'Everyone now, I believe, admits that uncontrollable sexual desires of her own play but a little part in inducing profligacy of the female.' Acknowledging that he is by no means the first to articulate a view about the essential passionlessness of the female, he begins by paying nearly rapturous tribute to Greg's 1850 review essay on prostitution: 'How beautifully is this [lack of sexual desire] alluded to in the following passage from the *Westminster Review*.'[68] Like Greg, Acton has to wrestle with contradictions in order to make his essentialising argument about passionlessness stick. Having asserted that the majority of women are not troubled by sexual feelings, he turns to a case involving a woman who, according to her husband, preferred masturbation to 'connexion', which she viewed with 'positive aversion'. Acton comments: 'So ruinous is the practice of solitary vice, both in the one and in the other sex, that it is carried on even in married life where no excuse can be devised, and is actually preferred to the natural excitement.'[69] This instance reveals the contradiction between the 'natural excitement' that women ought to prefer to self-abuse, and the 'natural repugnance' that women are generally supposed to feel about 'cohabitation' or 'connexion'. To deal with the contradiction, Acton admits that 'doubtless sexual feeling differs largely in different women. Although it is not my object to treat other than incidentally of the sexual economy in women, yet I may here say that the same causes which in early life induce abnormal sexual excitement in boys have similar effects in girls.'[70] Having taken pains to 'obtain and compare the opinions of large numbers of competent witnesses on this subject', Acton concludes that sexual excitement is abnormal in modest women.[71]

When Acton wrote his account of prostitution in 1857, he was evidently weary of definitions and distinctions between fallen women and habituated prostitutes. From his point of view, to insist on such distinctions was pointless because it was unlikely that one could tell a fallen woman from a prostitute, or any other woman, for that matter. Dispelling the notion that the prostitute is a detectable or recognisable deviation from the norm of womanhood, he wrote of prostitution as a 'transitory state, through which an untold number of British women are ever on their passage... multitudes are mothers before they become prostitutes, and other multitudes become mothers during their evil career'.[72] The whole point of Acton's chilling analysis of disease spreading undetected and unchecked is that prostitutes closet their pasts and mingle in society indistinguishable from other women; they enter and leave the ranks of respectable society without detection. Prostitutes are supposed to bear the signs of their evil lives, but, says Acton, 'if we compare the prostitute at thirty five with her sister, who perhaps is the married mother of a family, or has been a toiling slave for years in the over-heated laboratories of fashion, we shall seldom find that the constitutional ravages often thought to be necessary consequences of prostitution exceed those attributable to the cares of a family and the heart-wearing struggles of virtuous labour'.[73] Worse still, Acton observes, there is hardly a prostitute who has not had an opportunity of marriage 'above her original station'.[74] People are deluding themselves if they continue to hold to such vulgar errors as once a harlot, always a harlot; there can be no possible advance moral or physical in the condition of the actual prostitute; the harlot's progress is short and rapid. On the contrary, Acton's nightmare is a nation where disease spreads as women move unchecked and at will from sexual hire to marriage and motherhood. While Acton thoroughly agrees with Greg on the 'passionlessness' of most women, he accentuates the reversible career of the prostitute, offering a vision of society as one enormous closet of prostitutes, the only response to which can be damage control. Given the freedom with which prostitutes can move in and out of prostitution, those that can be identified should be registered and inspected.

In a climate where fears about detecting 'spoiled' women were mounting, Ruth's masquerade as a widow becomes highly charged. Although one would not call *Ruth* a governess novel, it is important that she has found employment as a governess to the Bradshaw girls, and holds that position when she is exposed. The fact that a 'spotted' woman is in contact with young charges makes her hidden past more culpable and her vilification greater. What seems to have bothered some reviewers was the fact that until Ruth's secret was out, no one in her community could have recognised her as fallen. An unsigned review in *Sharpe's* acknowledged that the blameless heroine should be accorded sympathy, but nevertheless found it unacceptable that she was allowed to act as governess to Mr Bradshaw's daughters – 'there is something revolting in such communion between the maiden girl and the spotted woman'.[75] What is especially revolting, it seems, is that the spots are invisible to the naked, social eye. A moral contaminant, Ruth suddenly conjures up fears by her mere presence of an invisible but deadly miasma of corruption.

The conditions under which Gaskell dramatises her exposure underscore the way in which the social circulation of the masquerading widow, secretly and sexually tainted, represents a threat of contamination and a fear that middle-class boundaries are alarmingly permeable. Gaskell's representation of Ruth, who falls apparently from 'pure unknowingness', obviously reflects topical representations of passionlessness; Ruth's gradual absorption into the community and eventual position as governess in a respectable family is the other side of that coin, playing into middle-class fears about inappropriate governesses, who instead of functioning as a 'bulwark against immorality and class erosion', might be the conduit through which sexual laxity could infect the home.[76] What is worse, although the governess was supposedly a 'tabooed woman', out of bounds to male servants, family members and acquaintances alike, Ruth is clearly attracting the attention of the supposed suitor of the eldest daughter of the Bradshaw family. Not only does she represent transgressive sexuality, she comes (unwittingly, as usual) to embody the threat of sexual competition. At this point, narrative attention shifts to Jemima, and the way in which the possession of Ruth's secret changes her perception of herself. While Gaskell's views coincide closely with Greg's and Acton's on the passionless fall, she develops a challenge to claims of female passionlessness through the headstrong and passionate Jemima. The first to possess Ruth's secret, Jemima spends some time before the secret is 'out' examining critically her own passionate nature and its social regulation. What does knowing mean? What does a condition of unknowing structure and protect?

Jemima Bradshaw is stunned and shocked when by merest chance she learns who Ruth really is. She feels her blood curdle as if 'she were a diver down in the depths of the sea' who has just encountered a 'ghastly lidless-eyed monster'. Gaskell repeats this metaphor of sin as a monster of the deep later when Ruth is confronted by Mr Bradshaw: 'The old offence could never be drowned in the Deep; but thus, when all was calm on the great, broad, sunny sea, it rose to the surface, and faced her with its unclosed eyes, and its ghastly countenance' (p. 337). Jemima has never imagined that she would come into contact with anyone who had committed sin, always counted on being guarded by all the respectable, family and religious circumstances of her life. By the 1860s the novel of sensation was developing and exploiting exactly the sort of reactions that Jemima here articulates. *Lady Audley's Secret*, for example, responded to (and, according to its critics, stimulated) desires to expose the respectable surfaces of genteel Victorian life in order to reveal underneath horrible 'lidless-eyed monsters' in the form of incestuous and bigamous relations, adulterous wives and mad mothers. Part of what was shocking and titillating in the sensation novels was that respectable surfaces were shown to be no guarantee against clanking skeletons in a myriad of sordid closets. Thus Lady Audley, beautiful to look at but not what she appeared to be, could be described as the lovely woman with the 'fishy extremities'. Indeed, the more rigidly respectable and genteel the surface, the more dark suppressed secrets one was likely to find. Who could trust appearances, especially the appearance of devoted and virtuous women? As Jemima asks herself, 'Who was to be trusted more if Ruth – calm, modest, delicate, dignified Ruth – had a memory blackened by sin?' But rather than exploiting the sensational, the text explores Jemima's condition of knowing as a powerful catalyst for examining her own ardent and passionate nature. Once told, Ruth's secret brings about 'the revelation of a powerful unknowing *as* unknowing, not as a vacuum or as the blank it can pretend to be'.[77] Thus Jemima moans aloud and upbraids circumstance 'for having deprived her of her unsuspicious happy ignorance' (p. 329). Believing Ruth to be a 'treacherous hypocrite, with a black secret shut up in her soul for years', living among the Bensons, she finds the very foundations of her mind are shaken. 'Who was true? Who was not?' (pp. 325–6). Jemima determines to keep the secret to herself and observe Ruth, who not unwarrantedly feels a cold sternness in her former friend's gaze.

Barely out of adolescence, Jemima is presented as struggling with the dictates of feminine obedience and tractability. She is described as turbulent, wild-hearted, wilful, uncurbed, perverse, vehement and impetuous. Although she loves Mr Farquar, we see her chafing against submission to feminine ideals, and wanting to be loved for her difference from rather than conformity to a desired pattern. From the repeated references to the 'depth of her love' her 'deep passionate regard' for Farquar and the 'full organ-peal of her love' (pp. 374, 375, 376), we see that she is as unhappily and searingly in touch with her feelings as Ruth has been dissociated from and oblivious to hers.

Jemima is angry with Ruth, suspecting that her friend has been enlisted by her father to make her pliant and pleasant to Farquar, whom he wants his daughter to marry. When she learns that her father wishes to reward Ruth for Jemima's civil behaviour one evening, she is enraged: 'Management everywhere! But in this case it was peculiarly revolting; so much so, that she could hardly bear to believe that the seemingly-transparent Ruth had lent herself to it' (p. 238). Her father's plans for her sicken her with their hypocrisy, since they seem to have meaning only in relation to patrimonial connections and authority. They override and distort her own wishes about what a relationship should mean. Like Mary Barton, who does indeed love the man her father wants her to marry, Jemima resents her father's disposition of her, and resents further having to submit to the public meanings that marriage symbolises:

> She would so fain have let herself love Mr. Farquar; but this constant manoeuvring, in which she did not feel clear that he did not take a passive part, made her sick at heart.… She felt as if she would rather be bought openly, like an Oriental daughter, where no one is degraded in their own eyes by being parties to such a contract (p. 240).

Initially she is a study of adolescent resistance, and then, as Mr Farquar begins to transfer his affections to the more submissive Ruth, she serves Gaskell's exploration of self-knowledge and sexual jealousy. Farquar grows weary of her rebellious and quarrelsome reception of him, and comes to feel that 'lovely, quiet Ruth, with her low tones and quiet replies, her delicate waving movements', is 'the very type of what a woman should be – a calm serene soul, fashioning the body to angelic grace' (p. 308). Jemima's apprehension of Farquar's growing interest in Ruth has a number of consequences. First it suggests, as Jemima's brother crudely puts it, that the governess is 'stealing a march' on her (p. 331). He even offers to buy his sister a nice bonnet to put her back in the race. Second, Jemima's hawk-like scrutiny of Ruth turns out to be the best testimony to Ruth's unimpeachable conduct. Both consequences draw the narrative into the young woman's developing knowledge about her own sexual and passionate feelings.

Jemima moves from her secret surveillance of Ruth, after she knows the secret of Ruth's past, to raise the question of what it would mean to identify with her as well as what it means to identify herself as against her.[78] Imagining Ruth as tempted and seduced, she admits that she might have been just like Ruth or even worse. 'It made me think of myself, and what I am. With a father and mother, and home and careful friends, I am not likely to be tempted like Ruth' (p. 365). But taking comfort in the protection that her strong family circle affords against transgression, she realises that she is still at risk, because she is more headstrong and passionate by nature than Ruth, and has 'yielded to every temptation that was able to come to me' (p. 365). Jemima passes, therefore, from horror at Ruth's secret and yet fascination with it, to judgement and rejection, and to identification and sympathy.

Awareness of Ruth's sexual past also helps Jemima to recognise her own 'passionate regard' for Farquar, and to distinguish between her resentment of authoritarian male management and her own vulnerable feelings, which masquerade as fierce, defensive pride. Such recognition enables her to soften her acerbic manner towards Farquar sufficiently to encourage him. After they have come to an understanding, Jemima, 'for some reason or fancy which she could not define', wants her engagement to remain a secret. Significantly, the person she longs to tell is Ruth, who has provoked her own knowledge of the turbulence and complexity of passionate and

UNSTABLE BODIES

vulnerable feelings. But despite Gaskell's emphasis on the way Ruth
functions as a catalyst in Jemima's self-knowledge and growth, the
representation of Jemima as rebellious, headstrong, and passionate,
but eventually happily tamed, is a problematic one. She seems too
handily colonised, as it were, and we find it difficult to believe that
she is not bothered when, after they have pledged themselves to each
other, Farquar clasps her more fondly as he thinks 'of the control
which he should have a right to exercise over her actions at some
future day' (p. 375). Gaskell also manipulates Jemima's feelings to
suit the plot: Jemima must love and admire Ruth, then turn away
from her in resentment and jealousy because of the attention Ruth is
attracting from Mr Farquar, and finally return to pity her and identify
with her. Yet it is through Jemima that Gaskell explores a version of
female passion, desire and yearning that contradicts the doctrines of
the essential passionlessness of women. What cannot be shown in
the case of Ruth, because it would heighten her culpability intoler-
ably, is explored in the case of Jemima, whose potential to fall
remains safely hypothetical. Although Jemima muses that if it were
not for the protection of her family, for the teaching and instilling of
prohibitions, passionate women like herself would be seriously in
danger, it is also clear that protection should not be confused with
ignorance of social realities or of one's own feelings. Mr Bradshaw's
rigid, tyrannical control over his children is shown to be far more
dangerous than their exposure to knowledge – in this case, knowledge of
Ruth's transgressive sexual past.

Since publication, the novel's ending has raised objections from
many readers, including Charlotte Brontë and Elizabeth Barrett
Browning, who didn't see why the *woman* had to die. The introduction
to a recent edition of the novel voices the same reaction: 'But even
the most generous criticism is bound to feel that the ultimate irony of
her death as a consequence of nursing her erstwhile seducer is ill
judged.'[79] But for one such as Gaskell, concerned with the responsibility
of seducers, the irony is not ill judged. Indeed, the ending is effective
as a way of refocusing the issue of male responsibility. While most
analyses of the problem of prostitution (Greg's, for example)
acknowledged that it is male desires and needs that create the
problem of prostitution, they did not dwell on how men ought to
share responsibility for the spread of disease. As if to point out that
blame belongs with those men who are the spoilers and the soilers,
Gaskell has her heroine contract typhus from her original seducer.

Ruth is quite able to nurse others to health and survive; the symbolic point is that she cannot survive her ex-lover's contagion. My argument depends of course on the association of the fallen woman with sources of contamination and disease: I see the plague that Bellingham spreads as a metaphor of sexual taint through which Gaskell engages with the public discourse of prostitution as a 'social evil' and anticipates the arguments of later feminists for the repeal of the Contagious Diseases Acts. Perverted men, feminists argued, spread syphilis and infected women, who were then subjected to registration, surveillance and the degradation of inspection. Through her metaphor Gaskell declares that it is the man – Bellingham/ Donne – who is the contagious, infecting presence that no woman's strength or immunity can withstand. While the text extols Ruth's selfless generosity, it also implicitly suggests that adherence to the self-sacrificial ideal of womanhood renders women susceptible to spoilers like Bellingham.[80]

Gaskell's exploration of the closeted identity of the fallen woman and her analysis of the structural relations it enables unsettled many of her readers. By examining at close quarters what it means to be respectable, what it means to have fallen, what the nature of female desire might be and how the conditions of knowing and ignorance shape and affect identity and self-knowledge, *Ruth* treads on new and threatening ground. Although the novel appears to be conservative – Ruth sins, Ruth repents, but Ruth dies anyway – it ventures critical and disturbing questions about mid-Victorian conceptions of female desire and sexual self-awareness. Through Ruth's well-kept, but subsequently divulged secret, Gaskell questions and challenges her culture's well-told tales about chastity, responsibility, sexual knowledge and ignorance.

Looking at Cleopatra: The expression and exhibition of desire in *Villette*

A central chapter in *Villette* focuses on Lucy Snowe's scrutiny of an ostentatious painting entitled *Cleopatra*, which depicts a voluptuous, semi-recumbent female figure. Charlotte Brontë supposedly based the painting she describes on a 'real' picture which she saw at the Brussels Salon in 1842, but this picture was not named *Cleopatra* at all and differs in significant ways from Brontë's fictional painting. Her 'recognition' of a rather ordinary Orientalist painting as a version of

Cleopatra illuminates how discourses of sexuality and race converge and overlap through longstanding western stereotypes of the Egyptian Queen and the burgeoning nineteenth-century fascination with the East and interest in Oriental exoticism. By loosening the knot of associations that the painting provokes, we can think about *Villette* in relation to mid-Victorian representations of female sexuality and their articulation in terms of race and class. Not only does the discourse of sexuality in *Villette* depend on the representation of an Eastern 'other', but also on stereotypical perceptions of prostitution, itself dependent on assumptions about physical characteristics (weight, shape, bodily functions, colour) and class.[81]

Throughout her narrative Lucy Snowe carefully scrutinises those around her, drawing attention not just to what she sees but also to the act of looking. References to gaze, glance, the exchange of looks, shafts of the eye, observations, and sight abound in her narrative, which dwells on moments of private, secret, or surreptitious scrutiny and their consequences. The narrative foregrounding of moments of looking encourages one to think about Lucy as spectator, in terms of recent critical discussions of the gaze.[82] At first sight, Lucy appears to disturb and perhaps invert the traditional positions of female 'to be looked-at-ness', and male looker.[83] When she stares at Dr John, recognising him as Graham Bretton, he immediately assumes that she has seen 'some defect' in him that attracts her usually averted eyes.[84] Later in the novel, Lucy curbs Paulina's admiration for Graham's beauty by casting him as the Medusa – a traditionally female role. She declares sarcastically that she avoids looking at him because the sight of him may strike her 'stone blind' (p. 520). Also, Lucy does not look at men as much as she looks at women, which seems further to unsettle traditional notions about the construction of the heterosexual subject. Although she watches Graham and Monsieur Paul closely, her observation of women – Madame Beck, Ginevra, the women in the audience at the concert, the subjects of paintings in the gallery, the actress playing Vashti – is closer still. Yet when we consider Lucy's position as one who looks, it is difficult to characterise her as simply subversive; she is not really the woman who refuses the position of object of the gaze thereby threatening the dominance of the male viewer. Since no one looks much at Lucy, or pays much attention to Lucy's looking, she can hardly be said to offer a disruptive, returning look 'from the place of the other'.[85] Her gaze does not usually unsettle those around her or allow her to appropriate control and power. Privately though, she does sometimes find bitter solace in her acute powers of observation. Moreover, when she refers to herself as a spectator, it is not to assert dominance, but to draw a contrast between herself as passive and the others, whom she sees as active players; she emphasises that she is merely someone who looks on as opposed to joining in. Hers is the gaze of the outsider.

It is precisely because Lucy's situation in the novel challenges without merely inverting the traditional binary formulation – female as the object of the gaze, male as dominating subject – that her spectatorship is important and interesting. Theoretical attention to the gaze is after all a way of articulating concerns with the formation of gendered subjectivity. In order to think about the process of gendering, we focus on the subject's pleasure in looking, the path of desire, the fantasies and conceptions of the self in relation to others, the perceptions of sexual difference. We are interested in the question of the gaze ('Who's zoomin' who?' as Aretha Franklin puts it) also because it directs attention to the power and politics of looking. Since *Villette* is so clearly a novel about desire, yearning, and invisibility, to consider Lucy in terms of the outsider's gaze is a way of engaging the novel's exploration of self-perception, desire and gendered subjectivity.[86]

Lucy is a keen observer of the dynamics of sexual attraction; she is shown, like Agnes Grey, looking to see what men see in other women and how women negotiate the problems of desire and its expression. She is also interested in the ways that they attract male attention and what male approbation affords as well as costs them. The fact that Lucy is often unseen, overlooked and unrecognised provokes both resentment and hurt. For, while she does not want to be appropriated as an object of visual pleasure (which is in the terms of current feminist discourse the effect of the male gaze) she also does not want to be invisible. Hence the narrative attention paid to Graham's failure to recognise her when he meets her ten years later, and the emphasis on looks and eyes in the scene where Lucy finds out that Monsieur Paul loves her. The effect, however, of her 'invisibility' is that she is excluded from the transactions of desire that patriarchy sanctions and as a consequence is extremely unsure whether she is desirable at all. We can think of the novel, then, as a chart of her difficulties in addressing the wish to be reflected as an admired and desirable self. The narrative explores the place of the desiring feminine subject and asks, 'What is the state between invisibility and making a "spectacle" of oneself?' Since the painting of Cleopatra does indeed make a spectacle of itself, Lucy spends some time describing and assessing it, its placement in the gallery, how the men around her respond to it and to her looking at it. She transgresses the boundaries of decorum by looking at this frankly sexualised female object; her position as a viewer of this painting is unorthodox, even illegitimate. Brontë draws attention to the fact that Lucy is the only unmarried woman in a group of largely male viewers who respond to the painting very differently from her, and as she coolly appraises the painting, Monsieur Paul chastises her for her 'temerity to gaze with sang-froid at pictures of Cleopatra' (p. 280).[87]

A painting called *Cleopatra* creates expectations that the subject is a representation of the historical queen, but the painting Lucy Snowe sees when she visits the art gallery in Villette depicts no particular anecdote associated with Cleopatra, nor includes any distinctive Cleopatra paraphernalia – asp, pearl dissolving in vinegar or wine, sumptuous barge, Antony or Caesar – though it does portray Cleopatra in a classic posture: lying on a couch in the midst of signs of excessive indulgence and feasting. Here is Lucy's deflating description:

> She lay half-reclined on a couch: why, it would be difficult to say; broad daylight blazed around her; she appeared in hearty health, strong enough to do the work of two plain cooks; she could not plead a weak spine; she ought to have been standing, or at least sitting bolt upright. She had no business to lounge away the noon on a sofa. She ought likewise to have worn decent garments; a gown covering her properly, which was not the case: out of abundance of material – seven-and-twenty yards, I should say, of drapery – she managed to make inefficient raiment. Then, for the wretched untidiness surrounding her, there could be no excuse. Pots and pans – perhaps I ought to say vases and goblets – were rolled here and there on the foreground; a perfect rubbish of flowers was mixed amongst them, and an absurd and disorderly mass of curtain upholstery smothered the couch and cumbered the floor (pp. 275–6).

As far as Cleopatra's well-documented orgiastic feasts are concerned, the description Lucy gives seems to correspond in essential details to standard 'classic' accounts of the feasts, such as that by Socrates of Rhodes: he too refers to the gold vessels (denigrated by Lucy as 'pots and pans'), the expensive roses ('a rubbish of flowers'), and the couch spreads (a disorderly, smothering 'mass of curtain upholstery').[88] The rubbish of flowers – Lucy later refers specifically to the roses, which she grudgingly concedes are nicely painted – brings to mind Cleopatra's extravagant floral budget: she is reputed to have spent large sums of money – 'a talent of silver' – on roses which were then strewn all over the floors like a carpet.

As a subject in Western pictorial art, Cleopatra has a long and varied history in which her representation takes as many different forms as the idea of woman she is used to represent – Guido Reni's Cleopatra looks very like his penitent Magdalena but very different from Artemesia Gentileschi's intense and passionate suicide or Tiepolo's regal Venetian princess.[89] With the rise of Orientalism in the nineteenth century, the figure of Cleopatra lends itself to representation as the acme of exotic Oriental sexuality, (a good example of such representation is Hans Makart's *Death of Cleopatra*, 1875).[90] Part of the developing nineteenth-century discourse of the Orient was the construction of the sexualised Eastern woman. As travellers and scholars began to map their knowledges of the East, they wrote in great numbers about the libidinous and lascivious character of the Egyptian woman. While there was a steady proliferation during the nineteenth century of scholarly texts, travels, and stories about the East, pictorial Orientalism also flourished in Europe, culminating in the establishment in Paris of the Salon des Peintres Orientalistes Francais in 1893. From *The Great Odalisque* of Ingres (1814) to the famous *Women of Algiers in Their Room* (1834) by Delacroix to Renoir's sultry *Odalisque* (1870), representations of Oriental women acquired a tradition and iconography in which a great many painters expressed their fantasies of harem life and Eastern sexuality.[91]

If we place Lucy's description of the lavish disorder surrounding her Cleopatra in the context of nineteenth-century versions of Oriental women, we see that it parodies not only Cleopatra's historic feasts, but also the way the harem and its inmates are represented in countless Orientalist paintings. Then again, both Cleopatra's sumptuous surroundings and the characteristically lush harem decor gesture toward an encompassing tradition in which the sensuality of a semi-recumbent female figure – she may be Venus, Cleopatra, or an anonymous odalisque – is suggested through contingent signs of luxury, excess and abandon. What Lucy challenges, therefore, in her withering account of the painting are the artistic traditions and contemporary fashions of representing the eroticised female subject.

The historic Cleopatra was, however, not the subject of the

Figure 1 Edward De Biefve, *Une Almé*

painting by Edouard De Biefve (1802–82) that Brontë saw at the
Brussels Salon in 1842.[92] De Biefve's canvas depicted an Egyptian
dancing girl lying semi-recumbent on a couch much as Lucy
describes the subject of the Cleopatra painting in *Villette*. De Biefve's
painting was entitled *Une Almé*.[93] Strictly speaking, *almeh* is the name
for a singer; dancing girls should be called *ghawazee*, as Edward Lane
refers to them. Edward Said notes that in Arabic *alemah* means a
learned woman. 'It was the name given to women in conservative
eighteenth-century Egyptian society who were accomplished
reciters of poetry. By the mid-nineteenth century the title was used as
a sort of guild name for dancers who were also prostitutes.'[94]

If we compare the lithograph of De Biefve's painting with *Villette's
Cleopatra*, (the painting itself I have been unable to trace) it appears
that Brontë magnifies and intensifies the figure's posture, dress, and
surroundings. Unlike Lucy's massive queen of the Nile, De Biefve's
subject looks rather contained – understated rather than underclothed.
Yet in 1842 the painting caused quite a stir both at its showing and in
press reviews, scandalising the Brussels viewers who considered it
flagrantly and ostentatiously sexual. A contemporary review suggested
that the painting was misnamed: rather than a dancing girl, the
reviewer reflected, this woman looked more like a voluptuous
odalisque – a better title would have been *A Slave of the Harem*.[95] The

remark is interesting because it suggests that the reviewer is drawing a distinction between the dancing girl and the odalisque, unaware that it was even then already blurred. Although some viewers of De Biefve's painting at the Brussels Salon in 1842 may have been puzzled that a dancing girl should be represented lying on a couch rather than dancing, worldly Orientalists at the time knew that *almeh* was practically a synonym for prostitute. In the iconography of the sexual woman in nineteenth-century Europe the almeh and odalisque are both Cleopatras in the sense that Lucy Snowe uses the name. Another writer reviewing the exhibition remarks that the head of De Biefve's figure 'has a somewhat vulgar character, the face of a woman of low degree'.[96] We may see implicit in this comment the sense that the subject's profession is that of a prostitute / dancer since nineteenth-century comparative anatomists invoked the shape of the prostitute's head and bone structure as signs of a pathological and atavistic sexuality. Perhaps too her unlowered eyes and unaverted gaze (like the look of the recumbent model / prostitute in Manet's *Olympia*) make the subject seem provocative and therefore vulgar and low. Just as it is difficult today to see what outraged viewers of *Olympia* in 1865 and how that painting transgressed and subverted traditional representational codes, so the scandalised reaction of the Brussels viewers is puzzling. As Gustave Charlier points out, *Une Almé* seems a rather mundane and restrained Orientalist representation, but in the Brussels of 1842 it struck some commentators as hypersexualised and sensational, drawing both salacious appreciation – one reviewer is enthusiastic about 'the devilishly' seductive 'almé' – and censorious opprobrium. Male viewers in *Villette* respond in similar ways to the *Cleopatra*.

Brontë explains and intensifies the actual painting by casting *her* odalisque as a Cleopatra, returning to earlier associations of exotic sexuality with the East – following the serpent of the Nile, as it were, to its source. And after all, one does not need to make a great leap in association to get from De Biefve's dancing girl who is not dancing but rather lying invitingly on a couch to well-known representations of Cleopatra, supine on a sumptuous couch, contriving to ensnare Antony and lose him half the world. To substitute the anonymous, recumbent odalisque for the very queen of recliners is a perfectly logical exchange in the realm of stereotypic female sexuality. Furthermore, by emphasising the iconographic markers of the Eastern *femme fatale* Brontë makes very clear that her subject epitomises a tradition of representation that embraces the legendary Cleopatra, the semi-nude pose of the subject, the lush harem interior, and the odalisque.

One can see from the ways that Brontë cites Cleopatra elsewhere that her particular references to Cleopatra here are deliberate and considered. In the Juvenilia, she refers to Cleopatra on a number of occasions, citing the Egyptian queen in company with other famous women, such as Helen of Troy and Madame de Staël; she even refers to 'the majesty of Cleopatra'[97] and compares the temptress Zenobia to Cleopatra in the following way:

> What eyes! what raven hair!... She is perfectly grand in her velvet robes and dark plume, and crown-like turban... the prima donna of the Angrian court, the most learned woman of her age, the modern Cleopatria [sic].[98]

The fact that Brontë can conceive of Cleopatra as a majestic and learned *femme fatale* emphasises, I think, that she did not generally associate her with large, coarse women. When Brontë labels the subject of her painting she is not thinking of Cleopatra as the intelligent, powerful, and ruthless Queen of Egypt, but rather of a dark, indolent, gipsy-queen, an association which makes Cleopatra, Queen of Egypt, synonymous with nineteenth-century stereotypes of Egyptian women – latter-day Cleopatras. What she chooses to blow up, as it were, in her fictional painting is the notion of Cleopatra 'i' the posture of a whore'.[99]

Consideration of the textual and visual sources of Lucy's description in accounts of Cleopatra and their relationship to the iconography of Orientalist art releases the full extent of the humour and parodic play by which Lucy deflates the diction and rhetoric of awe and splendour with her domestic, down-to-earth observations. Her pleasure in tartly puncturing high-flown descriptions is a manifestation of her desire to diminish the overblown Cleopatra type, for whom the catalogue of abundance, luxury, and laziness is a metonymy; glut is here inevitably associated with slut. Possibly, the undisciplined Cleopatra inspires envy and hence resentment in the hardworking Lucy, for whom life is no holiday. In an early chapter, Lucy teases the reader with a vision of the life she has *not* been living: 'Picture me then idle, basking, plump, and happy, stretched on a cushioned deck, warmed with constant sunshine, rocked by breezes indolently soft' (p. 94). The vocabulary of desirable ease and pampering – 'idle', 'plump', 'basking', and 'indolent' – is reminiscent of the language describing the 'Cleopatra' but in such a grossly exaggerated way as to make indolence and relaxation a sin. Lucy's response, however, is more than Protestant disapproval of any form of laxity. It is true that in order to register the chagrin of hardworking Lucy, Brontë draws attention to the laziness of the Cleopatra figure (who should have been doing the work of 'two plain cooks'), but the stress on sloth is also an indirect way of signifying that the 'Cleopatra' is like a prostitute. Rather than commenting directly on the sexualised quality of the figure, Lucy emphasises the sluggishness of her Cleopatra and the slovenliness of her surroundings. She is hardly pulling her weight (some fourteen to sixteen stone, Lucy estimates), lounging around unsuitably clad in broad daylight, amid clutter and disorder. Victorian studies of prostitution point repeatedly to grossness, stoutness, and excessive weight as characteristic of profligate women. A. J. B. Parent-Duchatelet, also referred to as the 'Newton of Harlotry', published *De la prostitution dans la ville de Paris* in 1836. This work, which was for a time the most widely read and influential study of prostitution, informed readers that prostitutes have a 'peculiar plumpness' on account of 'the great number of hot baths' they take. Their lassitude – they rise at ten or eleven in the morning and lead 'an animal life' – also helps to explain their plumpness.[100] Beliefs about the inclination of prostitutes to plumpness and lassitude are barely distinguishable from accounts and common conceptions of women in a harem. So persistent and common were assumptions about the luxurious sensuality and idleness of harem inhabitants, that some travellers and scholars were concerned to dispel the stereotypes:

> They do not, as the common descriptions of harem life lead us to believe, recline the live-long day on a soft divan enjoying *dolce far niente*, adorned with gold and jewels, smoking, and supporting upon the yielding pillow those arms that indolence makes so plump.[101]

When Harriet Martineau wrote about the harems she visited in the East, she described them as little better than brothels, implying also that excessive emphasis on sexuality – 'that which, with all our interests and engagements, we consider too prominent with us' – rendered Eastern women 'dull, soulless, brutish or peevish'.[102] Later when Martineau wrote an anonymous review of *Villette*, anticipating the responses of some twentieth-century feminist readers, she criticised it for its abiding concern with 'love' and a heroine who could only see life in terms of it. 'There are substantial, heartfelt interests for women of all ages, and under ordinary circumstances, quite apart from love: there is an absence of introspection, an unconsciousness, a repose in women's lives... of which we find no admission in this book.'[103] In her obituary of Charlotte Brontë, she remarked that 'passion occupies too prominent a place in her pictures of life' and regretted the 'morbid passion' of Brontë's heroines and their tendency to love too vehemently.[104] In *Eastern Life: Present and Past* she had written in a similar vein that it was dreadful to see the inmates of a harem in the grip of 'that one interest', expressing her concerns about women's work, scope and mental powers. In *Villette*, however, Brontë uses Oriental images to probe questions of desire, sexuality and representation. Although the two Englishwomen share assumptions about Eastern women as sexually excessive, sluggish, and indulged, Brontë uses her image in *Villette* of a woman 'half-reclined on a couch' to interrogate Victorian constructions of desire and to articulate a passionate if problematic subjectivity. Martineau, however, regards all interest in sexuality, passion and desire as inimical to female dignity.

Charlotte Brontë 'visited' the Orient only in her readings of *The Arabian Nights*, but like the women who actually travelled there she also associates the harem with tons of female flesh and registers an abhorrence of indolence and sexual availability. In *Jane Eyre*, shortly before Jane and Rochester are to be married, Rochester exclaims that he would not exchange 'this one little English girl for the Grand Turk's whole seraglio – gazelle eyes, houri forms and all!' Brontë writes: 'The Eastern allusion bit me again.' What is it that has bitten Jane Eyre except the implicit relegation of herself to the condition of a sexual slave? When she urges Rochester to go and buy whatever he fancies in the line of slaves, she describes him as having smiled on her as a sultan smiles on a favoured slave. He asks her what she will do while he bargains for 'so many tons of flesh'; Jane replies that she is going to liberate the enslaved, his harem inmates included.[105] She opposes the power Rochester has as 'a sultan' by seeking independence; it is after all her fear of being a 'kept' woman that urges her to write to her uncle in Madeira. With his wife locked secretly away, Rochester attempts to practise polygamy and become a kind of 'bashaw' or pasha, though a pasha would from all accounts have been able to rid himself of a troublesome wife (if he actually needed to) more easily than Rochester can. The insurrection in the harem imagined by Jane anticipates also the rebellion Bertha stages the night before Rochester's abortive wedding to Jane. In their sparring, Rochester and Jane evoke a context of male fantasies of the harem with its titillating availability of passive female flesh as well as the views of Victorian women travellers about the passivity, sloth and lassitude of harem women. Reflecting common cultural assumptions, Brontë's fiction represents female sexuality either as a passive, degenerate slump or as evil and overpowering; Bertha (large, dark, exotic, intemperate, with 'giant propensities') is the extreme to which *Villette*'s Cleopatra later points.[106]

In *Villette* the image of the pasha is evoked, significantly, in relation to Graham just when he 'abandons' Lucy for Paulina Home. Having waited seven weeks with no word from him, Lucy finally receives a letter from his mother in which she describes an occasion when Graham fell asleep and she 'invests his brows' with the 'grand adornment' of a sky-blue turban that he won as a prize at a concert: '[H]e looked quite Eastern, except that he is so fair.... [T]here was as fine a young bey, dey, or pacha improvised as you would wish to see' (p. 355). The characterisation of Graham as pasha recalls the images used as early as the third chapter, when the child Paulina is described as a 'little Odalisque, on a couch' (p. 87) and Graham, once he has won her affection, as 'the Grand Turk' who cannot be 'sufficiently well waited on' (p. 82).[107] Paulina could not be more unlike the sexualised women that Lucy later associates with the Cleopatra figure, but remember that Paulina's mother was a Ginevra, given to self-indulgent excess and pleasure just like her namesake, Paulina's cousin Ginevra. Home (which happens to be Paulina's last name) may be where the harem is, if one is in willing service to the pasha's self-absorption. This alternative scenario – being a slave to someone else's appetites – does not strike Lucy as better than being a slave to one's own.

If we return to Victorian assumptions about the sexualised woman as deviant and pathological, we see that they are underscored by the way that the prostitute became synonymous with disease.[108] Although in the 1850s representations of the prostitute increasingly focused on her similarity to other women, the sense persisted of the prostitute as physically and morally different from 'normal' women because of the association of prostitution with disease and contagion. In Lucy's response to the painting of Cleopatra, the discourse of prostitution is also evoked by the connotations of particular terms that Lucy uses in evaluating the picture as an 'enormous piece of claptrap' (p. 276). Claptrap, of course, means insincere or empty language, but it is also an artifice or ploy for winning audience approval. This piece of claptrap ensnares applause; it is an empty artifice seducing its viewers as Cleopatra is supposed to have seduced and ensnared hers. *Clapier* in French meant a brothel: what is trapped there is the clap, the connotations of which play into the stereotypic associations of the sexualised female with the prostitute, disease, and deviance.

Cleopatra is associated not only with a discourse of prostitution and sexuality, but also with the discourse of race. Brontë describes her Cleopatra figure as 'dark', 'dusky', 'mulatto', 'gipsy', as she draws on associations of Eastern and African women with excessive sexuality. While the foppish Colonel de Hamal is 'exceedingly taken' with the 'dusk and portly Venus of the Nile', Graham Bretton denies her charms, declaring that his mother is better looking, and that this 'mulatto' cannot compare with his Ginevra. The nice irony here is that the dark-complexioned Cleopatra that Graham slights and the pink and flaxen Ginevra are fundamentally similar: Ginevra too is material, self-indulgent, voluptuous, and driven by appetite – she often eats the 'lion's share' of Lucy's bread, cream and wine (p. 313). Most important, Ginevra elopes with Colonel de Hamal, who appreciates in her what he admired about Cleopatra – 'le type du voluptueux' (p. 282).

Since hypersexuality and race were strongly associated, the descriptions of Cleopatra as dark are significant. Sander Gilman has suggested that during the nineteenth century, the perception of the prostitute 'merged with that of the black', linking female sexuality to stereotypes of the primitive – the dark, savage 'lower' order of things.[109] While not exactly bestial, the Cleopatra figure is referred to as 'The Lioness'. In the context of nineteenth-century sexual stereotypes, her characteristics associate her with degeneration and a brutish life. Assumptions that blacks, seen as lacking in control, represented a primitive stage of civilisation merged with assumptions about dark women as threatening chaos in their unbridled sexuality. For the 'civilized orders', a loss of control would be marked by regression into such a dark past, a degeneration into primitive emotional and sexual license leading to madness. Indeed, *Villette* holds these two states – madness and sexual licentiousness – in a dangerous Scylla and Charybdis position, and it is interesting to note that not long before Lucy confronts the painting of the lascivious Cleopatra, she has suffered a 'breakdown' – madness – caused by being left at the school for the summer with only 'the cretin' to take care of (pp. 225–36). She is recovering at the home of the Brettons and enjoying the luxury of Dr Graham's attention and company.[110] Two versions of extreme derangement – madness and primitive sexuality – are thus counterpointed and associated. The fact that Lucy has been taking care of a cretin is also of relevance, given the way Victorian medical texts represent cretinism as an instance of immature and undeveloped sexuality.[111] Lucy's breakdown, occasioned by alienation and loneliness, is associated with the spectre of stunted sexuality, as her confrontation with Cleopatra later is associated with exaggerated and overblown sexuality.

It is important to note how Lucy interacts with the painting: more anxious than Agnes Grey about the 'animal' aspect of desire, she projects her own anxieties about laxity and displaces her own struggle for sexual identity onto it. Associated with the brutish and degenerate, the subject of the painting represents the claim of the primitive and the lack of control that Lucy fears in herself. License to recognise or own desire, especially libidinal desire, she immediately associates with licentiousness; relaxation becomes laxity. As Lucy indulges herself slightly at the gallery, her small shifts in the direction of permission are writ large in the distortion and magnification of the painting's subject. Just before stopping in front of the Cleopatra canvas, Lucy walks through the gallery glancing at the painting and discussing the familiar struggle within herself: part of herself demands that she admire what it is appropriate to admire, but part struggles against received canons of taste and withholds approbation. The division she experiences as she forms a judgement is fatiguing. After struggling for some time in this way, Lucy decides to let herself off the hook and simply to enjoy herself. The result is that she '[sinks] supine into a luxury of calm before ninety nine out of a hundred of the exhibited frames'. Her supine sinking anticipates the posture of the Cleopatra – 'She could not plead a weak spine; she ought to have been... sitting bolt upright' (p. 275). Does the portrait suddenly upbraid her for her own ease, slight as it is? Her lapse of vigilance must be punished, but since it is subconscious, it is projected onto the painting, which is then mocked and repudiated. The moment she relaxes, a backlash of punitive retribution follows. Should Lucy continue to give herself over to the luxury of self-indulgence, she would surely see herself exaggerated and distended in the gross and overblown way that she sees in the Cleopatra.

The subject of the painting is later described as a 'slug', a pulpy mass, which is, among other things, an image of massive regression. Asserting herself against the sight of the supine spineless slug Lucy does more than straighten up; she mounts a scathing attack on the part of herself that is expressed in the canvas. From this transaction, we can begin to summarise the characteristic displacement of her emotions in the narrative. Her fierce sense of secrecy and privacy about her feelings is born from her feeling that her own desires and yearning are unlikely to be reciprocated. Hence she counsels stoicism, anticipates neglect, and keeps her desires well under control. She likens herself to Jael, driving nails into the temples of her Sisera – desire. She also concludes that if her soft, tender feelings were to command attention they would have to be exhibited, paraded brazenly, which she refuses to do. The desiring self must therefore be hidden and stifled for two reasons: there is no one to recognise, summon, and cherish it, and secondly if desire asserts itself it will suffer disappointment. [112] Lucy's proleptic identification with Madame Beck, whom she sees as fighting desire and greeting the grisly hag of disappointment, confirms her expectation of disappointment. And if not disappointed, the desiring self will be spoiled, grow greedy and monstrous like Cleopatra, or conflagrate in demonic self-assertion like Vashti, in the theatrical performance Lucy watches later.

It is not only the subject of the painting that is gross and overbearing, but as far as Lucy is concerned the very painting itself – the whole 'preposterous' production which 'queens it' over all the others in the gallery. By what authority, Lucy asks, does such a representation command respect and attention? Not only is this canvas exhibited; it is itself exhibitionistic. By means of figurative transformation, the whole painting – that 'notable production' – is its subject. It is a production of 'pretentious size, set up in the best light, having a cordon of protection stretched before it, and a cushioned bench duly set in front for the accommodation of worshipping connoisseurs, who, having gazed themselves off their feet, might be fain to complete the business sitting' (p. 275). Indeed, Lucy sounds here much like John Berger in recognising how the evaluation of a 'work of art' is highly dependent on the logistics of its exhibition. The way the subject has been executed and framed solicits a certain viewing of her; it is Lucy's perverse pleasure therefore to take a dim view of such solicitation. But there is perhaps more to it than simply Lucy's objection to the painting's shameful call for male attention. If the definition of prostitution as a 'setting forth or placing in a public place' can be applied to the painting, it is clear from the response of those around Lucy that there are many clients available for seduction.[113] The idea of a public setting forth applies, of course, to Lucy's narrative, which is characterised by lies, evasions, and secrets never shared with the reader. Whereas Brontë could be accused of resorting to images of shipwreck when Lucy does not want to be specific about disappointment and pain, and whereas Lucy is infuriatingly withholding, reticent, and inscrutable at times, the narrative seems to ask the reader to work at knowing Lucy and meeting her, as it were, halfway. Brontë ensures that Lucy's narrative is no brazen publication. As readers we are hardly exempt from the consequences of the following point of view: 'There is a perverse mood of the mind which is rather soothed than irritated by misconstruction; and in quarters where we can never be rightly known, we take pleasure, I think, in being consummately ignored' (p. 164). Just as Lucy prefers to be ignored than to advertise or exhibit herself, so she maintains a private purity in the face of imagined misperception.

Cleopatra surfaces again later in the novel, in the context of another spectacle – the dramatic portrayal of Vashti. On this occasion Lucy compares her responses to the representations of Cleopatra and Vashti and delivers an impassioned diatribe against Rubens, whom she holds responsible for privileging women who look like the subject of the Cleopatra painting – large, buxom, 'Rubensesque' women. Paul Peter Rubens is not known for any depictions of Cleopatra, but at this point in the text 'Cleopatra' is functioning as a generic label for all fleshy, painterly subjects.

> Place now the Cleopatra, or any other slug, before her as an obstacle and see her cut through the pulpy mass as the scimitar of Saladin clove the down cushion. Let Paul Peter Rubens wake from the dead, let him rise from his cerements, and bring into this presence all the army of his fat women; the magian power or prophet-virtue gifting that slight rod of Moses, could, at one waft, release and re-mingle a sea spell-parted, whelming the heavy host with the down-rush of overthrown sea-ramparts (p. 340).

The paragraph is extraordinarily rich in conflating many aspects of the novel's concern with female sexuality and its artistic representation. I begin with the associations that Vashti, Saladin, Cleopatra, Moses, and Rubens raise here. Vashti offers a challenge to Rubens, who becomes a sign for the kind of painter who produced the *Cleopatra*. Although he is no Orientalist, he paints female subjects who remind Lucy of the women she labels as Cleopatras. Her implicit quarrel with such painters is that they have the power to represent women and to influence perceptions of beauty and desirability. The apostrophe to Rubens, whose women subjects are generally ample and fleshy, brings to mind paintings such as *The Judgement of Paris*, in which the naked women parade and compete for the prize. Beauty is rewarded; those not judged beautiful, as John Berger points out in *Ways of Seeing*, are not beautiful.[114] As an object of beauty the woman may be encouraged to enjoy her power over men and indeed to enjoy herself as a sight, though she may also be condemned as vain or narcissistic. The ramifications in Lucy's case are particularly interesting. Since she is judged not beautiful, Lucy is not encouraged to look upon herself as a sight that produces pleasure; in fact she is not encouraged to see herself at all. It is significant that her way of asking Monsieur Paul to declare that he loves and desires her is, 'Do I displease your eyes *much*?' (p. 583). Her stab at Rubens' fat ladies comes from one who has been so thinned as to vanish. In contrast to Cleopatra, half-reclined on a couch in the posture of the nineteenth-century whore, Lucy is secret, often self-effacing, denying her materiality and doubting at times her own substantiality.

In an amazing transference of association, the 'heavy host' refers not so much to the Egyptian enemies of Moses but to the stout gang of Cleopatras who have been the subjects (hosts) of many a painter like Rubens. Further, the contraction that converts 'heavenly' to 'heavy' is instructive. These are the divine creatures, graceful angels that men like Graham worship and adore, transformed by Lucy's critical eye into overweight slugs. Since she is slight, small, and thin, and since she associates large fleshy women with gross sexual parade, she fantasises with relish the slicing, paring, and cutting down to size. In a face-off between Rubens' flabby Cleopatras and Vashti, armed with Saladin's scimitar or the rod of Moses, Lucy envisions a triumphant trouncing. Her reference to Scott's *The Talisman* and the scimitar of Saladin that clove the down cushion underpins one fantasy of demolition; the rod of Moses another. The analogy of Moses and the Egyptians sustains the Eastern flavour of all the allusions and analogies Lucy makes here and elsewhere, but it has another significant function. Since Lucy is fantasising the dismissal of the artistic interpretations she despises and contrasting them with those she admires, Brontë invokes an Orientalist she respects – John Martin, whose *Destruction of Pharaoh's Host* she may very well have in mind here. Martin is an Orientalist painter in that many of his themes are Eastern and biblical, but instead of Cleopatra, his composition focuses on the rod of Moses and the power it derives from the dynamic sea and sky, which direct attention toward it. If we imagine Lucy thinking of this painting, we see that it is of course Lucy herself who occupies the powerful position of Moses here and would like to liquidate her imaginary army of fat women with the wave of her wand. Something needs to slice through all this blubber and cut both subjects and inflated painters down to size. The power that Lucy envisions in relation to this painting is a phallic power – Saladin's sword, Moses' wand. This perception raises interesting problems in the coding of power and fantasies of action as male.[115] Yet Lucy does not want to play the man, as her insistence on retaining female garb in the school dramatic production reveals. She articulates here the difficulty of envisaging a representation of female desire and sexuality that is not tantamount to looseness and 'giant propensities'. Further, the representation of Vashti's passionate self-expression suggests that the assumption of power by a woman is overwhelming, uncontainable. A female Moses might not be able to control the flood she summoned; in the same spirit the actress playing Vashti on this occasion seems actually to set the theatre alight.

It is significant that the impassioned gauntlet thrown down to Rubens and his army of fat women is made in the context of the biblical Vashti – one woman of the East who refused to be exhibited as the object of the male gaze. She contrasts interestingly with Cleopatra, whose exhibitionism and feasting and seductive manipulation of men define her. Lavish feasts, like those for which Cleopatra was famous, are described in the Book of Esther, which begins with Vashti's story: 'the beds were of gold and silver upon a pavement of red, and blue, and white, and black, marble. And they gave them drink in vessels of gold... and royal wine in abundance, according to the state of the king.'[116] Had she not shown some backbone, Vashti might have found herself in the supine position of Cleopatra. Commanded to appear so that all the distinguished guests could look upon her beauty – 'for she was fair to look on' – she refused to obey. She dies fighting, breathing mutiny and resisting the 'rape of every faculty' because she '*would* see, *would* hear' (p. 342).[117] If Cleopatra represents the regressive slump of dark, unbridled sexuality, and

Vashti the crimson flame of uncontainable and self-destructive passion, Lucy Snowe attempts to negotiate her path between these extremes. The alternatives seem unclear, however, for the woman who does not want to exhibit herself as a spectacle for male consumption, but who also realises the destructiveness of demonic and self-consuming anger.

What price visibility? Lucy Snowe's answer takes the form of a questioning of dominant discourses of desire in relation to the sexual woman and an assertion that passion and desire may exist in the woman who is not marked like the prostitute, just as passion and desire may be kindled for the woman who is not conventionally the object of the male gaze. Indeed, the ambiguous and troubling closure of the novel bears testimony to the difficult social negotiation of these differences. Lucy loves Monsieur Paul and is seen, recognised and rewarded by him, however problematic his despotic demeanour may be for modern readers. Lucy survives his loss, has economic independence, and is no man's slave. But Brontë does not allow her to keep in sight that which reflects her desiring, sexual self, and she becomes understandably associated with frost and cold. From what Brontë shows us in this novel, it is difficult to disturb entrenched patterns of gendered looking and what they imply about the expression of desire. Her closure will not preserve or seal, therefore, that dissenting scenario in which the outsider becomes a player in the exchange of mutually desiring gazes.

Notes

1. E. Blackwell, *The Laws of Life, with Special Reference to the Physical Education of Girls* (London, Sampson Low, 1859), p. 159.
2. G. Moore, *Conversations in Ebury Street* (London, 1924), p. 221.
3. 'Biographical notice of Ellis and Acton Bell', in T. Scott (ed.), *Agnes Grey: With a Memoir of her Sisters by Charlotte Brontë* (Edinburgh, John Grant, 1905), pp. 8–12.
4. See Charlotte's letter to W. S. Williams, 31 July 1848.
5. Emile Montegut, from an article in the *Revue des deux mondes* (1 July 1857); see M. Allott (ed.), *The Brontës: The Critical Heritage* (London, Routledge, 1974), p. 376.
6. I. Stina-Ewbank, *Their Proper Sphere: A Study of the Brontë Sisters as Early-Victorian Female Novelists* (London, Edward Arnold, 1966), p. 55.
7. See E. Langland, *Anne Brontë: The Other One* (London, Macmillan, 1989), pp. 96–117, who emphasises the way Agnes's story begins with the desire for self assertion and activity – the classic pattern of the male *Bildungsroman*.

8. Moore, *Conversations*, p. 221.

9. On this point, see also N. Armstrong, *Desire and Domestic Fiction: A Political History of the Novel* (Oxford, Oxford University Press, 1987), p. 79.

10. See M. Poovey, *Uneven Developments: The Ideological Work of Gender in Mid-Victorian England* (Chicago, University of Chicago Press, 1988), p. 128; Poovey's chapter on the changing aspects of the governess debate is the best treatment of mid-Victorian periodical literature on this subject.

11. A. Brontë, *Agnes Grey*, ed. R. Inglesfield and H. Marsden (Oxford, World's Classics, [1847] 1988), p. 1; all subsequent references are to this edition and will be incorporated in the text.

12. 'Hints on the modern governess system', *Fraser's Magazine*, 30 (November 1844), pp. 574–6.

13. H. Michie, *The Flesh Made Word: Female Figures and Women's Bodies* (Oxford, Oxford University Press, 1987), p. 23, notes that *Agnes Grey* subverts the usual motif of the male employer providing food and shelter.

14. See C. E. Russett, *Sexual Science: The Victorian Construction of Womanhood* (Cambridge, Mass., Harvard University Press, 1989), p. 72.

15. *Woman's Work: or Hints to Raise the Female Character* (London, Clarke, 1844), p. 121.

16. *Woman's Work*, pp. 124, 21.

17. For discussion of the relationship between woman and child see *The Woman Question*, p. 91; see also Russett, *Sexual Science*, for discussion of mainly late nineteenth-century science on the infantile nature of women, and L. Schiebinger, 'Skeletons in the closet: the first illustrations of the female skeleton in eighteenth-century anatomy', in C. Gallagher and T. Laqueur (eds.), *The Making of the Modern Body* (Berkeley, University of California Press, 1987), pp. 63–6.

18. Betty's resort to corporal punishment results in dismissal, and the fact that Agnes is later dismissed for the opposite reason – failing to take a firm enough hand with the children – demonstrates the impossible position of one hired to stand in the place of incompetent parents. Whether or not Agnes ought to have been authorised to thrash her delinquent pupils is not, as some critics have sought to argue, the issue; see P. J. M. Scott, *Anne Brontë: A New Critical Assessment* (London, Vision, 1983) who finds in *Agnes Grey* support for his views on the efficacy of corporal punishment.

19. E. Gaskell, *Life of Charlotte Brontë* (Edinburgh, John Grant, 1905), p. 154.

20. On the cultural currency of images of New Zealand inhabitants as most savage see 'Recent trials in lunacy', *Journal of Psychological Medicine and Mental Pathology*, 7 (1854), p. 617; Wm. Ryan, *Infanticide: Its Law, Prevalence, Prevention, and History* (London, Churchill, 1862), p. 253, and O. Moscucci, *The Science of Woman: Gynaecology and Gender in England, 1800–1929* (Cambridge, Cambridge University Press, 1990), p. 1.

21. See J. Stevens (ed.), *Mary Taylor, friend of Charlotte Brontë: Letters from New Zealand and Elsewhere* (Auckland, Auckland University Press, 1972), p. 82.

22. Letter to Ellen Nussey, 9 February 1849; quoted in Stevens, p. 82.

23. Poovey, *Uneven Developments*, p. 128.

24. Six sets of ellipses occur in the first four paragraphs of this chapter, signalling the narrator's discomfort with her confession.

25. A. Walker, *Woman Physiologically Considered As to Mind, Morals, Marriage, Matrimonial Slavery, Infidelity and Divorce* (London, Baily, 1840), p. 53.

26. See Moscucci, *The Science of Woman*, pp. 34–5, who remarks on the way aesthetic appreciation of the female body incorporated biological, social and moral aspects of women's sexual nature.

27. See A. Easson, 'Anne Brontë and the glow-worms', *Notes and Queries*, 224 (1979), pp. 299–300, who draws attention to Goldsmith as Brontë's source, but does not mention White's *History of Selborne* as the fourth reference on Natural History in Charlotte Brontë's letter to Ellen Nussey.

28. Wm. Acton, *The Functions and Disorders of the Reproductive Organs in Childhood, Youth, Adult Age, and Advanced Life, Considered in their Physiological, Social and Moral Relations* (London, Churchill, 1862), p. 81. The section is introduced by an account of the copulatory habits of various animals and insects: 'Nature has, however, not only given the adult animal these instincts, but provides in a most wonderful way for their gratification.'

29. Acton is quoting from Wm. Kirby and Wm. Spence, *An Introduction to Entomology: or Elements of the Natural History of Insects* vol. 2 (London, Longman, 1817), p. 428. Goldsmith notes also that the female is entirely a creeping insect, and is 'doomed to wait' for the male who flies to her (*History of the World*, vol. 8, p. 140). See Easson, 'Anne Brontë and the glow-worms', pp. 299–300.

30. Acton, *Functions and Disorders*, p. 101.

31. Acton, *Functions and Disorders*, p. 102.

32. Acton, *Functions and Disorders* 6th edn. 1885, p. 183; see above, Chapter One.

33. Acton, *Functions and Disorders*, p. 102.

34. On the glow-worm's ability to extinguish the light, see Kirby and Spence, *An Introduction to Entomology*. Gilbert White records that glow-worms regularly 'put out their lamps between eleven and twelve every night,' see *The Natural History and Antiquities of Selborne* (London, White, Cochrane, 1813), p. 524. White's *History of Selborne* was recommended reading on natural history, along with Bewick, Audubon, and Goldsmith, in Charlotte's letter to Ellen Nussey; see *The Brontë Letters*, selected and introduced by M. Spark (Great Britain, Peter Nevil, 1954), p. 47.

35. On ideals of middle-class manhood, see L. Davidoff and C. Hall, *Family Fortunes: Men and Women of the English Middle Class 1780–1850* (London, Hutchinson, 1987), pp. 110–13.

36. 'Hints on the modern governess system', *Fraser's Magazine*, 30 (November 1844), p. 573.

37. 'Queen bees or working bees?', *Saturday Review* (12 November 1859), p. 575.

38. See Kirby and Spence, *An Introduction to Entomology*, p. 122, where they explain that Aristotle's analogy is 'pushed rather too far', and imply that there are limits to the analogies that can usefully be made between one species and another.

39. W. R. Greg, 'False morality of lady novelists', *The National Review* (January 1859), p. 167.

40. W. R. Greg, 'Prostitution', *Westminster Review* (1850), pp. 448–506.

41. This is not to suggest, however, that the argument about passionlessness is without contradiction, as we see in the discussion of Greg and Acton below.

42. See J. Walkowitz, 'Male vice and female virtue: feminism and the politics of prostitution in nineteenth-century Britain', in A. Snitow, C. Stansell and S. Thompson (eds.), *Desire: The Politics of Sexuality* (London, Virago, 1984); and N. F. Cott, 'Passionlessness: an interpretation of Victorian sexual ideology, 1790–1850', *Signs*, 4 :2(1978), pp. 219–36.

43. See Walkowitz, 'Male vice and female virtue', pp. 421–2; see also E. J. Bristow, *Vice and Vigilance: Purity Movements in Britain since 1700* (Dublin, Gill and Macmillan, 1977) who notes that 'before feminism could make prostitution a paradigm for the condition of women, it took Josephine Butler and Ellice Hopkins to demonstrate to their sex that, in the words of Miss Hopkins, the fallen were "martyrs of purity"' (p. 62).

44. See E. K. Sedgwick, *Epistemology of the Closet* (Berkeley, University of California Press, 1990), pp. 72–5.

45. G. H. Lewes, *The Leader* (January 22 1853), p. 91.

46. Charlotte Brontë foresaw that critics would stick on the 'cover-up' by the minister; see her letter on *Ruth* in A. Easson (ed.), *Elizabeth Gaskell: The Critical Heritage* (London, Routledge, 1991), p. 201.

47. D. A. Miller, *The Novel and the Police* (Berkeley, University of California Press, 1988), p. 207.

48. To confront the world with one's perceived transgressions and have done with it was not an entirely simple matter, as he and Marian Evans would later learn. The openness of their unsanctioned union did not collapse the binarisms that defined them as transgressive, outsiders. Gaskell's own responses to their situation count as mild evidence in this regard. Although not intolerant of unconventional behaviour, she certainly expressed reservations about the Lewes/Evans union when she wrote to George Eliot congratulating her on *Scenes from Clerical Life* and expressing her delight in the work. In her typically forthright way, she added: 'I should not be quite true in my ending, if I did not say before I concluded that I wish you *were* Mrs Lewes. However that can't be helped, as far as I can see, and one must not judge others.' See J. A. V. Chapple and Arthur Pollard (eds.), *The Letters of Mrs Gaskell* (Manchester, Manchester University Press, 1966), p. 592. Earlier that year she had wondered what drew Marian Evans to someone like Lewes: '*How came she to like Mr Lewes so much?* I know he has his good points but somehow he is so soiled for a woman like her to fancy' (*Letters*, p. 587).

49. E. Gaskell, *Ruth* (Oxford, World's Classics, [1853] 1985), pp. 121–2; hereafter page references will be incorporated in the text.

50. Sally is prepared to support the lie that protects Ruth only when she has personally ensured that Ruth's sexuality is under control. In this way she anticipates what Judith Walkowitz finds in the attitudes of feminists of the 1860s, as well as more repressive moralists: the desire to protect working-class girls also masked impulses to control their sexuality; see Walkowitz, 'Male vice and female virtue', p. 427.

51. As critics of *Ruth* have noticed, the question of Ruth's desire is a highly problematic aspect of the novel; see P. Stoneman, *Elizabeth Gaskell* (Brighton, Harvester, 1987), pp. 100–2; H. Schor, *Scheherazade in the Marketplace: Elizabeth Gaskell and the Victorian Novel* (New York, Oxford University Press, 1992), pp. 45–79.

52. Sedgwick, *Epistemology of the Closet*, p. 68.
53. Chapple and Pollard (eds.), *Letters*, p. 227.
54. Greg, 'Prostitution', p. 448.
55. R. Wardlaw, *Lectures on Female Prostitution: Its Nature, Extent, Effects, Guilt, Causes and Remedy* (Glasgow, James Maclehouse, 1844), p.14.
56. Wardlaw, p. 72.
57. F. Mort, *Dangerous Sexualities: Medico-Moral Politics in England since 1830* (London, Routledge, 1987), p. 80.
58. M. Ryan, *A Manual of Midwifery, and Diseases of Women and Children* (London, Bloomsbury, 1831), p. 58.
59. R. Carlile, *Every Woman's Book or What is Love?* (abridged from *The Republican*, 18:11 ([c 1825], 1838), p. 42.
60. By the 1870s feminists were using ideas about female 'passionlessness' in attacks on state regulation. Feminists were also, however, the first to oppose a biology of 'passionlessness' when it became clear that such an ideology restricted women's knowledge of their own sexual functioning; see Cott, 'Passionlessness', p. 235, and Walkowitz, 'Male vice and female virtue'.
61. Greg, 'Prostitution', p. 450.
62. See Mary Poovey's analysis of Greg's article in 'Speaking of the body: mid-Victorian constructions of female desire', in M. Jacobus, E. Fox Keller and S. Shuttleworth (eds.), *Body/Politics: Women and the Discourses of Science* (London, Routledge, 1990), pp. 32–7.
63. Greg, 'Prostitution', p. 457.
64. Greg, 'Prostitution', p. 459.
65. Greg, 'Prostitution', p. 457.
66. Greg, 'Prostitution', p. 448.
67. Mort, *Dangerous Sexualities*, p. 79.
68. Wm. Acton, *Prostitution Considered in its Moral, Social and Sanitary Aspects* (London, Churchill, 1857), p. 20.
69. Acton, *Functions and Disorders* (1862), p. 104.
70. Acton, *Functions and Disorders* (1862), p. 104.
71. Acton, *Functions and Disorders* (1862), p. 101.
72. Acton, *Prostitution Considered*, p. 73.
73. Acton, *Prostitution Considered*, p. 63.
74. Acton, *Prostitution Considered*, p. 68.
75. Easson (ed.), *Elizabeth Gaskell*, p. 209.
76. See Poovey, *Uneven Developments*, p. 129.
77. Sedgwick, *Epistemology of the Closet*, p. 77.
78. See Sedgwick, *Epistemology of the Closet*, p. 61.
79. A. Helston (ed.), *Ruth* (Oxford, World's Classics, 1985), p. xix.
80. See Stoneman, *Elizabeth Gaskell*, pp. 113–16, who sees Ruth's final lack of self-awareness as an index of her denial of sexuality. But like other Gaskellian characters – Alice Wilson in *Mary Barton*, for example – the approach to death removes the subject to a fantasy of maternal fusion and reconnection.
81. While there has been some critical focus on the nature of buried or repressed desire and yearning in *Villette*, there has been relatively little attention paid

to the ways in which Brontë works out her version of female desire in opposition to traditional mid-Victorian notions about the sexualized woman. The most thorough and useful treatment of Brontë's views about sexuality is J. Maynard, *Charlotte Brontë and Sexuality* (Cambridge, Cambridge University Press, 1984); see also M. Jacobus, 'The buried letter', in *Reading Woman: Essays in Feminist Criticism* (New York, Columbia University Press, 1985); R. Fraser, *Charlotte Brontë* (London, Methuen, 1988), p. 173.

82. Feminist and psychoanalytic discussions particularly have explored Freud's emphasis on the gaze as a crucial aspect in the construction of male sexual identity. In terms of the Freudian scenario, the sight of the 'castrated' female is initially responsible for the production of male anxiety about sexuality and then, as the gazer asserts his difference, the anxiety is subsequently allayed. The domination of the 'looking' position is supposed to be a means of empowering the looker, a scenario that writes the power relations between the subject of the controlling gaze and its subordinated object. This opposition is further mapped onto the binaries of male / female, active / passive, and so on. See L. Mulvey, 'Afterthoughts on "Visual pleasure and narrative cinema" inspired by *Duel in the Sun*', in *Visual and Other Pleasures* (Bloomington, Indiana University Press, 1989), pp. 29–38; L. Gamman and M. Marshment (eds.), *The Female Gaze: Women as Viewers of Popular Culture* (Seattle, The Real Comet Press, 1989).

83. See Gamman and Marshment, *The Female Gaze*, p. 5.

84. C. Brontë, *Villette*, ed. M. Lilly (Harmondsworth, Penguin, [1853] 1979), p. 163; all subsequent page references are to this edition and will be cited parenthetically in the text.

85. See S. Heath, 'Difference', *Screen*, 19:3 (1978), p. 88; see also Beth Newman's discussion of Heath in '"The situation of the looker-on": gender, narration, and gaze in *Wuthering Heights*', *PMLA*, 105:5 (1990), pp. 1029–41.

86. My perspective on the gaze as a way of entering the novel's discourse of female desire and sexuality is indebted to Newman's discussion of *Wuthering Heights*.

87. For discussion of Brontë's treatment of the Cleopatra figure see L. Hughes-Hallett, *Cleopatra: Histories, Dreams and Distortions* (London, Vintage, 1990), pp. 230–1; M. Hamer, *Signs of Cleopatra* (London, Routledge, 1993), p. 44.

88. See *Athenaeus: The Deipnosophists*, trans. C. B. Gulick (Cambridge Mass., Harvard University Press, 1961) vol 4, pp. 147–8. Brontë's knowledge of Cleopatra's feasts may have come from her readings in ancient history. Charles Rollin's *The Ancient History of the Egyptians, Carthaginians, Assyrians, Babylonians* (London, printed for Cowie, 1827) was apparently recommended for study by Miss Wooler at Roe Head, and indeed Rollin offers an expansive treatment of the most famous classical accounts of Cleopatra's conspicuous consumption and sexual politics.

89. Renaissance depictions often show her with the asp, a familiar metonymic signifier of her identity. While death scenes continued to be popular, the Restoration favoured scenes showing the famous episode in Pliny where Cleopatra dissolves a fabulously valuable pearl in a glass of wine in order to win a wager with Antony about who was the bigger spender. Unlike the nineteenth century, the seventeenth century was disposed to admire and

indulge, even idealise, extravagant sensual love.

90. Having been 'seduced by Egypt' Makart altered his conception of Cleopatra, which he had previously treated in a 'generalized Baroque manner'. Influenced by Egyptologist Georg Ebers, he also invented genre scenes with an Egyptian flavour. His *Ancient Egyptian Dancing Girl* is clothed (or unclothed) in a costume identical to that of his Cleopatra.

91. Although the realistic style of painters who actually lived and worked in the East (John Frederick Lewis and Gerome, for example) was at one time held to reflect Oriental reality with scientific exactitude and objectivity and to advance the West's 'knowledge' of Eastern women, such claims are today rigorously deconstructed. See L. Nochlin, 'The imaginary Orient', *The Politics of Vision: Essays on Nineteenth-Century Art and Society* (New York, Harper and Row, 1989), pp. 3–60; Joanna de Groot, '"Sex" and "race": the construction of language and image in the nineteenth century', in S. Mendus and J. Rendall (eds.), *Sexuality and Subordination* (London, Routledge, 1989), pp. 89–128.

92. The identification of this painting and the one described in *Villette* was originally put forward by G. Charlier, 'Brussels life in *Villette*', *The Brontë Society Transactions*, 5 (1955), pp. 386–90, who points out that Brontë both misnames and misdescribes the painting by De Biefve. Charlier was also able to show that another painting at the Salon is recognisable in Lucy's description of 'La vie d'une femme'. For information on De Biefve see P. Berko, *Orientalist Painters* (Brussels, Laconti, 1982), who lists his name among Belgian Orientalists but offers no commentary on his work; see also P. Berko and V. Berko's *Belgian Painters: A Dictionary of Belgian Painters born between 1750 and 1875* (Brussels, Laconti, 1981), which has a short entry on De Biefve but does not mention Orientalist themes at all. He was known for his portraits and his historic, mythological, and religious scenes. Also remarked on is his penchant for the large canvas depicting pomp and circumstance; *Une Almé* is not mentioned.

93. Beneath the lithograph printed in *La Renaissance*, the following explanatory lines accompanied the title of the painting:
    Les almes de l'Egypte, agiles bayaderes,
    Aux longs cheveux flottants, aux tuniques légères…
    [Egyptian almées, light-footed dancing-girls
    With filmy draperies and long floating curls…]

94. E. Said, *Orientalism* (New York, Pantheon, 1978), p. 186; see also the section on 'dancing girls' in C. B. Klunzinger, *Upper Egypt, its People and its Products* (New York, Scribner, 1878), pp. 30–2.

95. See Charlier, 'Brussels life in *Villette*', p. 389.

96. 'Salon National de 1842', *La Renaissance: chronique des arts et de la litterature*, 4 (1842–43), p. 92.

97. See T. J. Wise and J. A. Symington (eds.), *The Miscellaneous and Unpublished Writings of Charlotte and Patrick Branwell Brontë* (The Shakespeare Head Brontë, 1936 and 1938) vol. 2, p. 390; see also C. Alexander, *The Early Writings of Charlotte Brontë* (Oxford, Blackwell, 1983).

98. Quoted in W. Gerin, *Charlotte Brontë: The Evolution of Genius* (Oxford, Clarendon, 1967), p. 51.

99. *Antony and Cleopatra*, V.ii. 219.
100. Quoted in S. L. Gilman, *Difference and Pathology: Stereotypes of Sexuality, Race and Madness* (Ithaca, Cornell University Press, 1985), p. 94; see also J. Walkowitz, *Prostitution and Victorian Society* (Cambridge, Cambridge University Press, 1980), pp. 36–44, for discussion of Parent-Duchatelet's influence on British social scientists.
101. C. B. Klunzinger, *Upper Egypt, its People and its Products* (New York, Scribner, 1878), p. 162.
102. H. Martineau, *Eastern Life: Present and Past* (London, Moxon, [1848] 1875), p. 239.
103. Quoted in Fraser, *Charlotte Brontë*, p. 433.
104. Fraser, *Charlotte Brontë*, pp. 486–7.
105. C. Brontë, *Jane Eyre* (Harmondsworth, Penguin, [1847] 1966), pp. 297–8.
106. Brontë, *Jane Eyre*, p. 334.
107. On the representation of male vanity and sense of entitlement, see Martineau, *Autobiography* (1877):

> I had heard all my life of the vanity of women as a subject of pity to men; but when I went to London, lo! I saw vanity in high places which was never transcended by that of women in their lowlier rank... There was Bulwer, on a sofa, sparkling and languishing among a set of female votaries, – he and they dizened out, perfumed and presenting the nearest picture to a seraglio to be seen on British ground-only the indifference or hauteur of the lord of the harem being absent.

108. See Gilman, *Difference and Pathology*, pp. 99–101; see also Mary Poovey's discussion of the different versions of desire that developed in response to public concern about contagious diseases in 'Speaking of the body', pp. 30–7.
109. Gilman, *Difference and Pathology*, p. 99.
110. He introduces her to Villette culture and often takes Lucy to the galleries, leaving her as she prefers for some hours to view the exhibitions on her own.
111. See S. L. Gilman, 'Sexology, psychoanalysis, and degeneration: from a theory of race to a race about theory', in J. E. Chamberlin and S. L. Gilman (eds.), *Degeneration: The Dark Side of Progress* (New York, Columbia University Press, 1985), p. 74:

> Marguerite Gors, twenty-three years old... appears like a ten-year-old girl. She is not quite 977mm tall and weighs about 20kg. Noticeable is the lack of any sign of puberty and the retention of all her milk teeth. Her genitalia are no more developed than those of a seven or eight-year-old child. The pubis is totally hairless. The feeling of shame seems not yet to have been awakened. The examination of Dr. Destrade, the family doctor, who accompanied me on my visit, actually seemed to cause her no embarrassment.

112. Graham confirms this by repeatedly failing to recognise her as a woman, and Monsieur Paul refutes it by endorsing and responding to that desiring, sexual self. John Maynard, *Charlotte Brontë and Sexuality*, p. 170, observes that Monsieur Paul is the only male viewer who responds to 'the sexual reality behind the poor and foolish painting'; see also p. 200, for his discussion of Monsieur Paul's sexual and passionate nature.

113. C. Bernheimer, *Figures of Ill-Repute: Representing Prostitution in Nineteenth-Century France* (Boston, Harvard University Press, 1989), p. 1.
114. J. Berger, *Ways of Seeing* (London, BBC and Penguin, 1972), p. 52.
115. See Mulvey, 'Afterthoughts', p. 37.
116. Book of Esther I: 6–7.
117. See the discussion of Vashti and Cleopatra in S. M. Gilbert and S. Gubar, *The Madwoman in the Attic: The Woman Writer and the Nineteenth-Century Literary Imagination* (New Haven Yale University Press, 1979), pp. 399–440.

Chapter four

Maternal deviance

> The generative organs reach their greatest state of development in the human species, and consist of parts adapted to coitus, ovulation, menstruation, impregnation, utero-gestation, parturition, and lactation – functions which are placed in relation to the highest affection and parental love (W. Tyler Smith, 'On the theory and practice of obstetrics', *Lancet*, 1 (1856), 4).

If medico-scientific representations of the mother underwrote cultural conceptions of woman as specially framed for reproduction and equipped with maternal instinct, how did Victorian discourses of motherhood accommodate or respond to obvious departures from this ideal of 'the highest affection and parental love'? In the first part of this chapter, I discuss representations of maternal functioning in the late-1850s and 1860s in medical debates about wet-nursing and treatises on infanticide. The controversy about the causes and incidence of infanticide reinforces the recognition that constructions of motherhood and maternal instinct were ideologically central, if internally inconsistent.[1] Conceptions of maternal instinct function to legitimate approved mothering behaviour, while constructions of deviance designate as unnatural the kind of mother that departs from the norm. The discourse of maternal instinct and its perversions serves to inscribe class differences as differences among women, and to naturalise the distinctions between middle-class mothers and deviant others. Turning to fictional representations of maternal aberration in George Eliot's *Adam Bede* (1859) and Lady Emma Caroline Wood's *Sorrow on the Sea* (1868), I consider how they reflect and reflect on contemporary constructions of maternal instinct.

Wet-nurses, infanticide and the discourse of motherhood

One way to recuperate the all-sacrificing, ministering mother in the face of apparently monstrous maternal acts was to argue that certain classes of women were losing their natural instincts through the effects of their physical and moral conditions. As we saw in Chapter one, biomedical discourse emphasised the instability of sexual difference; adverse social conditions could distort or destroy natural provisions. As texts on infanticide and infant morality expressed shock and horror at the evils of burial clubs, baby-farming and baby-dropping, so they reinforced the representation of working-class mothers as having lost their 'natural propensities' through the acquisition of debased morals and habits.[2]

> The voice of nature is strong enough to speak for the child to the mother's heart until stifled by vicious habits, or crushed out by absolute want of the necessaries of life. Sometimes, indeed, it happens that that which should be cherished by the mother as her own life is regarded as an encumbrance, and she sets a price on the head of her child. How else are to be interpreted those dark and almost incredible doings occasionally brought to light? Do we not hear of mothers insuring the means of burying, not in one, but in several burial clubs, for the sake of the gain to be obtained by the death of their infants?[3]

Representations of aberrant working-class motherhood were characteristic of early social science and anti-factory texts, but the debates about motherhood and wet-nursing of the 1850s and 1860s focus attention also on delinquent middle-class mothers who selfishly refuse to nourish their children as Nature intended: 'Oh! let those who have any influence in this matter pause ere they help to sever those holiest and purest of earthly ties which Nature has intended, with wise purpose, should exist between a mother and her child.'[4] Nature, however, cannot be blamed for mothers failing to nurse their children. 'The artificial mode of life which leads to these evils must be blamed, and not Dame Nature, who is innocent of such offence.'[5] Mothers who cross Dame Nature not only harm their children, but run the risk of incurring disease themselves. As one surgeon pointed out: 'The very great prevalence of uterine and mammary disease now known to exist... is in some degree, attributable to the increase of this interference with one of Nature's most established laws.'[6] Deploring the rate of infant mortality in Britain, Mary Anne Baines, of the Ladies' National Association for the Diffusion of Sanitary Knowledge, is firmly convinced that 'society' has interfered with the workings of instinct: 'It might be interesting and instructive to enquire how far the present constitution and requirements of 'society' militate against the development of the domestic virtues especially against the exercise of the maternal affections.' Infant mortality, she suggests, is the consequence of the 'habitual absence of the mother from the home – no matter in what station of life this practice prevails'.[7] The result of women working, argued Dr Arthur Leared, along the lines of early anti-factory tracts, is a new breed of woman, who lacks the finer instincts and sympathies which adorn her sex and is 'selfish, calculating, masculine, and even violent in her conduct'.[8]

In response to a mortality among children that 'out-Herods Herod', the *Lancet* proposed in 1859 that mothers who can't or won't suckle their own children should not be allowed to endanger the lives of other children by buying the milk of their mothers. To inhibit the rise of delinquent mothers it was thought necessary to police mothering functions: official medical referees should be paid to provide certificates of the buying mother's need and the selling mother's competency. 'Such an official referee … would be a check to these proceedings, and could moreover register the names of women fitted to undertake the duties of wet-nurse when absolutely required.'[9] The vanity of middle-class mothers and the callous inefficiency of working-class nurses each contribute to the maternal deviance which medical regulation must now monitor. As the presiding image of Lady Macbeth in this article signifies, aberrant maternity is the villain of this piece, intervention and control by the medical profession the saviour. It is not coincidental that debates about nursing and motherhood peak at what is also a moment of increased feminist activity, growing criticism of the sexual double standard, and assertion of women's needs for education and economic independence.

In the next few years, the *Lancet* and the *British Medical Journal* featured lead articles and a vigorous correspondence debating the perceived link between wet-nursing and infanticide, and assessing the dangers of employing wet-nurses from the ranks of fallen women. Why at this time did the figure of the wet-nurse arouse such controversy? Wet-nursing was, after all, a custom centuries old.[10] Medical advice texts had frequently counselled mothers on the choice of a surrogate, and among the duties of the accoucheur were that surrogate's examination and approval.[11] At one time, doctors advised that a woman known to have had many children would be a good wet nurse, because she was clearly inured to leaving her own child for her work.[12] Now, however, middle-class mothers were supposedly assisting infanticide by buying the nurse's milk and keeping it from her own child.

A number of factors converge at this time to make the wet-nurse a very controversial figure, more destabilising and anxiety-provoking than even the governess. Herself a mother, she is called upon to do the work of another mother – one who has turned away from her maternal duties, but has the means to hire someone to perform them for her. The wet-nurse, however, is seldom a respectable mother, because if she were it is unlikely that she would be hiring her services out, leaving her husband and children. If a married woman hired herself out to nurse another's child, Mary Anne Baines asserted, her own must suffer. More importantly, her 'husband's comforts are not attended to, and thus temptations offer to *wean* a man from home and to contract irregular habits' [my italics].[13] The husband, it would seem, is also in the position of the nursing child, weaned only at the responsible wife/mother's peril. The metaphoric use of 'wean' in this context suggests the husband as a permanent suckling to the home breast, and articulates attempts to naturalise the domestic function of the respectable wife: domesticity, like nursing one's child, is seen as a natural function of womanhood.

Worse than the threat of maternal and conjugal irresponsibility was the suspicion of sexual immorality. More likely to be a fallen mother than a respectably married woman, the wet-nurse had probably already, as one doctor put it, embarked on a 'fornicating course of life', and her maternity could be taken as evidence of her transgressive sexuality. [14] She stood for disorder and immorality as much as for convenience. The wet-nurse, therefore, as one of a swelling number of fallen women could be seen as polluting the homes of middle-class mothers, encouraging them in the loss of their maternal capacities, and leaving a glut of unwanted, illegitimate babies on the public conscience. She focused anxieties about the way supply and demand in nursing bodies and babies was sorting itself out according to the laws of the market, anxieties that often helped to lead to analysis and revelation of some of the unpleasant aspects of Victorian economic structures and sexual mores. But from an essentially biological perspective the wet-nurse was also seen literally as a conduit through which contaminating moral and hereditary influences could flow. If advice books and medical attention offered to supervise and control every aspect of the mother's state during pregnancy to ensure that middle-class reproduction was healthy and pure, the substitution of an unruly and unregenerate maternal body at the crucial stage of nursing threatened to undo the effects of such good regulatory work.

At the same time, therefore, as some doctors were expressing concern for the babies of wet-nurses deprived of their sustenance, they were also asserting the danger of that sustenance for the middle-class baby. 'Wet-nurses from the fallen' warns against the dangers of hiring unmarried mothers to nourish good middle-class babies.[15] The disordered and irregular life that such women must have led is the worst possible preparation for a wet-nurse, who could through her milk pass on her temperament to the child; proven lack of self-control in nursing mothers could be life-threatening for the infant. 'A burst of rage, a passion of grief, a sudden emotion that passes off like a shadow from the mother, and leaves her unchanged, produces so marked an effect on the milk as seriously to prejudice the health of the infant during many days and weeks.'[16] This dramatic account of the effect of emotion on milk is understated in comparison with others. For example, William Carpenter, a respected physiologist, discussed the immediately fatal effect that a nursing mother's thoughts could produce. He cites one alarming if not very enlightening instance where a mother, while suckling her child, had a depressing fear that the baby might, like its siblings, succumb to a convulsive disorder. As soon as she left-off nursing, the child was seized with a convulsion-fit and died almost instantly.[17] If the emotions of even a stable mother were a danger, how much more dangerous the unruly emotions of a transgressive woman?

Anxieties about the capacity of wet-nurses to transmit not just diseases like syphilis but undesirable moral qualities, disposition and hereditary characteristics reached new proportions in medical debates at this time. Citing Forbes Winslow, an expert on insanity who argued for the capacity of criminal parents to transmit their tendencies to their children, C. H. F. Routh warned of the effects of undesirable milk on the health of future generations. If blood was the medium through which the inheritance of criminality or insanity was passed, was not milk a vital and essential fluid like blood? Routh cites a long list of ancient and classical authors who testify to the power of milk to transmit moral qualities. Because Romulus was suckled by a wolf, we learn, he was cruel, passionate, and patient of discomfort; Nero's parents were most benevolent, but he was suckled by a cruel nurse, which accounts for the fact that he later killed his mother.

Routh concedes that these examples are only allegorically persuasive, but proceeds to cite various medical opinions (including Carpenter's) on the determining of constitution through infant nourishment. 'I myself', writes Routh, with stunning lack of concern for confounding variables, 'have known two cases: one a lady suckled by a bad woman, who in youth was full of like bad passions, till converted by the gospel truth; and another of a gentleman suckled by a nurse of strong sexual passions, who has inherited all her propensities.' Numerous examples follow to show that we are what we eat, that different nations exhibit different temperaments because of their diet and that a change in the quality of one's food influences constitutional change. Given the importance of child-feeding, then, fallen mothers ought only to be allowed to do menial work under surveillance in large hospitals or prisons, if they are to be employed as nurses at all.[18]

When William Acton in a letter to the *Lancet* (1859) endorsed the employment of unmarried wet-nurses, he scoffed at the notion that breast milk unblessed by the Church, or unsanctified by the registrar's office, could be a deadly moral poison. He was not, after all, proposing to employ prostitutes (who, as everyone knew, hardly ever had children), but healthy, first-time offenders. Acton saw the employment of the fallen as a happy situation in which demand was being supplied by the very class of women who needed help. Instead of becoming a prostitute, the unlucky serving maid could have an opportunity of useful employment and a chance to redeem herself and support her child. Contrasting the sickly, dyspeptic, fashionable mother who is feeble and nervous, with the healthy, strong and penitent servant, he asked rhetorically who was likely to have the healthiest milk.[19]

Acton's support for wet-nurses from the fallen unleashed strong responses: some asserted the dangerous properties of 'fallen' milk; others reiterated that hiring wet-nurses was tantamount to supporting infanticide, a transaction 'entirely selfish and ... so revolting to humanity' that amounted to the 'bribing of a needy woman to part with that on which the health, frequently the life, of her own child depends'.[20] The week after Acton's letter, an answer signed 'Mater' begged Acton to think of the poor girl's child, a sacrifice to the 'tyrant custom, *wet-nursing*', that also serves the 'demon *Infanticide*' which claims vast numbers of illegitimate children.[21] 'Mater' calls on middle-class mothers to leave off luxurious and selfish habits, condemning 'the habitual neglect of the maternal duty' that forms a 'foul blot on the moral escutcheon of the mothers of England!'[22]

Manifest in the wet-nurse debates and subsequent discussions of infanticide is a Victorian politics of reproduction declaring the ideological centrality of the maternal body to the doctrine of separate spheres for men and women and the maintenance of well-defined class divisions. What characteristically emerges in the spate of letters over this period is a middle-class fear of contamination expressing itself as an urgent need to police class boundaries. At the same time, ethical injunctions about wet-nursing address the problem of reinforcing the domestic and mothering functions of the middle-class wife. Stop her from purchasing the milk that rightfully belongs to other babies, and she will have to provide for her own child as Nature intended. Operative in most of these medico-polemical texts is the assumption that sexually transgressive women must be aberrant mothers; keeping them and their milk separate from the middle classes is a primary regulatory impulse. Concerned medical men and middle-class mothers as well as sanitary reformers are all anxious to retrench the doctrine of separate spheres and maintain a strict demarcation among classes.

To talk about the middle-class mother and the employment of wet-nurses in terms of the purity of milk or the encouragement of infanticide among the lower classes was largely to bypass uncomfortable questions about the relationship of mothering to social structures and economic pressures. In discussions of infanticide over the next decade, analysts disagreed about whether economic pressures affected the capacity to mother. Could economic stress and destitution account for rising infanticide rates? In 1834, the Poor Law Commissioner's Report had discounted economic motives for infanticide: 'We believe that in no civilized country, and scarcely in any barbarous country, has such a thing ever been heard of as a mother's killing her child in order to save the expense of feeding it.'[23] William Burke Ryan, whose prize-winning essay on infanticide in its medico-legal relations was expanded and published in 1862, also dismissed economic privation as a relevant consideration, using the example of the Irish to make his point. Ryan is perplexed about the rising rates of infant deaths, but dismisses poverty as a factor because in Ireland, which should not, he says, be pilloried with her sister kingdoms, there is relatively little infanticide: 'Could anything excuse so heinous a crime as infanticide – and nothing can, – extreme poverty might do it; but with poverty of the most extreme degree infanticide is happily almost unknown.'[24] Since Ryan has already spent some time detailing the heinous practices of the burial clubs in Manchester and other manufacturing districts, his dismissal of material want as a cause of infanticide is too easily managed through the Irish example.

Convinced that deviation from the doctrine of separate spheres produces distortions in child-rearing capacities, Arthur Leared attempted to think about the relationship between infant mortality and the economic pressures that send mothers out to work. 'England is regarded as the head-quarters of the domestic virtues, and we boast of the word "Home" as a national possession', but, he goes on, one would not be able to say so after considering the state of the home in the lowest ranks of life.[25] Since Leared is convinced that the destruction of 'home associations' destroys womanly instincts, he attributes all depravity to the effects of mothers going out to work. While other observers doubt the financial necessity that drives women to work, Leared is prepared to acknowledge that the need is real, but in struggling with the question of women's work, he soon finds that the economic knots are too difficult for him to untie:

> It is sad to think that certain branches of our commercial greatness depend on what is truly a social evil. The family of the industrious working man is sacrificed because his wages are insufficient for their support. Why this should be, is a question for merchant princes and political economists to decide. At present we have only to do with the results.[26]

One of his recommendations is that women from the 'better classes' should exert their 'civilizing influence' and 'all the lights of science' to dispel ignorance among the poor and help them to regain their maternal instincts. It is clear that infant mortality and its close relationship to infanticide is conceived as a question of class; unnatural mothers are contained within the working-classes and the industrial poor, and Leared believes that no mothers of the 'higher classes' are so depraved or desperate as to dispose of their children. But as the midwife and baby-farming exposés of the following years revealed, there were indeed many clients from those 'better classes' who required the discreet services of a midwife adept at producing a 'quiet 'un'.[27] For the most part, the Victorians avoided recognising that, across class, women were attempting to exercise choice and control over their reproductive capacities, both before and after the fact of pregnancy.

Those who dismissed poverty as a provocation for infanticide, concentrate, like Ryan, on the constraining pressures of respectability and call for the relaxation of savage and hypocritical rules about sexual relations. Commentators argue that the middle classes need to encourage their sons to marry earlier, and suggest that regulative attention be paid to the 'profligate seducer' rather than the 'seduced victim'.[28] Some supported the establishment of foundling hospitals as institutions that might put a stop to infanticide by 'throwing the mantle of charity and secrecy over the fallen woman', but such institutions were also seen to be encouraging vice by helping to care for its progeny.[29] Andrew Wynter, a former editor of the *British Medical Journal* argued further that if such institutions are effective they must themselves procure wet-nurses. The hospital in his own district goes out 'into the market and asks two hundred mothers in the counties of Kent and Surrey to sell their milk ... This is nothing more or less than an indirect method of bringing about infanticide – an infanticide of the legitimate by their own parents, that the illegitimate may live.'[30] The way Wynter starkly depicts the competition among babies for mothers' milk makes it clear that, in his view, not all babies are equal. He discloses therefore the impasse in which those outraged about the delinquency of the middle-class mother find themselves. It is one thing to say piously that no mother should purchase 'alien nourishment', or attempt to buy the 'life-blood' of other children; another to ponder how abandoned women without work or recourse to foundling hospitals are to preserve their children. As soon as women deviate from the ideologically approved scenario of each mother ministering to her husband and children, confusion reigns and amid the ethical and social confusion of the marketplace legitimate maternal bodies end up in service to illegitimate babies. Not surprisingly, then, the only solution Wynter can envision is a renewal of male responsibility and a reinforcement of female dependency on male provision. The fathers of illegitimate children, he argues emphatically in a modern vein, should be made to contribute substantially to their support. Wynter acknowledges, however, that since 1834, the law has not aided unwed mothers to claim assistance from delinquent fathers.[31] The Malthusian rationale behind the 1834 Poor Law Report assumed that curtailing the putative father's accountability would indeed reduce the rate of abortions and infanticide, since it was the man, supposedly, who was usually the first to suggest these crimes. As one commissioner submitted: the female, 'left to herself, from maternal feelings and natural timidity, would seldom make the hazardous attempt to destroy her offspring'.[32] By the late 1850s, it was alarmingly clear to many that large numbers of women were desperate enough to disregard maternal instincts and conventional prohibitions.

As the immorality of upper- and middle-class seducers became a target in debates about the great 'Social Evil' of prostitution, feminists blamed male profligacy, but not without defensive retort. A particularly aggressive article in the *Saturday Review* (1866) challenged assertions that seducers should shoulder the responsibility for the problem of fallen women and infanticide. First, there is no proof, the writer argues, that the number of infanticides is as great as asserted. Second, he denies that such child-murders are perpetrated by 'girls whose maternity is the result of "seduction"'.[33] The assertion that very few mothers actually poison or suffocate their children paves the way for a claim that many infant deaths are caused simply by fatal and often deliberate neglect. The real culprits are poor and working-class mothers, married as much as unwed, who are desirous of getting rid of costly incumbrances:

> The care of providing for a large family, and the hard life which it entails, reconcile many a mother, who in other circumstances would be tender and affectionate, to a bereavement which at all events diminishes her expenses, just as the irksome duty of toiling for a child she rarely sees reconciles the servant or factory-girl to the loss of her illegitimate infant. It is not absolutely necessary to invent the hypothesis of collusive or indirect murder.[34]

The writer acknowledges that poverty strains the capacity of the mother to preserve and nurture her children, but this acknowledgement serves to produce only a distancing complacency. In their circumstances, he implies, one can quite understand the responses of such women. Working-class mothers are not monstrous – under other conditions they would be 'tender and affectionate' – they are merely facing Malthusian realities. Such cold understanding works insidiously to dissolve the problem, as if limited resources and excessive population among the 'lower classes' were better left to sort themselves out and represented no challenge to the self-definition, empowerment and socio-economic privilege of the 'higher' classes.

On the subject of male seducers, the author asserts that for every one case of 'one-sided' seduction, there are fifty of 'mutual and consentient unchastity'. Few men go out looking for beauty and innocence to corrupt; on the contrary, those young women who are too lazy to earn a living in a 'menial' situation are only too ready to offer themselves for a 'light' one. 'Hard work disagrees with their health and sensibilities. They dislike sweeping and scouring, but they are ready to take any "light" situation, and the lighter it is the better it suits them.' The 'much-lauded extension of education' to women is to blame, since it has fitted them for reading novels and spoiled them for housemaids. The structure of the argument in 'Seduction and Infanticide' targets female responsibility. Working-class mothers are responsible for infant deaths (but who can blame them?) because they are too hard-pressed to care for all their large families. Lower middle-class women, spoiled by education, are too lazy to work; only too ready to trade their chastity for an easy life, they cannot claim to be seduced. The argument further relies on attacking both the notions of infanticide and seduction in an attempt to prove that these problems have nothing to do with middle-class men.

In the next few years, the views expressed in 'Seduction and Infanticide' provoked strong responses from feminists. When Josephine Butler, Beth Wolstenholme and Lydia Becker formed 'The Committee to Amend the Law in Points wherein it is Injurious to Women' (CALPIW), they issued a pamphlet 'Infant mortality: its causes and remedies', in which they attempted to focus attention on male irresponsibility in sexual and family matters and to draw the blame for infant mortality away from the negligence of mothers and nurses.[35] They objected to the Infant Life Protection Bill, introduced in 1871, because it proposed state interference in women's lives, gave medical men great power over women, and penalised women alone for infant death, paying no attention to male seduction and betrayal. Regulating baby-farming, as the bill proposed to do, did not address the true causes of infant mortality – women's oppression – and it failed to recognise factors such as ignorance, poverty, seduction, and, above all, the difficulties in the way of unmarried mothers supporting themselves and their children.

'The unnaturalness of her crime': infanticide and maternal instinct in *Adam Bede*

George Eliot's *Adam Bede* was one of the literary successes of the *annus mirabilis* 1859. Although the action of the novel takes place at the turn of the century, the representation of the desperate, pregnant

Hetty, who leaves home to have her illegitimate child in secret and then abandons it, speaks to contemporary concerns about infanticide and maternal instinct. The 'germ' of the story was, as George Eliot explains, the trial of a young woman for child-murder and her subsequent contrition and repentance. Although her Methodist Aunt Samuel (Elizabeth Tomlinson) told Marian Evans this story round 1839, she writes that she did not recall the anecdote until 1856, when she recounted it to Lewes. The case of Mary Voce, executed in 1802, fitted right in with the topicality of infanticide in the 1850s and the upsurge of concern about the decline of maternal instinct.[36] Cases similar to that of Hetty Sorrel, particularly in relation to the method of disposal of the child, were tried through the decade. In 1851, Maria Clarke was convicted of murdering her illegitimate child and sentenced to hanging; she had clumsily buried her child alive. Her sentence was later commuted by the Home Secretary. In 1855, at the Bedford Assizes, Elizabeth Lound, 18, was found guilty of the wilful murder of her child and sentenced to fourteen years transportation. It was reported that she 'actually buried the child alive', placing it in the ground and covering it with loose earth and sods.[37]

One reason for thinking that George Eliot responds to contemporary concerns about maternal instinct is the way she alters the emphasis of her aunt's story in the final chapters of *Adam Bede*. Her aunt had put her emphasis on the sinning mother's confession, which enabled her contrition. While Hetty opens her heart to Dinah and apologises to Adam, her contrition is subordinate in the novel to the function of her confession as testimony in prevailing debates about maternal instinct.

What would have been lost had Hetty remained stubbornly closed and gone to her transportation and subsequent death? Through the confession, Hetty supposedly rejoins (and indicts) her community; the confession scene is also a fine picture of Dinah's powerful effect on people. But what is really accomplished is the satisfaction of the reader's desire to know what the witnesses cannot tell – whether Hetty really meant to murder her child and how she feels about it. By providing, ultimately, an account of what Hetty thought and felt the novel breaks new ground. The confession focuses issues of subjectivity and relationship and has an important bearing on the question of what makes a mother. This is a question with which the narrative is consistently concerned. From the early scenes of Adam Bede's interaction with his plaintive mother, to Timothy's Bess nursing one of her maternal jewels, Mrs Irwine's fondness for her 'Dauphin' and disregard of her daughters, and Rachel Poyser's special tenderness for little Totty, the diversity of mothers and mothering testifies to the novel's interest in maternal relationships. Hetty is only the most dramatic instance through which the novel explores the implications of being or becoming a mother.[38]

One way to approach the maternal discourse in the novel is through its parodic treatment. George Eliot uses Bartle Massey's habit of dispensing with the distinction between women and animals to table a range of topics relating to wives and motherhood which, although treated humorously, also resonate seriously with the novel's concerns. In all his strictures about women, the misogynist Massey reduces them to insects or animals: he avers that young women will turn to 'stinging gnats', and he sees Hetty's kind as 'vermin', better put out of the world. Massey is also in the habit of addressing his dog Vixen as if she were a woman: 'He always called Vixen a woman', notes the narrator, 'and seemed to have lost all consciousness that he was using a figure of speech'.[39] Massey clearly has a past involving some suffering at the hands of a woman: he has been 'a fool' himself in his time, as he says, and the only female with whom he is prepared to trust himself is Vixen, with whom he can always be master, berate and abuse womankind, but also safely show and receive tenderness and love. Significantly, Adam finds at one point that Bartle Massey has been absent from church because Vixen has just had a litter of puppies, which allows Bartle to be a concerned father, as well as to bluster about how he should have 'strangled the mother and the brats with one cord', and how he has to feed his dog though she does nothing with the food except 'nourish those unnecessary babbies. That's the way with these women – they've got no head-pieces to nourish, and so their food all runs either to fat or to brats' (pp. 284–5). It won't escape any reader's notice that Bartle Massey's hardboiled pose and insulting grumbles about women pithily echo biomedical discourse, which emphasises that women are governed by a body specialised for reproduction rather than by a rational, highly-developed mind. They also anticipate later medical warnings about the dangers of female education, in which doctors worried that if women did nourish their 'head-pieces' they would redirect the body's energies from its specialised reproductive functions. Bartle's reference to 'fat and brats' recalls the following summary of female function: 'The great purpose of life in woman is secretion, whether it regard the formation of the superficial adipose substance which invests her with beautiful and attractive forms, or the nutrition of the new being which is the object of her attractions and of her life.'[40]

Massey sees Adam to the gate accompanied by Vixen but as he watches the young man stride off, the dog runs back to the house twice to 'bestow a parenthetic lick on her puppies' (p. 292). Massey chides her for her foolishness in having consorted with Will Baker's 'hulking bull-terrier', and as Vixen runs back into the house again with her tail tucked between her legs, the narrator exploits the breakdown of distinction between dog and woman: 'Subjects are sometimes broached which a well-bred female will ignore' (p. 292). The schoolteacher caustically comments that it is no use talking to a woman with babies, for she has 'no conscience – it's all run to milk!' (p. 292). The ingredients of this scene are the unwisely indulged sexuality of the 'woman', but also her unquestionable maternal instinct in caring for and nursing the offspring sourly said to be unwanted and better strangled. These ingredients parody similar concerns in the main action of the novel – Hetty's unwisely indulged sexuality and questionable maternal instinct. Along with the humorous mileage that George Eliot extracts from tracking across the line between animal and human behaviour, the situation raises the serious question of how that line is to be drawn. If Massey obliterates a crucial distinction by losing consciousness that he uses a figure of speech as he persistently calls Vixen a woman, perhaps equations of human sexuality and reproductive instincts with those of animals represent a similar loss of consciousness or blind-spot on the part of social scientists and medical writers. The novel's concern with whether human mothers are born or made explores that blind spot.

Bartle Massey's comment about the way reproductive functions such as nursing subsume all female attention and energy echoes the narrator's description of Timothy's Bess, described as standing at her door nursing her baby, and 'feeling as women feel in that position – that nothing else can be expected of them' (p. 239). The distinction between the two Besses in the novel is pertinent to Hetty's representation and her failure to assume the role of the mother. The first Bess we meet is likened to Hetty in her love of finery and the nature of her petty hopes and anxieties; she possesses the pair of large earrings with false garnets, renounced temporarily after Dinah's preaching. The second is her cousin, defined, not by her earrings but by a 'handsome set of matronly jewels' (p. 64). Later at the celebration for Arthur's birthday, Chad's Bess, who has taken to her earrings again, wins a race and, expecting a handsome prize, is bitterly disappointed with the 'grogram gown and a piece of flannel' bestowed on her. Her disappointment is contrasted to the practical and domestic responsibility of her 'discreet matronly cousin' who is happy to carry off the grogram to make clothes for her children (p. 322). The crucial difference between the two Besses, the narrator points out, is that one is a matron, the other a maiden. Hetty is strongly aligned with Chad's Bess, imagistically through her fondness for earrings – Arthur gives her a pair with real garnets and pearls – and specifically through the narrator's commentary. Whether Chad's Bess may one day come to have a set of 'matronly jewels' that she values more highly than her false garnets, depends on how she makes the transition from maiden to matron. It is exactly that transition that George Eliot suggests is so difficult in Hetty's case. As Martin Poyser says of his niece: 'Them young gells are like th' unripe grain; they'll make good meal by-and-by, but they're squashy as yit. Thee't see, Hetty'll be all right when she's got a good husband an' children of her own' (p. 201). His words are usually quoted to show how wrong he is and how right his wife is about Hetty's hard heart. But there is a way in which the text takes Poyser's view seriously. Just as Chad's Bess may turn out 'all right', so might Hetty, under other circumstances, have managed motherhood better. The distinction between the maiden Bess and the matron Bess, between valuing baubles rather than babies, draws attention to Hetty's problem, which is that she must make her transition suddenly, alone and without support.

Motherhood may be a biological process and a social identity, but the narrative demonstrates that it is pre-eminently a relational activity demanding a special kind of self-forgetting love. The text very carefully, even laboriously, prepares the reader to see why Hetty rejects the encounter with such 'an other' as her own baby. She is repeatedly shown to be narrow, vain, childish, incapable of loving unselfishly. Totty Poyser will not go to her, but in a pointed contrast allows Dinah to carry her off; Hetty hates nasty little lambs, hates hatching time, and finds the Poyser children 'as bad as buzzing insects that will come teasing you on a hot day when you want to be quiet' (p. 200). In a passage of heavy foreshadowing, we learn that nothing seems to give her a turn i' th' inside, not even when we thought Totty had tumbled into the pit. To think o' that dear cherub! And we found her wi' her little shoes stuck i' the mud an' crying fit to break her heart by the far horse-pit. But Hetty niver minded it, I could see, though she's been at the nussin' o' the child iver since it was a babby. It's my belief her heart's as hard as a pibble (p. 201).

Of this passage, Blackwood wrote to George Eliot: 'I was positively affected at the illustration [Mrs Poyser] gave of Hetty's supposed strong indifference to the child she had handled from its cradle'.[41] Despite the wish contained in Blackwood's comment, there is nothing 'supposed' about Hetty's indifference. Though as responsive as anyone to Hetty's extraordinary beauty, Mrs Poyser, who has a reputation for seeing and telling the truth about people, can also see her as a cherry with a hard stone of a heart; we should not be surprised therefore that Hetty fails to respond to and preserve her own child. The dangerous assumption that Adam and others make is that Hetty, so child-like herself, will dote upon her children, and again we see the dubious value of human/natural analogies: 'She is almost a child herself, and the little pink round things will hang about her like florets round the central flower' (p. 198). Hetty's child-like qualities, however, indicate her own need to be parented rather than her capacity to parent.[42] By the end of the novel, we see that Adam has revised his reasoning about what makes a suitable mother when he observes of Dinah, 'It's a pity she shouldna be a mother herself', since children are so fond of her (p. 548). In the first place, Adam considers that Hetty, so child-like herself, would look well with children about her; in the second he sees that children are drawn to Dinah. Interestingly, neither view takes into account the wishes or desires of the woman in question.

In the course of the narrative, continued comparisons between Dinah and Hetty allow the narrator to suggest that maternal feeling is a particular and concentrated instance or manifestation of a more general capacity. Strong and unselfish maternal love is akin to fellow-feeling, a sympathetic identification with the lot of another. In *Adam Bede*, as in all George Eliot's novels, those with a capacity for loving others deepen and extend it through their own suffering.[43] Thus Adam Bede himself learns what love is by means of the alphabet of grief, first through his father's death and then through his tribulations with Hetty and Arthur. To the extent that Adam's love for Hetty exemplifies unselfishness and a high degree of sympathetic identification, it approaches mother love, which, at Hetty's trial, is the way the narrator represents it:

> Others thought she looked as if some demon had cast a blighting glance upon her, withered up the woman's soul in her, and left only a hard despairing obstinacy. But the mother's yearning, that completest type of the life in another life which is the essence of real human love, feels the presence of the cherished child even in the debased, degraded man; and to Adam, this pale hard-looking culprit was the Hetty who had smiled at him in the garden under the apple-tree boughs – she was that Hetty's corpse, which he had trembled to look at the first time, and then was unwilling to turn away his eyes from (p. 477).

Adam occupies metaphorically the position of the mother, who identifies most fully in the life of another and whose posture toward the other is the 'essence of real human love'. If Adam's capacity to feel for Hetty approaches 'the mother's yearning', and if, as the text has emphasised, Hetty's pretty face does not guarantee a maternal heart, there would appear to be nothing universal, instinctual or innate about maternal love. And yet, as Hetty's confession shows, George Eliot is clearly reluctant to let go of the notion of a natural and involuntary bond between mother and child.

Hetty's final softening and confession to Dinah informs us that although she had experienced her baby as a heavy weight round her neck, she has also felt an instinctual bond that she cannot sever. Despite the *Saturday Review*, which had remarked on Hetty's 'utter want of mere motherly *instinct* in the manner of the murder of her child', George Eliot is careful to allow Hetty a minimal bond with her newborn infant.[44] A force draws her back after she abandons it and will not allow her to leave the place where she has tried to bury it:

> I turned back the way I'd come. I couldn't help it, Dinah; it was the baby's crying that made me go: and yet I was frightened to death. I thought that man in the smock-frock 'ud see me, and know I put the baby there. But I went on, for all that: I'd left off thinking about going home – it had gone out o' my mind. I saw nothing but that place in the wood where I'd buried the baby... I see it now (p. 500).

Hetty's responses are represented as marginal, involuntary, beyond the exercise of will, amounting to a magnetic pull to the place where she covered the baby in woodchips and turf and the unbearable resounding of the baby's cries in her head. Nevertheless, these rudimentary responses are sufficient to paralyse her plans of escape

173

and hold Hetty in the blank impasse in which she is eventually found. In this way, George Eliot preserves a notional maternal instinct, but distinguishes it from the will and responsibility needed to mother adequately. The text reveals that the biological fact of motherhood is itself but the smallest of passports to maternal responsibility and attachment. Rather, it suggests (as Marian Lewes would later demonstrate with Lewes' sons) that mothering is a conscious and relational activity that requires its own specific capacity.

The text demonstrates how that capacity is shaped and impinged upon by changing circumstances and conditions. Although the narrator's and Mrs Poyser's pronouncements about Hetty anticipate her failure to nourish and protect her child, the narrative of Hetty's flight and her confession call into question some of those earlier judgements. When the narrator describes Hetty as a plant without roots, he (a George Eliot persona) invokes an image that immediately follows and comments ironically on the view of Hetty as a beautiful flower, her eyelids delicate as petals, her long lashes curled like stamens. Around this central flower, her children will hang about her like florets. Undermining – indeed replacing – this image, the narrator describes Hetty rather as one of those plants 'that have hardly any roots: you may tear them from their native nook of rock or wall, and just lay them over your ornamental flower-pot, and they blossom none the worse' (p. 199). But in fact, Hetty cannot be torn from her native nook and blossom none the worse. Going home becomes the strongest motivation after she has given birth: 'I longed so to go back again…. I longed so to be safe at home' (pp. 498–9). At this point, the narrator has to reconsider such earlier judgements as: 'I think she had no feeling at all towards the old house, and did not like the Jacob's Ladder and the long row of hollyhocks in the garden better than other flowers' (p. 199). But though Hetty has no repository of affections bound up with local habitation, no Wordsworthian memories that root her consciously in past and place, she is not without roots. Even if she is not conscious to begin with of her attachment to home, and although she does not live with a sense of appreciation of her surroundings, we see nevertheless how, when in trouble, home is all she can think of. Caught finally between two powerful motivations, she is the runaway child who longs to be home as well as the unwed mother bound to her baby and unable to go home. The text suggests that Hetty's minimal capacity for relationship and rootedness is a primary factor in her failure as a mother; in contradiction it also supports current views of infanticide that emphasise the shame of being seduced and abandoned and the power of community scorn and ostracisation.

As we have seen, George Eliot is concerned to dispel notions of the automatic match between the capacity to mother and the beauty that men find irresistible and associate with a womanly ideal. While Anne Brontë's *Agnes Grey* frankly acknowledges the function of beauty as a means of sexual attraction, George Eliot also admits its power but directs considerable irony and splenetic criticism toward its overvaluation and the tendency to equate physical charms with psychological and moral virtues. As critics of George Eliot have often noted, she writes against the view that 'goodness and beauty in woman' are 'in strict relation to each other; and the latter will be seen always to be the external sign of the former', or the idea that 'the most beautiful and perfect [women], physically, are the most excellent and perfect mentally'.[45] In *Adam Bede* she uses Hetty's case deliberately to undermine the common assumption in biomedical and social discourse that female beauty is evidence of the fittedness of woman for her role as mother:

> It is that portion of the body in immediate connexion with those parts peculiar to her organization, that the greatest beauty of form is found in woman.... Nature ever lavishes her favours on woman in respect of forms; in her the outlines are always undulating and full of grace and suppleness.... The pelvis is the manifestation of the [maternal] instinct – the bust expresses the sentiment of love; within the recesses of the one the embryo man is conceived and nourished; upon the other, whether babe or adult, he is hushed to slumber or soothed in suffering.[46]

Where social and medical discourse on the function of female beauty lauded the wisdom of Nature and the happy equation of external and internal attributes, George Eliot challenged that equation and expressed scepticism about our confidence in our ability to read Nature: 'Nature has her language, and she is not unveracious; but we don't know all the intricacies of her syntax just yet, and in a hasty reading we may happen to extract the very opposite of her real meaning' (p. 198).

There is a moment, however, when the narrator defends Adam's susceptibility to Hetty's beauty, elevating his apparent weakness to a strength, like the capacity to respond to harmonious music. Beauty is here represented not as an attribute of a particular woman, or a mechanism of sexual selection, but as an expression of something

> beyond and far above the one woman's soul that it clothes, as the
> words of genius have a wider meaning than the thought that prompted
> them: it is more than a woman's love that moves us in a woman's
> eyes – it seems to be a far-off mighty love that has come near to us,
> and made speech for itself there; the rounded neck, the dimpled arm,
> move us by something more than their prettiness – by their close
> kinship with all we have known of tenderness and peace (p. 400).

Through reference to a 'far-off mighty love' and 'all we have known
of tenderness and peace' the narrator articulates the desire that
beauty excites in a way that suggests desire for the psychic mother,
the promise of love and wholeness – the illusory oneness of the
imaginary. Indeed, the 'rounded neck, the dimpled arm' might just as
well be attributes of the baby as of the beautiful woman as mother.
This dovetailing image suggests a fusion or oneness in which there is
no subjectivity, no differentiation. Just as we saw the narrator
describe the 'mother's yearning' as the 'essence of all human love', so
the 'far off, mighty love' recalls the child's yearning for the maternal
imago. All love, the narrator suggests here, holds the promise of the
idealised mother, and is composed of projection and desire: 'We look
at the one little woman's face we love, as we look at the face of our
mother earth, and see all sorts of answers to our own yearnings' (p. 254).

Just as George Eliot would argue that ideas of God represent
humankind's best self-conception, so the idealised mother is a
projection of collective yearning for the most unselfish love. Associations of the idealised mother are therefore never far away from the
novel's meditations about human love. But what relationship does
George Eliot's representation of love as the longing for the mother or
the mother's longing for the child bear to the 'real' mothers in the
novel? Since the narrative is very interested in social mothers and
repeatedly focuses on what goes into choosing a wife, and what
makes a mother and shapes her position in the household and
community, we need to explore this relationship further. In *Motherhood and Representation*, E. Ann Kaplan distinguishes the discursively
constructed mother in three representational spheres: the historical,
psychoanalytic and fictional. The first construct is the mother in her
institutional role; the second, the mother in psychoanalytic
discourse, the mother in the unconscious, through whom the subject
is constituted; and the third is the mother in fictional representations
who 'combines the institutionally positioned mother, and the

unconscious mother'.[47] This clarifying scheme is useful for considering the discourse of motherhood in *Adam Bede*, where the idealisation of mother love as the 'completest type of the life in another life which is the essence of real human love' contrasts with the flawed and complex relationships of 'social' mothers.[48]

Lisbeth Bede is not only far from idealised, but her representation allows George Eliot to mark the differences between idealised mother love, and the complexities and ambivalences of 'real' mothers in social situations. On one level, she is important in the novel because her relationship with Adam demonstrates his emotional growth; he becomes more tolerant of a mother who is sometimes burdensome in her dependency. On another, she reveals the combination of power and powerlessness in a mother whose identity is drawn almost exclusively from her maternal status. In the opening scenes, the narrator is critical of her fretting and self-abnegation, which is also a way of inducing guilt. She is the instance from which he generalises about complaining women. When Adam's dog is treated more kindly than his mother, the narrator asks rather cruelly whether we are not kinder to 'the brutes that love us than to the women that love us' because the brutes are dumb (p. 86). We also learn that while Adam resembles his mother, he certainly did not inherit his full brow and intelligence from her.[49] Nevertheless, it is Lisbeth who first articulates the narrator's judgements of both Hetty and Dinah, and Lisbeth, ultimately, who prods her son to see what she has seen – that he and Dinah love each other. Opening Adam's eyes, she chides him: 'thee think'st thy mother knows nought, but she war alive afore thee wast born'(p. 545). Although Seth warns her not to interfere, she is prepared at this point to take a risk in order to facilitate Adam's happiness. This is not to say that Lisbeth's exertions for Adam's happiness are either self-sacrificing or disinterested. If Adam's wife ought to be a care-giving replacement for his mother – 'An' what wut do when thy mother's gone, an' nobody to take care on thee as thee gett'st a bit o' victual comfortable i' the mornin'?' (p. 543) – this care-giver is also meant to tend to Adam's mother. It is not insignificant that Dinah's children are named Adam and Lisbeth.

Early in the novel, Lisbeth admits to Dinah that she is glad not to have had daughters of her own, since they are 'poor queechy things, gells is; I allays wanted to ha' lads as could fend for theirsens' (p. 155). Her verdict on daughters suggests a fear of her own vulnerability as a woman. As the mother who derives satisfaction from her strong son – Adam is as tall and upright as a poplar tree – her relationship to him exemplifies Freud's notion of the child's meaning for the mother as phallus. Subordinate and self-sacrificing, she can be seen as the mother in abjection. She is also, in some measure, the phallic mother, whose claims for herself are expressed through jealous possessiveness. In Adam's dreams of Hetty, for example, she appears as the angry inhibitor of his love's fulfilment, and he later chides her that she ought not to want to rule over him 'body and soul' (p. 260). We note that it is only in relation to this strong elder son that Lisbeth's passionate maternal feelings are engaged. In an undisguised partiality that quite eclipses Seth, she sets Adam idolatrously at the centre of her existence. Because she loves him and derives her sense of self from his being, she is contradictorily 'patient and complaining, self-renouncing and exacting' (p. 87). The narrator points to the mixture of idolatry and possessiveness she experiences at Arthur's birthday feast:

> Poor Lisbeth was suffering from a strange conflict of feelings. Her joy and pride in the honour paid to her darling son Adam was beginning to be worsted in the conflict with the jealousy and fretfulness which had revived when Adam came to tell her that Captain Donnithorne desired him to join the dancers in the hall. Adam was getting more and more out of her reach; she wished all the old troubles back again, for then it mattered more to Adam what his mother said and did (p. 326).

The tensions that gather in George Eliot's representation of Lisbeth are felt when she is first described in Chapter four, and the narrator is using Adam's likeness to her to talk about the nature of family resemblances. The difficulty of reading Nature's syntax, which the narrator demonstrates in Adam's assumptions about Hetty, is also manifest in trying to understand oneself as similar yet distinct from one's close relatives. Besides being syntactically tricky, Nature is also a great tragic dramatist, who 'knits us together by bone and muscle, and divides us by the subtler web of our brains; blends yearning and repulsion; and ties us by our heartstrings to the beings that jar us at every movement' (pp. 83–4). This passage directs us to think not only about the apparent lottery of inheritance, but about how the meanings of physical attributes change as they manifest themselves in successive incarnations. It is the dissonance between the first form and subsequent forms that makes familial relationship so poignant and complex, as when we hear a 'voice with the very cadence of our own uttering the thoughts we despise' (p. 84). We see eyes so like our mother's, but averted in alienation. The generalised meditation implies Adam's situation as it focuses on the shameful father from whom he inherits his mechanical instinct, and the anxious mother whose likeness he bears, but whose difference from himself he needs to assert. A slight change in tone occurs as the narrator looks ahead to the recognition of the mother, 'whose face we begin to see in the glass as our own wrinkles come' (p. 84). As we age, physical changes may recall the 'long-lost mother' and demand a reassessment of who we are now in relation to how we understood her then. Thus the fretting and irrationally persistent mother materialises in the glass as Adam looks at himself, and demands a continual revisiting of self and (m)other. What began as a thought about how jarringly we experience Nature's work of wedding us through our physicality to our kin, ends as the return of the 'long-lost mother' in our aging faces. At that point, the narrator implies that rather than feeling the need to distance ourselves from our resemblance to the mother, we may welcome the finding of the 'long-lost' and stand in new relation to our impatient younger selves. More than anyone else, the mother in this meditation represents the conditions of self-knowledge and the means by which we are continually marking both differentiation and kinship.

The representation of Adam's mother is complex because it articulates a range of sometimes contradictory perceptions about mothering: the narrator's dismissive, slightly patronising treatment of the complaining mother, an understanding of the way maternal possessiveness in relation to a strong son reflects on the social position of women, a sense of the mother's subjectivity and conflict, and a perception that to accept and honour the mother is a sign of one's own growth and maturity. By considering Hetty's failure as a mother in relation to the larger discourse of mothering in the novel, we can see that although the narrative idealises mother love as 'the essence of real human love', it also qualifies idealising and naturalising accounts of motherhood and attempts to negotiate the complexities of mother-child relationships and the way social constructions of motherhood shape subjectivities.

Sorrow on the Sea: The business of maternity

The feeble wail of murdered childhood in its agony assails our ears at every turn, and is borne on every breeze.... In the quiet of the bedroom we raise the box-lid, and the skeletons are there. In the calm evening walk we see in the distance the suspicious-looking bundle, and the mangled infant is within. By the canal side, or in the water, we find the dead child. In the solitude of the wood we are horrified by the ghastly sight; and if we betake ourselves to the rapid rail in order to escape the pollution, we find at our journey's end that the mouldering remains of a murdered innocent have been our travelling companion; and that the odour from that unsuspected parcel truly indicates what may be found within.[50]

With its catalogue of suspicious-looking bundles, skeletons in boxes, mouldering remains and mangled infants, William Ryan's treatise on infanticide summons heightened rhetorical power to make its audience see and feel the epidemic of child-murder that Ryan claims is sweeping through England. The rhetoric moves into the realm of the sensational as it attempts to represent the horrible spectre of mass infanticide. In 1865, the *Saturday Review* wrote of the prevalence of infanticide as a 'foul current of life, running like a pestilential sewer beneath the smooth surface of society'.[51] Similar terms describe the subject matter of sensation novels of this decade, which were accused of dwelling on 'the sinks and sewers of society' and portraying the 'obscene birds of night'.[52] The particular 'foul current' of which the *Saturday Review* speaks is, however, one which very few works of fiction at this time cared to tap. Bigamy, murder, seduction, wrongful incarceration, may have been common subjects for sensational treatment, but infanticide and child-murder were not.[53]

In 1868 Tinsley Brothers published Lady Emma Caroline Wood's *Sorrow on the Sea*, a fast-paced, lurid sensation novel. According to the scanty accounts available, its genteel author was a talented, determined woman, who began her career as a novelist at the age of sixty-six, shortly after her clergyman husband left her a widow. In the next dozen years she produced fourteen novels. She had also already produced some thirteen children, among whom were the notorious Katherine O'Shea, Field Marshal Sir Evelyn Wood, and the novelist Anna Steele.[54] *Sorrow on the Sea* was found to be objectionable; it shocked and outraged readers especially on account of its sexually predatory villain, and its graphic depiction of baby disposal and unscrupulous midwifery. A review in the *Athenaeum* declared that 'the details of these volumes are literally unfit for presentation in any language'.[55] Lady Wood's brother-in-law, Baron Hatherley, reputedly bought up all available copies shortly after publication and had them burned.[56]

Since *Sorrow on the Sea* is a little-known work, I will briefly summarise the action before turning to discuss its purchase on topical issues relating to the construction of maternal instinct. Cora Noble, the beautiful but penniless daughter of a naval officer killed in action, is offered a position as lady's companion in the Helmingham household. There she meets Rufus, charming and unscrupulous, and Edmond, his elder brother, a scarred but brave and honest naval officer. (Rufus reads *Tom Jones*, not for the story, but only for the satirical observations at the beginnings of chapters – a sure sign, the narrator hints, that he is morally corrupt.) By the end of the second volume, Cora has secretly married Edmond, despite the satanic plots of the jealous Rufus to part them. After one brief night of wedded bliss, Edmond must depart on his latest naval command. Cora soon learns that she is expecting a child and also that Edmond's vessel has been wrecked. Although he is presumed dead, we know he is in fact stranded on a desert island in the unsettling company of a young but precociously developed maiden, the improbable but not impossible offspring of an Otaheite woman and a Scots mutineer from the Bounty. Rufus learns of Cora's marriage and pregnancy through intercepting her letters, and, concerned that her marriage and production of an heir will interfere with his inheritance of his father's estate, determines to have Cora and her child removed from the scene. Through a contact in London, he arranges matters with Mrs Drury of 'Off-Hand Farm'.[57] He then contrives an advertisement for a lying-in house, and brings it slyly to Cora's attention: 'Ladies requiring temporary retirement might be attended with perfect secrecy and safety, and the infant provided for on reasonable terms' (p. 14). Cora takes the bait, corresponds with a female agent in London and is sent to the 'The Retreat' (alias 'Off-Hand Farm') in Essex.

In *Sorrow on the Sea*, the vulnerability of a young mother attempting to save her child from the clutches of a midwife employed by her evil brother-in-law provides occasion for sensational and melodramatic treatment. While the heroine, Cora Noble, is a paragon of virtuous and instinctive motherhood, the callous midwife, herself the mother of a Caliban-like son whom she despises and exploits, contradicts any notion of natural and intrinsic mother love. It may be argued that Wood's representation of mothering is inflected by issues relating to both class and race. The narrator describes Mrs Drury and her son in terms of savage, primitive nations and the 'more noble brutes'. Hugh Drury has a coarse, animal face, and his legs, 'the point in a figure where savage nations are most deficient in symmetry, were bandy and devoid of calves'(p. 19). He regards his mother with profound awe and pays her the obedience which the 'Indians yield to the Devil'. Nancy Drury is herself not an ill-looking woman, but her face is similarly coarse and sensual. It is hinted that Hugh is the illegitimate son of the proprietor of the farm; Nancy Drury was once his favourite servant, and he has supposedly placed her and her son in the position they hold 'from motives of gratitude for former services' (p. 21). But while Wood's representation of the evil midwife and baby-farmer depends on notions of class and degeneration, she also unsettles current tendencies to demonise the baby-farmer and sanctify the innocent mother.

The journalist James Greenwood's account of baby-farming in *The Seven Curses of London* described the likes of Mrs Drury as 'those monsters in woman's clothing who go about seeking for babies to devour'.[58] By demonising the child-minders, he could preserve the innocence and purity of young mothers who were forced to farm out their babies while they worked. Wood's novel certainly associates Mrs Drury with the age-old superstition of witchcraft and evil that surrounded midwives, and figures her as low, brutal and degenerate, but she destabilises accounts like Greenwood's that vilify the baby-farmer and midwife.[59] We learn that the many clients for Mrs Drury's business in paid infanticide come from all classes, and far from being duped, her clients are well aware of the nature of their contracts with her. By having the midwife dilate on the various services she performs for both rich and poor, provincial and metropolitan clients, Lady Wood expresses a topical anxiety that the numbers of women in need of a Mrs Drury may be disturbingly high, and that such women are drawn not only from the ranks of the 'lower classes'.

Concern with criminal baby-farming practices grew during the press exposures of the 1860s. The much-publicised trial of Charlotte Winsor, who took in and 'put away' illegitimate children occurred in 1865.[60] In the same year, the *British Medical Journal* carried a story about 'some country districts of England where child-killing by opium is monstrous'.[61] In 1868 the same journal ran its exposé of baby-farming and baby-murder, which revealed that under the moral and legal pressures of Victorian social organisation, pregnancy, childbirth and childcare spawned needs with significant commercial potential.[62] Undercover investigations, in which Dr Alfred Wiltshire visited many advertised lying-in houses, disclosed that they varied from straightforward maternity homes, struggling to provide decent care, to establishments that would procure abortion, guarantee stillbirth, or arrange for baby-planting or adoption.[63] These articles attracted wide publicity in the press.[64] Operating from a farmhouse in what is effectively and ominously described as a 'thinly populated' part of Essex, Mrs Drury's establishment offers both local and metropolitan clients a range of chilling services similar to those detailed in recent press coverage. Before Rufus arrives at 'Off-Hand Farm', we witness Mrs Drury's interviews with a number of local women. One wants something from 'the wise woman' to still her fractious babe at night. The child is illegitimate and its father refuses to contribute to its upkeep. Mrs Drury observes: 'Them chance-children have a bad life on 't. They're best out of the world'(p. 28). It transpires that the young woman has someone who wishes to marry her, but does not want the responsibility of the child. Mrs Drury asks if he'd marry her if she *put the child out to nurse?*' (p. 28). In the interchange, conducted by innuendo and euphemism, a price is negotiated and Mrs Drury promises to put the child to sleep in her bed. '"*My* children all sleep sound", she added with a little laugh' (p. 29).

Mrs Drury's conversation with Rufus is conducted through similar indirect means. He suggests that it would be a mercy were heaven to take the infant, and she observes that babies often die: 'Sometimes the mother's milk don't seem to agree with 'um; sometimes they fare sleepy, and go off so' (p. 35). She dispenses with delicacy, however, when they quarrel over terms of payment: 'When gentlefolks go a murdering they must pay for it' (p. 36). He threatens to complain to her friends in London; she retorts that she merely pays them a percentage for a recommendation, and she has nothing to fear from his threat. They need her more than she needs them. Mrs Drury then explains the many occasions that call for her talents: sometimes her London contacts want a baby saved and kept, just as you do a puppy, so that women who can't 'breed' can make their husbands a present of a living child. 'Sometimes them as breeds out of course, when their husbands are in foreign parts, like to come down here, and I put 'em to bed and keep the child for them, all close and comfortable, and the good man don't suspect when he comes home' (pp. 37–8). Her clients bless her, and call her their saviour, but occasionally she has to blackmail them when times are tough. While the narrator is officially condemnatory of these practices, the image of a grateful clientele hints at the pressures created by the moral, legal and economic regulation of reproduction, and the attempts that women contrive to alleviate those pressures and to negotiate the demands and limitations of the social system in which they function.

In a subsequent chapter, Nancy Drury explains to her doltish son that Cora's child, now sleeping peacefully with his mother upstairs, has to remain alive until Rufus sees it, because otherwise he is unlikely to pay up. She reiterates the point to Rufus: 'I find I don't get paid for my job if the kids are still-born. They say 'twas the hand of God and not my hand, and they shirk my dues – no, no; if things are to be done, I must see my money down first, as you've seen the babe alive and likely to live' (p. 50). When Rufus asks how she accomplishes her task, she is again happily expansive, and details her various techniques of suffocation and exposure.

In the scene where the unsuspecting Cora and her newly-born son sleep upstairs, while the midwife and her son discuss the situation downstairs, the narrator escalates tension and stimulates suspense by lingering on Cora's new maternal bliss: 'Heaven has given to human and brute mothers such intense enjoyment in the first possession of their newly-born progeny. To fall asleep with these heavenly treasures close to the maternal bosom seems enough to compensate for suffering past and to come' (p. 45). By invoking the notion of compensation, Wood may seem to be articulating a view similar to Maudsley's on maternal instinct. Maudsley observed that if it wasn't for maternal instinct, a mother would hardly be prepared to provide the 'base services which the child exacts' from her.[65] But while Maudsley saw parturition and nursing as excretory and secretory processes that no one would perform unless driven by instinct, Wood represents nursing as an intensely pleasurable, erotic experience: 'But of the future she was content not to think, when the small blind lips of her boy sought his nourishment from her breast, and when his tiny fingers expanded and contracted in their pressure over the heart which throbbed with the intensity of her joy' (p. 47). Yet even as she dwells on maternal pleasure, the narrator insists on the brevity of bliss, apostrophising the mother to warn that this moment of fusion and tenderness cannot last: 'Caress the smooth head, yet unplotting of evil, gentle Mother! Press the tiny crimson lips to thy bosom, which as yet cannot wound thee by expressions of petulance or indifference ... Poor mother! Thy elysium is when thy infant sleeps at thy breast' (pp. 46–7). Quite apart from the horrors being prepared downstairs, there are sufferings aplenty to be endured in the ordinary course of mothering. In one way, the narrator's prophesies evoke the topos of the self-sacrificing mother. Despite ingratitude and without recompense, she must persistently minister to the needs of this growing other. But in another way, they go beyond that. For a brief moment, a maternal space opens in Wood's novel where the mother's future experience and reactions are imaginable. The narrator's warnings seek to represent the mother's experience of wounding, worry, separation and finally marginalisation. Her focus on the mother's subjectivity and vulnerability anticipates modern explorations of the maternal space. 'One does not give birth in pain', writes Kristeva, 'one gives birth to pain: the child represents it and henceforth it settles in, it is continuous. Obviously you may close your eyes, cover up your ears, teach courses, run errands, tidy up the house, think about objects, subjects. But a mother is always branded by pain, she yields to it.'[66]

Like other sensation novels of the 1860s, this one abounds in incident and its plot is shaped by a constant succession of climaxes.[67] Its graphic account of Mrs Drury's trade and methods relies on topical material, indicating the book's typicality, but it does not share all the characteristic features of the sensation novel. The *Quarterly* observed that 'a tale which aims at electrifying the nerves of its reader is never thoroughly effective unless the scene be laid in our own days and among the people we are in the habit of meeting'.[68] Unlike the typical sensation novel, *Sorrow on the Sea* is set at the end of the eighteenth century, partly perhaps to accommodate that section of the plot that has the hero marooned on a desert island with the daughter of a mutineer from the Bounty, and partly to pretend that the shocking practices of Mrs Drury are a thing of the past. The pretence is thin, however, for apart from the dating of the action, the world of the novel is thoroughly mid-Victorian. Winifred Hughes suggests that the sensation novel takes over the form and trappings of popular stage melodrama but radically alters their meaning. Melodrama depends on the unproblematic distinction between good and evil and on unambiguous resolution; it leaves a final stasis in which good triumphs and evil is trounced. While sensation fiction appears to do the same, it actually unsettles the very codes and standards on which assessments of good and evil are based. Beneath the cosy and respectable domestic surfaces lurk taint and corruption, so that even when perpetrators are brought to justice, the troublesome sense of association between respectability and corruption remains.[69] Despite this novel's conventional happy ending, domestic bliss is not unalloyed. The narrator hints that far from being all to each other, both husband and wife have had their greatest emotional and physical crises without each other. The hero's domestic happiness is slightly undercut by his memory of the exotic island girl who surpassed his wife: she did not just endure faithfully, but actually died for him, sacrificing herself to the cannibals who were hunting him. For evermore he keeps a lock of her hair in his diary. In contrast, the great crisis of the heroine's life has been a maternal, not a romantic one. Rather than saving or being saved by the hero as a prelude to marriage, her greatest agonies and strongest exertions have been on behalf of her child, who displaces the husband's prime position in the advised hierarchy of family relations. The ending upholds middle-class domestic ideals, while suggesting simultaneously that such ideals conceal undermining flaws.

But more importantly, the closing dispensation of the power of evil and good is less than resounding, for evil is dispersed rather than disposed of. Rufus, the villainous brother, disappears, but we learn that he has merely left the country for a successful legal career in America. What is more alarming is that the unscrupulous midwife makes for London, where she will presumably find an extensive clientele and set up in business once more. In the city, the narrator observes darkly, the only competition for her kind of work is the Thames, which, as everyone knew, was a favoured place for disposing of infant bodies.[70] Mrs Drury's survival suggests that she and the clients she serves are uncomfortable facts of social life that not only jar with prevailing ideals of motherhood and constructions of maternal instinct but call them into question.

Lady Audley's Secret: Madness and badness

The debates about wet-nursing and infanticide preserve the notion of an idealised maternal instinct by blaming distortions of it on the effects of a corrupt society or different class values and practices. Another not unrelated mode of recuperating the notion of a natural and instinctive maternal function in the face of contradictory evidence was to represent maternal deviance as insanity. Thus one of the medical witnesses in the controversial Brough infanticide case of 1854 declared:

> We cannot, for a single instant, believe that any mother, however lost to all sense of shame, and deeply steeped in vice, could, in violation of one of the most powerful instincts wisely implanted in the human heart, proceed deliberately, in defiance, and in total disregard of

appeals that would have roused even the affection and wrung the heart of a Hottentot or New Zealand savage, destroy six of her unoffending and innocent children! [71]

In his insistence on the maternal as 'one of the most powerful instincts' and its comparison of the accused with a 'Hottentot or New Zealand savage', the witness makes clear that if Mrs Brough is not found to be insane, maternal instinct and civilisation itself are threatened. Given such an enormous ideological investment in motherhood, Victorian courts were prone to find infanticide *prima facie* evidence of insanity. Yet angry responses to the successful insanity plea in Mrs Brough's case denounced the masquerade of badness as madness, and pointed to the perilous state of civilised life if every 'homicidal orgasm' was to be construed as an attack of insanity.

In spite of the 'unnaturalness of her crime', mothers accused of killing their infants were, paradoxically, objects of considerable public sympathy in mid-Victorian England. None of the thirty-one women convicted of infanticide between 1849 and 1864 was executed.[72] Reflecting public feeling, the courts took a very lenient and exculpatory attitude towards women facing infanticide charges, and the Home Secretary responded to an awareness that the public would not countenance hanging.[73] Expressing the stark moralistic side of the debate, William Ryan was incensed at the way the courts appeared to bend over backwards to exculpate the women charged: Lord Russell's opinion that the law ought not to affix capital punishment to the murder of children under a certain age, say six months, scandalised him.[74] To act on this doctrine, said Ryan, would be to 'out-Herod Malthus'.[75] Unencumbered apparently by the scientific and theological complexities of today's abortion debate, Victorian law did not recognise an infant as a separate legal being unless there was evidence of independent circulation, and until it was fully born and separate from the mother's body. If it could not be proved that the child was thus separate from the mother at the time of the killing, a charge of infanticide could not be upheld.

But as the author of 'Child-murder and its punishment' recognised:

If entire proof of live-birth be in all cases rigorously demanded on trials of child-murder, it is scarcely possible when the prisoner is ably defended, that any convictions for the crime should take place…. The child is proved to have lived and breathed, but the medical evidence fails to show that the living and breathing took place or continued after entire delivery.[76]

187

In a case where the head of the infant had been almost severed from its body, Justice Earle reminded his jury that medical life did not necessarily correspond with legal life. The law incensed reformers who spoke angrily of the fact that in England it was 'no crime to strangle a child with a cord, to smash its skull with a hammer, or to cut its throat from ear to ear' if at the time its lower extremities were within the mother's body.[77]

Among those who called for the execution of convicted infanticides, Mary Anne Baines deplored the courts' inconsistencies and hoped that while the sentence of capital punishment remained on the statute book, the law 'not be made exceptional in favour of Infanticide'. Just because the poor, erring woman was alone made to bear the whole burden of her obloquy, and her sinning partner enjoyed 'all but complete immunity' did not mean that no one was to be held responsible for the crime of infanticide. To satisfy its conscience, 'society' was too ready to bestow 'an undue amount of sympathy upon her whom it has doubly wronged'.[78] Baines's views raise two interesting problems in infanticide convictions – the question of responsibility and the nature of public conscience. She reasons that the first wrong (women are left to face the consequences of sexual transgression alone) gives rise to a second (no one is punishable and no one to blame). This means that justice is defeated and the 'present state of things is the consequence'. Her views are grounded in the assumption that punishment functions as a deterrent: someone must bear responsibility or the slaughter of infants will continue.[79] She articulates, I think, the impasse in which courts found themselves. Since most of the infanticide convictions involved illegitimate children, the aberrant mother was readily conceived of as a victim, just as the representation of prostitutes at this time emphasised their victim status. If juries and judges were sympathetic to the 'poor, erring woman' who had to bear the shame alone, how could they also allow punishment to fulfil its function as a deterrent?

One way out of this impasse was to accept that the accused was acting with diminished responsibility. Recommendations of mercy in cases of conviction meant that 'the guilty were often reprieved as criminal lunatics'.[80] Many factors converged in the acceptability of the insanity plea in cases of maternal aberration: cultural assumptions of female dependency, passivity and lack of responsibility, medical representations of the instability of female reproductive functioning, the need to preserve the ideologically important construct of maternal instinct, the reluctance to probe questions of poverty, class, and the economic implications of the sexual double standard. But the medicalisation of infanticide also brought with it a host of problems that exposed ideological contradictions in the construction of motherhood. On the one hand, 'mother' meant instinctive care, nurturing, responsibility and self-sacrifice; on the other the mother's 'parturition' and 'confinement' became associated with precarious mental health, derangement, emotional perversity, and murderous destructiveness. By the 1870s, L. S. Winslow's *Manual of Lunacy* described puerperal mania not merely as derangement after childbirth, but as the new mother's desire to harm or murder her infant.[81]

Medico-legal representations of maternal insanity are concerned with how to draw the fine line between badness and madness. 'If I were inclined to sophistry', wrote Dr Robert Semple, 'it would not be very difficult to show that crime itself is a species of insanity; for the law having been made for the good of all, whether individuals or communities, it is clear that he who commits a crime is really injuring himself, and as his so doing is contrary to the common instincts of human nature, he ought to be considered insane.'[82] The crime of infanticide was indeed seen as a species of insanity. Semple argued that if so many women were found to be disturbed because of milk fever or puerperal insanity, then why were they not more carefully watched beforehand? 'Why did not some of the witnesses, and especially the Medical ones, keep a watchful eye upon the conduct of these unhappy mothers, and thus prevent the commission of horrible infanticide? Why is the commission of murder to be the only valued evidence of insanity?'[83] These questions ground a rationale for the medical profession's control and surveillance of the postpartum period. 'Confinement' becomes a very literal usage, suggesting that the time after birth is when the female system is most unstable and requires most medical supervision.

Maternal insanity is itself a slippery term that signifies both madness occasioned by becoming a mother (puerperal insanity) as well as madness inherited from the mother (insanity transmitted through the maternal line). This discourse of insanity allows matters of class, economic and social position to be represented as the instability of the female body, and its propensity to pass on such instability to its female issue. To construct deviation or aberration as internal malfunctioning is one way of silencing arguments about the social factors that bear on constructions of deviant behaviour. Mary Elizabeth Braddon's popular sensation novel, *Lady Audley's Secret*, exposes what it means to explain deviance in terms of an inherently unstable female body, whose instability is most evident when it becomes a maternal body. The text explores many aspects of the construction of maternal insanity, both in the sense of the insanity occasioned by motherhood, and in the way insanity was thought to pass from mother to daughter.

In Lady Audley's maternal history, women go mad at the point that they become mothers. Braddon's figuring of childbirth and new motherhood as a time of great instability is consonant with the representations of medical discourse, but rather than suggesting that such instability is the result of a fragile and highly wrought reproductive mechanism, she shows that it is a response to specific cultural and socio-economic conditions. Motherhood is a time of heightened dependency and vulnerability, when previous self-identification is challenged and a new subject position develops. Becoming a mother may also mean confronting the ways in which one 'becomes' one's mother. Motherhood, as Lady Audley conceives it, is a process of reduplication proving that a woman's only identity is to become her mother. Lady Audley repeatedly associates her mother's madness with dependency, drudgery and poverty. On becoming a mother herself, she confronts exactly what she sought to avoid – drudgery and dependency and want – and she experiences fits of madness which cease when she takes action to make a new and better life for herself. Such action, as befits a good sensation novel, involves abdicating the care of her son, changing her married name, passing herself off as a governess, committing bigamy, attempting murder, and plotting arson.

In so far as Braddon hunts with the hounds, Lady Audley is shown to be a beautiful but wicked imposter, who must be punished for her attempts to muscle in on the class position and privilege to which she is not entitled. Braddon encourages us to see Lady Audley's confession of madness as a ploy to avert prosecution for her many crimes. When cornered, she melodramatically confesses her history of maternal insanity, thereby, she thinks, trumping her detective nephew. She plays the card of her own history of puerperal insanity and its hereditary pedigree through her maternal line, knowing that proof of it is likely to win her clemency in the courts. Not only does she come from a long line of madwomen, she says, but her own imbalance was triggered by the birth of her child. She knows too that her case will never get to court, for her nephew is unlikely to bring 'everlasting disgrace' on the family name he venerates: "'They'll put me away somewhere, I suppose", my lady thought. "That's the worst they can do for me."'[84]

Braddon teases her readers with the vexed distinction between madness and badness, vice and insanity, but she draws on their familiarity with the controversial insanity plea less to hint that crime may masquerade as insanity than to point out that her society would rather accept an explanation of madness than confront the implications of female transgression and deviance. We see her running with the hare, therefore, as she explores the way transgressive behaviour and insanity may both be responses to thwarting and confining social conditions. The novel manipulates the discourse of madness provocatively to make the reader think about maternal inheritance in a symbolic way, not as a matter of biological organisation and bodily functioning, but in terms of legal, social and economic position, and psychologically in relation to the formation of subjectivity.

Critics of the Victorian novel have commented on the 'pervasive motherlessness' of the heroine, and the way young women are 'wildly unmothered' even where they are not motherless. In a number of fictional situations, however, the mother's legacy asserts itself as a determining and inescapable inheritance.[85] Dead mothers live on in their daughters' inherited propensities; daughters are trapped in what their mothers pass on. A mild instance of such determinism is the hapless heroine of *East Lynne* whose momentary lapse means that she loses all. She had a mother, we recall, who was a perfectly admirable and steady woman but for one 'mad act' – she was persuaded to elope and married without a settlement. This brief history of Lady Isabel's mother offered in the opening pages of the novel accounts not only for her daughter's portionless position, but registers a maternal instability that will later be tapped in Isabel's one 'mad act', also under persuasion and described as a 'blind leap in a moment of wild passion'.[86] The implication, never explicit, is that the otherwise unimpeachable Isabel inherits her propensity for passion, flight and persuasion from her otherwise unimpeachable mother. Far more explicit is the relationship, in *Jane Eyre*, between Bertha Rochester and her mother. Although we learn that Bertha's excesses have nurtured the seeds of madness she inherited, she appears also to have inherited the tendency to excess. As Rochester puts it, his wife is the 'true daughter of an infamous mother'. Neither *East Lynne* nor *Jane Eyre* is concerned with the daughter's responses to her mother or how the knowledge of her mother's temperament and fate shape her own sense of self; each woman is simply determined by the mother's nature.[87] In *Lady Audley's Secret*, however, the heroine's struggle to avoid her maternal inheritance is the wellspring of her actions, and the novel explores maternal insanity as a metaphor for the daughter's social and psychic inheritance rather than using it to signify her biological instability.

For a work that addresses itself in many ways to the question of madness, *Lady Audley's Secret* broaches the topic only as it nears its conclusion. In the mechanics of this sensation novel, madness is the most melodramatic of a series of scandalous disclosures, all of which may have been anticipated, but the history of madness, conventional as it is, startles even the canniest reader, since Lady Audley appears throughout the novel to be perfectly sane. This last secret is also the means by which the novel effects closure: after she has been certified insane, Lady Audley can be handily dispatched to a home-like asylum. On the face of it, madness is the secret now told, but it functions in significant ways more as 'cover-up' than disclosure.[88]

While we are asked to associate the disclosure of madness with a 'coming out' – the latent hereditary taint is made patent to explain the heroine's conduct – I want to argue that Braddon shows how the discourse of madness displaces the economic and class issues already raised in the novel and deflects their uncomfortable implications. Elaine Showalter has argued that Braddon's novel is subversive because it demonstrates that deviance from a norm of womanly submission and obedience is likely to be labelled madness.[89] But Braddon's sensation novel goes further than criticising Victorian constructions of femininity; it points a finger at the work done by discourses of morality and madness in establishing and protecting class boundaries. What makes *Lady Audley's Secret* a fascinating text is that it apprehends social and medical discourses in the act of enunciating the nature of an aberrant 'other' in order to shape a healthy, middle-class self. Until madness is pulled out of the hat as a solution and the means of plot resolution, what seems primarily to be the matter with Lady Audley is that she threatens to violate class boundaries and exclusions, and to get away with appropriating social power beyond her entitlement. Having married Sir Michael, she has made an immense shift from powerlessness to a position of considerable influence. It does not escape the notice of his household that, having been little better than a servant when she was the governess in the doctor's house, she now controls Audley Court's household keys, an important signifier of domestic and class power, which declare Lady Audley's new role in managing the 'lower' orders rather than being one of their number.[90] The events of Lady Audley's life, which are gradually revealed as the novel progresses toward her final confession, emphasise her bid for a position of power and comfort, which the keys of Audley Court symbolise. She first refuses to accept her position as the daughter of a mad and impoverished mother; later she refuses to be crushed when her attempt to marry money fails because the wealthy father of the oafish dragoon, George Talboys, has cut him off. Instead of capitulating, she sets about making a new life for herself after George deserts her to seek his fortune in Australia. Male susceptibility to female beauty being what it is, the narrator acknowledges, Lucy has a golden opportunity to remake her life when Sir Michael falls in love with her. It may seem implausible that Sir Michael would readily accept her story of her background – an orphanage and a quiet secluded convent school life. But the way in which Sir Michael dupes himself is exactly the shocking point. When inappropriate connections are made, disaster can be expected to follow; an adequate background check is dispensed with, quality control fails and social ranks open to the wrong kind. Playing on current fears about the wrong kinds of women passing themselves off as governesses, Braddon thrills and horrifies her readers with the proposition that the usurper may look right, but who knows what tainted depths her beauty conceals?

When Sir Michael proposes, Lucy briefly hints at her mother's problems of poverty and deprivation but does not mention madness: 'My mother – But do not let me speak of her. Poverty, poverty, trials, vexations, humiliations, deprivations! You cannot tell; you, who are amongst those for whom life is so smooth and easy; you can never guess what is endured by such as we' (pp. 10–11). Lucy Audley's difference ('you' as opposed to 'we') is signalled here in terms of her family's socio-economic position just as in the course of the novel as a whole, what is outside – a matter of economic stress and social need – is inscribed and represented as inside, a deviant and disruptive force within the unacceptable woman that wreaks havoc on traditional stabilities and pieties. While madness receives most attention as the sensational secret, social position and poverty are really the issues at stake. Indeed, the desire to change the latter is what leads to the actions that symptomise the former.

Although her biographer Robert Wolff claims that only in later novels did Mary Elizabeth Braddon learn to satirise Victorian social life 'so skilfully that her readers need not see her doing it', *Lady Audley's Secret* offers strong evidence that her skills are already finely honed.[91] She writes with an eye on the circulating libraries as custodians of middle-class morality, and with deference to those readers who would be happy to see Lady Audley put away discreetly for her wickedness, and without public scandal. Taking care not to offend, she closes her story hoping that 'no one will take objection to my story because the end of it leaves the good people all happy and at peace' (p. 447). The 'bad' heroine, whose allure may have fooled us as it initially captivated her step-nephew, Robert Audley, is punished and her badness rationalised through its representation as madness. But the emerging picture of Lady Audley's life history and sense of abandonment does elicit sympathy, even though the narrator never fails to comment censoriously and sanctimoniously on her heroine's thoughts and behaviour. But then again, the narrator often undermines sanctimoniousness or teases a complacent reader, trustful of appearances, as she hints at the dire thoughts and dangerous motivations that may be going on under the superficial calm of gracious, socially-approved behaviour. At times the narrator seems to favour Robert Audley and to look upon his final marriage and assumption of a career with approval, but the narrative tone also encourages us to see him as self-righteous and even misogynistic.

While the narrator endorses and blesses Robert's union with Clara, the domestic idyll she presents of Robert, Clara, and her brother George is a mocking parody of respectable upper middle-class aspirations. For though Robert Audley comes from a family of landed gentry, his development through the novel from a lethargic and purposeless drifter to a model husband, father, and provider is a parable of solid middle-class virtue: he proceeds from upper-class dissolution and the idle pursuit of pleasure to a life of energy, discipline, work and duty. It is the self-appointed task of exposing and expelling Lady Audley and winning Clara Talboys that prompts him to put away his Meerschaum pipes and his French novels. (We note, however, that while his reading of these French novels may sap his energy, it leaves his morals intact. He is less susceptible than Lady Audley, who is also an avid and corrupted reader of romances and yellow-papered novels, thought by vituperative critics to be dangerous to feminine health and moral well-being.) Whereas he comes to symbolise the stable future of respectable English society, she represents what threatens it. Most tellingly, Robert marries for love; Lucy Audley has married for position and money. We remember that Sir Michael dismisses his first marriage as a 'dull jog-trot bargain made to keep some estate or other in the family' and deludes himself that with Lucy he has found love at last (p. 6). But Sir Michael's second marriage is shown to be a grotesque parody of love supposedly triumphing over class alliance. It contrasts with Robert's choice of Clara, who represents the right and natural dictation of the heart; he could after all have made a more fiscally-minded alliance with his receptive cousin, Alicia Audley. What is right about Clara, we suspect, is that she is a proper civiliser of men, the conduct books' exemplary wife whose function was to regulate and socialise from the domestic space. She urges Robert to use his 'talents and opportunities' and to undertake a life of 'serious work' being 'useful to his fellow-creatures and gaining a reputation for himself' (p. 437). He presumably does just that for the last we hear of Robert is that he makes his name and his fortune as a barrister. Suggesting that he now profitably rubs shoulders with the members of an exclusive class from which his clientele is drawn, the narrator tells us that Robert comes to fame in a breach of promise case – Hobbs vs. Nobbs.

In order to see how the novel implicates the discourse of madness in redistributing questions of class and power as matters of biological inheritance and gendered pathology, I want now to focus on the way it invokes notions of moral, hereditary and puerperal madness. Braddon deliberately distinguishes her heroine from the stereotype of the demonised lunatic: 'All mental distress is, with some show of reason, associated in our minds with loose disordered garments, and dishevelled hair, and an appearance in every way the reverse of my lady's' (p. 397). Lady Audley herself has imagined her own mad mother as a maniacal demon. Lucy Audley (who begins as Helen Maldon, becomes Helen Talboys, changes her name to Lucy Graham and then Lady Audley) is a child when she learns from the taunts of her abusive foster mother that her own mother is mad. She lives tormented by the image of her mother as a lunatic 'in a cell with a hideous garment that bound her tortured limbs', who would pounce on her and kill her if she came near; she dreams of her mother's 'icy grasp around her throat and heard her ravings in her ear' (pp. 348-9). But lo, when Lucy does actually visit her mother one day – a plot mystery rationalised only by the novel's concern to exploit yet dislodge the stereotype of the demonic madwoman – her mother is a charming, pretty, girlish, blue-eyed creature. She 'skipped towards us with her yellow curls decorated with natural flowers, and saluted us with radiant smiles, and gay, ceaseless chatter' (p. 350). This madwoman does not look mad: she has no lurid visage, swollen lips, matted hair and so on. She appears to be Victorian patriarchy's idealised other – a blue-eyed, curly-headed, infantilised angel. Her fictional predecessor is not mad Bertha in *Jane Eyre*, the deranged animal of giant propensities, but rather someone like Dora Spenlow, the angel who (had she lived to become a mother) may have had the same trouble balancing her mind she had with the household accounts.

The cool Lady Audley illustrates very well, therefore, what moral insanity was thought to be: a morbid perversion of the moral disposition and natural impulses that did not seem to come from any remarkable disorder or defect of the intellect, and that did not result in delusions or hallucinations. The doctrine of 'moral insanity' articulated the Victorian tendency to regard crime or sin as a species of insanity; it referred to madness as the experience of inappropriate emotions rather than the result of defective reasoning or cognitive impairment. James Cowles Prichard, physician and ethnologist, and later Commissioner of Lunacy, introduced the term 'moral insanity' in 1833, defining it as follows: 'This form of mental disease... consists of a morbid perversion of the feelings, affections, habits, without any hallucination or erroneous conviction impressed upon the under-standing; it sometimes coexists with an apparently unimpaired state of the intellectual faculties.'[92] The definition drew attention to anti-social or deviant behaviour, as emotional and ethical confusion resulting from the immoderate, excessive and undisciplined passions. One patient diagnosed as morally insane described her experience of herself thus: 'I have my reason, but I have not the command of my feelings. Circumstances in life create feelings and prejudices which prevent my passing through life smoothly. My *intellect* is not insane; it is my *feelings* I cannot control.'[93] Lady Audley herself muses: 'Have I ever been really *wicked*, I wonder? ... My worst wickednesses have been the result of wild impulses, and not of deeply-laid plots. I am not like the women I have read of, who have lain night after night in the horrible dark and stillness, planning out treacherous deeds, and arranging every circumstance of an appointed crime' (p. 297).

Moral lunatics posed a special conundrum because they brought the problematic crime/insanity boundary into focus.[94] 'Persons so affected present great difficulties to the medical man', wrote L.S. Winslow in his *Manual of Lunacy*. 'The line of demarcation between vice and insanity is most difficult to perceive or define.'[95] By mid-century, moral insanity had become an extremely controversial notion in medical and legal discourse, considered by many subversive and mischievous because associated with the evasion of criminal responsibility and accountability. Nevertheless, it is not difficult to see why the Victorians were fascinated by the relationship between vice and insanity: 'In a society as concerned with morality as was Victorian England, a theory which seemed to ascribe moral perversity to insanity was bound to have a strong appeal.'[96] If insanity can be understood as the consequence of defective moral agency, behaviour judged deviant then becomes a symptom. George Eliot invokes such views for our wry amusement when she writes of the tendency among Middlemarchers to see non-conformity as equivalent to lunacy: 'Sane people did what their neighbours did, so that if any lunatics were at large, one might know and avoid them.'[97] The statement itself seems a humorous exaggeration, but the implied corollary is altogether serious: if you didn't do what your neighbours did – if your behaviour was considered deviant – they were quite justified in calling you a lunatic. Mrs Cadwallader exemplifies this view by insinuating that Dorothea Brooke's unconventional attitudes to life and her choice of Casaubon as a husband provide evidence of 'a little crack in the Brooke family', and that Dorothea was suffering from a 'deeper and more constitutional disease' than Mrs Cadwallader had been willing to believe. Had Dorothea married Sir James, Mrs Cadwallader opines, there was a chance 'of her becoming a sane, sensible woman'.[98] In the same vein, the narrator of *Lady Audley's Secret* observes innocently that had Lucy Graham refused Sir Michael, everyone would have thought it 'something more than madness in a penniless girl to reject such an offer' (p. 9).

To have argued, however, that the heartless Lady Audley was merely morally insane would not have been sensational enough; nor would it have allowed Braddon sufficient scope to explore the way discourses of madness help to construct gender. Hereditary disposition, manifesting itself in puerperal insanity, allows Braddon to explore the social reproduction of classed and gendered positions. Lady Audley explains: 'My baby was born, and the crisis which had been fatal to my mother arose for me' (p. 352).[99] It should not surprise us either that Lucy's mother was 'sane up to the hour of my birth; but from that hour her intellect had decayed, until she became what I saw her' (p. 350). In case we have missed the point about the tyranny of maternal inheritance, Lucy Audley throws in her grandmother, who was also mad. Her mother's madness 'was an hereditary disease transmitted to her from her mother, who had died mad' (p. 350). Medical opinion held that one of the most dangerous states of excitement and turbulence was the puerperal state, which either predisposed a woman to insanity, or brought it out when there was hereditary disposition or 'peculiar pre-aptitude'.[100] Since postpartum women were highly susceptible to both moral and hereditary factors, puerperal insanity could be induced by any powerful influence of 'fright, surprise, or other strong emotions … acting on a mind already disposed to mania by some hereditary influence'. 'Sympathy of the brain' for the disordered state of uterine function could account for many cases, but the increased 'nervous excitability' and the influence of moral causes led some physicians to argue that cases arising from *moral* causes were four times as many as those produced by *physical*. Considering that the 'physical and moral causes of disturbance' were so rife during pregnancy and labour, Dr James Reid thought it surprising that there were not more cases of such insanity.[101] Since a woman could not exert the usual and necessary control over her impulses and urges at this time, the 'religious and moral principles' which alone give 'strength to the female mind' collapsed, allowing the 'subterranean fires' to smoulder and flame.[102] Not unexpectedly, the sudden moral decline of a hitherto respectable woman constituted evidence of madness. Shrieking obscenities at the doctor and her husband, demonstrating a dislike for her new-born baby, refusing to carry out household duties and exhibiting other inappropriate behaviour were symptoms of deep malaise. Considering the sexual etiology of much female insanity, and the notion that women were specialised for reproduction, we can understand why Victorian doctors regarded times of change or crisis in a woman's reproductive life to be especially dangerous. The onset of menses and the process of menopause were equally high risk periods in which minds might become unhinged.[103] Some medical texts go so far as to represent the condition of being female as inherently pathological and regard the line between biological function and disease as blurred. 'It is generally admitted' wrote E. J. Tilt, 'that pathology and physiology are inseparable, and the female organs of generation afford, perhaps, the best illustration of the axiom.'[104]

When we examine the maternal madness that Lady Audley claims is responsible for her behaviour, we see that it deflects attention from distressing material conditions and the opportunities Lady Audley seizes to escape them. Indeed, Braddon takes care not to omit from Lady Audley's confession an account of her legacy of poverty, privation and fear. After her child was born, Lucy says that her mother's disease rose up in her. Although she escaped, she was left 'much more irritable perhaps after my recovery; less inclined to fight the hard battle of the world; more disposed to complain of poverty and neglect' (p. 352). Her husband then deserted her to seek his fortune in Australia, leaving a note that she would not see his face again till he made good. Since he could not find a job in England, she is not filled with optimism or a sense of security. 'The hereditary taint that was in my blood had never till this time showed itself by any one sign or token; but at this time I became subject to fits of violence and despair' (p. 353). Although this characterisation fits very well with the emphasis in medical discourse on the moral susceptibility of women who succumb to puerperal insanity, we can see Braddon actually suggesting that Lucy Audley is not deranged, but desperate – not mad (insane) but mad (angry). It is not surprising, therefore, that her fits of violence and despair cease when she determines to run away from her wretched situation – just as her husband did, we may note, except that his abandonment of his wife and child to find gold 'down under' is condoned, whereas her departure from her child and abandonment of her married name is seen as demonic and unwomanly, a crime against nature. Afraid that poverty, labouring for a pittance, and diminishing hope for the return of a husband who has deserted her are likely to wear her down, Lucy Audley seeks to rely on herself for comfort and security, recalling Jane Eyre, who, when Brocklehurst questioned her about what to do to avoid going to hell, replied that she should stay healthy and not die. Jane's generally unpopular, but frankly self-preservatory answer is similar to the solution that Braddon's heroine derives to protect her sanity. She must avoid poverty and privation, themselves acknowledged causes of madness in men as well as women.[105]

Poverty is a dreaded state for Lucy Audley and avoidance of it a primary motivation.[106] As Robert Audley closes in on her, she considers running away. 'But where could I go? I must go back to the old, hard, cruel, wretched life – the life of poverty, and humiliation, and vexation, and discontent. I should have to go back and wear myself out in that long struggle, and die – as my mother died, perhaps' (p. 316). From the time she was a young woman, the fear of turning into her mother has made her alert to opportunities of avoiding such a fate and she seeks to capitalise on the social value of female beauty: 'My ultimate fate in life depended upon my marriage, and I concluded that if I was indeed prettier than my schoolfellows, I ought to marry better than any of them' (p. 350). Her installation at Audley Court means that, like her portrait, painted splendidly in the Pre-Raphaelite manner, she becomes one of Sir Michael's prized possessions. The very specific inventory of lavish, material treasures in her bedroom titillates the reader with a feast of conspicuous consumption as it suggests that Lady Audley's beauty, ornamentality, and apparent conformity are purchased and rewarded by such prizes as Marie Antoinette cabinets, Gobelin tapestries, Pompadour china, Benvenuto Cellini glasses, Leroy and Benson ormolu clocks. As if to emphasise that her crimes are linked to her efforts to maintain the luxuries that signify her elevated station, she is shown (post-confession) mourning the loss of the precious things in her luxurious apartment and thinking of how much – literally, not morally – they have cost (p. 373).

Lady Audley's Secret was written shortly after a period of 'lunacy panic' in England, during which the horrifying possibilities of involuntary and wrongful incarceration were frequently and dramatically brought to public attention in the law courts and the press. One such case concerned Edward Bulwer-Lytton, the mentor and correspondent of Braddon to whom Lady Audley's Secret is gratefully dedicated. In 1858, a few years before Braddon began her novel, Bulwer-Lytton had his wife committed to Inverness Lodge, Brentford. There was a public outcry about the fact that Lady Lytton was made to spend a month at an asylum (even if it was a rather exclusive home-like establishment) before she was able to arrange to be released. It is intimated that those in charge tried to conceal from her the kind of place to which she was being taken. Her indignant biographer relates that when

Lady Lytton asked whether the unfortunates roaming in the grounds were incarcerated there, the woman in charge replied evasively, 'Those ... are our ladies. They are out gathering strawberries.' Much like the pet-shop owner in the Monty Python skit who insists that a clearly dead parrot is not dead, the head of the establishment himself is said to have assured her: 'Madhouse! madhouse! nonsense, Lady Lytton! this is no madhouse... those are my children.'[107] Similarly, when Lady Audley asks the woman in charge if her place of exile is the madhouse she suspects it is, the answer she gets is far from reassuring: '"Ah, but no, Madame", the woman answered, with a shrill scream of protest. "It is an establishment of the most agreeable, where one amuses oneself –"' (p. 387). Though she anticipated confinement when she confessed to madness, Lady Audley is furious to have her suspicions confirmed and accuses Robert Audley of using power basely and of bringing her to a living grave. Newspapers such as *The Somerset County Gazette* and *The Daily Telegraph* made much of the Lady Lytton affair, defending her sanity and decrying the infringement of the rights and liberties of a subject of the realm:

> It is a question of deep importance whether it is not utterly wrong, and most dangerous to the liberties of individuals, that upon the word of two medical men persons may be taken to a madhouse, when, if not already insane, they are undoubtedly placed in circumstances in every way calculated, by their horrible and frightful character, to destroy reason and produce insanity.[108]

The *Gazette* then went on to call for a public inquiry before anyone were to be committed: 'Society in general demands this; helpless women require it .... It is true that investigation into cases like that of Lady Lytton is compelled when demanded by friends of the incarcerated person; but the system is altogether contrary to the general equity of British laws and customs.'[109] While it is remarkable how closely the confinement of Lady Audley parallels accounts of the occasion on which Lady Rosina Lytton was committed, there is no evidence from Braddon's correspondence with Bulwer-Lytton that she based her representation of incarceration on circulated accounts of Lady Rosina's confinement.[110] Both Braddon's novel and Lady Rosina Lytton's manuscript autobiography (used later in Louisa Devey's biography) are highly conscious of the 'genre' of wrongful incarceration, which contemporary sensation novels and case histories are helping to form.

In exploiting the topicality of wrongful confinement, *Lady Audley's*

Secret operates as a typical sensation novel. But novels like Charles Reade's *Hard Cash* and Wilkie Collins' *The Woman in White* that set out to play on the horror of a conspiracy to incarcerate must present protagonists who are clearly sane or else blur the question of wrongfulness and cheat the reader of the horrible thrill that a sane person is being unjustly committed. If *Lady Audley's Secret* is examined by such criteria, problems immediately arise. Whether we think of the committal as wrongful depends on whether we believe Lady Audley's confession of madness or how we understand the doctor's initial and then reconsidered verdict after he has examined her. What also distinguishes the question of wrongful confinement here from typical treatments is that it marks Lady Audley's end instead of being a starting point or a complicating factor provoking a rescue narrative. The chapter that describes Lady Audley's incarceration is entitled 'Buried Alive', which has a particularly grisly ring to it because no chapter of rescue follows. From the conventional point of view that the narrator officially adopts, the ending functions on the principle of 'just desserts', for who can deny that Lady Audley has been very wicked and deserves punishing? Yet the ending also shows the extent of her powerlessness. For someone who has been so devious and clever, she hardly puts up a good fight, though it seems for a short time that her gambit of accusing Robert of madness may provide a match worth watching:

> 'Robert Audley is mad,' she said decisively. 'What is one of the strongest diagnostics of madness – what is the first appalling sign of mental aberration? The mind becomes stationary; the brain stagnates; the even current of the mind is interrupted; the thinking power of the brain resolves itself into a monotone. As the waters of a tideless pool putrefy by reason of their stagnation, the mind becomes turbid and corrupt through lack of action; and perpetual reflection upon one subject resolves itself into monomania. Robert Audley is a monomaniac' (p. 287).

In addition to deploying the discourse of monomania with some sophistication, she also uses the fact that Robert's father was a known eccentric to apply the received wisdom about maternal madness and daughters to fathers and sons: 'Do you know, Alicia, that madness is more often transmitted from father to son, than from father to daughter, and from mother to daughter than from mother to son?' (p. 278). But Lady Audley does not add that, as Andrew Wynter put it: 'The tendency of the mother to transmit her mental disease is, however, in all cases stronger than the father's; some physicians have, indeed, insisted that it is twice as strong.'[111] Robert Audley's father may have been eccentric, but his son was more likely to inherit income, position, and privilege than madness.

Cornered after trying unsuccessfully to murder Robert by setting fire to the inn where he is lodging, Lady Audley melodramatically discloses her hereditary taint. Robert briskly makes arrangements with a *maison de sante* and procures the documents for his step-aunt's certification. When Robert tells the most grave Dr Mosgrave the facts of the case, omitting his suspicions of murder and arson, the doctor's expert medical opinion is that she is not mad. He reasonably points out that she ran away from marriage and motherhood because her life was unpleasant and committed bigamy to obtain fortune and position. When she found herself in a desperate position, she did not grow desperate but intelligently carried out a conspiracy. She is sane but immoral, which is not, Dr Mosgrave implies, the same as morally insane. Her mother may have been insane, but that does not necessarily mean that she is insane, and he recognises Robert's desire that his aunt be certified to muffle the shame on his uncle's house. Robert has then reluctantly to confide his suspicions that she may have murdered her first husband, George Talboys, which changes Dr Mosgrave's mind about Lady Audley. After an interview with her, he reconsiders his initial diagnosis and confirms that there is latent insanity, which might arise under 'extreme mental pressure'. The lady is not mad, he equivocates, but she has the hereditary taint in her blood and the 'cunning of madness with the prudence of intelligence' (p. 379). Dr Mosgrave's revised judgement is in keeping with lamentations in professional journals at the time about the difficulty of reaching a diagnosis until a crime had actually been committed: 'Why is the commission [or in this case, attempted commission] of murder to be the only valued evidence of insanity?'[112]

Dr Mosgrave's reversal of diagnosis is startling and allows Braddon to satirise the medical profession's claims to objectivity and impartiality. First the 'mad doctor' announces that no jury would entertain an insanity plea on the evidence that Robert disclosed; then, after hearing of Lady Audley's attempt at murder he finds that she is prone to insanity. He judges, however, that there is not enough evidence to link her to the supposed death of her husband: no jury would find her guilty of murder. This dismissal of the case allows him to salve his conscience about obstructing the course of justice or circumventing the trial. He can then advise that she had better be put away, and there is no need for the family to bear the *esclandre* of a public trial. He is, of course, persuaded by Robert's needs, but does not wish to appear collusive. He warns Robert that he will not be party to any hugger-mugger smuggling of her out of the reach of justice, but insists that he does not (unlike the reader) see any reason to suspect that she has murdered her missing first husband. Since Robert's suspicions on this score were what prompted him to revise his initial diagnosis, the doctor's collusion in her incarceration under a mask of cool, medical impartiality and objectivity is hardly ambiguous.

The asylum functions in the novel as a final and effective closet into which to push the family skeleton. Robert, however, presents it to Lady Audley as a penitentiary, a convent, where confinement will bring about remorse, contrition and purification. Robert sanctimoniously assures his deviant aunt that her fate is not so bad: 'You will live a quiet and peaceful life, my lady, such a life as many a good and holy woman in this Catholic country freely takes upon herself, and happily endures unto the end' (p. 391). If you were a pure and religious woman, he seems to say, you would willingly take on a life of seclusion in a convent; my sending you here is nothing terrible. The demonstrated function of the asylum – to bury Lady Audley alive – together with Robert's sanctimonious attitude to her incarceration underscores the text's interest in the relationship between transgressive behaviour and definitions of madness. The ending exposes rather than resolves the confusion created by defining madness in terms of immoral behaviour and punishing such behaviour by means of the institutions set up to deal with madness. It points to that confusion, however, as a screen for issues that bear on class interests and boundaries.

While invoking the discourse of maternal insanity, the text directs us to think of maternal heritage in terms of positionality and social power rather than physicality and embodiment. Wrongful confinement and inheritance take on, then, a metaphorical quality, if one thinks of them in terms of relegation to a category entailing privation and impotence. The novel emphasises that Lady Audley seeks to avoid 'dependence, drudgery and humiliation' and allows her finally and pathetically to reiterate that she has been motivated in all her actions by fear of her mother's horrible inheritance, fear of poverty and of the men with power over her. We remember that as a child she went away after seeing her mother, knowing that 'the only inheritance I had to expect from my mother was – insanity' (p. 350). If she has been motivated by the fear of becoming her mother, there is the final irony that she dies, like her mother, in a madhouse, not mad, we believe, but trapped in her efforts to avoid her mother's fate. The time of her greatest vulnerability is when she becomes a mother, that is, becomes most like her own mother. The act of becoming a mother emphasises therefore the completed trans- mission of her own maternal legacy and threatens her with her own mother's fate, making her confront the fulfilment of a social destiny, naturalised in the discourse of madness as a biological inevitability.

Notes

1. On the contradictions in ideologies of motherhood, see S. Shuttleworth, 'Demonic mothers: ideologies of bourgeois motherhood in the mid-Victorian era', in L. Shires (ed.), *Rewriting the Victorians: Theory, History, and the Politics of Gender* (London, Routledge, 1992), pp. 31–51.
2. The term baby-farming covers a number of child-minding practices. For example, another name for a crèche might be a baby-farm. The term took on insidious and sinister connotations in the scandals of the 1860s where numbers of illegitimate babies were 'farmed out' for nursing and care. Baby-farming became synonymous with paid infanticide. Baby-dropping refers to abandonment or infanticide.
3. A. Leared, *Infant Mortality and Its Causes* (London, Churchill, 1862), p. 10 (originally published as an essay in the *English Woman's Journal*); the phenomenon of burial clubs is referred to in Chadwick's *Sanitary Inquiry Supplement*, 'Interment in towns', (1843). See Wm. B. Ryan, *Infanticide: Its Law, Prevalence, Prevention and History* (London, Churchill, 1862), pp. 20–2, who cites Chadwick on the depravity of Manchester parents, some of whom had insured payments in nineteen different burial clubs; women were also known to refer to subscribed children in the following way: 'Aye, aye, that child will not live; IT IS IN THE BURIAL CLUB.'
4. M. A. Baines, 'Excessive infant mortality', (London, John Churchill, 1862), pp. 13–4; see also her 'The practice of hiring wet-nurses – especially from the "fallen"– considered as it affects public health and public morals', (London, John Churchill, 1859). Mrs Baines, often cited as an authority on infant feeding, also wrote 'A few friendly words to young mothers', By One of the Maternity (1856).
5. Mater, 'Wet-nurses from the fallen', *Lancet*, 1 (1859), pp. 200–201.
6. 'Wet-nursing', *British Medical Journal*, 1 (1861), p. 129.
7. 'Excessive infant mortality', p. 3; she also argues that during the Preston strikes the rate of infant mortality actually declined, because working mothers were shut out of the factories and forced to stay home with their children. See also H. M. Davidson, *The Two Babies: A Sketch of Everyday Life* (London, 1859).

8. Leared, *Infant Mortality*, p. 11.
9. 'Murder of the Innocents', *Lancet*, 1 (1858), p. 346.
10. See V. Fildes, *Wet Nursing: A History from Antiquity to the Present* (Oxford, Basil Blackwell, 1988).
11. See, for example, H. P. Chavasse, *Advice to Wives on the Management of Themselves During the Periods of Pregnancy, Labour and Suckling* (London, Longman, 1843), pp. 77–9; T. H. Barker, 'On the diet of infancy and childhood', *British Mothers Magazine*, 8 (1852), pp. 193–7; T. Graham, *On the Management and Disorders of Infancy and Childhood* (London, 1853).
12. For further discussion of wet-nursing customs, see A. Roberts, 'Mothers and babies: the wetnurse and her employer in mid-nineteenth-century England', *Women's Studies*, 3 (1976), pp. 279–93.
13. Ryan, *Infanticide*, p. 122; Ryan is quoting Mrs Baines.
14. C. H. F. Routh, 'On the selection of wet nurses from the fallen', *Lancet*, 1 (1859), p. 580.
15. Routh, 'Wet-nurses from the fallen', *Lancet*, 1 (1859), pp. 113–4.
16. Routh, 'Wet-nurses from the fallen', p. 114.
17. W. Carpenter, *Principles of Human Physiology; with Their Chief Applications to Pathology, Hygiene and Forensic Medicine* (London, Churchill, 1842), pp. 346–7.
18. *Lancet*, 1 (1859), p. 581. See also *Lancet*, 1 (1859), p. 637, for a response to Routh's diatribe against morally tainted milk; Acton's response, 'Child-murder and wet nursing', *British Medical Journal*, 1 (1861), p. 184; and further defence of Routh in the *Lancet*, 2 (1859), pp. 71–2.
19. Acton, 'Unmarried wet nurses', *Lancet*, 1 (1859), pp. 175–6.
20. 'Wet-nurses', Letter from Graily Hewitt, M.D, *British Medical Journal*, 1 (1861), p. 129.
21. Mater, 'Wet-nurses from the fallen', *Lancet*, 1 (1859), p. 201.
22. Mater, 'Wet-nurses from the fallen', p. 201. Maternal escutcheons were not the only ones felt to be blotted. In 1866, a lead article in the *British Medical Journal* called on the medical brethren to urge mothers to nurse their own children. Is it not also the case, the writer asked, that mothers who are desirous of nursing are 'by their own doctors forbidden to do so? This great and most serious blot (as we view the matter) upon the escutcheon of medical practice always, we confess, shows itself black and staring to us when we read of infanticide' ('Infanticide and wet-nursing', *British Medical Journal*, 2 [1866], p. 614). The rhetoric of escutcheons in these letters reveals the alliance between the medical profession and middle-class women in helping to create an empowered (if highly regulated) class of mothers that exemplified and reproduced middle-class values and exclusions.
23. Quoted in G. Behlmer, 'Deadly motherhood: infanticide and medical opinion in mid-Victorian England', *Journal of the History of Medicine*, 34 (1979), p. 418.
24. Ryan, *Infanticide*, p. 62.
25. Leared, *Infant Mortality*, p. 13.
26. Leared, *Infant Mortality*, p. 11. See also Baines, 'Excessive infant mortality', p. 5, where she blames the 'supposed necessity that induces working mothers to seek industrial employment'.

27. On the history of baby-farming and the execution of Margaret Waters see R. Pearsall, *Night's Black Angels* (London, Hodder and Stoughton, 1975) and L. Rose, *Massacre of the Innocents: Infanticide in Britain 1800–1939* (London, Routledge, 1986), pp. 96–107.

28. Ryan, *Infanticide*, p. 52.

29. Ryan, *Infanticide*, p. 92.

30. A. Wynter, *Curiosities of Toil*, vol. 2 (London, Chapman, 1870), pp. 198–9.

31. Wynter, *Curiosities*, pp. 194–208. For discussion of the Poor Laws in the context of infanticide see Rose, *Massacre of the Innocents*, pp. 24–6.

32. Poor Law Commission Report, 1834; quoted in Behlmer, 'Deadly motherhood', p. 418. Frances Trollope's *Jessie Phillips: A Tale of the Present Day* (1843) responds to both the New Poor Law and this commissioner's perception by having her heroine's seducer take advantage of her with a sense of fiscal impunity, and then later kill the infant. Her representation is less radical, therefore, than George Eliot's *Adam Bede*, discussed below. For a contrasting view, see A. R. Higginbotham '"Sin of the age": infanticide and illegitimacy in Victorian London', *Victorian Studies*, 35 (1989), p. 322.

33. 'Seduction and infanticide', *Saturday Review*, (22 October 1866), p. 481.

34. 'Seduction and infanticide', p. 481.

35. See M. L. Shanley, *Feminism, Marriage and the Law in Victorian England, 1850–1895* (London, Tauris, 1989), p. 90.

36. Sally Mitchell goes so far as to suggest that another 'germ' may have been the culminating scene in Frances Trollope's *Jessie Phillips*, which is very similar to that of *Adam Bede*; see S. Mitchell, *The Fallen Angel: Chastity, Class and Women's Reading, 1835–1880* (Ohio, Bowling Green University Popular Press, 1981), p. 67.

37. For an account of the case, see Ryan, *Infanticide*, p. 74.

38. Having assumed the masculine mask of George Eliot, and about to assume the role of 'Mutter' to Lewes's sons, Marian Evans is herself positioned in a complicated way as the author of *Adam Bede*.

39. George Eliot, *Adam Bede*, ed. S. Gill (Harmondsworth, Penguin, [1859] 1980), p. 284; all further references are to this edition and are cited parenthetically in the text.

40. A. Walker, *Beauty: Illustrated by an Analysis and Classification of Beauty in Woman* (London, 1846), p. 229.

41. G. S. Haight (ed.), *The Letters of George Eliot*, (New Haven, Yale University Press, 9 vols 1954–78), vol. 2, p. 510.

42. On Hetty's position as an abandoned child see M. Harris, 'Infanticide and respectability: Hetty Sorrel as abandoned child', *English Studies in Canada*, 9:2 (1983), pp. 177–96.

43. But fellow-feeling is also at times figured as a kind of sibling solidarity. The novel's feminised 'Nature' is sometimes personified as the most unmindful and impersonal 'mother' of all. Her very indifference to her vast family demands that the sibling community of human beings turn to each other for nurture and support: 'We are children of a large family, and must learn, as such children do, not to expect that our little hurts will be made much of – to be content with little nurture and caressing and help each other the more' (p. 338).

44. *Saturday Review* (26 February 1859), p. 250.
45. Walker, *Beauty*, p. 4; 'Woman in her psychological relations', *Journal of Psychological Medicine and Mental Pathology*, 4 (1851), p. 21.
46. 'Woman in her psychological relations', pp. 19–20; the author is quoting from Fan and Knox's *Anatomy of the External Forms of Man*; on the discourse of beauty and female sexuality see the discussion of Walker, *Beauty*, Chapter one, and O. Moscucci, *The Science of Woman: Gynaecology and Gender in England, 1800–1929* (Cambridge, Cambridge University Press, 1990), p. 35; on George Eliot's responses to Spencer's construction of female beauty see N. L. Paxton, *George Eliot and Herbert Spencer: Feminism, Evolutionism, and the Reconstruction of Gender* (Princeton, Princeton University Press, 1991), pp. 43–68.
47. E. A. Kaplan, *Motherhood and Representation: The Mother in Popular Culture and Melodrama* (London, Routledge, 1992), pp. 6–7. For a distinction between the psychic mother and the social mother see N. Wood, 'L'ane dossier: an introduction', *m/f: A Feminist Journal*, 8 (1983), pp. 17–21, who observes that 'feminism has primarily sought to expose and reclaim the "social" mother by illuminating all her material tasks and functions' while psychoanalysis 'conjures a maternal "imago" whose relationship to any bodily counterpart is greatly attenuated'.
48. K. Brady, *George Eliot* (London, Macmillan, 1992), p. 25, notes that 'maternal love appears in both Eliot's life and her fiction as a significant and tantalising gap'. I am arguing here, however, that it is not as great a gap as recent critics have suggested, though it is certainly a matter of considerable ambiguity and complexity.
49. To say that Adam Bede is a 'virtual orphan' is an extreme form of the way critical treatment of the novel discounts her; see Harris, 'Infanticide and respectability in *Adam Bede*', p. 187.
50. Ryan, *Infanticide*, pp. 45–6.
51. 'Infanticide', *Saturday Review* (August 1865), pp. 161–2.
52. 'New novels', *Athenaeum*, 29 (1866), pp. 732–3. On the relationship between sensation fiction and the press of the period, see T. Boyle, *Black Swine in the Sewers of Hampstead: Beneath the Surface of Victorian Sensationalism* (Harmondsworth, Penguin, 1989).
53. See J. Greenwood, *The Seven Curses of London* (London, Stanley Rivers, 1869), pp. 21–58, who repeatedly draws himself up and attempts to avoid sensationalising his account of baby-farming.
54. The story of her rescue of her son Evelyn, then a junior naval officer, from the hospital in Scutari where he lay injured, is a dramatic account of motherly determination and devotion. Despite Florence Nightingale's insistence that it was impossible to take the young man back to England in his condition, she did return him to the family home in Essex and there nursed him back to health; see J. Marlow, *The Uncrowned Queen of Ireland: The Life of 'Kitty' O'Shea* (London, Weidenfeld, 1975), p. 12.
55. *Athenaeum*, 31 (1868), p. 624.
56. See Marlow, *The Uncrowned Queen*, p. 22.
57. Lady Emma Caroline Wood, *Sorrow on the Sea* (London, Tinsley Brothers, 1868), vol. 3, p. 18. Page references are to this edition and will be given

hereafter parenthetically in the text.

58. See Greenwood, *The Seven Curses of London*, p. 35.

59. For discussion of charges of scapegoating in the case of Margaret Waters, who was convicted of murder in 1870 and subsequently hanged, see Rose, *Massacre of the Innocents*, pp. 101–2; I. Pinchbeck and M. Hewitt, *Children in English Society*, vol. 2 (London, Routledge, 1973), pp. 613–18.

60. Greenwood discusses the trial of 'Mrs Winser, a year or so ago' in *The Seven Curses of London*, Chapter 3.

61. See P. W. J. Bartrip, *Mirror of Medicine: A History of the British Medical Journal* (Oxford, British Medical Journal and Clarendon Press, 1990), p. 99.

62. For a more detailed discussion of Wiltshire's expose, see Rose, *Massacre of the Innocents*, pp. 79–93. I am indebted to Rose's references to Mrs Drury, which directed me to Lady Emma Caroline Wood's *Sorrow on the Sea*.

63. See Rose, *Massacre of the Innocents*, pp. 90–2; his term 'baby-planting' refers to the procedure whereby a woman would pretend to be pregnant and the midwife or accoucheur would smuggle in a live baby and fake the scene of birth.

64. See Rose, *Massacre of the Innocents*, p. 82.

65. H. Maudsley, *The Physiology and Pathology of the Mind* (London, Macmillan, 1867), p. 389; see also Chapter One.

66. J. Kristeva, 'Stabat mater', *The Kristeva Reader*, ed. T. Moi (New York, Columbia University Press, 1986), p. 167.

67. For discussion of the characteristics of sensation novels, see W. Hughes, *The Maniac in the Cellar: Sensation Novels of the 1860s* (Princeton, Princeton University Press, 1980), p. 19.

68. [H. L. Mansel], 'Sensation novels', *Quarterly Review*, 113 (April 1863), pp. 488–9.

69. See Hughes, *Maniac in the Cellar*, p. 14.

70. See Ryan, *Infanticide*, p. 49, who quotes the *Lancet* 2 (1861) on the numbers of bodies retrieved from the Thames.

71. [F. Winslow] 'Recent trials in lunacy', *Journal of Psychological Medicine and Mental Pathology*, 7 (1854), p. 617.

72. R. Smith, *Trial by Medicine: Insanity and Responsibility in Victorian Trials* (Edinburgh, Edinburgh University Press, 1981), p. 145, cites thirty nine convictions.

73. See Smith, *Trial by Medicine*, p. 147.

74. On perceptions of infanticide as abortion after the fact see E. Badinter, *The Myth of Motherhood: An Historical View of the Maternal Instinct*, trans. R. DeGaris (London, Souvenir Press, 1981); on the ethics of infanticide in relation to abortion debates see M. Tooley, *Abortion and Infanticide* (Oxford, Clarendon Press, 1983).

75. Ryan, *Infanticide*, p. 67.

76. 'Child-murder and its punishment', *Social Science Review*, 2 (1864), pp. 454–5.

77. G. Greaves, 'Observations on some of the causes of infanticide', *Transactions of the Manchester Statistical Society* (1862–63), p. 5; cited in Behlmer, 'Deadly motherhood', p. 411.

78. M. A. Baines, 'A few thoughts concerning infanticide', *Journal of Social Science*, 2 vols in 1 (1866), p. 537.

79. Baines then suggests ways to control infant care (inspection of burial clubs, registration of still births, registration and inspection of the practices and premises of midwives and 'wet' or 'dry' nurses) as well as ways to help and reform erring mothers (a refuge, lying-in hospital and nursery).

80. Behlmer, 'Deadly motherhood', p. 413; but see also Higginbotham, 'Sin of the age', p. 330, whose sample of cases tried in the Central Criminal Court, London, 1839–1906 shows only about 5 per cent not guilty by reason of insanity.

81. L. S. Winslow, *Manual of Lunacy* (London, Smith Elder, 1874), p. 292.

82. R. H. Semple, 'On criminal responsibility', *Medical Times and Gazette*, 12 (1856), p. 58.

83. Semple, 'On criminal responsibility', p. 59.

84. M. E. Braddon, *Lady Audley's Secret*, ed. D. Skilton (Oxford, World's Classics, [1862] 1987), p. 372; all references are to this edition and will be given henceforth parenthetically in the text.

85. See for instance M. Hirsch, *The Mother/Daughter Plot: Narrative, Psychoanalysis, Feminism* (Bloomington, Indiana University Press, 1989), p. 46.

86. Mrs H. Wood, *East Lynne* (Great Britain, Dent, [1861] 1984), p. 289.

87. It is exactly this awareness and responsivity that Jean Rhys imagines in *Wide Sargasso Sea*.

88. See D. A. Miller, 'Sensation and gender in *The Woman in White*', in C. Gallagher and T. Laqueur (eds.), *The Making of the Modern Body: Sexuality and Society in the Nineteenth Century* (Berkeley, University of California Press, 1987), pp. 110–22. Miller draws attention to the way *Lady Audley's Secret* 'blows the cover' on desires that are socially deviant. He says the secret is not whether Lady Audley is a madwoman, but that she must be treated as one whether she is or not (p. 121).

89. E. Showalter, *A Literature of Their Own: British Women Novelists from Brontë to Lessing* (London, Virago, 1977).

90. See E. Langland, 'Nobody's angels: domestic ideology in the Victorian novel', *PMLA*, 107:2 (1992), pp. 290–304.

91. See R. L. Wolff, *Sensational Victorian: The Life and Fiction of Mary Elizabeth Braddon* (New York, Garland, 1979), p. 8.

92. J. C. Prichard, *A Treatise on Insanity* (London, Marchant, 1833), p. 14; for a discussion of Prichard's views see E. Carlson and N. Dain, 'The meaning of moral insanity', *Bulletin of the History of Medicine*, 36 (1962), p. 131; V. Skultans, *English Madness: Ideas on Insanity 1580–1890* (London, Routledge, 1979), pp. 65–8.

93. See J. C. Bucknill and D. H. Tuke, *A Manual of Psychological Medicine* (New York, Hafner, [1858] facsimile 1968), pp. 188–9.

94. See Smith, *Trial by Medicine*, p. 116.

95. Winslow, *Manual of Lunacy*, p. 74.

96. P. McCandless, 'Liberty and lunacy', in A. Scull (ed.), *Madhouses, Mad-Doctors, and Madmen: The Social History of Psychiatry in the Victorian Era* (Philadelphia, University of Pennsylvania Press, 1981), p. 355.

97. George Eliot, *Middlemarch: A Study in Provincial Life*, ed. G. Haight, (Boston, Riverside, 1956), p. 7.

98. George Eliot, *Middlemarch*, p. 45.

99. Biographies of Mary Elizabeth Braddon reveal that the subject of puerperal madness must have been of some interest to her. John Maxwell, the man with whom she lived, had a wife who had, he said, become mentally 'defunct' after the birth of their children, and had been confined to an institution for many years. Braddon took over the care of his five children and produced a further six, the eldest of whom appeared during the writing of *Lady Audley's Secret*.

100. See A. Morison, *Outlines of Mental Diseases*; quoted in V. Skultans, *Madness and Morals: Ideas on Insanity in the Nineteenth Century* (London, Routledge, 1975), p. 32; and Reid, 'On the causes, symptoms, and treatment of puerperal insanity', *Journal of Psychological Medicine*, 1 (1848), p. 136.

101. Reid, 'On the causes, symptoms and treatment', pp. 128, 143; see also the continuation of this article in *Journal of Psychological Medicine*, 1 (1848), pp. 284–93.

102. Bucknill and Tuke, *Manual of Psychological Medicine*, p. 273.

103. See K. P. Morgan, 'Women and moral madness', in L. Code, S. Mullett and C. Overall (eds.), *Feminist Perspectives: Philosophical Essays on Method and Morals* (Toronto, University of Toronto Press, 1988), pp. 146–67, who suggests that moral madness should be understood as a state of genuine confusion that the experience of lived gender in contemporary western society can produce. Such experience can distort and even destroy a woman's moral voice and her sense of moral integrity.

104. E. J. Tilt, *On Diseases of Women and Ovarian Inflammation* (London, Churchill, 1853), p. 1.

105. For a discussion of poverty as a cause of insanity see R. Hunter and I. Macalpine, *Psychiatry for the Poor: 1851 Colney Hatch Asylum-Friern Hospital 1973* (London, Dawsons, 1974), p. 199.

106. Avoiding poverty was also a very real issue for Braddon, who went on the stage to support her mother and herself. She confessed unabashedly that she wrote sensationally and prolifically to earn a living. When the spectre of poverty was banished, she told Edward Bulwer-Lytton, she would write deeper and worthwhile fiction – now her books had to sell.

107. L. Devey, *Life of Rosina, Lady Lytton* (London, Swan, 1887), p. 299.

108. *Somerset Country Gazette*, (July 13th, 1858); quoted in Devey, *Life of Rosina*, p. 317.

109. Devey, *Life of Rosina*, p. 318.

110. Her rather cryptic and tantalising letter to Bulwer-Lytton, shortly after the publication of *Lady Audley's Secret*, does not suggest that she knew anything of his knowledge of English lodges for the wealthy insane but merely that she erred in placing her *maison de santé* abroad rather than in England: 'I wrote the third & some part of the second vol of "Lady A." in less than a fortnight, & had the printer at me all the time. I had no one to consult about "*Maisons de Sante*" & it was only when the book was printed that I heard from a lady whose husband was an inmate of such a house, that what I had done abroad was more impossible than it would have been at home.' See R. Wolff, 'Devoted disciple: the letters of Mary Elizabeth Braddon to Sir Edward Bulwer-Lytton, 1862–1873', *Harvard Library Bulletin*, 22 (1974), pp. 5–35; 129–61. What, we may wonder, was 'more

impossible' abroad? Especially among the well-to-do, the private rest-home offered a solution to care giving as well as a way of muffling social shame, but did Braddon imagine that such home-like institutions were typically English or is she saying that only in England were corrupt certification practices common? David Skilton (ed.), *Lady Audley's Secret*, p. 454, suggests that Braddon is referring to the ease with which Lady Audley is confined. On the domestication of madness, see E. Showalter, *The Female Malady: Women, Madness, and English Culture, 1830–1980* (Harmondsworth, Penguin, 1987), p. 28; on the state of Belgian licensed houses, see Winslow, *Manual of Lunacy*, pp. 216–19.

111. A. Wynter, *The Borderlands of Insanity* (London, Strand, 1877), p. 48; see also H. Maudsley, *The Pathology of The Mind: A Study of its Distempers, Deformities, and Disorders* (London, Macmillan, 1895), p. 216, who remarks that insanity descends more frequently from the mother than the father, and from mother to daughter than to son.

112. Semple, 'On criminal responsibility', p. 59.

Chapter five

From hysteria to maternity: Saint Teresa and the Madonna in *Middlemarch*

Presumptions about the effect of sexed being on the minds of men and women, their differences and relative capacities, permeate Middlemarch conversation and influence behaviour and expecta-tions. Sir James, for example, is comfortable in the assumption that a man's mind will always be superior to a woman's, 'as the smallest birch-tree is of a higher kind than the most soaring palm, – and even his ignorance is of a sounder quality'.[1] Lydgate styles himself the bear in relation to Rosamond as the exquisite bird and avers that 'an accomplished woman almost always knows more than we men, but her knowledge is of a different sort' (p. 118).[2] Mr Brooke, though he doesn't deny the possibility of intellectuality in a woman – especially in his own family – believes that intelligence has a masculine bias. On hearing that Dorothea is bent on Casaubon, he seems to understand what startles everyone else:

> But you must have a scholar, and that sort of thing? Well, it lies a little in our family. I had it myself – that love of knowledge, and going into everything... though that sort of thing doesn't often run in the female line; or it runs underground like the rivers in Greece, you know – it comes out in the sons. Clever sons, clever mother (p. 33).

The mother may be a bearer of intelligence, which lies latently or recessively in women and manifests itself only in their male offspring. For her part, Dorothea imagines that knowledge is the only lamp to light the way for an ardent seeker, and that learned men alone keep its oil. Since her own education has given her only a 'toy-box history of the world', the equivalent of the 'nibblings and judgments of a discursive mouse', she must indeed have a scholar.[3] For his part, Mr Casaubon has imagined that in marrying Dorothea he would acquire a pleasant young wife whose great excellence like that of all her sex would be her capability of 'ardent self-sacrificing affection' and who would observe his scholarly efforts with no more critical questioning than 'an elegant-minded canary-bird' (pp. 37, 149). Although Dorothea's problem turns out to lie much deeper than the acquisition of knowledge, the narrator makes it clear that the social valuation of female intelligence and the nature of female education are important issues.

In the 1870s, debates about 'sex in mind' and the advisability of higher education for women gathered steam. George Eliot shared with the 'sex in mind' debates an interest in the way pronouncements about women's natural propensity for maternity and reproduction underwrote prescribed social roles for women and constrained their opportunities to find avenues of self-expression other than through marriage and maternity. But her interest in the gendered cultural opposition between productive and reproductive energies was broader than the question of educational opportunities. She did, after the first edition of *Middlemarch*, delete a specific barb about women's education, which indicted society for its 'modes of education which make a woman's knowledge another name for motley ignorance' (p. 612, n.1). Education is only one area ruled by the pervasive (if often challenged) Victorian assumption that the female body is primarily a reproductive body and that nothing should impede the fulfilment of its reproductive function. The representation of Dorothea explores this assumption and the cultural and political attitudes and practices that it validates.

George Eliot begins the novel by registering her awareness that the social regulation of women's lot depends on binding potentially destabilising energies to the purpose of marriage and motherhood. On such regulation, as Herbert Spencer later put it, depend the requirements of the race and the continuance of the species.[4] Such regulation, according to George Eliot, exacts a toll on those who vary from the prescribed norm, yet she also recognises that the question of how to accommodate variation and alter assumptions about female needs and desires is extremely complex. In an early review dealing with Margaret Fuller and Mary Wollstonecraft (1855), Marian Evans refers to 'the folly of absolute definitions of woman's nature and absolute demarcations of woman's mission' and quotes Fuller with approval: '"Nature", she says, "seems to delight in varying the arrangements, as if to show that she will be fettered by no rule; and we must admit the same varieties that she admits."'[5] Nature may delight in variations such as Dorothea but her social world does not. The question about Dorothea – 'What could she do, what ought she to do?' – meets with a constraining answer that shapes the narrative's exploration of the costs of conformity (p. 20). Dorothea's story hinges on the way energies considered excessive, unstable and vague are contained ultimately in essentially reproductive purposes. Why this happens, the novel suggests, is that the split between productive and reproductive energies is so culturally reinforced and produces such strong gendered associations in areas that appear to have nothing to do with sexuality, that dissolving it is the work of generations. Indeed, the narrator's language and system of valuations themselves reproduce the gender assumptions that the novel struggles to destabilise.

In attempting to represent Dorothea's dilemma as a split between productive and reproductive energies, George Eliot associates Dorothea with two important figures – cultural images – whose work in the novel's representation of sexuality and maternity I want to explore. Saint Teresa is evoked as a paradigm of the productive woman, whose path Dorothea cannot follow, while images of the Madonna associate Dorothea with the most elevated Mother and work to reconcile us to the importance of Dorothea's maternal status. Both these figures, I will suggest, are problematic and unstable signifiers. Just as Saint Teresa raises the question of a repressed and hysterical sexuality in relation to productivity, so the Madonna signals the subsumption of sexuality in maternity, itself arguably a form of hystericisation.

Although hysteria was a condition that perplexed, infuriated and divided Victorian doctors, many agreed that its cause was sexual repression or sexual excitement.[6] Most likely, the hysterical patient was a woman whose sexual energies were not happily bound in service to motherhood. According to Samuel Ashwell's *Practical Treatise on the Diseases Peculiar to Women*, those who marry late, or after

> great delay and who, from disparity of age or mutual dislike, bear children at long intervals; and those who either from the claims of fashionable life, or other insufficient reasons, do not suckle; young widows and the single; in all of whom some uterine derangement may be suspected, and in many ascertained to exist; such individuals are the common subjects of the disease.[7]

It was not surprising that doctors found, therefore, that women who menstruated healthily, married happily, became mothers at a sufficiently early age, and nursed their young were rarely hysterical.

'Many believe that hysteria is never anything more than a morbidly increased or excited sexual desire', wrote Graily Hewitt, Professor of Midwifery and Diseases of Women at University College. But while he proposed that the 'sexual tendencies require to be kept in subjection', he also admitted that 'it is not easy to say how far, or in what special manner this part of the treatment should be carried out... for hardly two cases admit of being treated alike'.[8] The idea was to take the hysterical patient's mind off her desires, admittedly so difficult to police and repress: 'Revolutions, sieges or other public events of absorbing attention and interest to the community, are favourable to the cure of hysteria.'[9] More mundanely, a change of scene, some new occupation, an increase of locomotive exercise were thought to be effective, but medical consensus was that the most effective cure for hysteria was marriage.[10]

While some doctors may have recognised that social conventions fostered sexual repression, they did not therefore suggest that social conventions change. Robert Brudenell Carter, for example, advocated that it was best to arrange a marriage, 'even a relatively undesirable one', when signs of hysteria began to manifest themselves. Better such a marriage for the hysterical patient than a growing addiction to medical examination and the speculum, the use of which, he warned, was reducing young women 'to the mental and moral condition of prostitutes'.[11] Edward Tilt noted that 'the absolute privation of sexual stimulus is no doubt a cause of sub-acute ovaritis in women whose passions are strong, especially when they are excited to their satisfaction by many of the fashionable amusements of civilised society. Then women suffer from one of the many forms of hysteria, sometimes caused by ovarian inflammation.' He claimed that 'psychical causes' tend to inflame and exaggerate desires which, 'though natural in themselves, may be pampered by bodily and mental inactivity, and unduly excited by thoughts, books, pictures, conversation, music, and the fascinations of social intercourse – burning desires, which cannot be quenched'.[12] Tilt alludes to social provocations in fashionable life, but the etiology of hysteria is almost always a question of biological and specifically reproductive functioning. Even though later in the century the neurologist, Horatio Bryan Donkin, did think about hysteria as a response to cultural oppression, he 'preferred the biological argument that hysteria came from unsatisfied sexual and maternal drives to the cultural argument that women were unsatisfied and thwarted in other aspects of their lives'.[13]

Although Dorothea Brooke is by no means an hysteric, she has something in common with young women thought to be prone to hysterical behaviour. In the 1860s, F. C. Skey noted that hysterical girls were often passionate and energetic, 'exhibiting more than usual force and decision of character, of strong resolution, fearless of danger, bold riders, having plenty of what is termed *nerve*'.[14] Describing the qualities of adolescents who are likely later to become hysterical, Josef Breuer himself also pointed to their energy of will and lively, gifted, intellectual natures: 'They include girls who get out of bed at night so as secretly to carry on some study that their parents have forbidden from fear of their overworking.'[15] Dorothea not only gets worked up about things that Middlemarchers cannot conceive of as a source of impassioned response, but she is also capable of staying up all night to read and of fasting like a Papist. Breuer suggests that during puberty, with the awakening of sexuality, the excitability of the hysteric releases 'free nervous energy available for the production of pathological phenomena'. Dorothea certainly tends towards self-mortification, sacrifice and suppression. She is also embarked on a displacement of the physical and sensual into the 'higher' search for truth and knowledge and useful service. In the opening chapters of *Middlemarch* the narrator is careful to convey a sense of Dorothea's struggle with sensuality and physical pleasure. She is always looking forward to giving up horseback riding, which she enjoys but regards as mere sensual indulgence, and her fondness for self-denial and asceticism is figured as a sublimation of uneasy sexuality.

Commenting on her chances of marriage, the narrator asks why such a handsome and accomplished young woman should not marry. The exclamation that follows (it is not an answer) leaves us to wonder whether Dorothea's excess and unsanctioned ardour will respond to the cure of marriage, or if it will complicate her chances of taking her place in the ordinary scheme of things: 'A young lady of some birth and fortune, who knelt suddenly down on a brick floor by the side of a sick labourer and prayed fervidly as if she thought herself living in the time of the Apostles – who had strange whims of fasting like a Papist, and of sitting up at night to read old theological books!' (p. 7). But the Middlemarchers who know her feel sure that her yearnings for a noble cause will be happily forgotten in marriage: 'As to the excessive religiousness alleged against Miss Brooke, [Sir James] had a very indefinite notion of what it consisted in, and thought that it would die out with marriage' (p. 16). Mrs Cadwallader also asserts that Dorothea is full of 'a flighty sort of Methodistical stuff' (p. 42). If not for Miss Brooke's engagement to Casaubon, she would have assured Sir James that 'these things wear out in girls'. Sir James responds with disgust to the announcement of Dorothea's engagement, and Mrs Cadwallader opines that 'this marriage to Casaubon is as good as going to a nunnery' (p. 43). Rather than a stabilising regulation or containment for Dorothea's unfixed desires, she implies, this marriage marks a grotesque displacement of sexuality.

The difference between the narrator's view and Middlemarch opinion is that the latter regards Dorothea's idealism wholly as a symptom of aberrant energy and believes that if and when her womanly energies are put to use in the only proper sphere she will behave like a normal person. Her idealistic desire to be productive is (mis)interpreted in the dominant ideology as a displacement of the natural desire to be reproductive. While the text hints that Dorothea's passion for social causes does indeed signal a displaced sexual energy, the narrator is not ready to write off her yearning for service as sublimation. We can see the narrator carefully raising the problem of how women like Dorothea can satisfy idealistic yearnings without having to jettison emotional and sexual fulfilment. Indeed, George Eliot clearly structures Dorothea's predicament in terms of a disjunction between ideals and the 'common yearning of womanhood' first articulated in the Prelude. Speaking of young Englishwomen like Dorothea, she says:

> With dim lights and tangled circumstance they tried to shape their thought and deed in noble agreement; but after all, to common eyes, their struggles seemed mere inconsistency and formlessness; for these later-born Theresas were helped by no coherent social faith and order which could perform the function of knowledge for the ardently willing soul. Their ardour alternated between a vague ideal and the common yearning of womanhood (p. 3).

Desire is directed toward both lofty and common realms. Dorothea associates the world of ideals, the lofty realm, with male learning, knowledge, and truth: 'Surely learned men kept the only oil?' (p. 64). This world of knowledge and ideals is symbolically the realm of the Father. Feminine affections and the yearnings of womanhood, at first so severely devalued in Dorothea's hierarchy of worth, are associated with the Mother. Indeed, Dorothea lives the distinctions between the mother and the father that Freud articulated so categorically in *Moses and Monotheism*: 'This turning from the mother to the father points [to]… a victory of intellectuality over sensuality – that is, an advance in civilisation, since maternity is proved by the evidence of the senses, while paternity is a hypothesis based on an inference and a premiss. Taking sides in this way with a thought process in preference to a sense perception has proved to be a momentous step.'[16] Casaubon is of course presented as the 'thought process', the Father/reader under whose tutelage Dorothea imagines that she too will learn to 'read', be wise, and align herself with progressive advances in civilisation. In Dorothea's system of valuation, an elevating desire is the desire for the power of knowledge and language in a world that privileges male speakers and where, according to Dorothea, only the Father sees truly, and only service to the Father is the route to plenitude, knowledge, and voice. It is after all Casaubon's imagined phallic power in language that draws Dorothea toward him in the first place.

What is complicated about Dorothea's dilemma is her expectation that marriage to Casaubon should be a way of satisfying not only desire for the ideal, but also the 'common yearning of womanhood'. Although Dorothea does not want to marry the virile Sir James, and responds with 'revulsion' and 'disgust' to the thought that he is interested in her, she does not, as Mrs Cadwallader puts it, marry Casaubon in order to go 'to a nunnery'; and if her distress in Rome and her later responses to Ladislaw are any evidence, Dorothea clearly does not expect to remain virginal after her marriage.[17] She assumes unconsciously, confusedly that this husband/ father/reader will satisfy all desires. The text explores therefore whether it is possible to connect the 'ardent' and 'theoretic' without sacrificing 'feminine affections'. Getting lucky, the narrator implies, means that the route through the 'theoretical' coincidentally satisfies 'common yearning'. Had Casaubon been a learned man who also kept some sexual and emotional oil, Dorothea's ardour may have been happily fuelled in both spheres. Service to the father, which in this case amounts to being Mr Casaubon's reader, should in the text's logic also covertly locate and satisfy the needs associated with the Mother, which are loosely signified as 'feminine affections'. Dorothea chooses Casaubon because she imagines that through him she will come to know what now seems dark and find the world of knowledge and truth accessible. Her fear that she should prove illegible in quarters where she desires to be read, prompts her to rewrite her acceptance letter for Casaubon three times. Since she imagines that

Casaubon is the means by which she will become a reader as well as a read text, she must continue to present herself to him as legible/eligible. If Dorothea can give her eyes to Casaubon, then she may see with his: the exchange has a strange but not unfamiliar logic. 'Those provinces of masculine knowledge seemed to her a standing-ground from which all truth could be seen more truly' (p. 47). Greek and Latin and Hebrew texts are high places, unreachable by a woman unless she is given a lift by a male textual mediator. But if we pursue the language of textuality, Casaubon is a moribund text himself, incapable of giving anyone a lift. Mrs Cadwallader, a rather practical semiologist, recognises this in her relegation of him to the level of punctuation, when she dismisses him as a bunch of semi-colons and parentheses.

But even if Dorothea's desire for such reading/service leads to a blighted bid for truth and knowledge, all would not be lost if her ardour could at least be channelled toward the satisfaction of so-called feminine needs. Hence the narrator states explicitly that if, in a crucial moment of disappointment on her honeymoon, Dorothea had been able to hang upon Casaubon's sleeve and find in him a responsive affection that might have been enough:

> With all her yearning to know what was afar from her and be widely benignant, she had ardour enough for what was near, to have kissed Mr Casaubon's coat-sleeve, or to have caressed his shoe latchet, if he would have made any other sign of acceptance than pronouncing her, with his unfailing propriety, to be of a most affectionate and truly feminine nature, indicating at the same time by politely reaching a chair for her that he regarded these manifestations as rather crude and startling (p. 147).

Before they are married, all that Casaubon says seems to her like the 'inscription on the door of a museum which might open on the treasures of past ages' (p. 24). Later in Rome, Dorothea comes to see not so much that her husband is no great scholar, but that he is incapable of animated response. When Casaubon suggests that she might like to go to the Farnesina to see some of Raphael's frescoes, Dorothea wants to know if Casaubon *cares* about them. He responds with a pedantic assessment that since some of the frescoes represent the fable of Cupid and Psyche, which is 'probably the romantic invention of a literary period' they cannot be reckoned a genuine 'mythical product'. Dorothea's disappointment is clearly not in the frescoes: 'After parting from him she went on through the museum out of mere listlessness as to what was around her' (p. 150). Clearly, the literal correlative (stony inscriptions) of the entrance that Casaubon now represents serves to highlight not the emptiness of the museum that was supposed to stock for her the treasures of past ages (truth, knowledge, the theoretical) but emotional entombment. 'See Rome and die', quips Casaubon, altering the adage in Dorothea's case to 'See Rome and live henceforth a happy wife'. The attempt at humour is stilted; with the bitter irony of his words it reinforces the sense of sterility and impotency that now comes to define their marriage. Married yet virginal, Dorothea is left unread, darkly indecipherable, and confused about reading without ardour: '"I will write to your dictation, or I will copy and extract what you tell me: I can be of no other use." Dorothea, in a most unaccountable, darkly-feminine manner, ended with a slight sob and eyes full of tears' (p. 148).

The different realms assigned in the text's discourse to the symbolic functions of Father and Mother are further suggested by horizontal and vertical axes that function as important mapping and evaluating devices. Height expresses the superiority that men are supposed to have over women. Breadth or broadness is associated with the pedestrian and with the diffusion and invisibility to which the finale draws attention. Unfortunately, to be immersed in the quotidian preoccupations of the personal lot means dispersal and seepage and silence. Broadness has also to do with sexuality; so Mr Brooke tells the ailing Casaubon to get Dorothea to read him light things (*Roderick Random* and *Humphrey Clinker*). They are a 'bit broad' but she can read anything now that she is married. 'Broad' is clearly available to Dorothea after her marriage, but the question is can she get high.

It is in this regard that George Eliot's reliance on the figure of Saint Teresa becomes significant, since the saint is represented as an ardent seeker whose desires for a productive life were satisfied. The Saint Teresa of *Middlemarch* does not apparently bear much resemblance to such versions of her as Bernini's ecstatic visionary pierced with the arrow of Christ, Breuer's patron saint of hysterics, or the star of 'Visions of Ecstasy', a British television film banned in 1989, which depicts the saint 'caressing and kissing Christ and is undercut with shots of her being erotically touched by a female character meant to represent her psyche'.[18] Nevertheless, Saint Teresa's recurrent presence in representations of erotic sublimation and in the discourse of hysteria does draw attention to a Teresa who would perhaps have been an appropriate 'patron saint' for the incipiently hysterical

Dorothea. A hysterical Saint Teresa returns as the repressed in *Middlemarch* to call attention to problematic assumptions about femininity and sexuality.

The particular and specific ways in which Teresa is evoked in *Middlemarch* as a paradigm emphasise her epic life and achievements rather than her ecstasy. George Eliot's Saint Teresa is not an ecstatic visionary, pierced with the arrow of Christ, but a practical idealist with determination and a purposeful faith; there is no mention of her famous experience of transverberation or her passionate recordings of mystical unions with Christ, accounts of which were widely known in the nineteenth century. Whereas Henry Maudsley's *The Pathology of Mind* refers to Saint Teresa in discussing hallucination and the mania of persecution, George Eliot's saint is nowhere associated with pathology.[19] The Church of the Cornaro, which houses Bernini's sculpture of the ecstasy of the transcendentally ravished woman, is just around the corner from where George Eliot places the weeping Dorothea in Rome, yet this version of the saint is miles away, as it were, from the Teresa in *Middlemarch* – the founder of a new conventual order. It is, however, the practical and energetic Teresa whom Breuer invokes when he sets out in *Studies on Hysteria* to correct the common misconception that young women who suffered from hysteria were listless and unproductive. In the same vein as some Victorian medical treatises on hysteria, Breuer argues that hysteria does not preclude strong mental faculty and 'solid mental endowment'. He continues: 'The patron saint of hysteria, Saint Theresa, was a woman of genius with great practical capacity.'[20] She was after all responsible for the reform of a conventual system. Like George Eliot, but in service of a different design, Breuer focuses on the energy of will, purpose, and practical capacity of Teresa. But whereas Breuer moves on to suggest that high achievement and hysterical response are by no means mutually exclusive, George Eliot dwells on the way that social structures and conditions can thwart or accommodate energetic and purposeful women. The tone of her emphases is similar to that of the summary of Teresa's life in the 1861 edition of Chamber's *Encyclopedia*: 'The most notable and permanent fruit of the enthusiastic spirituality of Teresa is the reform of the Carmelite order, of which she became the instrument.' 'Enthusiastic spirituality' has a robust, wholesome quality, describing a productive faith the effects of which are imaged in terms of fertility and reproductivity. As the agent of reform, whose considerable energies were channelled into a far-reaching and long-lived productivity, why should Teresa not be an ideal for other young, spiritually enthusiastic women? From Breuer's point of view such descriptions of Teresa's efficacy are accurate but incomplete. He would want to add that, although figuratively presented as a fruit bearer, literally she was a sterile hysteric. Breuer's discourse is informed by overt oppositions such as literal and figurative, sterile and productive; in *Middlemarch* too such alternatives and oppositions are operative even if in a covert manner.

Mary Jacobus briefly draws the contexts of Breuer and George Eliot together in her provocative discussions of hysteria in *Reading Woman*. Quoting Breuer's remark that hysterics are sterile and beautiful like double flowers, she writes: 'Not just flowers (as women should be), but double flowers, hysterics are represented as being at once more decorative than other women, and reproductively sterile; at best they can hope to resemble, like George Eliot's Dorothea Brooke, the woman whom Breuer calls "the patron saint of hysteria" – Saint Theresa, a woman of good deeds.'[21] Jacobus' remarks tacitly link Dorothea Brooke and the hysteric through their relationship to Saint Teresa: both can at best hope to emulate the productive and useful woman. The implication is that the hysteric, as Breuer conceives her, may be productive but not reproductive. As metaphorical Mother in her conventual order, Saint Teresa epitomises Breuer's observations and it is exactly in these terms that George Eliot anticipates Breuer in her representation of Dorothea, since Dorothea's dilemma in the novel is structured implicitly by the difficulty of reconciling *productive* and *reproductive*: as a latter-day Saint Teresa, Dorothea is 'foundress of nothing', but she does eventually produce a number of children, and she is 'only known in a certain circle as a wife and mother' (p. 611).

Although George Eliot explores Dorothea's case in terms of alternatives that depend on repression and exclusion, she declines to deal with Saint Teresa in like terms. The possibility that Teresa's epic achievement and productivity demanded the repression of her sexual or reproductive self is not considered because George Eliot's focus is on the failure of nineteenth-century English social structures to nurture ardent questers. Saint Teresa is evoked in the context of yearning and higher purpose, preparing the ground for the representation of Dorothea Brooke as a latter-day Saint Teresa with reduced heroic opportunity in early Victorian England. Breuer's concern, by contrast, is with what kinds of sexual repression produce hysterical symptoms and what kinds of women suffer these symptoms. Yet these different approaches both allow a point of convergence. George Eliot's critique of educational practices and cramping attitudes toward women's capacities indicts constructions of gender, while Breuer's (and Freud's) focus on the sexual etiology of hysteria stops short of examining hysteria as a response to ideological and cultural constraints. But if George Eliot pre-dates Breuer and Freud because her attention is not focused on sexual issues alone, her emphasis on the wider social issues that constrain and frustrate self-expression also tentatively anticipates post-Freudian attention to social structures and cultural forces as agents and causal factors in hysterical response. Increasingly, contemporary critiques of Freud point out that the history of psychoanalysis and its theorising of hysteria yields a range of problematic assumptions about the nature of 'femininity' and female sexuality, rather than a definitive understanding of a clinical pathology – hysteria.[22]

What did Saint Teresa signify for George Eliot's readers and how would they have known about her? The narrator is able to draw on Saint Teresa as a paradigm of the epic seeker because cultivated nineteenth-century readers were probably acquainted with her in these terms. The novel begins with the question: 'Who that cares much to know the history of man and how the mysterious mixture behaves under the varying experiments of Time, has not dwelt, at least briefly, on the life of Saint Theresa?' (p. 3). The assumed answer is, of course, 'I have.'[23] The 'at least briefly' suggests that while readers may not have intensive knowledge, a passing acquaintance with the saint's biography can reasonably be expected.[24] Not only was a spate of popular biographies published during the century, but encyclopedias began to include specific entries about her. In the 1817 edition of the *Encyclopedia Britannica*, for example, there is no entry on Teresa, but by the end of the century a lengthy and full account of her life, her mysticism, and her works can be found. Teresa does not occupy a great deal of narrative time – she is invoked in the Prelude, mentioned a few times in the course of the narrative, and cited briefly in the finale. Yet the terms in which the narrator frames her representation of Dorothea are heavily dependent on the inspiring vision of this heroic woman: she is set up as a paradigm against which the narrator measures Dorothea's ardent nature and longing for a cause or outlet that will demand and channel that ardour. George Eliot recognises that problematic desire is what Saint Teresa and Dorothea have in common; they diverge, the narrative is at pains to emphasise, because of their different social contexts. Had Dorothea lived in sixteenth-century Spain, she too might have found her 'epos' in a conventual order; instead provincial England in the 1830s gives her 'the home epic' in which to make her mark and find satisfaction: marriage is the site in which her ardent spirit must crusade to find martyrdom or fulfilment.

It becomes clear that the example of Teresa is very carefully managed by the narrator to underscore two important aspects of George Eliot's focus: that ordinary mortals have to accept limitation and limited satisfaction, but that a recognition of thwarting and constraining social conditions may enable us to improve them. According to the narrator, Teresa lived at a time, when, for a variety of reasons, heroic deeds were still possible. Not only was a coherent social faith available to structure idealism, but the opportunity to effect significant change was greater than in England at the time of the First Reform Bill. The epilogue informs us that 'the medium of ... ardent deeds is forever gone', and the nineteenth-century likes of Antigone and Saint Teresa have to contend with different social realities and historical conditions.

Not all early readers accepted the narrator's readiness to write off opportunities in their own time for the expression of idealistic energy. One such reader was Florence Nightingale, who objected to George Eliot's portrayal of Dorothea as a frustrated Saint Teresa. She pointed out that there were women around – Octavia Hill, for example – who were making their philanthropic ideals 'very real indeed'.[25] The objection makes one see that it is not only the ostensible issue of philanthropic practice that is at stake (or the fact that Octavia Hill was not born until 1838) but the complex problem of passion and suffering and sacrifice for an ideal. Teresa and Antigone are not easily matched by Octavia Hill and, moreover, Teresa is a more useful paradigm than Antigone exactly because of the submerged associations she has with bodily privation and religious ecstasy. Despite the narrator's emphasis on the saint's productive energies, therefore, the text also inscribes the association of Teresa with suffering and self-denial, qualities that have traditionally defined the highest ideal of femininity.[26]

George Eliot uses her insight 'that the medium of ardent deeds is gone' to reconcile the reader to the inevitable limitation of satisfaction that we ordinary mortals have to accept – men and women alike. So, for example, later in the novel when the narrator describes Lydgate's dreams and ambitions, she suggests that we know of the great founders and originators only after they have been elevated and enshrined:

> Each of those 'Shining Ones' had to walk on the earth among neighbours who perhaps thought much more of his gait and his garments than of anything which was to give him a title to everlasting fame: each of them had his little local personal history sprinkled with small temptations and sordid cares, which made the retarding friction of his course towards final companionship with the immortals (p. 109).

But 'retarding friction' is often the facilitating grit of fiction; it is what interests the novelist who is not writing so much of the 'Shining Ones' but of struggling ones, successful or otherwise. Although George Eliot is not concerned with her in this passage, Saint Teresa is a very good case in point. She may be enshrined and elevated, but she too, as her autobiography bears testimony, experienced a great deal of 'retarding friction' en route to companionship with the immortals. Because she is interested in Teresa as a paradigm of one who desired, sought, and found an epic life, the narrator does not focus on the extraordinary friction of Saint Teresa's life, which even the briefest biographical accounts usually acknowledge.

Nor does the opening question of the novel foreground Teresa as a woman struggling with the desires and yearnings that are specifically problematic for women. She is presented initially as an interesting example in the 'history of man' – the generic, perhaps ungendered seeker whose demand for an epic life illustrates that passion, rapture, and their expression in a transcendent cause are enduring human problems. The paragraphs that follow the introduction to Saint Teresa hint that in latter-day Saint Teresas such problems need to be considered in relation to constructions of gender and in terms of the split in women between 'vague ideals' and 'the common yearning of womanhood'.

The narrator does not point out what a brief scrutiny of the saint's autobiography reveals: like Dorothea, Teresa did struggle with prevailing devaluations of what is associated with the feminine. She too felt that learned men kept the only oil: 'I praise God greatly – we women, and those who are unlearned, ought always to render him unceasing thanks – because there are persons [priests] who, by labours so great, have attained to the truth, of which we unlearned people are ignorant.'[27] Convalescing at the home of her revered and religious uncle, Teresa was exposed to learned and pious books – a contrast to the corrupting, time-wasting romances she associated with her mother. As George Eliot writes:

> Theresa's passionate, ideal nature demanded an epic life: what were many-volumed romances of chivalry and the social conquests of a brilliant girl to her? Her flame quickly burned up that light fuel; and, fed from within, soared after some illimitable satisfaction, some object which would never justify weariness, which would reconcile self-despair with the rapturous consciousness of life beyond self (p. 3).

To 'get high' she had to leave all that was associated with lowly female desires, and she did so more decisively than Dorothea Brooke. But what is conveniently occluded in *Middlemarch* is George Eliot's perception of the costs of such leave-taking. For an important part of the spiritualisation of desire in Teresa's case was the mortification of the body; her autobiography does not lack evidence of the enormous physical suffering she experienced. She describes how, as a young woman, she lay once for four days presumed dead. Wax was placed on her eyelids and when she awoke, her tongue was bitten to pieces; there was choking in her throat and for the next three years she was quite unable to walk. Such accounts describe a paradox – a hysterical split – validated and underwritten by religious approval: 'When I was ill, I was well with God.'[28] Perhaps this paradox is most forcefully evidenced in the accounts of her visions, which record with intense passion and ecstasy the 'sweetness of excessive pain'. Describing how a seraph holding the arrow of Christ has pierced her with fiery love, she writes:

> I saw in his hand a long spear of gold, and at the iron's point there seemed to be a little fire. He appeared to me to be thrusting it at times into my heart and to pierce my very entrails; when he drew it out, he seemed to draw them out also and to leave me all on fire with a great love of God. The pain was so great that it made me moan; and yet so surpassing was the sweetness of this excessive pain that I could not wish to be rid of it.... It is a caressing of love so sweet which now takes place between the soul and God.... I wished to see or speak to no one, but only to cherish my pain, which was to me a greater bliss than all created things could give me.[29]

Bernini depicts this account in sexualised terms in his famous sculpture of the saint being pierced by the seraph with the fiery arrow of Christ's love. Descriptions of the work usually associate the saint's posture with sexual ecstasy: her swoon, or her ecstatic trance, the lips that hang inert and numb, her eyes that are half-closed and her mouth 'opened in an almost audible moan'.[30]

In twentieth-century discourse on hysteria, the subordination of the body and the 'sweetness of excessive pain' become important signifiers of hysterical repression.[31] Having made a connection between hysteria and sexual repression, psychoanalytic discourse examines the 'jouissance' of hysterical displacement. If the 'hysterogenic body is produced when the sexualisation of the erotogenic body has somehow been disrupted', then what is it that attains the ecstasy which supposedly belonged to the sexualised body?[32] About a century after George Eliot cited Teresa as exemplary of epic female achievement, Lacan published his seminars on jouissance with a photograph of Bernini's sculpture on the cover – Saint Teresa as the 'insatiably orgasmic woman'.[33] Julia Kristeva, writing about the jouissance of the saint, notes that the saint's passion for the symbolic depends on making 'her own body the exalted, sanctioned sign of denial' – a particularly apt description of Teresa's case, where the ground of ecstasy is the suppression and mortification of the body.[34]

'Maternity knots and unknots paranoia, the ground on which hysterics stand'[35]

If Saint Teresa as the patron saint of hysterics returns as the repressed in *Middlemarch* to destabilise notions of ideal and common yearnings, the figure of the Madonna also plays an important but problematic part in the representation of Dorothea and its engagements with constructions of female sexuality. Throughout the novel Dorothea is quietly associated with the iconography and pictorial representations of the Madonna and the Blessed Virgin. Although Dorothea's lot is that of ordinary womankind – marriage and actual motherhood – her association with Western culture's highest Mother, allows her to be figured inspirationally as a type of motherhood. George Eliot enlists the image of the Madonna to give Dorothea, earthly wife and mother, a special status. But just as Saint Teresa, through her hovering presence in the text, reinforces rather than transcends the

costs of productivity, so the Madonna images elevate the reproductive sphere, but only by reinforcing the synonymity of sexuality
and maternity.

An obvious difference between the use of Saint Teresa and the
Madonna in the novel is that George Eliot evokes specifically visual
images of the Madonna, and invites the reader to look at Dorothea as
if she were a subject for a painting. George Eliot had once responded
to a visual representation of the annunciation, writing about the
Madonna in a way that imagined the young woman's reactions to
being chosen for an extraordinary position:

> A young maiden, believing herself to be on the eve of the chief event
> of her life – marriage – about to share in the ordinary lot of woman-
> hood, full of young hope, has suddenly announced to her that she is
> chosen to fulfil a great destiny, entailing a terribly different experi-
> ence from that of ordinary womanhood.[36]

One might invert the terms of this evocative narrative to produce
Dorothea's story, or point to the parallels between this account of the
Virgin and that of Dorothea in *Middlemarch*, which begins, 'a young
lady of some birth and fortune...' (p. 7). My point is, however, that
the Madonna in *Middlemarch* is no longer imagined as a young
woman whose reaction to her great destiny solicits our identification; rather she functions as a powerful and inspirational icon that
seeks to imbue Dorothea's destiny of ordinary womanhood with an
aura of greatness.

In order to see why the figure of the Madonna is evoked specifically in the form of visual images in the novel, we must look for a
moment at the debates about representation between Ladislaw and
his friend, the artist Naumann. They argue about whether painting
or language is a 'finer medium' for the representation of women.
Naumann desires to paint Dorothea, referring to her as the 'most
perfect young Madonna' he has ever seen, to which Ladislaw responds:

> Language gives a fuller image, which is all the better for being vague.
> After all, the true seeing is within; and painting stares at you with an
> insistent imperfection. I feel that especially about representations of
> women. As if a woman were a mere coloured superficies! You must
> wait for movement and tone ... they change from moment to
> moment (p. 142).

Language is a better medium of representation than painting, Will
suggests, because painting would not be able to represent motility

and voice. If the medium of language can give Dorothea voice, then presumably she can be heard rather than being merely observed. And since language is the better for being vague, Dorothea would not, Will implies, be fixed in the specular space of pictorial representation, but read in the fullness of language's flexible evocation.

These remarks about the representation of women are significant beyond their immediate context – Ladislaw's Romantic aestheticism and his slightly competitive appropriation of Dorothea. They draw attention to the way George Eliot handles the representation of Dorothea using the medium that gives a 'fuller image'. Yet that representation does draw strongly on visual images and responses to painting. The connection between Dorothea's association with the Madonna and the opposition in the novel between verbal and visual media lies in the role of the image, especially the image of the Madonna, which plays a large part in George Eliot's attempts to synthesise word and image and to counteract their traditional gender associations. By thinking about aspects of the representation of Dorothea in the context of the claims for verbal over visual in matters of representation, we can see how George Eliot attempts to negotiate the opposition between productive and reproductive energies raised by the references to Saint Teresa.

Ladislaw's preference for the verbal as a 'finer medium' than the visual depends on a view of language that we can characterise as Romantic. In his study of iconology, W. J. T. Mitchell discusses what Romantic writers claim in their conception of the image: '[they] assimilate mental, verbal and even pictorial imagery into the mysterious process of "imagination" which is typically defined in contrast to the "mere" recall of mental pictures... and (in painting) the "mere" depiction of external visibilia, as opposed to the spirit, feeling or "property" of a scene'.[37] When imagination comes into the picture, as it were, the very concept of imagery is divided between the 'pictorial or graphic image which is a lower form – external, mechanical, dead and often associated with the empiricist model of perception – and a "higher" image which is internal, organic and living'.[38] As Will says: 'And what is a portrait of a woman? Your painting and Plastik are poor stuff after all. They perturb and dull conceptions instead of raising them. Language is a finer medium' (p. 142). Furthermore, his reservations about the expressive capacity of painting invoke an old argument in which poetry or the verbal concerns itself with motion, sound and continuous time, whereas painting deals with space, silence and stasis.[39] It is not surprising therefore that Will, who wants to write and be a poet, and who hears the sound of the Aeolian harp in Dorothea's voice, later tells Dorothea that she is a poem, which is presumably much preferable to being a portrait (p. 166).

Poetry and painting as media of representation carry longstanding gender associations: the history of debates about the relative merits of the arts reveals that while poetry is a 'manly' art, painting has traditionally been aligned with conceptions of the feminine.[40] Ephraim Gotthold Lessing's influential *Laokoon* provides a good example of such gender attributions and is particularly apposite since we know that George Eliot thought very highly of it. Mitchell's interpretive paraphrase of Lessing's views allows us to explore the implications for gender in Lessing's views of genre:

> Paintings, like women, are ideally silent, beautiful creatures designed for the gratification of the eye, in contrast to the sublime eloquence proper to the manly art of poetry. Paintings are confined to the narrow sphere of external display of their bodies and of the space which they ornament, while poems are free to range over an infinite realm of potential action and expression, the domain of time, discourse and history.[41]

Dorothea herself seems familiar with some of the implications of these views: her distaste for the fine arts and music lies partly in the belief they are light-weight and domestic, by implication associated with feminine inconsequentiality and ornamentation. When she thinks of writing and 'poems', however, she thinks of great masculine texts, such as those of Hooker and Milton. While the narrator through humour and irony distances herself from such unsubtle gender attributions, through Dorothea's story she pleads for the mutual valuation of these polarities more than she imagines their dissolution. In terms of oppositions between high and broad, Mother and Father, and word and painting, Dorothea's story can be understood as her pursuit of the symbolic Father and the word through her relationship to Casaubon, and her subsequent relinquishment of what the word *in extremis* has stood for. Learning the expressive capacity of the image, Dorothea symbolically finds Mother and herself takes on the qualities of an inspiring image of motherhood. The text makes literal that symbolic finding, revealing that if Dorothea is to find expression of emotional, 'womanly' needs, she has to conform to the patriarchal logic of women = Woman = Mother.[42] In this regard, the Madonna images function as a means of elevating the maternal; the implication is that Dorothea in the ordinary role of wife and mother is worthy of the same reverence and respect that Western culture's highest Mother commands.

The narrator's discourse works at incorporating the emotional power associated with visual images in the medium of language; her attempt to translate and appropriate for textuality some of the representational qualities of painting blurs the boundaries between verbal and visual and can perhaps be seen as an attempt to feminise the word and to fuse thought and feeling. One of the ways in which the narrative itself works strenuously at an amalgamation of Mother and Father is by subsuming the emotionality of 'image' into 'text' in the act of representing Dorothea's movement toward emotionality, sexuality and maternity.[43] Throughout the novel, the narrator invests considerable energy in urging the reader to learn how to 'read' with the benefit of a Romantic synthesis of image and word, emotion and intellect. Since paintings and the responses to painting function throughout the novel as indices of emotional capacity, to be blind to pictorial art is a failure of emotional openness, a repression of what the novel associates pre-eminently with the 'feminine'. It is significant, therefore, that we are taught about 'reading' through the following example that deals with painting. Just prior to the exchange between Naumann and Will quoted earlier, the narrator delivers a little warning on the misreading of Christian art:

> In those days, the world in general was more ignorant of good and evil by forty years than it is at present. Travellers did not often carry full information on Christian art either in their heads or their pockets; and even the most brilliant English critic of the day mistook the flower-flushed tomb of the ascended Virgin for an ornamental vase due to the painter's fancy (pp. 139-40).

It is to be hoped, the narrator is saying, that you, reader, would be able to tell the Virgin's tomb from an ornamental vase. (In the Finale she hopes similarly that the reader appreciates the significance of *this* Madonna's 'unvisited tomb'.) The narrator continues, explaining why these days are different from those:

> Romanticism, which has helped to fill some dull blanks with love and knowledge, had not yet penetrated the times with its leaven and entered into everybody's food; it was fermenting still as a distinguish-able vigorous enthusiasm in certain long-haired German artists at

Rome, and the youth of other nations who worked or idled near them were sometimes caught in the spreading movement (p. 142).

As well as offering an ironic smile at Ladislaw's heady fervour, the narrator is making a claim for Romantic aesthetics as a mode of apprehending that can dispel the sort of mistake even the 'most brilliant' critic could make. Why does Romanticism help us to know the 'flower-flushed tomb' of the ascended Virgin for what it is? The reference to 'love and knowledge' is a crucial directive for right reading since love (construed as a catholicity of emotion) leads to sympathetic understanding and knowledge. The ways of knowing that are valued here are those which have their root in emotional openness. Romanticism, as the narrator presents it, is flexible and embracing and opposed to all that is narrow, censoring and exclusive. Because of its attention to emotion and the expressive potential in language and painting, Romanticism is capable of generating a powerful fusion of thought and feeling. It does the work here of reclaiming an alien past – the icons and figures of Catholicism, for example – and making that past relevant and accessible. Romanticism recuperates the wide emotional appeal of the image without accepting its status as a Papist icon. Similarly, we may say that Dorothea, associated with images of the Madonna, acquires some of the powerful effect that those images produce without having to embrace a self-sacrificial saintliness.

If the 'best English critic' of Dorothea's day can mistake the tomb of the ascended Virgin for a vase due to the painter's fancy, then Romanticism has certainly some work cut out for it. (The critic is Hazlitt. He apparently misread the iconography of Raphael's *The Coronation of the Virgin* in the Vatican Museum.)[44] That something of great spiritual significance could be overlooked or dismissed as an empty decoration, is testimony to the need for love and knowledge. Similarly, if Dorothea's world cannot recognise her significance, those who come after her should. The text wants, therefore, a 'Romantic' reader, whom the narrator's solicitations set out to educate: 'She walked briskly in the brisk air, the colour rose in her cheeks, and her straw bonnet (which our contemporaries might look at with conjectural curiosity as at an obsolete form of basket) fell a little backward. She would perhaps hardly be characterised enough if it were omitted that she wore her brown hair flatly braided' (p. 20). The first sentence establishes the reader's connection to the narrator in a realm beyond Dorothea's, enlisting the reader in an enlightened perspective and marking the passage of time through references to Dorothea's old-fashioned bonnet. The narrator then tells us how Dorothea would be seen by the observers in her own world through whose hypothetical gaze we are often invited to see: 'All people, young or old (that is, all people in those ante-reform times), would have thought her an interesting object if they had referred the glow in her eyes and cheeks to the newly-awakened ordinary images of young love.' The narrator emphasises that Dorothea would have been thought an interesting object only if the cause of her glow fulfilled the traditional romance script. Dorothea's unreadability in her world is translated for us, as the narrator implies that we (now) as opposed to them (then) will find her an interesting object even if the glow in her cheeks is not attributable to the sanctioned anticipations of the 'blooming matron'.

In contrast to the fortunate reader, who has the guidance and direction of the narrator, and can be nudged toward right reading, Dorothea, both an unskilled reader and a short-sighted viewer, has to figure things out for herself. On account of her interest in reading the books of great men and the world that lies behind the words of men, Dorothea has overvalued the word. One could say that she moves from being a repressed reader of texts to being a receptive viewer of paintings, a movement which signals her capacity to acknowledge her own emotions and sexuality. Dorothea's growth manifests itself in learning to license emotions that are personal and gratifying even if they are not immediately part of a grand plan for improving the human condition. When Dorothea meets Ladislaw for the first time as he is sketching, she says to Mr Brooke:

> You know, uncle, I never see the beauty of those pictures which you say are so much praised. I suppose there is some relation between pictures and nature which I am too ignorant to feel – just as you see what a Greek sentence stands for which means nothing to me (p. 58).

Dorothea's analogy is misleading: while there is, as Ladislaw points out, a language to art that one can learn, response is also a matter of feeling and sensitivity to beauty. Dorothea cannot read Greek because she has not learned its sign system; this is an intellectual problem. She can't respond to paintings because, in her ascetic terms, emotionality that is not directed to the universal good is unlicensed and ought to be denied, like her pleasure in horseriding. The subtle links between responses to painting, pleasurable emotions, sexual feelings, and the feminine are thus made.

Taking up the subject of art and appreciation again, Ladislaw says: 'I fear you are a heretic about art generally.' Dorothea replies:

I should like to make life beautiful – I mean everybody's life. And then all this immense expense of art, that seems somehow to lie outside life and make it no better for the world, pains one. It spoils my enjoyment of anything when I am made to think that most people are shut out from it (pp. 162-3).

Initially, Dorothea's confused emotional investments and blockages are well signalled by the fact that she can respond to music and painting only when they overpower her. She confesses that she sobbed hearing the music of the great organ in Freiburg; she also admits that at times she feels overwhelmed by paintings, at least momentarily:

At first when I enter a room where the walls are covered with frescoes, or with rare pictures, *I feel a kind of awe* – like a child present at great ceremonies where there are grand robes and processions; *I feel myself in the presence of some higher life than my own*. But when I begin to examine the pictures one by one, the life goes out of them, or else is something violent and strange to me (p. 153; my emphasis).

The language of the passage points to Dorothea's potential for experiencing emotions viscerally – the way George Eliot herself responded to the Sistine Madonna in 1858, when she visited the Dresden Gallery: 'I sat down on the sofa opposite the picture for an instant; but *a sort of awe, as if I were suddenly in the living presence of some glorious being, made my heart swell*' [my emphasis].[45] Evidently she went back several times during her stay to see the painting and was thus overpowered each time. Not only does she use the same kind of terms to describe the effect that paintings have on Dorothea, but some deleted phrases from the manuscript version of *Middlemarch* reveal that she was thinking about Dorothea as affecting others in a way that is as powerful as the Sistine Madonna had been to her. When Dorothea arrives to speak to Rosamond in Chapter 81, George Eliot originally wrote: 'Dorothea's face had become animated; and as it beamed on Rosamond very close to her, *she felt something like <awe> of a <supernatural> presence*' [my emphasis].[46] Without making too much of a passage that was after all deleted, I think one can argue that in writing this scene George Eliot was searching for a way to show that Dorothea can make even Rosamond experience the same kind of response that George Eliot herself had towards Raphael's Madonna. Dorothea is represented so as to elicit powerful feelings conducive to actions which in turn constitute 'the growing good of the world' – she becomes an inspiration to others, as Rosamond's response is the first case to testify. All her life Rosamond keeps in 'religious remembrance the generosity which had come to her aid in the sharpest crisis of her life' (p. 610).

But Dorothea can occupy her status as a powerful emotional influence and inspiration only when she has learned the value of emotionality in its various forms. One of the ways that George Eliot represents her growing awareness of the value of emotion is through Dorothea's own response to paintings. As Dorothea finds herself moving painfully from an ascetic puritanism (characterised by repressed emotions and ignorance or suspicion of art) she is on the way to embracing an aesthetic catholicism that indicates a new psychological freedom and integrity.

The beginning of her conversion to 'reading' through the emotions, seems in retrospect like a 'disease of the retina' and, befitting a conversion, takes place in Rome. Since Rome is where she begins to discover how she has misread Casaubon, the reference to the disease of the retina points to an awareness of a vision more distorted than she knew. More significantly, the scenes that she sees in Rome seem to erupt in emotions which unsettle the orderly and straitened channels for expression that she has known. Rome represents the unintelligible welter of emotions (sexual and passionate, among others) that Dorothea has avoided facing; the city's panorama seems therefore to her a lurid carnival or promiscuous kaleidoscope of different art forms that force on her deep impressions against which she has no defence and which she lacks means to interpret. [47]

By the time Naumann paints Casaubon, Dorothea, though still sceptical about painting, has begun to doubt that Casaubon is indeed the province from which truth can be seen more truly. As Naumann gives them 'little dissertations' on his finished and unfinished subjects and Will chimes in to praise his friend's work, the narrator comments:

> Dorothea felt that she was getting quite new notions as to the significance of Madonnas seated under inexplicable canopied thrones with the simple country as a background…. Some things which had seemed monstrous to her were gathering intelligibility and even had a natural meaning, but all this was apparently a branch of knowledge in which Mr Casaubon had not interested himself (p. 159).

Besides inviting us to smile at Naumann's Nazarene symbolism, the passage also marks an opening up for Dorothea and the beginnings of a recuperation of feelings and ardour from the narrow intellectual world represented by Casaubon in which she has invested so much. The passage is richly suggestive of the widening of Dorothea's frame of reference, not only about paintings but more importantly about herself. For what is it that formerly seemed monstrous but now seems intelligible, even natural? Is Dorothea making strides as a 'reader' of paintings, becoming an aesthete? Hugh Witemeyer's view about Dorothea's aesthetic capacity is that 'As the novel progresses, Ladislaw becomes less the aesthete, but Dorothea does not become more the connoiseuse.'[48] I would suggest, however, that the text is not really concerned with Dorothea's progress as an aesthete except in so far as it marks a growing awareness of her 'womanly' needs. Eliot's textual strategy is to use Dorothea's aesthetic interest and response as a way of signifying a subtext about her increasingly poignant emotional hunger and emerging capacity for sexuality and passion. Discussion of Naumann's paintings and her response to them is apparently about aesthetic response, but since emotional aesthetic response is here a signifier for displaced sexuality, terms such as 'monstrous' and 'natural' are interesting markers in Dorothea's evolution as a sexual and passionate woman. The self-denying Dorothea who early in the book abjures horseriding and feels guilty about her desire for her mother's emerald ring has regarded all forms of sensuality as 'monstrous'; now she is becoming capable of accepting such feelings as 'natural'. And that indeed, as the narrator points out ostensibly in relation to art, but really in relation to emotions and sexuality, is not something that Casaubon knows anything about.

Yet while what we may call the aesthetic subtext traces Dorothea's emotional awakening, the narrative's association of her with images of the Madonna suggests her status as an inspirational type of motherhood and confirms the representation of sexuality as maternity. Although in her letters and novels George Eliot invokes the Madonna most often to represent feminine saintliness and goodness, she occasionally uses artistic representations of the Madonna to suggest stasis or fixity, a contrast to living women who struggle with problematic lives. In *The Mill on the Floss* the narrator comments on Raphael's fixed and unadaptable Madonnas where she describes Mrs Tulliver's inadequacies in dealing with Maggie:

> I have often wondered whether those early Madonnas of Raphael, with the blond faces and somewhat stupid expression, kept their

placidity undisturbed when their strong-limbed, strong-willed boys got a little too old to do without clothing. I think they must have been given to feeble remonstrance, getting more and more peevish as it became more and more ineffectual.[49]

'Blond faces' and 'stupid expressions' may get by well enough with docile infants, but mothers had better look sharper than those 'early Madonnas of Raphael's when they have to deal effectively with active, questing children. George Eliot makes the point that idealised representations of motherhood do not take into account the emotional responsiveness required by 'real' women living through the daily demands of children and domesticity. Similarly, in her impassioned analysis of Margaret Fuller and Mary Wollstonecraft, Marian Evans castigates the reluctance of men to treat women with 'justice and sober reverence', instead of making them 'idols, useless absorbents of precious things'.[50] Such an idol is 'fit for nothing but to sit in her drawing-room like a doll-Madonna in her shrine'. There is, however, a world of difference between the stupid expressions of Raphael's early Madonnas or the static ornamentality of doll-Madonnas and the emotionally compelling Sistine Madonna – this 'sublimest picture' she called it.

Marina Warner writes in *Alone of All Her Sex* about the subtle denigration of women implicit in the 'very celebration of the perfect human woman'.[51] Like Warner, recent feminist critics examining the ideological functions of Madonna mythology and the cult of the Virgin have argued that the image of the Madonna in Western culture represents both a sanctification and colonisation of the female body. Woman as defined by the image of the Madonna is 'sanctified' because carnality is eliminated in the 'virginal Maternal'; she is thought of as 'colonised' when she serves an ideology which dictates that her dominant function is to reproduce.[52]

While George Eliot does not suggest that the Madonna is a model of femininity that traps Western women, she is implicitly critical of ideals or models of womanhood that cramp female potential. We can understand therefore why her novels are persistently concerned to explore madonnahood and which aspects of it seem mutually contradictory or incompatible. It is useful to think of the many meanings 'madonna' has for George Eliot as a function of possible combinations of three categories: motherhood, sexuality, saintliness. The paradigm of madonnahood – the Virgin Mary presented with the Christ child – clearly combines first and last, miraculously bypassing the middle term through the notion of Virgin Birth. Throughout her fiction George Eliot has run experiments on the nature of female longing and aspiration and the social circumstances of its limited satisfaction. While responsibility to duty and the renunciation of personal passion or fulfilment may purchase what may be called saintliness, the rewards of such self-denial are in most cases circumscribed. For example, Romola as a madonna figure is primarily saint, but also quasi-mother since she ends up taking care of her late but unlamented husband's illegitimate children. Despite Romola's exalted status, her fate has repeatedly failed to please or satisfy readers.[53] The end of the novel sacrifices the possibility of a personal, passionate and sexual life for Romola, which simply confirms the commonplace that satisfied sexuality and saintly stature are mutually exclusive. Although her madonnahood can accommodate a vicarious form of maternity, it must apparently exclude the middle category: sexuality. (Saint Teresa also combines sainthood and metaphorical motherhood – she is mother in her new conventual order.) By contrast, Esther Lyons in *Felix Holt* is most clearly the heroine whose emotional and sexual fulfilment is not a tragic choice, but then she does not have the passionate aspiration for selfless service that characterises Dorothea at the start of *Middlemarch*. Indeed, Esther is specifically described as 'verging neither towards the saint nor the angel'. What is interesting about the representation of Dorothea is George Eliot's struggle to incorporate the middle term, sexuality, and to negotiate its compatibility with some degree of saintliness. Since George Eliot does not wish to sacrifice Dorothea's emotional and sexual needs, motherhood and sexuality will be the strong terms of the combination, if she is to be a madonna figure at all. In so far as her representation manifests the subtle interrelationship and balancing of all three terms of madonnahood, Dorothea is George Eliot's most delicate and complex case.

One of the first details given about Dorothea is that her hands and wrist are 'so finely formed that she could wear sleeves not less bare of style than those in which the Blessed Virgin appeared to Italian painters' (p. 5). The narrator asks here that we link Dorothea, through the image of her unadorned dress, to Renaissance representations of the Madonna. Later in Rome, the painter Naumann declares he would like to paint Dorothea and describes her as the most perfect young Madonna he has ever seen. Apart from Lydgate's reference to Dorothea – she has 'a heart large enough' for the Virgin Mary – most of the associations between Dorothea and the Madonna are in the context of Christian art and its iconography of idealised motherhood. When Naumann sees her she stands against a pedestal near the marble voluptuousness of the 'reclining Ariadne', thought at that time, the narrator informs us, to be a sculpture of Cleopatra. Critics have discussed the importance of the comparison between Dorothea and the sculpture, but do not acknowledge the significance of the statue's mistaken identity.[54] In *Villette*, as we have seen, the representation of an Egyptian dancing-girl as a Cleopatra figure has much to say about cultural associations of sexuality and oriental exoticism; in *Middlemarch* a statue described as voluptuous and taken as a representation of Cleopatra serves to emphasise Dorothea's spirituality. The Cleopatra-like Ariadne is surely the antithesis of Dorothea, a contrast reinforced by the 'Quakerish' drapery and the 'sort of halo' made by Dorothea's white beaver bonnet. The reference to her 'beautiful ungloved hand' links her to the opening image, as her hand evokes Renaissance representations of the Blessed Virgin (p. 140). She is also described as 'unshamed' by the Ariadne, which suggests that in contrast to pagan sensuousness, her sexuality is spiritualised. Like the Madonna, whose gaze in many Renaissance paintings is meditative and unseeing, Dorothea stares abstractedly before her, not even seeing the statue, her 'large eyes fixed dreamily on a streak of sunlight' on the floor (p. 140). About to be rescued from emotional and sexual entombment with Casaubon (signified through disappointed readership), Dorothea's linkage to images of the Madonna lifts her fate of mothering and marriage out of the ordinary. This a compensatory way of giving breadth some height.

A well-remarked scene in the novel is that in which Dorothea discovers her passionate love for Will. Critical commentary usually passes over Dorothea's anguished self-recognition to attend to her 'moment of transcendence' – the experience of connection to the world outside as she looks out of the window the next morning. It is significant, however, that Dorothea's discovery of passionate love is represented in terms that evoke the experience of labour and the giving of birth; she becomes metaphorically a mother. The 'very little seed', planted and kept alive 'since the days in Rome' leads to this 'mysterious incorporeal might' which has Dorothea stretched on the floor, her 'grand woman's frame' shaking as she lies there sobbing. (Metaphorically, this is a version of Virgin Birth; impregnated by the seed planted in Rome, Dorothea is, through the course of the narrative, unknowingly in a state of gestation.) Dorothea discovers her passion for Will in the very moment of her knowledge of separation and loss. As she pictures Will and stretches out her arms towards him she is pierced by the knowledge that this nearness is a parting vision – maternity signified as parturition.[55] The narrator describes her anguish as a response to the vivid images that she sees within. The wrench of finding and losing is also depicted in terms of a mother's feelings:

> There were two images – two living forms that tore her heart in two, as if it had been the heart of a mother who seems to see her child divided by the sword, and presses one bleeding half to her breast while her gaze goes forth in agony towards the half which is carried away by the lying woman that has never known the mother's pang (p. 576).

Metaphoric transfer allows Dorothea, childless though she is herself, to occupy the position of mother against Rosamond as the lying woman who has never known what it is to be a mother. Careless and irresponsible, Rosamond loses her unborn child, we remember, through her wilful insistence on going horseriding. The loss seems not to affect Rosamond greatly; she is sure she would have had a miscarriage anyway, even if she had not gone riding. The suggestion is that she is too selfish for love or motherhood, both of which demand a heightened emotionality and a capacity for intense connectedness. Dorothea, however, who has never been pregnant, is at this point in the text now emotionally attuned to 'know the mother's pang' and feels it in her discovery of love and loss in the same moment. This process of self-discovery is aptly imaged as a birth, but the representation of the discovery of passion in terms of motherhood is an illuminating metaphor that functions as a sudden swaddling to wrap sexuality in maternity so that the two become synonymous or indivisible. The next step is the ideological enlisting of the maternal self, demonstrated in Dorothea's response to what she sees through the window the next morning. What she sees, framed by the window, is a picture that represents ordinary human life, family and toil. She feels connected to her newborn vision: 'that involuntary, palpitating life' figured in the man and the woman carrying a baby. It is further a picture weighted towards the power of the concrete, living form as opposed to abstract principle. Dorothea is no longer drawing cottage plans for farm labourers, but responding to a view of the broad commonality of all living human beings. If 'art is the nearest thing to life' it is through this 'picture' that Dorothea approaches life. The following words spoken by Daniel Deronda can draw attention, among other passages in George Eliot's work, to her belief that our moral and psychological perceptions can be shaped by aesthetic experience:

> 'I wonder whether one oftener learns to love real objects through their representations, or the representations through the real objects,' he said, after pointing out a lovely capital made by the curled leaves of greens, showing their reticulated underside with the firm gradual swell of its central rib. 'When I was a little fellow these capitals taught me to observe, and delight in, the structure of leaves.'[56]

The passage is useful in highlighting the interaction between real objects and representations. Although Dorothea sees 'real objects' through the window, we can say, since what she sees is framed, that her vision also functions as an artistic representation of pedestrian life. Emotionality in response to the picture coalesces here with an extension of sympathies to the 'real objects' and signals Dorothea's coming of age. In turn, paradoxically, the reader is asked to look through the frame of fiction at Dorothea, a representation, and experience her as a 'real object'.

This Madonna steps out of her frame when in the Finale Dorothea becomes a 'real' mother. Shortly after she is widowed, Dorothea is amusingly described as having to sit, as if she were a model for Raphael's Saint Catherine, looking rapturously at Celia's baby. By the end of the novel, we might anticipate a vision of Dorothea as Madonna, holding her own infant. But this would be taking the work of the image too far, for the text does not freeze Dorothea in the timeless pose of the Madonna. The advent of Dorothea's first child commands some attention in the Finale, where we are told that Dorothea has nearly died giving birth, suggesting not only the real dangers of pregnancy and childbirth, but the symbolic costs to Dorothea as well. Significantly, the birth of her son is an occasion for healing the breach between Dorothea and Celia even though the baby affects the inheritance prospects of Celia's own children. Celia may argue with her husband that Dorothea has erred in marrying Will, but she is no longer 'the dangerous part of the family machinery' (p. 596). Having taken her place as woman/mother, Dorothea can now be embraced by Celia not only as a sister but also because they both share the 'broad sameness' of the female lot.

Productivity has its price, as the history and representations of Saint Teresa show, actually reinforcing what the narrator means to bring home specifically about Dorothea's England. If we have dwelt even a little on the life of Saint Teresa we know that the medium of ardent deeds that she was lucky enough to be born into also exacted considerable costs in her experience of hysteria and sexual bodily privation. The challenge is not just to see what it is that one should do, or to respond to commandments of a higher authority, but to deal with the internal effects of socially unsanctioned choices. In Dorothea's case the 'higher authority' or structuring faith is less the issue than the version of female desire that Victorian culture articulates. As the novel represents it, desire is not only split: its forms are oppositional and largely incompatible. It suggests that all women share the *common* (or broad) yearning of womanhood, but that some women also have *lofty* desires. The text wants to say that as long as such ideal yearnings are socially coded as masculine, women like Dorothea will suffer. Yet its thrust is to put Dorothea in touch with her emotional/sexual needs, to lead her – and to ask us – to value these more highly, and to reconcile us to the intractability of gender associations. We have been told that if Dorothea were to write a book, she could not do it unless, like Saint Teresa, she were 'under the command of an authority that constrained her conscience' (p. 64). If she cannot find that higher authority that will permit voice, she must be consigned to silence, a condition often linked with hysteria. To the extent that the text upholds the dominant ideology of motherhood, that silence, though regrettable, is not an unhealthy one; it is the silence of the self-sacrificing wife and mother upon whose unhistoric acts the 'growing good' of the world depends. The novel lets stand the traditional Victorian notion that satisfied motherhood, which signals an appropriate channelling of sexual energies, is as yet largely incompatible with voice, resonant action, productivity and fame.

The narrator's sadness about Dorothea's silent and diffusive influence is unmistakable. Although Dorothea finds cure in becoming Will's wife and bearing his children, and although her significance as mother is heightened through the text's recurrent association of her with images of the Madonna, the narrator also sees Dorothea's fine energies as wasted. The folk in Middlemarch may think it a pity that so 'rare a creature' as Dorothea should have been absorbed into the life of another and be only known as a wife and mother. 'But no one stated exactly what else that was in her power she ought rather to have done' (p. 611). The tone of reproof here signals the narrator's own frustration with the problem of desires that are ill-accommodated by prevailing versions of sexual difference and their far-reaching gender associations. The representation of Dorothea is both a telling critique of nineteenth-century society and a regretful accommodation to its judgements and contradictory expectations of women. If female sexuality is understood in terms of motherhood, and productivity is associated with the world of ideals and achievements and understood as a male realm, then clearly it is difficult to envision either psychologically or practically a woman who brings these divided and oppositional desires together. George Eliot herself could manage it only by holding various identities and names in fragile poise – the pseudonymous George Eliot to the public; 'Mutter' or 'Madonna' in her own familial circle.

Notes

1. George Eliot, *Middlemarch: A Study in Provincial Life*, ed. G. Haight (Boston, Riverside, [1872] 1956), p. 16. Subsequent references are to this edition and will be cited parenthetically in the text.
2. George Eliot's interest in medical issues – new scientific research, clinical treatment and professional organisation and reform – informs her portrait of Lydgate. See P. M. Logan, 'Conceiving the body: realism and medicine in *Middlemarch*', *History of the Human Sciences*, 4:2 (1991), pp. 197–222. Since *Middlemarch* is closely concerned with cultural assumptions about female nature and the social lot of women, we may wonder why she did not create a young medical man whose research might articulate some of the ideas about women that the novel critically explores. Centred on the discovery of primitive tissue, Lydgate's research interests run in quite another direction from the medical concern with sexual specialisation discussed in previous chapters. Yet the links between Lydgate's medical interests and his views about female nature are significant. As Peter Logan shows, Lydgate's naive stance in relation to his medical labours – an overconfidence in the methodology of science and in the referentiality of scientific concepts – extends also to his naive assumptions about women. When, after his experiences with the actress Laure, he determines to take a 'strictly scientific view of woman' he promises himself that he will entertain 'no expectations but such as were justified beforehand' (p. 114). Quite apart from the fact that Lydgate is not able to legislate his feelings and responses, his justified expectations in relation to Miss Vincy proceed from the mistaken belief that signs and referents are in perfect harmony. Reading the signs of Miss Vincy's body as he reads the bodies of his patients, he assumes that meaning and representation show a one-to-one correspondence (Logan, pp. 209–10). Lydgate similarly regards plain women like other 'severe facts of life, to be faced with philosophy and investigated by science' (p. 70). In her representa-

tion of the sympathetic and promising young surgeon, George Eliot subtly reveals the costs that his views of women entail. Cultural assumptions about 'Woman' provide an implicit connection between his story and that of Dorothea Brooke, whose narrative may be seen as the other side of the same coin in that she bears the cost of her culture's attempts to regulate the lives of women on the basis of definitions about their absolute nature.

3. George Eliot, *Middlemarch: A Study of Provincial Life*, ed. G. Haight (Boston, Houghton Mifflin, [1871–2] 1956), pp. 64, 21, 63.

4. The terms are Herbert Spencer's in *The Principles of Ethics*, vol. 1 (London, 1904), p. 520.

5. 'Margaret Fuller and Mary Wollstonecraft', in Thomas Pinney (ed.), *Essays of George Eliot* (London, Routledge, 1963), p. 203. See Gillian Beer's discussion of George Eliot's emphasis on variety in *Darwin's Plots: Evolutionary Narrative in Darwin, George Eliot, and Nineteenth-Century Fiction* (London, Routldge, 1983).

6. Although almost all medical texts admit that hysteria is not a disease confined only to women, they discuss it as a specifically female malady. The discourse of hysteria as a problem of sexual suppression or excitement contradicts, of course, the doctrine of female passionlessness discussed in Chapter Three.

7. S. Ashwell, *A Practical Treatise on the Diseases Peculiar to Women* (London, Samuel Highley, 1844), pp. 229–30.

8. G. Hewitt, *The Diagnosis, Pathology, and Treatment of Diseases of Women, including the Diagnosis of Pregnancy*, 2nd edn. (London, Longmans, 1868), pp. 383, 384.

9. Hewitt, *Diagnosis, Pathology and Treatment of Diseases of Women*, p. 383.

10. See J. Elliotson, *The Principles and Practice of Medicine* (London, Butler, 1846), p. 681.

11. R. B. Carter, *On the Pathology and Treatment of Hysteria* (London, Churchill, 1853), p. 69; see also I. Veith, *Hysteria: The History of a Disease* (Chicago, Chicago University Press, 1965), p. 206.

12. E. J. Tilt, *On Diseases of Women and Ovarian Inflammation* (London, Churchill, 1853), pp. 147, 148.

13. E. Showalter, *The Female Malady: Women, Madness, and English Culture, 1830–1980* (Harmondsworth, Penguin, 1987), p. 131.

14. F. C. Skey, *Hysteria*, 2nd edn. (London, Longmans, 1867), p. 77.

15. The references to Freud are to *The Standard Edition of the Complete Psychological Works of Sigmund Freud*, 24 vols., ed. J. Strachey (London, 1953–74), hereafter cited *SE* with volume and page number(s); *SE* 2, p. 240. Freud and Breuer collaborated on *Studies on Hysteria* (1893–95), a compilation of case histories and theoretical discussion.

16. Freud, *SE* 23, p. 114.

17. See D. Lodge, 'Mimesis and diegesis in modern fiction', in A. Mortimer (ed.), *Contemporary Approaches to Narrative* (Tubingen, Gunter Narr Verlag, 1984), pp. 989–1008.

18. This was the first film to be banned in Britain under a law for blasphemy that originated in the seventeenth century. The film was produced for television by Axel Ltd., an independent film company. An account of the banning,

handed down in September 1989, is given in 'Britain bans St Theresa's visions', *Globe and Mail* (Toronto) (December 11, 1989).

19. H. Maudsley, *The Pathology of Mind: A Study of its Distempers, Deformities, and Disorders* (London, Macmillan, 1895), pp. 218, 299.

20. Freud, *SE* 2, p. 232.

21. M. Jacobus, *Reading Woman: Essays in Feminist Criticism* (New York, Columbia University Press, 1985), p. 203.

22. See *In Dora's Case: Freud – Hysteria – Feminism*, ed. C. Bernheimer and C. Kahane (New York, Columbia University Press, 1985). The radicalisation of traditional views is well illustrated in this volume of essays; see particularly T. Moi, 'Representations of patriarchy: sexuality and epistemology in Freud's Dora'.

23. E. D. Ermarth, 'Th' observed of all observers: George Eliot's narrator and Shakespeare's audience', in J. Hawthorn (ed.), *The Nineteenth-Century British Novel* (London, Edward Arnold, 1986), pp. 127–40, points out that most readers nowadays would have to answer in the negative.

24. Although Benedict Zimmerman notes that the saint's life and character have always been 'favourite studies for men and women of various schools of thought', the nineteenth century saw an increase in publications about Teresa. See *The Life of St. Teresa of Jesus Written by Herself*, trans. D. Lewis, ed. B. Zimmerman, 5th edn. (London, Baker, 1916), p. xxxix.

25. See F. Nightingale, 'A note of interrogation', *Fraser's Magazine*, 87 (1873), p. 567; quoted in J. Uglow, *George Eliot* (New York, Virago, 1987), p. 68.

26. If nineteenth-century versions of Teresa associated her desire for self-denial and suffering with a yearning for martyrdom, the twentieth century has interpreted that as masochistic rather than gloriously altruistic. For example, the masochistic Olive Chancellor (a character in Henry James's *The Bostonians* who has mastered the 'history of feminine anguish') is described by Irving Howe as 'a sort of St. Theresa'; quoted in C. S. Wiesenthal, 'A Jamesian vision of "American nervousness": masculine disease and diseased femininity in *The Bostonians*', *English Studies in Canada*, 15 (1989), pp. 447–97.

27. Zimmerman (ed.), *The Life of St Teresa*, p. 105.

28. Zimmerman (ed.), *The Life of St Teresa*, p. 58; on the question of Saint Teresa and hysteria see Benedict Zimmerman's annotated bibliography of works dealing with her. He refers to a number of works that attempt to discredit her visions by attributing them to 'animal magnetism' and 'hysterical derangements' (p. xxxiv). Zimmerman also cites P. Gregoire de S. Joseph, *La pretendue hysterie de Sainte Therese*, a work which 'has ably summed up and disposed of' the arguments about hysteria. See also A. Weber, *Teresa of Avila and the Rhetoric of Femininity* (New Jersey, Princeton University Press, 1990), p. 140.

29. Zimmerman (ed.), *The Life of St Teresa*, pp. 267–8.

30. See R. Wittkower, *Gian Lorenzo Bernini: The Sculptor of the Roman Baroque* (London, Phaidon Press, 1955), pp. 28–9; and R. T. Peterson, *The Art of Ecstasy: Teresa, Bernini, and Crashaw* (London, 1970).

31. Freud noted that 'it is owing to no chance co-incidences that the hysterical deliria of nuns during the epidemics of the Middle Ages took the form of violent blasphemous and unbridled erotic language' (*SE* I, pp. 126–7). He was much influenced by Charcot and Desire Magloire Bourneville, whose

scholarship was directed to showing that certain Catholic religious beliefs were based on misunderstood hysterical phenomena; see Wm. J. McGrath, *Freud's Discovery of Psychoanaylsis: The Politics of Hysteria* (Ithaca, Cornell University Press, 1986), pp. 156–7. Charcot's text does not mention Saint Teresa, but I am suggesting a context in which psychoanalytic discourse, as anticipated by Breuer, for example, would see her as an hysteric.

32. See M. David-Menard, *Hysteria From Freud to Lacan: Body and Language in Psychoanalysis*, trans. C. Porter (Ithaca, Cornell University Press, 1989), p. xiv.

33. Lacan's Saint Teresa is described thus by J. Todd, *Feminist Literary History* (London, Routledge, 1987), p. 54.

34. J. Kristeva, *Desire in Language: A Semiotic Approach to Literature and Art*, ed. L. S. Roudiez (New York, Columbia University Press, 1980), pp. 279–80.

35. Kristeva, *Desire in Language*, p. 280.

36. See G. Haight, *George Eliot: A Biography* (New York, Oxford University Press, 1968), p. 376.

37. See W. J. T. Mitchell, *Iconology: Image, Text, Ideology* (Chicago, University of Chicago Press, 1986), p. 24.

38. Mitchell, *Iconology*, p. 25.

39 Mitchell, *Iconology*, p. 48.

40. While a number of critics have set Ladislaw's Romantic fervour in the context of early nineteenth-century aesthetics, no one has paid attention to the way the debate between language and painting focuses issues of gender and sexual difference in the novel.

41. Interestingly, George Eliot mentions the Laokoon in Chapter 22 when Will inquires about Dorothea's sentiments about it and the Madonna di Foligno. For a full discussion of Lessing's influence on George Eliot's theory of *ut pictura poesis* see H. Witemeyer, *George Eliot and the Visual Arts* (New Haven, Yale University Press, 1979), pp. 40–3.

42. T. de Lauretis, *Technologies of Gender: Essays on Theory, Film, and Fiction* (Indiana, Indiana University Press, 1987), p. 20.

43. Mitchell points out how the 'sublimation of the image reaches its logical culmination when the entire poem or text is regarded as an image or "verbal icon" and this image is defined, not as pictorial likeness or impression, but as a synchronic structure in some metaphorical space' (*Iconology*, p. 25). The very representation of Dorothea in the medium of language whilst harnessing the emotional power of the image is an attempt to fuse poetry and painting in a 'verbal icon'.

44. 'Referring to a vase of flowers, Hazlitt fails to recognise the Marian resurrection symbolism of the lilies and roses that spring from the Virgin's sarcophagus' (Witemeyer, *George Eliot and the Visual Arts*, p. 85). See also J. Wiesenfarth, '*Middlemarch*: The Language of Art', *PMLA*, 97 (1982), p. 371. The 'unromantic' reader of *Middlemarch* may similarly overlook its 'Marian' symbolism.

45 J. W. Cross, *George Eliot's Life as Related in her Letters and Journals*, vol. 2, arranged and edited by her husband (Edinburgh and London, Blackwood, 1885), p. 58.

46. J. Beaty, *Middlemarch from Notebook to Novel: A Study of George Eliot's Creative Method* (Urbana, University of Illinois Press, 1960), p. 115.

47. T. Chambers, 'Clinical lectures on hysteria', *British Medical Journal*, 2 (1861), p. 652, warned fellow physicians to keep hysterical patients clear of the Eternal City, a place known to bring on hysteria. He attributed Rome's 'bad pre-eminence' in this regard to its climate, but George Eliot's representation of Rome as provoking emotions that Dorothea is unable to understand or process nevertheless resonates interestingly with Rome's reputation in relation to hysteria.
48. Witemeyer, *George Eliot and the Visual Arts*, p. 152.
49. George Eliot, *The Mill on the Floss*, ed. G. Haight (Oxford, World's Classics, [1862] 1980) vol.2, p. ii.
50. T. Pinney (ed.), *Essays of George Eliot* (London, Routledge, 1965), p. 205.
51. M. Warner, *Alone of All Her Sex: The Myth and Cult of the Virgin Mary* (London, Picador, 1976), p. xxi.
52. See Jacobus, *Reading Woman*, pp. 137–93; J. Kristeva, 'Stabat mater', in T. Moi (ed.), *The Kristeva Reader* (New York, Columbia University Press, 1986); Warner, *Alone of All her Sex*.
53. V. A. Neufeldt, 'The madonna and the gypsy', *Studies in the Novel*, 15 (1983), pp. 44–54.
54. Both Witemeyer and Wiesenfarth discuss, from different points of view, Dorothea's similarity to the Ariadne figure. The former sees Ariadne as a pagan element that prompts Naumann to a more comprehensive definition of womanhood which is a synthesis of classical, pagan and Christian and therefore tempers Dorothea's representation as a 'Christian heroine' (Witemeyer, *George Eliot and the Visual Arts*, p. 86). Wiesenfarth sees Dorothea as Ariadne waiting for the rescuing Will/Bacchus and draws attention to the posture of cheek pillowed in hand that she and the statue share ('*Middlemarch*', p. 372).
55. My observation about Dorothea here is indebted to the discussion of maternity in M. Jacobus's 'Dora and the pregnant Madonna'.
56. George Eliot, *Daniel Deronda*, ed. B. Hardy (Harmondsworth, Penguin, 1967), p. 476; see Witemeyer, *George Eliot and the Visual Arts*, p. 156, on George Eliot and the shaping of perception through aesthetic experience.

Conclusion

The question of sexual instability, as I have explored it in a variety of social, medical and literary texts, expresses anxiety that the 'natural' distinctions between men and women are mutable and capable of being eroded by culture. Such anxiety, I have argued, produces the powerful reiterations of incommensurable difference that have come to be associated with the Victorians. But my focus on sexual instabilities has also revealed that the notion of sexuality as culturally and environmentally responsive, offered ways of defining differences among women of different classes, nationalities and races. And given the instability of representations and their capacity to be used in oppositional or subversive contexts, ideas about unstable sexual difference were available to be mobilised to undermine the very ideologies with which they have been associated.

Victorian preoccupations with both the biological and cultural bases of sexual instability live on. In the late-twentieth century we have witnessed an upsurge of interest in the biological, genetic bases of sexuality. The 1990s, for example, has been called 'the decade of sex differences in the brain'.[1] In *Myths of Gender*, Anne Fausto-Sterling describes the discovery at the end of the nineteenth century of sex hormones; research on their production and biochemistry followed. It was then imagined that separate male and female hormones defined the essence of masculinity and femininity through their gonadal functions. When scientists found that males produced oestrogen and females testosterone they had to entertain a quantitative model of the kind that endures today. But, writes Sterling, describing current tendencies to attribute sexual orientation to genetic causes, 'no longer do hormones simply define the gonad (and the gonad the man – or woman). Now they can even define the brain, and the brain then gets to define the man or woman.'[2] As the key to all sexual orientations, the brain must surely manifest the differences between homosexuals and heterosexuals.

But if the 1990s has been labelled the decade of 'brain sex' and has seen a flurry of activity in the long tradition of biological explanations for differences among human beings, it has also produced the discourse of gender as performance, as stylisation. A fascination with cross-dressing and sexual masquerade, gender confusion and instability emerges in popular culture in a rich variety of forms. Yet when historicising the advent of cultural preoccupations with the instability of gender identity, scholars have typically turned attention to modernist constructions of gender, possibly looking to the 'sexual anarchy' of *fin de siècle* writers as early precursors of those who broke from the rigidity and fixity of Victorian conceptions of gender.[3] If, however, we acknowledge that in their own specific ways Victorians were perpetually alert to the question of sexual instability, we need to think further about the continuities between Victorian and modernist culture and to revise the histories of sexuality that associate Victorians with an insistence on the commensurable nature of sexual difference. The various ways in which Victorians responded to ideas about sexuality must influence how we read the Victorian enterprise of 'othering' abroad, as well as how notions of a gendered and classed 'self' were produced at home. *Unstable Bodies* has sought to articulate some of the discursive contradictions that allowed women writers to mobilise an army of fictional possibilities in representing sexuality and maternity. How the Victorian preoccupation with sexual ambiguity and approximation inflected the construction of masculinity and also of childhood during the period awaits further exploration.

Notes

1. Anne Fausto-Sterling, *Myths of Gender: Biological Theories about Women and Men* (New York, Basic Books, 1992), p. 224.
2. Sterling, *Myths of Gender*, p. 224.
3. The term 'sexual anarchy' is from Elaine Showalter's *Sexual Anarchy: Gender and Culture at the Fin de Siècle* (Harmondsworth, Penguin, 1990).

Select bibliography

Primary texts

Acton, Wm., *The Functions and Disorders of the Reproductive Organs in Childhood, Youth, Adult Age, and Advanced Life, Considered in their Physiological, Social, and Moral Relations*, London, Churchill, 1862.

— *Prostitution Considered in its Moral, Social and Sanitary Aspects, in London and Other Large Cities, with Proposals for the Mitigation and Prevention of Its Attendant Evils*, London, Churchill, 1857.

— 'Unmarried wet nurses', *Lancet*, 1 (1859), pp. 175–6.

— 'Child-murder and wet nursing', *British Medical Journal*, 1 (1861), pp. 183–4.

Allan, J. M., 'On the real differences in the minds of men and women', *Journal of the Anthropological Society*, 7 (1869), pp. cxcv–ccxix.

Anderson, E. G., 'Sex in mind and education: a reply', *Fortnightly Review*, 15 (1874), pp. 582–94.

Ashwell, S., *A Practical Treatise on the Diseases Peculiar to Women*, London, Samuel Highley, 1844.

Athenaeum, (2 May 1868), pp. 623–4, [Review of *Sorrow on the Sea*].

Athenaeus: The Deipnosophists, trans. C. B. Gulick, Cambridge, Harvard University Press, 1961.

'Baby-farming and baby-murder', *British Medical Journal*, 1 (1868), pp. 127–8.

'Baby-farming and baby-murder', *British Medical Journal*, 1 (1868), pp. 175–6.

'Baby-farming in Marylebone', *British Medical Journal*, 2 (1868), p. 315.

Baines, M. A., 'Address to the National Association for the Promotion of Social Science', *National Association for the Promotion of Social Science Transactions*, (1859), pp. 531–2.

— 'A few friendly words to young mothers', by One of the Maternity, London, 1856.

— 'A few thoughts concerning infanticide', *Journal of Social Science*, 2 vols in 1 (1866), pp. 535–40.

— 'Excessive infant mortality', London, John Churchill, 1862.

— 'The practice of hiring wet-nurses – especially from the 'fallen' –

considered as it affects public health and public morals', London, John Churchill, 1859.

Barker, T. H., 'On the diet of infancy and childhood', *British Mothers Magazine*, 8 (1852), pp. 193–7.

Blackwell, A. B., *The Sexes Throughout Nature*, New York, 1875.

Blackwell, E., *The Laws of Life, with Special Reference to the Physical Education of Girls*, London, Sampson Low, 1859.

— *The Human Element in Sex: Being a Medical Enquiry into the Relation of Sexual Physiology to Christian Morality*, 2nd edn, London, J. and A. Churchill, 1884.

Braddon, M. E., *Lady Audley's Secret*, ed. D. Skilton, Oxford, World's Classics, 1987.

Brontë, A., *Agnes Grey*, ed. R. Inglesfield and H. Marsden, Oxford, Oxford University Press, 1988.

Brontë, C., 'Biographical notice of Ellis and Acton Bell', in *Agnes Grey: With a Memoir of her Sisters by Charlotte Brontë*, ed. T. Scott, Edinburgh, John Grant, 1905.

— *Villette*, ed. M. Lilly, Harmondsworth, Penguin, 1979.

— *Jane Eyre*, Harmondsworth, Penguin, 1966.

— *The Brontë Letters*, ed. M. Spark, Great Britain, Peter Nevil, 1954.

Bucknill, J. C. and D. H. Tuke, *A Manual of Psychological Medicine*, New York, Hafner, [1858] 1968 facsimile.

Carlile, R., *Every Woman's Book or What is Love?*, abridged from *The Republican*, 18:11 (*c.* 1825).

Carpenter, Wm., *Principles of Human Physiology; with Their Chief Applications to Pathology, Hygiene and Forensic Medicine*, London, Churchill, 1842.

Carter, R. B., *On the Pathology and Treatment of Hysteria*, London, Churchill, 1853.

Chadwick, E., *Report on the Sanitary Condition of the Labouring Population of Gt. Britain*, ed. M. W. Flinn, Edinburgh, Edinburgh University Press, [1842] 1965.

Chambers, T., 'Clinical lectures on hysteria', *British Medical Journal*, 2 (1861), pp. 651– 5.

Chavasse, H. P., *Advice to Wives on the Management of Themselves During the Periods of Pregnancy, Labour and Suckling*, London, Longman, 1843.

'Child-murder and its punishment', *Social Science Review*, 2 (1864), pp. 454–5.

'Child-murder: its relations to wet-nursing', *British Medical Journal*, 1 (1861), p. 68.

Combe, G., *Elements of Phrenology*, Edinburgh, Maclachlan and Stewart, 1855.

Conquest, J. T., *Letters to a Mother*, London, 1848.

Darwin, C., *The Descent of Man, and Selection in Relation to Sex*, 2nd edn., London, John Murray, 1874.

— *The Variations of Animals and Plants Under Domestication*, vol. 20, *The Works of Charles Darwin*, ed. P. H. Barrett and R. B. Freeman, London, William Pickering, 1988.

Davidson, H. M., *The Two Babies: A Sketch of Everyday Life*, London, 1859.

Devey, L., *Life of Rosina, Lady Lytton*, London, Swan, 1887.

Drummond, J. and C. B. Upton, *The Life and Letters of James Martineau*, 2 vols, London, James Nisbet, 1902.

Eliot, G., *Adam Bede*, ed. S. Gill, Harmondsworth, Penguin, 1980.

— *Middlemarch: A Study in Provincial Life*, ed. G. Haight, Boston, Riverside, 1956.

— *The Mill on the Floss*, ed. G. Haight, Oxford, World's Classics, 1980.

— *The Letters of George Eliot*, ed. G. Haight, 9 vols, New Haven, Yale University Press, 1954–78.

Elliotson, J., *The Principles and Practice of Medicine*, London, Butler, 1846.

Essays of George Eliot, ed. T. Pinney, London, Routledge, 1963.

Faucher, L., *Manchester in 1844: Its Present Condition and Future Prospects*, trans. with copious notes appended by a member of the Manchester Athenaeum, Manchester, Heywood, 1844.

'Female labour', *Fraser's Magazine*, 61 (1860), pp. 359–71.

Freud, S., *The Standard Edition of the Complete Psychological Works of Sigmund Freud*, 24 vols, ed. J. Strachey, London, 1953–74.

Gaskell, E., *Mary Barton*, ed. E. Wright, Oxford, World's Classics, 1987.

— *Ruth*, ed. A. Shelston, Oxford, World's Classics, 1985.

— *Life of Charlotte Brontë*, Edinburgh, John Grant, 1905.

— *The Letters of Mrs. Gaskell*, ed. J. A. V. Chapple and A. Pollard, Manchester, Manchester University Press, 1966.

Gatty, M., *Parables from Nature*, London, Bell and Daldy, 1855.

Graham, T., *On the Management and Disorders of Infancy and Childhood*, London, 1853.

Greenwood, J., *The Seven Curses of London*, London, Stanley Rivers, 1869.

Greg, R., *The Factory Question and The Ten Hours Bill*, London, James Ridgway, 1834.

Greg, W. R., *An Inquiry into the State of the Manufacturing Populations*, London, James Ridgway, 1831.

— 'False morality of lady novelists', *The National Review*, (January 1859), pp. 148– 9.

— 'Prostitution', *Westminster Review*, 53 (July 1850), pp. 238–68.

Hewitt, G., *The Diagnosis, Pathology, and Treatment of Diseases of Women, including the diagnosis of Pregnancy*, 2nd edn, London, Longmans, 1868.

— 'Wet-nursing', *British Medical Journal*, 1 (1861), pp. 128–9.

'Hints on the modern governess system', *Fraser's Magazine*, 30 (November 1844), pp. 571–83.

Hompes, M., 'Mrs. E. C. Gaskell', *Gentleman's Magazine*, 55 (1895), pp. 124–38.

'Infanticide and wet-nursing', *British Medical Journal*, 2 (1866), pp. 613–14.

Johnson, W., *The Morbid Emotions of Women: Their Origin, Tendencies, and Treatment*, London: Simpkin, 1850.

Kay, J. P., *The Moral and Physical Condition of the Working Classes Employed in the Cotton Manufacture in Manchester*, Manchester, James Ridgway, 1832.

Kirby, Wm. and Wm. Spence, *An Introduction to Entomology: or Elements of the Natural History of Insects*, 4 vols, London, Longman, 1815–26.

Klunzinger, C. B., *Upper Egypt, its People and its Products*, New York, Scribner, 1878.

Kydd, S., *The History of the Factory Movement*, 2 vols, London, Simpkin, 1857.

Lamb, A. R., *Can Woman Regenerate Society?*, London, Parker, 1844.

Lane, E., *The Manners and Customs of The Modern Egyptians*, London, Dent, [1836] 1908.

Laycock, T., *A Treatise on the Nervous Diseases of Women: Comprising an Inquiry into the Nature, Causes, and Treatments of Spinal and Hysterical Disorders*, London, Longman, 1840.

Leared, A., *Infant Mortality and Its Causes*, London, Churchill, 1862.

Martineau, H., *Eastern Life: Present and Past*, London, Moxon, [1848] 1875.

Maudsley, H., 'Sex in mind and in education', *Fortnightly Review*, 15 (1874), pp. 466–83.

— *The Physiology and Pathology of the Mind*, London, Macmillan, 1867.

— *The Pathology of Mind: A Study of its Distempers, Deformities, and Disorders*, London, Macmillan, 1895.

'Murder of the innocents', *Lancet*, 1 (1858), pp. 345–6.

'New novels', *Athenaeum*, 29 (2 June 1866), pp. 732–3.

Nicholson, H. A., 'The generative expenditure of man', *Edinburgh Medical Journal*, 18 (1872), pp. 332–8.

Nightingale, F., 'A note of interrogation', *Fraser's Magazine*, 87 (1873), p. 567.

Parkes, B. R., *Remarks on the Education of Girls, with Reference to the Social, Legal, and Industrial Position of Women in the Present Day*, 3rd edn., London, John Chapman, 1856.

Prichard, J. C. *Natural History of Man*, 2nd edn., London, Balliere, 1845.

— *A Treatise on Insanity*, London, Marchant, 1833.

'Queen bees or working bees', *Saturday Review*, (21 February, 1857), pp. 172–3.

'Queen bees or working bees?', *Saturday Review*, (12 November, 1859), pp. 575–6.

[F. Winslow], 'Recent trials in lunacy', *Journal of Psychological Medicine and Mental Pathology*, 7 (1854), pp. 572–625.

Reid, J., 'On the causes, symptoms, and treatment of puerperal insanity', *Journal of Psychological Medicine*, 1 (1848), pp. 128–51; 284–93.

Roberton, J., *Essays and Notes on the Physiology and Diseases of Women, and on Practical Midwifery*, London, John Churchill, 1851.

— 'On the period of puberty in Esquimaux women', *Edinburgh Medical and Surgical Journal*, 63 (1845), pp. 57–65.

Rollin, C., *The Ancient History of the Egyptians, Cartheginians, Assyrians, Babylonians*, London, printed for Cowie, 1827.

Routh, C. H. F., 'On the selection of wet nurses from among fallen women', *Lancet*, 1 (1859), pp. 581–2.

Ryan, M., *A Manual of Midwifery*, 4th edn., London, Bloomsbury, 1841.

Ryan, Wm. B., *Infanticide: Its Law, Prevalence, Prevention, and History*, London, Churchill, 1862.

'Salon national de 1842', *La Renaissance: chronique des arts et de la litterature*, 4 (1842–3), p. 92.

'The sanitary condition of the milliners and dressmakers of London', *Lancet*, 1 (1853), pp. 519–20.

'Seduction and infanticide', *Saturday Review*, (22 October, 1866), p. 481.

'Selection of wet nurses from among fallen women', *Lancet* 2 (1859), pp. 71–2.

'Selection of wet nurses from among fallen women', *Lancet* 1 (1859), pp. 637–8.

Semple, R. H., 'On criminal responsibility', *Medical Times and Gazette*, 12 (1856), pp. 58–60.

[H. L. Mansel], 'Sensation novels', *Quarterly Review*, 113 (April 1863), pp. 481–514.

Simpson, Sir J. Y., 'Hermaphroditism', in Sir W. G. Simpson (ed.), *The Works of Sir James Y. Simpson, Bart*, 3 vols, Edinburgh, Adam Black, 1871.

Skey, F.C., *Hysteria*, 2nd edn., London, Longmans, 1867.

Smith, W. T., Introductory lecture to a course of lectures on obstetrics, delivered at the Hunterian School of Medicine, 1847–48, *Lancet*, 2 (1847), pp. 371–4.

— On the theory and practice of obstetrics, *Lancet*, 1 (1856), p. 4.

Spencer, H., *Principles of Sociology*, 3rd edn., London, Williams and Norgate, 1897–1906; reprint, Westport, Conn., Greenwood, 1975.

Terry, H., 'Wet-nursing', *British Medical Journal*, 1 (1861), p. 129.

Tilt, E. J., *On Diseases of Women and Ovarian Inflammation*, London, Churchill, 1853.

Trollope, F., *Jessie Phillips: A Tale of the Present Day*, London, H. Colburn, 1844.

Walker, A., *Woman Physiologically Considered as to Mind, Morals, Marriage, Matrimonial Slavery, Infidelity and Divorce*, London, Baily, 1840.

— *Beauty: Illustrated by an Analysis and Classification of Beauty in Woman*, London, 1846.

Wardlaw, R., *Lectures on Female Prostitution: Its Nature, Extent, Effects, Guilt, Causes and Remedy*, Glasgow, James Maclehouse, 1844.

West, C., *Lectures on the Diseases of Women*, 3rd edn., London, John Churchill, 1864.

'Wet-nurses from the fallen', *Lancet*, 1 (1859), pp. 113–14; 1 (1859), pp. 200–01.

White, G., *The Natural History and Antiquities of Selborne*, London, White, Cochrane, 1813.

Winslow, L. S., *Manual of Lunacy: A Handbook*, London, Smith Elder, 1874.

Wollstonecraft, M., *A Vindication of the Rights of Woman: With Strictures on Political and Moral Subjects*, London, J. Johnson, 1792.

'Woman in her psychological relations', *Journal of Psychological Medicine and Mental Pathology*, 4 (1851), pp. 18–50.

Woman's Work: or Hints to Raise the Female Character London, Clarke, 1844.

Wood, Lady E. C., *Sorrow on the Sea*, 3 vols, London, Tinsley Brothers, 1868.

Wood, Mrs H., *East Lynne*, ed. S. Davies, Great Britain, Dent, 1984.

Wynter, A., *Curiosities of Toil*, 2 vols, London, Chapman, 1870.

— *The Borderlands of Insanity*, London, Strand, 1877.

Secondary texts

Alexander, C., *The Early Writings of Charlotte Brontë*, Oxford, Blackwell, 1983.

Alexander, S., *Women's Work in Nineteenth-Century London: A Study of the Years 1820–1850*, London, Journeyman's Press, 1983.

— 'Women, class and sexual differences in the 1830s and 1840s: some reflections on the writing of a feminist history', *History Workshop Journal*, 17 (1984), pp. 125–49.

Allott, M. (ed.) *The Brontës: The Critical Heritage*, London, Routledge, 1974.

Armstrong, N., *Desire and Domestic Fiction: A Political History of the Novel*, Oxford, Oxford University Press, 1987.

Ashton, T. S., *Economic and Social Investigations in Manchester 1833–1933: A Centenary History of the Manchester Statistical Society*, London, King, 1934.

Badinter, E., *The Myth of Motherhood: An Historical View of the Maternal Instinct*, trans. R. DeGaris, London, Souvenir Press, 1981.

Bartrip, P. W. J., *Mirror of Medicine: A History of the British Medical Journal*, Oxford, British Medical Journal and Clarendon Press, 1990.

Beaty, J., *Middlemarch from Notebook to Novel: A Study of George Eliot's Creative Method*, Urbana, University of Illinois Press, 1960.

Beer, G., *George Eliot*, Sussex, Harvester, 1986.

— *Darwin's Plots: Evolutionary Narrative in Darwin, George Eliot and Nineteenth-Century Fiction*, London, Routledge, 1983.

Behlmer, G., 'Deadly motherhood: infanticide and medical opinion in mid-Victorian England', *Journal of the History of Medicine*, 34 (1979), pp. 403–27.

Benhabib, S., 'The generalized and the concrete other', in S. Benhabib and D. Cornell (eds.) *Feminism as Critique*, Cambridge, Polity Press, 1987.

BIBLIOGRAPHY

Bennett, T., *Outside Literature*, London, Routledge, 1990.

Berger, J., *Ways of Seeing*, London, BBC and Penguin, 1972.

Berko, P., *Orientalist Painters*, Brussels, Laconti, 1982.

Berko, P. and V., *Belgian Painters: A Dictionary of Belgian Painters born between 1750 and 1875*, Brussels, Laconti, 1981.

Bernheimer, C., *Figures of Ill-Repute: Representing Prostitution in Nineteenth-Century France*, Boston, Harvard University Press, 1989.

— and C. Kahane (eds.) *In Dora's Case: Freud – Hysteria – Feminism*, New York, Columbia University Press, 1985.

Bewell, A., '"Jacobin plants": botany as social theory in the 1790s', *Wordsworth Circle*, 20:3 (1989), pp. 132–9.

Birkin, L., *Consuming Desire: Sexual Science and the Emergence of a Culture of Abundance, 1871–1914*, Ithaca, Cornell University Press, 1988.

Bodenheimer, R., 'Private grief and public acts in *Mary Barton*', *Dickens Studies Annual*, 9 (1981), pp. 195–216.

Bowlby, R., 'Walking, women and writing: Virginia Woolf as *flaneuse*', in I. Armstrong (ed.) *New Feminist Discourses*, London, Routledge, 1992.

Boyle, T., *Black Swine in the Sewers of Hampstead: Beneath the Surface of Victorian Sensationalism*, Harmondsworth, Penguin, 1989.

Brady, K., *George Eliot*, London, Macmillan, 1992.

Branca, P., *Silent Sisterhood*, London, Croom Helm, 1975.

Bristow, E. J., *Vice and Vigilance: Purity Movements in Britain since 1700*, Dublin, Gill and Macmillan, 1977.

Burney, E., *Cross Street Chapel Schools*, Manchester, Didsbury, 1977.

Butler, J., *Gender Trouble: Feminism and the Subversion of Identity*, London, Routledge, 1990.

— and J. W. Scott (eds.), *Feminists Theorize the Political*, London, Routledge, 1992.

Carroll, D. (ed.), *George Eliot: The Critical Heritage*, London, Routledge, 1971.

Charlier, G., 'Brussels life in *Villette*', *Brontë Society Transactions*, 5 (1955), pp. 386–90.

Costello, P. H., 'A new reading of Anne Brontë's *Agnes Grey*', *Brontë Society Transactions*, 3:19 (1987), pp. 113–8.

Cott, N., 'Passionlessness: an interpretation of Victorian sexual ideology, 1790– 1850', *Signs*, 4:2, (1978), pp. 219–36.

Cross, J. W., *George Eliot's Life as Related in her Letters and Journals*, arranged and edited by her husband, 3 vols, Edinburgh and London, Blackwood, 1885.

Curtis, L. P., Jr., *Apes and Angels: The Irishman in Victorian Caricature*, Washington, D.C., Smithsonian Institute Press, 1971.

— *Anglo-Saxons and Celts: A Study of Anti-Irish Prejudice in Victorian England*, Bridgeport, University of Bridgeport, 1968.

David-Menard, M., *Hysteria From Freud to Lacan: Body and Language in Psychoanalysis*, trans. C. Porter, Ithaca, Cornell University Press, 1989.

Davidoff, L. and C. Hall, *Family Fortunes: Men and Women of the English Middle Class 1780–1850*, London, Hutchinson, 1987.

— '"Adam spoke first and named the orders of the world": masculine and feminine domains in history and sociology', in H. Corr and L. Jamieson (eds.), *Politics of the Everyday: Continuity and Change in Work and the Family*, Basingstoke, Macmillan, 1990.

— and J. Newton (eds.), *Sex and Class in Victorian Britain*, London, Routledge, 1983.

Davidson, C. and E. M. Broner (eds.), *The Lost Tradition: Mothers and Daughters in Literature*, New York, Frederick Ungar, 1980.

de Groot, J., '"Sex" and "race": the construction of language and image in the nineteenth century', in S. Mendus and J. Rendall (eds.), *Sexuality and Subordination: Interdisciplinary Studies of Gender in the Nineteenth Century*, London, Routledge, 1989.

de Lauretis, T., *Technologies of Gender: Essays on Theory, Film, and Fiction*, Bloomington, Indiana University Press, 1987.

— (ed.), *Feminist Studies/Critical Studies*, Bloomington, Indiana University Press, 1986.

Dews, P., 'Power and subjectivity in Foucault', *New Left Review*, 144 (1984), pp. 72–95.

Easson, A. (ed.), *Elizabeth Gaskell: The Critical Heritage*, London, Routledge, 1991.

— 'Anne Brontë and the glow-worms', *Notes and Queries*, 224 (1979), pp. 299–300.

Edmond, R., *Affairs of the Hearth: Victorian Poetry and Domestic Narrative*, London, Routledge, 1988.

Ermarth, E. D., 'Th' observed of all observers: George Eliot's narrator and Shakespeare's audience', in J. Hawthorn (ed.), *The Nineteenth-Century British Novel*, London, Edward Arnold, 1986.

Fildes, V., *Wet Nursing: A History from Antiquity to the Present*, Oxford, Basil Blackwell, 1988.

Foucault, M., *The History of Sexuality*, vol. 1, trans. R. Hurley, Harmondsworth, Penguin, 1981.

Fraser, R., *Charlotte Brontë*, London, Methuen, 1988.

Fryckstedt, M. C., *Elizabeth Gaskell's* Mary Barton *and* Ruth: *A Challenge to Christian England*, Stockholm, Almqvist & Wiksell, 1982.

Gallagher, C., *The Industrial Reformation of English Fiction: Social Discourse and Narrative Form 1832–1867*, Chicago, Chicago University Press, 1985.

— and T. Laqueur (eds.), *The Making of the Modern Body: Sexuality and Society in the Nineteenth Century*, Berkeley, University of California Press, 1987.

Gamman, L. and M. Marshment (eds.), *The Female Gaze: Women as Viewers of Popular Culture*, Seattle, The Real Comet Press, 1989.

Gay, P., *The Bourgeois Experience: Victoria to Freud*, vol. 2, New York Oxford University Press, 1984–6.

Gerin, W., *Charlotte Brontë: The Evolution of Genius*, Oxford, Clarendon, 1967.

Gilbert, S. and S. Gubar, *The Madwoman in the Attic: The Woman Writer and the Nineteenth-Century Literary Imagination*, New Haven, Yale University Press, 1979.

Gilman, S., *Sexuality: An Illustrated History Representing the Sexual in Medicine and Culture from the Middle Ages to the Age of AIDS*, New York, John Wiley, 1989.

— *Difference and Pathology: Stereotypes of Sexuality, Race and Madness*, Ithaca, Cornell University Press, 1985.

Gilman, S. C., 'Political theory: left to right, up to down', in J. E. Chamberlin and S. L. Gilman (eds.), *Degeneration: The Dark Side of Progress*, New York, Columbia University Press, 1985.

Greenblatt, S., 'Shakespeare and the exorcists', in P. Parker and G. Hartmann (eds.), *Shakespeare and the Question of Theory*, London, Methuen, 1985.

Grossberg, L. and C. Nelson (eds.), *Marxism and the Interpretation of Culture*, London, Macmillan, 1988.

Haight, G. S., *George Eliot: A Biography*, New York, Oxford University Press, 1968.

Hamer, M., *Signs of Cleopatra*, London, Routledge, 1993.

Harris, M., 'Infanticide and respectability: Hetty Sorrel as abandoned child', *English Studies in Canada*, 9:2 (1983), pp. 177–96.

Heath, S., Difference, *Screen*, 19:3 (1978), pp. 51–112.

Helsinger, E. K., R. L. Sheets and Wm. Veeder (eds.), *The Woman Question: Society and Literature in Britain and America, 1837–1883*, 3 vols, Manchester, Manchester University Press, 1983.

Higginbotham, A. R., '"Sin of the age": infanticide and illegitimacy in Victorian London', *Victorian Studies*, 35 (1989), pp. 319–37.

Hirsch, M., *The Mother/Daughter Plot: Narrative, Psychoanalysis, Feminism*, Bloomington, Indiana University Press, 1989.

Homans, M., *Bearing the Word: Language and Female Experience in Nineteenth-Century Women's Writing*, Chicago, Chicago University Press, 1986.

Howard, J., 'The new historicism in Renaissance studies', in A. Kinney and D. Collins (eds.), *Renaissance Historicism: Selections from English Literary Renaissance*, Amherst, University of Massachusetts Press, 1987.

Hughes, W., *The Maniac in the Cellar: Sensation Novels of the 1860s*, Princeton, Princeton University Press, 1980.

Hughes-Hallett, L., *Cleopatra: Histories, Dreams and Distortions*, London, Vintage, 1990.

Hunter, R. and I. Macalpine, *Psychiatry for the Poor: 1851 Colney Hatch Asylum— Friern Hospital 1973*, London, Dawsons, 1974.

Jacobus, M., *Reading Woman: Essays in Feminist Criticism*, New York, Columbia University Press, 1985.

Jalland, P. and J. Hooper (eds.), *Women from Birth To Death: The Female Life Cycle in Britain 1830–1914*, New Jersey, Humanities Press, 1986.

Jones, D., 'Women and Chartism', *History*, 68:222 (1983), pp. 1–21.

Jordanova, L. (ed.), *Languages of Nature: Critical Essays on Science and Literature*, London, Free Association Books, 1986.

— *Sexual Visions: Images of Gender in Science and Medicine between the Eighteenth and the Twentieth Centuries*, Great Britain, Harvester, 1989.

Kaminsky, A. R. (ed.), *The Literary Criticism of George Henry Lewes*, Lincoln, University of Nebraska Press, 1964.

Kaplan, E. A., *Motherhood and Representation: The Mother in Popular Culture and Melodrama*, London, Routledge, 1992.

Kendrick, W., *The Secret Museum: Pornography in Modern Culture*, New York, Viking, 1987.

Kristeva, J., *Desire in Language: A Semiotic Approach to Literature and Art*, ed. L. S. Roudiez, New York, Columbia University Press, 1980.

— 'Stabat mater', in T. Moi (ed.), *The Kristeva Reader*, New York, Columbia University Press, 1986.

Langland, E., *Anne Brontë: The Other One*, London, Macmillan, 1989.

— 'Nobody's angels: domestic ideology and middle-class women in the Victorian novel', *PMLA*, 107:2 (March 1992), pp. 290–304.

Laqueur, T., *Making Sex: Body and Gender from the Greeks to Freud*, Cambridge, Mass., Harvard University Press, 1990.

Levine, G. (ed.), *One Culture: Essays in Science and Literature*, Madison, University of Wisconsin Press, 1987.

Levy, A., *Other Women: The Writing of Class, Race, and Gender, 1832–1898*, New Jersey, Princeton University Press, 1991.

Lodge, D., 'Mimesis and diegesis in modern fiction', in A. Mortimer (ed.), *Contemporary Approaches to Narrative*, Tubingen, Gunter Narr Verlag, 1984.

Logan, P. M., 'Conceiving the body: realism and medicine in *Middlemarch*', *History of the Human Sciences*, 4:2 (1991), pp. 197–222.

Mahood, L., *The Magdalenes: Prostitution in the Nineteenth Century*, London, Routledge, 1990.

Marcus, S., *The Other Victorians: A Study of Sexuality and Pornography in Mid-Nineteenth-Century England*, New York, Basic Books, 1966.

Marlow, J., *The Uncrowned Queen of Ireland: The Life of 'Kitty' O'Shea*, London, Weidenfeld, 1975.

Maynard, J., 'The worlds of Victorian sexuality: work in progress', in D. R. Cox (ed.), *Sexuality and Victorian Literature*, Tennessee Studies in Literature, vol. 27, Knoxville, University of Tennessee Press, 1984.

— *Charlotte Brontë and Sexuality*, Cambridge, Cambridge University Press, 1984.

McCandless, P., 'Liberty and lunacy', in A. Scull (ed.), *Madhouses, Mad-Doctors, and Madmen: The Social History of Psychiatry in the Victorian Era*, Philadelphia, University of Pennsylvania Press, 1981.

McGrath, Wm. J., *Freud's Discovery of Psychoanaylsis: The Politics of Hysteria*, Ithaca, Cornell University Press, 1986.

McNay, L., *Foucault and Feminism: Power, Gender and the Self*, Cambridge, Polity Press, 1992.

Meyer S., 'Colonialism and the figurative strategy of *Jane Eyre*', in J. Arac and H. Ritvo (eds.), *Macropolitics of Nineteenth-Century Literature: Nationalism, Exoticism, Imperialism*, Pennsylvania, University of Pennsylvania Press, 1991.

Miller, D. A., *The Novel and the Police*, Berkeley, University of California Press, 1988.

— 'Sensation and gender in *The Woman in White*', in C. Gallagher and T. Laqueur (eds.), *The Making of the Modern Body: Sexuality and Society in the Nineteenth Century*, Berkeley, University of California Press, 1987.

Mitchell, S., *The Fallen Angel: Chastity, Class and Women's Reading, 1835–1880*, Ohio, Bowling Green University Popular Press, 1981.

Mitchell, W. J. T., *Iconology: Image, Text, Ideology*, Chicago, University of Chicago Press, 1986.

Michie, H., *The Flesh Made Word: Female Figures and Women's Bodies*, Oxford, Oxford University Press, 1987.

Moore, G., *Conversations in Ebury Street*, London, 1924.

Morgan, K. P., 'Women and moral madness', in L. Code, S. Mullett and C. Overall (eds.), *Feminist Perspectives: Philosophical Essays on Method and Morals*, Toronto, University of Toronto Press, 1988.

Morgan, R., *Women and Sexuality in the Novels of Thomas Hardy*, London, Routledge, 1988.

Mort, F., *Dangerous Sexualities: Medico-Moral Politics in England since 1830*, London, Routledge, 1987.

Moscucci, O., *The Science of Woman: Gynaecology and Gender in England, 1800– 1929*, Cambridge, Cambridge University Press, 1990.

— 'Hermaphroditism and sex difference: the construction of gender in Victorian England', in M. Benjamin (ed.), *Science and Sensibility: Gender and Scientific Enquiry 1780–1945*, Oxford, Basil Blackwell, 1991.

Mulvey, L., 'Afterthoughts on "Visual pleasure and narrative cinema" inspired by *Duel in the Sun*', in *Visual and Other Pleasures*, Bloomington, Indiana University Press, 1989.

Nead, L., *Myths of Sexuality: Representations of Women in Victorian Britain*, New York, Basil Blackwell, 1988.

Neufeldt, V. A., 'The madonna and the gypsy', *Studies in the Novel*, XV (1983), pp. 44–54.

Newman, B., '"The situation of the looker-on": gender, narration, and gaze in *Wuthering Heights*', *PMLA*, 5:105 (1990), pp. 1029–41.

Nochlin, L., *The Politics of Vision: Essays on Nineteenth-Century Art and Society*, New York, Harper and Row, 1989.

Paxton, N. L., *George Eliot and Herbert Spencer: Feminism, Evolutionism, and the Reconstruction of Gender*, Princeton, Princeton University Press, 1991.

Pearsall, R., *Night's Black Angels*, London, Hodder and Stoughton, 1975.

Perkin, J., *Women and Marriage in Nineteenth-Century England*, London, Routledge, 1989.

Peterson, R. T., *The Art of Ecstasy: Teresa, Bernini, and Crashaw*, London, 1970.

Pinchbeck, I. and M. Hewitt, *Children in English Society*, vol. 2, London, Routledge, 1973.

Poovey, M., *Uneven Developments: The Ideological Work of Gender in Mid-Victorian England*, Chicago, University of Chicago Press, 1988.

— 'Speaking of the body: mid-Victorian constructions of female desire', in M. Jacobus, E. Fox Keller and S. Shuttleworth (eds.), *Body\Politics: Women and the Discourses of Science*, London, Routledge, 1990.

Riley, D., *'Am I That Name?': Feminism and the Category of 'Women' in History*, Minneapolis, University of Minnesota Press, 1988.

Roberts, A., 'Mothers and babies: the wetnurse and her employer in mid-nineteenth-century England', *Women's Studies*, 3 (1976), pp. 279–93.

Rose, L., *Massacre of the Innocents: Infanticide in Britain 1800–1939*, London, Routledge, 1986.

Russett, C. E., *Sexual Science: The Victorian Construction of Womanhood*, Cambridge, Mass., Harvard, 1989.

Said, E., *Orientalism*, New York, Pantheon, 1978.

Sawicki, J., 'Feminism and the power of Foucauldian discourse', in J. Arac (ed.), *After Foucault: Humanistic Knowledge, Postmodern Challenges*, New Brunswick, Rutgers University Press, 1988.

Sayers, J., *Biological Politics*, London, Tavistock, 1982.

Schiebinger, L., 'Skeletons in the closet: the first illustrations of the female skeleton in eighteenth-century anatomy', in C. Gallagher and T. Laqueur (eds.), *The Making of the Modern Body*, Berkeley, University of California Press, 1987.

— 'The private life of plants: sexual politics in Carl Linnaeus and Erasmus Darwin', in M. Benjamin (ed.), *Science and Sensibility: Gender and Scientific Inquiry, 1780–1945*, Oxford, Basil Blackwell, 1991.

Schor, H., *Scheherazade in the Marketplace: Elizabeth Gaskell and the Victorian Novel*, New York, Oxford University Press, 1992.

Scott, J., *Gender and the Politics of History*, New York, Columbia University Press, 1988.

Scott, P. J. M., *Anne Brontë: A New Critical Assessment*, London, Vision, 1983.

Scourse, N., *Victorians and Their Flowers*, London, Croom Helm, 1983.

Sedgwick, E. K., *Epistemology of the Closet*, Berkeley, University of California Press, 1990.

Seed, J., 'Unitarianism, political economy and the antinomies of liberal culture in Manchester 1830–50', *Social History*, 7:1 (1982), pp. 1–25.

Shanley, M. L., *Feminism, Marriage and the Law in Victorian England, 1850–1895*, London, Tauris, 1989.

Shelston, A., 'Elizabeth Gaskell's Manchester (1)', *Gaskell Society Journal*, 3 (1989), pp. 41–82.

Showalter, E., *A Literature of Their Own: British Women Novelists from Brontë to Lessing*, London, Virago, 1977.

— *The Female Malady: Women, Madness, and English Culture, 1830–1980*, Harmondsworth, Penguin, 1987.

Shuttleworth, S. and J. Christie (eds.), *Nature Transfigured: Science and Literature, 1700–1900*, Manchester, Manchester University Press, 1989.

— 'Female circulation: medical discourse and popular advertising in the mid-Victorian era', in M. Jacobus, E. Fox Keller and S. Shuttleworth (eds.), *Body\Politics: Women and the Discourses of Science*, London, Routledge, 1990.

— 'Demonic mothers: ideologies of bourgeois motherhood in the mid-Victorian era', in L. Shires (ed.), *Rewriting the Victorians: Theory, History, and the Politics of Gender*, London, Routledge, 1992.

Skultans, V., *English Madness: Ideas on Insanity 1580–1890*, London, Routledge, 1979.

— *Madness and Morals: Ideas on Insanity in the Nineteenth Century*, London, Routledge, 1975.

Smart, C., 'Disruptive bodies and unruly sex: the regulation of reproduction and sexuality in the nineteenth century', in C. Smart (ed.), *Regulating Womanhood: Historical Essays on Marriage, Motherhood and Sexuality*, London, Routledge, 1992.

Smith, R., *Trial by Medicine: Insanity and Responsibility in Victorian Trials*, Edinburgh, Edinburgh University Press, 1981.

Smith-Rosenberg, C., 'Puberty to menopause: the cycle of femininity in nineteenth-century America', in M. Hartman and L. W. Banner (eds.), *Clio's Consciousness Raised: New Perspectives on the History of Women*, New York, Harper, 1974.

Spivak, G. C., 'A literary representation of the subaltern', in *In Other Worlds: Essays in Cultural Politics*, London, Methuen, 1987.

Stallybrass, P. and A. White, *The Politics and Poetics of Transgression*, London, Methuen, 1986.

Stevens, J. (ed.), *Mary Taylor, friend of Charlotte Brontë: Letters from New Zealand and Elsewhere*, Auckland, Auckland University Press, 1972.

Stina-Ewbank, I., *Their Proper Sphere: A Study of the Brontë Sisters as Early-Victorian Female Novelists*, London, Edward Arnold, 1966.

Stocking, G. W., Jr., *Victorian Anthropology*, New York, Free Press, 1987.

Stoneman, P., *Elizabeth Gaskell*, Brighton, Harvester, 1987.

Taylor, B., *Eve and the New Jerusalem: Socialism and Feminism in the Nineteenth Century*, London, Virago Press, 1983.

Thompson, D. (ed.), *The Early Chartists*, London, Macmillan, 1971.

— *The Chartists*, London, Temple Smith, 1984.

Thompson, F. M. L., *The Rise of Respectable Society 1830–1900*, London, Fontana, 1988.

Tillotson, K., *Novels of the Eighteen-Forties*, London, Oxford, 1954.

Todd, J., *Feminist Literary History*, London, Routledge, 1987.

Todd, R. B., *Cyclopaedia of Anatomy and Physiology*, 5 vols, London, Sherwood, 1839–54.

Tooley, M., *Abortion and Infanticide*, Oxford, Clarendon Press, 1983.

Uglow, J., *George Eliot*, New York, Virago, 1987.

Valverde, M., 'Love of finery: fashion and the fallen woman in nineteenth-century social discourse', *Victorian Studies*, 32:2 (1989), pp. 169–88.

Veith, I., *Hysteria: The History of a Disease*, Chicago, Chicago University Press, 1965.

Vicinus, M., 'Sexuality and power: A review of current work in the history of sexuality', *Feminist Studies*, 8 (1982), pp. 133–56.

Walkowitz, J., 'Male vice and female virtue: feminism and the politics of prostitution in nineteenth-century Britain', in A. Snitow, C. Stansell and S. Thompson (eds.), *Desire: The Politics of Sexuality*, London, Virago, 1984.

— *Prostitution and Victorian Society: Women, Class, and the State*, Cambridge, Cambridge University Press, 1980.

Warner, M., *Alone of All her Sex: The Myth and the Cult of the Virgin Mary*, London, Picador, 1976.

Weber, A., *Teresa of Avila and the Rhetoric of Femininity*, New Jersey, Princeton University Press, 1990.

Webster, C. (ed.), *Biology, Medicine and Society 1840–1940*, Cambridge, Cambridge University Press, 1981.

Weeks, J., 'Foucault for historians', *History Workshop*, 14 (1982), pp. 114–16.

— *Sex, Politics and Society: The Regulation of Sexuality since 1800*, London, Longmans, 1981.

— *Sex, Politics and Society: The Regulation of Sexuality Since 1800*, 2nd edn., London, Longmans, 1989.

Wiesenfarth, J., '*Middlemarch*: the language of art', *PMLA*, 97 (1982), pp. 363–77.

Wiesenthal, C. S., 'A Jamesian vision of "American nervousness": masculine dis-ease and diseased femininity in *The Bostonians*', *English Studies in Canada*, 15 (1989), pp. 447–97.

Williams, P., 'Women, medicine and sanitary reform: 1850–90', in M. Benjamin (ed.), *Science and Sensibility: Gender and Scientific Inquiry 1780–1945*, Oxford, Basil Blackwell, 1991.

Wise, T. J. and J. A. Symington (eds.), *The Miscellaneous and Unpublished Writings of Charlotte and Patrick Branwell Brontë*, 2 vols, 1936 and 1938.

Witemeyer, H., *George Eliot and the Visual Arts*, New Haven, Yale University Press, 1979.

Wittkower, R., *Gian Lorenzo Bernini: The Sculptor of the Roman Baroque*, London, Phaidon Press, 1955.

Wolff, R., 'Devoted disciple: the letters of Mary Elizabeth Braddon to Sir Edward Bulwer-Lytton, 1862–1873', *Harvard literary Bulletin*, 22 (1974), pp. 5–35, 129–61.

— *Sensational Victorian: The Life and Fiction of Mary Elizabeth Braddon*, New York, Garland, 1979.

Wood, N., 'L'ane dossier: an introduction', *m/f: A Feminist Journal*, 8 (1983), pp. 17–21.

Yeazell, R. B., 'Why political novels have heroines: *Sybil*, *Mary Barton* and *Felix Holt*', *Novel*, 18 (1985), pp. 126–44.

Index

abortion 182, 187

Acton, William 13, 15, 45-7, 49, 90, 106-8, 114, 124-6, 127, 162

Adam Bede (Eliot)
    and beauty 172, 175-6
    Hetty compared with Ruth 3
    and Hetty's abandonment of her baby 3, 4, 167-8
    infanticide in 1, 3, 4, 167-8
    and maternal deviance 16, 157
    and maternal instinct 157, 167-79
    treatment of pregnancy 1-3

adoption 183

Agnes Grey (Brontë)
    and the 'animal side of life' 90-113
    and beauty 92, 103, 105-6, 108, 175
    Charlotte and 91, 99
    children in 96-8, 100
    confession in 16, 89, 93-4, 95, 104, 105, 108, 113
    desire in 16, 89, 104, 108, 112, 113
    even and orderly narrative 91
    fledgling bird incident 91, 98-9
    flower imagery 96
    glow-worm analogy 15, 106, 108
    and governessing 89, 92-9, 102, 104, 110, 111
    and passion 89, 91, 95, 97, 98, 102, 103
    secrecy in 89, 112
    treatment of middle-class values 93, 109-10, 112-13
    and working as 'hireling' v self-employment 111
    zoological imagery 96-7

agriculture,
    and masculinisation 60

alcoholism, and wet-nursing 69

Allan, J. McGrigor 34-5

Alone of All Her Sex (Warner) 238

Anderson, Elizabeth Garrett 13, 25, 27

androgyny 23, 26, 33, 40

animals
    behaviour compared with human 15
    and control of sexual development 28-9
    and growth rapidity 34
    on 'heat' 15, 31, 45, 107

    instincts 41
    reproduction 15, 30, 31

anti-factory tracts 158, 159

Arabian Nights, The 140

Aristotle 112

Armstrong, Nancy 8, 12

Ashwell, Samuel 215

Athenaeum 180

baby-dropping 158

baby-farming 158, 182
    and maternal instinct 13
    and motherhood 16
    regulated 167

baby-planting 183

Baines, Mary Anne 158-9, 160, 188

beards, female development of 29, 33, 38

beauty,
    and *Adam Bede* 172, 175-6

beauty, and *Agnes Grey* 92, 103, 105-6, 108, 175

Becker, Lydia 167

bee behaviour 15, 28-9, 39-40, 111-12

Beer, Gillian 3

behaviour,
    human and animal compared 15

Berger, John 144, 146

Bernini, Giovanni Lorenzo 221, 222, 228

Bewell, Alan 76

biological cycles 35

biology
    and 'essential nature' 9
    and relation of the sexes 10
    reproductive 7, 8, 22, 23, 49

biomedical discourse
    analogies between humans and plants/animals 15, 28-9, 30, 31
    and desire 43
    distinction between male and female bodies 10
    and fecundation 43
    limited circulation and readership of texts 13
    and maternity 4
    and ovulation 43
    and sex 22
    and sexual difference 5, 10, 49, 158

closeting
  by prostitutes 125
  of fallen women 115, 131
  homosexual 115, 120
  in *Ruth* 120, 131
Coleridge, Samuel Taylor 76
Collins, William Wilkie 33, 202
colour-blindness 69
Combe, George 43
Committee to Amend the Law in Points
  wherein it is Injurious to
  Women (CALPIW) 167
conception
  female passion unnecessary for 43, 44
  as involuntary and periodic 122
confession
  in *Agnes Grey* 16, 89, 93-4, 95, 104, 105,
    108, 113
  in *Ruth* 89
contagious diseases legislation 11, 114, 131
Cott, Nancy 11
cretinism 143
criminality, and wet-nursing 69
cross-dressing 250
culture
  control of 25
  medicine and 24
  and nature 8, 10, 24, 25, 36-40, 47, 57
  and sexual development 36-40
  and sexual difference 8, 24
  working-class 48, 64
cultures,
  proving inferiority of other 48, 57, 113
Cyclopaedia of Anatomy and Physiology (Todd)
  29, 35, 37, 44

Daily Telegraph 201
Daniel Deronda (Eliot) 242
Darwin, Charles 10
  and children 97
  and female 'inferiority' 28
  and hermaphroditism 23, 38
Darwinism,
  and menstruation 37
De Biefve, Edward *136*, 136-7
De la prostitution dans la ville de Paris (Parent-
  Duchatelet) 139
death rate,
  public discussion of 13
degeneration,
  of the body 6, 9, 39
Delacroix, Eugène 135
Descent of Man, The (Darwin) 10, 38-9
desire 16, 49, 83, 89

in *Agnes Grey* 16, 89, 104, 108, 112, 113
as an unreliable indicator of the 'true' sex
  36
and evolution of feelings of love 42
female seen as analogous to male 44-5
and male puberty 123
in *Middlemarch* 218-20, 237, 244
origins of 26
in *Ruth* 16, 89, 114, 119, 120, 121, 131
as unwomanly 94
and *Villette* 90, 133, 140, 144, 148
within marriage 122
Desire and Domestic Fiction (Armstrong) 12
Devey, Louisa 201
domesticity
  and factory system 59
  and gendered social hierarchy 58
  in *Mary Barton* 56, 64, 65, 82
  and 'real' women 238
  'slovenly' 63-4
  statistics recorded 57
  and Unitarian Domestic Mission 62
  working-class 57, 58, 61
Donkin, Horatio Bryan 216
dressmaking 67
Duchatelet, Parent 48

Earle, Justice 188
East Lynne (Wood) 191, 192
Eastern Life: Present and Past (Martineau) 140
Edgeworth, Maria 71
education
  for females 25, 27, 39, 159, 167
  and feminism 39
  for men and women 26
  and middle class 40
  statistics recorded 57
  and threats of 'sexlessness' 39
  and ugliness/sterility 41
  Wollstonecraft on 76-7
education, higher,
  and reproduction 10, 214
Eliot, George
  and education 214, 224
  exploration of Madonnahood 238-9
  and the fallen woman as unmarried
    mother 3
  and female sexuality 3
  and human/animal behaviour 15
  praised by gynaecologist 1
  and sensational novels 16-17
  and Sistine Madonna 235, 238
Ellis, Havelock 97
embryology 29, 30

and animal behaviour 15
attempts to recuperate a notion of 13, 16
ideologically important construct of 189
perversions of 58
society's interference with 158-9
maternity
and biomedical discourse 4
and child as oppressive burden 4
competing and contradictory representations of 11
and factory system 58
in *Middlemarch* 215, 228, 229, 237
representation in literature 2, 3
and social scientific discourse 4
maternity homes 182
Maudsley, Henry 13, 25-7, 31, 39, 41-2, 97, 184, 222
medical texts 6, 9
and condition of being female 199
and cretinism 143
and discussion of sex 13, 25
on hysteria 222
and 'medicine of sex' 2
predict dire bodily responses to cultural developments 39
and sexual kinship 24
and sexuality 4, 13, 49
and sociological v ontological sex 36
and womanhood 4
Medical and Times Gazette 42
melodrama 181, 185
menopause 106, 198-9
menstruation
advice about onset of 47
age of 58
as an effect of civilisation 37
as 'flowers' 30
and human/animal behaviour 15
and insanity 198-9
as involuntary and periodic 122
late onset among Western women 48
male 24, 35
and surplus nutritive material 27
middle class
and childbirth 38
claims to moral superiority 109, 115
constructions of class difference 56
and culture's degree of civilisation 57
and education 40
and fertility 65
and reproduction 160-61
sexuality 47
and wet-nursing 158, 159-60, 162-3
and women's writing 12

and working-class women 11
Middlemarch (Eliot)
desire in 218-20, 237, 244
and femininity 222
and hysteria 215-17, 221-3
and insanity 197
and the Madonna 215, 228-33, 237, 239-40, 242
maternity in 215, 228, 229, 237
painting/language debate 229-31
and productive/reproductive energies 214, 215, 218, 223, 229, 230, 243, 244
and productive/reproductive work 16
and Romanticism 230, 232-3
and Saint Teresa 215, 221-30
sexuality in 215, 217, 222, 228, 229, 237
and yearnings of womanhood 218, 219, 226, 243
midwifery, and superstition 182
Mill on the Floss, The (Eliot) 237-8
Miller, D.A. 116-17, 120
millinery 67
Milton, John 231
Mitchell, W.J.T. 230, 231
monkeys, sexuality of 15, 42
monogamy 48
Moore, George 91, 92
moral conditions,
and sexual difference 17
moral feelings,
and desire 42
moral insanity 196
morality
attainment of present standard 38
and factory life 48
of governesses 89
and lady novelists 13
middle-class 194
and poverty 59
as province of literature and medicine 2
working-class 6, 56, 57, 58, 61
Mort, Frank 124
Moscucci, Ornella 24, 32
Moses and Monotheism (Freud) 218-19
Moses, and *Villette* 145-7
motherhood
advice about 47
contradictions in representations of 16
demands of 241
discourse of 157
Gaskell's treatment of 56
and governessing 95, 110, 111
idealised 238

and race 16, 25
  representations in literary texts 2, 3
  as 'science' 14
  and social scientific discourse 4, 6
  and sociocultural moulding 9
  subject as an important arena 60-61
  women's conceptualising of own 13
  working-class 13, 16, 25, 56, 58, 61, 65
Sharpe's 126
Showalter, Elaine 192
Simpson, Professor James Young
  and *Adam Bede* 1, 2
  on breasts 35
  and embryology 29-30
  and hermaphroditism 26, 33-4, 36
Skey, F.C. 217
Smart, Carol 21-2
Smith, W. Tyler 157
social formation
  differentiation of power in 12
  process of 11
social life,
  and sexual difference 25
social power,
  and female passionlessness 11
social relations
  and science 7
  and sexual differences 8
social science,
  birth of Victorian 57
social scientific discourse
  and maternity 4, 158
  and sexuality 4, 6
  and working-class women 11, 16
Somerset County Gazette 201
Sorrow on the Sea (Wood)
  baby disposal in 180-86
  on breast-feeding 184
  and maternal deviance 16, 157
  melodramatic treatment 181
  and middle-class domestic ideals 186
  as a sensation novel 180, 181, 185
  shocks readers 180
South Sea Islanders 37, 57
Spencer, Herbert 28, 38, 214
Steele, Anna 180
stillbirth 183, 184
Studies on Hysteria (Breuer) 222
Symposium (Plato) 26
syphilis 124, 131, 161
Talisman, The (Scott) 146
Taylor, Mary 100
temperance 57
Ten Hours Bill 59

Tenant of Wildfell Hall, The (Brontë) 91, 92
Tennyson, Alfred, Lord 26, 40
Teresa, St, and *Middlemarch* 215, 221-30, 239, 243
testes
  and female as inverted male 29-30
  and male characteristics 32-3
  and ovaries 28
  removal of 32, 48
testosterone 249
Thomson, Dr Allen 35
thrift 57, 62
Tiepolo, Giovanni Battista 135
Tillotson, Kathleen 77
Tilt, Edward 32, 44-5, 49, 114, 199, 216
Tinsley Brothers 180
Todd, R.B. 29, 35, 37, 44
Tom Jones (Fielding) 181
Tomlinson, Elizabeth 168
trade unions 61, 64, 80
'Training and Restraining' (Gatty) 79

unemployment,
  Gaskell's treatment of 56
Unitarian Domestic Mission 62, 63
upper class,
  and childbirth 38

Variations of Animals and Plants Under Domestication, The (Darwin) 39
Vashti, and *Villette* 145-8
Vicinus, Martha 4, 11
Victoria, Queen 59
Villette (Brontë)
  Cleopatra painting in 90, 131, 134-5, 136, 137-9, 141-6, 240
  and De Biefve's *Une Almé* 131-2, 135-7
  and desire 90, 133, 140, 144, 148
  and the gaze 132-4, 148
  and harem 135, 138, 141
  and insanity 142-3
  and invisibility 133-4
  Martineau reviews 139-40
  passion in 90, 148
  and prostitution 132, 139, 148
  secrecy in 144, 145
  and the sexualised Oriental 16, 90
  and yearning 133, 144
Vindication of the Rights of Women, A (Wollstonecraft) 76-7
'Visions of Ecstasy' (television film) 221
Voce, Mary 168

Walker, Alexander 40-41

INDEX